# America's
# Chess Heritage

# America's
# Chess Heritage

From
Benjamin Franklin
to Bobby Fischer
*—and Beyond*

Walter Korn

DAVID McKAY COMPANY, INC.
*New York*

Library of Congress Cataloging in Publication Data
Korn, Walter.
    America's chess heritage.
    Includes indexes.
    1.  Chess—United States—History.  2.  Chess players—
United States—Biography.  I.  Title.
GV1323.K67        794.1′0973        78–16224
ISBN 0–679–13200–7

10 9 8 7 6 5 4 3 2 1

# Preface

When working on an earlier book *American Chess Art: 250 Portraits of Endgame Study*, it struck me that amid the flood of books on the general history of chess, no modern volume existed which dealt specifically with the total American chess scene and its immense contribution to the game—nationally and globally.

Unfolding chronologically against a historical background, *America's Chess Heritage* depicts the flow of American chess, its impact locally, and its contributions (and controversies) in the international arena. In style of context, in the selection of the games given, in the character of the annotations to the moves, I have tried to reflect accurately the changing fashions and periods from the past to the present, including the future benefits to chess of existing technology and promising social attitudes.

*America's Chess Heritage* compares the achievements and values of chess in America and on the world scene. Rolling several topics into one, it goes into the psychological, sociological, and even economic issues as they relate to trends in chess, the chess periods under scrutiny, the players' personal idiosyncrasies, and the geopolitical climate of the era, thus embracing the totality of chess.

This volume is not a minute collation of every detail of the body of chess in the United States. It is an independent, and to my best intent, a scrupulously objective narration of the general picture, interspersed with some novel or personal observation. It is written by a recreation-oriented, chess-loving generalist and should relate to the enthusiast of any strength who is interested in the background of the game and its players. It is a record by an historian, trying not to be blanked out by the professional specialist alone, or by the specter of the record-breaker, with the often dangerous accompaniment of sports medicine, energizers, even hypnotism and other "isms."

While many opinions in this book might be my own responsibility, I have tried my utmost to verify and review the facts, statements, documents, and relevant writings as referred to; to rectify erroneous beliefs; explode myths; and provide a complete record of any essential American national chess data. I apologize for any innocent omission of any important fact, or of personages who might have done much for chess nationally or regionally. Quite reasonably, a line had to be drawn where, beyond the essentials, some technicality could not be accommodated because of the limits on space, cost, and price of the publication.

The idea for this work was conceived in 1974 and through extraneous circumstances it took four years to come to fruition. That means that some observations about the present and the future of chess might have sounded clairvoyant then and that some others are *déjà vu* to me now. On the other hand, the delay has allowed further updating and the sifting out of outdated material. Nevertheless, fresh names and events constantly make their debut in an ever-changing world; it is in the hands of upcoming generations to provide the substance for a continuing task as is presented by this volume.

San Mateo, California                                      Walter Korn

# Acknowledgments

Foremost in my thought is my gratitude to my late Wife, Herta, whose continued and invaluable assistance was lovingly given to me in the creation of this book. Without her support and help, this and other of my books might never have been written. It is to her that I dedicate this book.

My thanks to Professor Christopher Becker for helpful advice when the outlines of the idea for this title were taking shape; to Rudite J. Emir of San Francisco for her conscientious copy-editing of the manuscript; to David S. Lake and Joan Wolfgang of Pitman-Fearon Inc., Belmont, California; and to Alan Tucker and Barbara Anderson of the David McKay Company of New York for their excellent author–publisher rapport. Special mention is also due to Mr. Ian Herbert of Pitman Publishing, London, whose initial confidence in the success of this particular topic provided the needed impetus.

As concerns the medical data touched upon, I am indebted to Martin Becker, MD, of East Orange, New Jersey, for checking professional details and phraseology. I thank Dr. V. Koressaar of the Slavonic Division, New York Public Library, for his counsel pertaining to proper transcription and Mrs. Alice N. Loranth of the Cleveland Public Library's John G. White Collection for the loan of rare literature and photos and for other information.

Last not least, I have received instant responses from many chess players and functionaries whenever I made a request and I hope that I have not omitted any such relevant mention within the pages of this volume.

# Contents

# Explanatory Notes

The variations are evaluated by means of generally known symbols as follows—

++   after White's (or Black's) move: White (Black) has a clear winning advantage.

+   after White's (Black's) move: White (Black) has a distinct superiority, although there is no immediate forced win.

±   White has slightly better chances.

∓   Black has slightly better chances.

=   The position offers even chances.

!   Good moves—or *best choice among several alternatives.*

?   Weak move.

!?   Speculative attempt to complicate.

∞   Unclear position, with judgment reserved, or *open to further experimentation.*

ch   "Check" (incorporating "discovered check" and "double check").

e.p.   Taking a pawn *en passant.*

MCO   *Modern Chess Openings,* usually supplemented by the number of the edition; published in descriptive notation, in one compact volume.

ECO   *Encyclopedia of Chess Openings,* published in Yugoslavia in algebraic notation and in consecutive volumes.

USCF   United States Chess Federation.

CL&R   *Chess Life & Review* magazine.

FIDE   Fédération Internationale des Échecs (World Chess Federation).

# Comparative Chart of Chess Notations

For the benefit of those not familiar with the English (descriptive) notation, we give a diagram of the board with a comparison of the English and algebraic definition of the squares, and a table of international equivalents for the English symbols for the chessmen.

In the English notation, the symbol before the hyphen indicates which piece is being moved, the symbol following the hyphen the square to which it is moved. On the board below, the notation in brackets indicates Black's moves, with the board seen from Black's point of view.

|   | a | b | c | d | e | f | g | h |   |
|---|---|---|---|---|---|---|---|---|---|
| **8** | (QR1) QR8 | (QN1) QN8 | (QB1) QB8 | (Q1) Q8 | (K1) K8 | (KB1) KB8 | (KN1) KN8 | (KR1) KR8 | **8** |
| **7** | (QR2) QR7 | (QN2) QN7 | (QB2) QB7 | (Q2) Q7 | (K2) K7 | (KB2) KB7 | (KN2) KN7 | (KR2) KR7 | **7** |
| **6** | (QR3) QR6 | (QN3) QN6 | (QB3) QB6 | (Q3) Q6 | (K3) K6 | (KB3) KB6 | (KN3) KN6 | (KR3) KR6 | **6** |
| **5** | (QR4) QR5 | (QN4) QN5 | (QB4) QB5 | (Q4) Q5 | (K4) K5 | (KB4) KB5 | (KN4) KN5 | (KR4) KR5 | **5** |
| **4** | (QR5) QR4 | (QN5) QN4 | (QB5) QB4 | (Q5) Q4 | (K5) K4 | (KB5) KB4 | (KN5) KN4 | (KR5) KR4 | **4** |
| **3** | (QR6) QR3 | (QN6) QN3 | (QB6) QB3 | (Q6) Q3 | (K6) K3 | (KB6) KB3 | (KN6) KN3 | (KR6) KR3 | **3** |
| **2** | (QR7) QR2 | (QN7) QN2 | (QB7) QB2 | (Q7) Q2 | (K7) K2 | (KB7) KB2 | (KN7) KN2 | (KR7) KR2 | **2** |
| **1** | (QR8) QR1 | (QN8) QN1 | (QB8) QB1 | (Q8) Q1 | (K8) K1 | (KB8) KB1 | (KN8) KN1 | (KR8) KR1 | **1** |
|   | a | b | c | d | e | f | g | h |   |

| Fig. | Eng. | Czech | Dut. | Fr. | Ger.[1] | It.[2] | Pol. | Roum. | Russ. | FIDE |
|---|---|---|---|---|---|---|---|---|---|---|
| ♚ | K | K | K | R | K | R | K | R | Кр | K |
| ♛ | Q | D | D | D | D | D | H | D | ф | D |
| ♜ | R | V | T | T | T | T | W | T | л | T |
| ♝ | B | S | L | F | L | A | G | N | C | S |
| ♞ | N[3] | J | P | C | S | C | S | C | К | N |
| ♟ | P | (P) | (P) | (P) | (B) | (P) | (P) | (—) | (П) | — |

[1] These are also used in the Scandinavian and Yugoslav notations.
[2] These are also used in the Portuguese and Spanish notations.
[3] N for Knight in modern usage, replacing the archaic symbol Kt.

# Early Pioneers

# 1.

# The Ideologies and Heresies
# of Chess

Modern chess has most likely been put on the map by the United States. By "modern" we mean the combination of dynamism and pragmatism that accompanied the dawning technological period of the late nineteenth and the twentieth century.

## EARLY FOUNDATIONS

Chess had had an earlier foundation in Europe, which had inherited the game from Arabia; which, in turn, had been intrigued by this Sino-Indian game.

Each culture changed the game to suit its own society. Thus, the Occident transformed the symbolism and the static, contemplative nature of chess into a speedier game with extended power for the pieces. The process of change spread over half a millennium.

During the late Middle Ages, chess was clothed in the ideological structure of the day—as behooved that era of faith and conviction. Its new-gained respectability made acceptance all the more rapid, and it quickly gained in popularity.

The character of chess at that time accurately reflected the social beliefs of the period and was so treated in allegorical literature. To quote H. J. R. Murray,[1]

> Quite a number of works were devoted to the allegorical explanation of chess, generally on the broad line that the game was emblematic of the social condition of the time. These works were widely known by the name of *Moralities*. . . . They exercised a potent influence on the nomenclature of the pieces; they may have carried a knowledge of chess to circles where it had not penetrated before . . . [they]

[1] *A History of Chess* (Oxford: 1913, reprinted 1962), pp. 537–38.

3

helped break down prejudice against the game . . . [they] directed attention of chess players to the moral instruction, which was the ultimate purpose of the "morality."

The most prominent author of a chess morality was Jacobus de Cessolis, of whose works the Cleveland (Ohio) Public Library owns some first editions; i.e., *De Ludo Scacchorum* (Lombardy: 1290), with several facsimiles also available in other American libraries.

One fact is useful to keep in mind: during the game's transition from the Orient to the Occident, its development was not always a smooth one. At times, it was strongly objected to. The gentry, often secluded and with little to do, embraced chess as a welcome pastime. However, this indulgence was frowned upon by the watchful clergy, who remembered how chess was played with dice in its earlier days. Nor did the universities approve; they considered chess, and other games, to be a waste of scholastic time. The game was for noblemen's hedonistic pursuits during their leisure hours, when no pressing matters were at hand. Merchants and the working class were not encouraged to participate.

Between 1300 and 1600 A.D., with the advent of the Renaissance and the "Burgher States," the social barriers to the game crumbled and its popularity spread rapidly. From the seventeenth century onward, the elements of Western chess were defined first by Spanish and Italian chroniclers,[2] and then by Phillip Stamma of London, a native Syrian who helped introduce Central Europe (but not England!) to the algebraic chess notation then used in the East.

France was next in popularizing chess. The Encyclopédists in chess under the guidance of André Danican Philidor, converted the game from an empirical to a theoretical endeavor. This methodological trend continued in central Europe and Imperial Britain (e.g., under William Staunton), and the total achievements of that long period bore fruit in the First International Chess Tournament in London in 1851. Attended by sixteen of the world's leading players, it was won convincingly by the German-Scandinavian Adolph Anderssen, a schoolmaster from Berlin, who thus became an uncrowned chess champion of the world.

Mature play as we know it had not yet set in, though. Philidor, Staunton, and Germany's Bilguer had provided the cornerstones for systematic opening analysis and terminology; but practical play was not yet thought of as an interrelated, cohesive whole. Although the prophetical La Bourdonnais had begun to show the way, there still was little continuous flow. The middlegame was handled as a sepa-

[2] Greco, Lucena, Ruy Lopez of Spain; later Cozio, Del Rio, Lolli, Ponziani, Salvio of Italy.

rate entity, and play was often more combinative than sound—decorative rather than positional; nor was transition to a favorable ending then known. The technical aspects of the game's final phase were only beginning to be explored. The style consisted of daring thrust and reckless counterthrust! Cautious defense and favorable simplification were looked upon as cowardice.

True, the great masters of that period used their own improvisational resourcefulness and produced their masterpieces. Yet, as with any set of theorems laboriously arrived at and clung to, the codified chess heritage of the mid-nineteenth century contained a core of dogmatism and rigidity that might have spelled stagnation, for it was bound to a mouth-to-mouth tradition with too little evaluative criticism.

Fortunately, two dominant personalities of the young, muscle-flexing United States were destined to leave their revolutionary imprint. First came Benjamin Franklin, the founding father of American chess. He preached its virtues vigorously, and—to good diplomatic advantage—was himself a strong practitioner of the game. Second came Thunderbolt Paul Morphy—in his ethics, a disciple of Franklin; in his practice, a meteoric chess phenomenon.

## AMERICA'S CHESS DIPLOMATS

Benjamin Franklin (1706–1790) embodied the Horatio Alger rise from Poor Richard's rags to the stature of eminent scientist and early American statesman. Less known, except among "the club," was his strong and sound game of chess. His treatise, *The Morals of Chess*, gave both educational and practical advice about chess conduct and drew parallels with life.[3] These maxims, coming from his authoritative pen, were widely acclaimed in European and American circles and drew the attention of players and laymen alike.

Franklin's influence was so profound that in 1791 a translation from the French reprint of *The Morals of Chess* was published in Russian in St. Petersburg under the title *Pravila dlia shashechnoi igry* (*Rules for the Game of Chess*). The title uses the word *shashechnoi* ("checkers") instead of *shakhmatnoi* ("chess"), a word coined later; but it is actually the first original book on chess published in Russia, and the title page and table of contents acknowledge Franklin's authorship.[4]

---

[3] Composed in 1779, it was published the same year by C. & J. Robinson in London, and reproduced in a refined version in *The Columbian Magazine* in Philadelphia in 1786.

[4] Compare the listing in N. I. Sakharov, *Soviet Chess Bibliography* (Moscow: 1968), p. 33; and Cleveland Public Library index card.

Continuing in the footsteps of the medieval moralities, but on an advanced level, Franklin thus laid down an American constitution for chess and its own pursuit of happiness. He was also aware of the sedentary drawbacks of the game compared to physical exercise, as is attested to in Ralph K. Hagedorn, *Franklin and Chess in Early America* (Philadelphia: 1958), and of the risk of its becoming an obsession.

As the game took roots, the demand for chess books grew so strong that beginning in 1802 the first domestic manuals were marketed. According to the records in the Cleveland Public Library, the first one in the United States was printed in 1805 by W. Pelham of Boston. It can be considered the first because, notwithstanding the reference to Philidor, whose games were given, the book contained independent thoughts and instruction. It was probably authored by William Blagrove, the publisher's nephew and an enthusiastic amateur. Though based on Philidor's games, the book's title was *The Elements of Chess*.

In the creation of mass appeal for chess, the "Automaton," a mechanical chess-playing contraption, nicknamed "The Turk," may have had significant effect. It was exhibited in the States between 1826 and 1854, drawing crowds of curious people unaware of the hoax: hidden cleverly inside the machine was a grandmaster who responded to the moves made on the board. Still it might have prompted sensible onlookers to get behind the game's mystique and become seriously interested. A monograph by Charles Michael Carroll, *The Great Chess Automaton* (New York: Dover, 1975), describes the history, background, and operators of this and similar inventions in up-to-date detail.[5] "Ajeeb" entered the United States in 1898 and during its earlier appearances was operated, among others, by Pillsbury. Godfrey Gumpel's "Mephisto" even entered the (English) Counties Chess Association Handicap tournament in 1878 and placed first. The strong master E.G. MacDonnell refused to participate because of the unknown identity of the player hidden inside (it was Gunsberg). The same question of the "secret opponent" was to come up again, although in different form, a century later (see Chapter 14).

Qualitatively, chess progressed steadily up to 1857 with the appearance of the periodical *The Chess Monthly*. It was edited by Daniel Willard Fiske and, for a time, coedited by Paul Morphy. Its problem section was taken care of by the world-famous composer

[5] These details were further augmented by Donald M. Fiene (of the University of Tennessee, Knoxville, in "Kempelen's Turk" (*The British Chess Magazine*, August/September 1977). Also in 1977, the same magazine ran a series on similar contraptions; namely on "Ajeeb" and on "Mephisto."

Eugene B. Cook (1830–1915), whose chess library is in the custody of Princeton University in New Jersey. *The Chess Monthly* ended its run in 1861.

D. W. Fiske was born in Ellisburg, New York, in 1831, was educated at Copenhagen and at the Swedish University of Uppsala, became a professional American diplomat and professor of North European linguistics at Cornell University in Ithaca, New York.[6] Later on he assumed the position of Librarian of the institution, where his archives were housed and on the grounds of which he was buried. He is said to have mastered about forty languages.

An active supporter of chess publications and a fine organizer of chess events, he wrote a scholarly volume, published posthumously, *Chess in Iceland and in Icelandic Literature* (Florence, Italy: 1905). It supplied some of the more important source material for H. J. T. Murray's *A History of Chess*. Also after his death appeared the manuscript *Chess Tales and Chess Miscellanies* (New York: 1912), an anthology which faithfully mirrors the chess life of the period and contains articles about Morphy and about the history of chess, a number of fables, and also problems by Loyd, etc.

Fiske helped organize the First American Chess Congress in New York in 1875. It was won by the greenhorn Paul Charles Morphy, followed by young Louis Paulsen, with Lichtenhein third. Thirteen more American players followed suit sedately. In 1859, Fiske brought out the tournament book, one of the most accurate and readable American chess books ever written, a classic. America had arrived at master chess and Hurricane Morphy was approaching.

---

[6] Another three notable chess players-diplomats, who will take their bows later, were Max Judd, James Mortimer, and Raul Capablanca.

# 2.

# Morphy: A Chess Player's
# Fame and Failure

Upper-class breeding, the study of law, and the enjoyment of music were the initial ingredients in the makeup of Paul Charles Morphy. He came to be, inescapably, the symbol for chess genius. He was born in New Orleans, Louisiana, in 1837, as son of Louise Thelcide, nee Le Carpentier, a Creole, and Louisiana Supreme Court judge Alonzo Michael Morphy.

Morphy's grandfather, James Diego Morphy, who died in 1814 in New Orleans, was born to his Portuguese mother in Malaga, Spain, in 1765. His great-grandfather, Miguel Morphy, had arrived in Madrid, Spain, in 1753 from Ireland as "Michael Murphy," and from 1793 to 1799 filled the position of U.S. Consul for southern Spain.

## THE YOUNG CELEBRITY

Paul Morphy learned the game of chess at the age of ten, became a New Orleans chess celebrity two years later, and moved decisively into the international limelight in 1875, when he topped the First American Chess Congress in New York.

The Congress consisted of a number of elimination matches. In his encounter with Paulsen in the last round, Morphy chalked up 5 wins and 2 draws, with only 1 loss. Getting 6 out of 8 possible points had the makings of a stampede, as Paulsen was no pushover. Born in Germany in 1833, he had picked up the game at the age of four, and during his residency in the States between 1854 and 1860, had quickly secured top rank. He was feared for his methodical innovations in the openings.

The Paulsen System of the Sicilian Defense is still as alive as ever. He was the first theoretician to demonstrate the superiority of two bishops over two knights in the endgame. He was a tenacious defender in closed positions, which were one of Morphy's few weak spots; he never felt too comfortable with a constricted game.

Morphy was by far not so infallible as he was often made out to be. The masters of future generations became better technicians than he was. Comparisons between the strength of leading players of different epochs are very difficult because each player is the child of his own intellectual climate. The early masters were builders of first prototypes, geniuses compared to their contemporaries. In the first game given below, the stratagems, novel or faulty, the sparks and the deficiencies of a human struggle—all show up in full force. But Morphy, the doer, embodies a young mind's reaction against too much groping for deeper meaning still insufficiently supported by any massive experience.

Morphy exemplified *development*. He speedily placed his pieces in their most effective locations, and his games thus became the first incarnations of time, space, and mobility in chess. But against the rock of Paulsen's staying power, these features could not come to the fore so manifestly as against opponents of lesser strength. Thus, Morphy's encounters with Paulsen showed ups and downs and lapses on both sides until Morphy finally prevailed.

The 6th match game, played on November 8, 1857, in the 4th round, holds a prominent place among these encounters.

**FIRST AMERICAN
CHESS CONGRESS**

Round 4
New York 1857
*Four Knights' Defense*

L. PAULSEN          P. MORPHY

1 P-K4          P-K4
2 N-KB3          N-QB3
3 N-B3

Typical for Paulsen's style, which in those days was "modernistic," that is, positional. He preferred this cautious approach to the volatile Scotch Game or Gambit, or the Evans Gambit.

3 . . .          N-B3
4 B-N5          B-B4

A Morphy natural. The consensus of sophisticated opening analysis, since Morphy leans toward 4 . . . N-Q5 or 4 . . . B-N5; but the final distillate of 4 . . . B-B4 concedes White only a minimal edge.

For Morphy, moving the knight twice so early in the game by 4 . . . N-Q5 was an inconceivable loss of tempo, notwithstanding the later principles of the modern school.

To play 4 . . . B-N5 would have meant a symmetrical, hence positional, answer falling in line with Paulsen's own style, and Morphy may have discarded the move in favor of psychologically more disturbing tactics. Instead, in his own way, he developed a piece on the diagonal with the widest range.

5 O–O        O–O
6 NxP       R–K1

The point of divergence of the old and the new. The latter now prefers 6 . . . NxN 7 P–Q4 B–Q3 8 P–B4 N–B3 9 P–K5 B–N5 10 P–Q5 P–QR3 11 B–K2 B–B4ch 12 K–R1 NxQP 13 QxN, with only a minimal edge (Keres). 6 . . . N–Q5 is another choice.

As is his habit, Morphy picks a move (6 . . . R–K1) that occupies an open rank and after the next exchange also opens a file for his bishop.

7 NxN

The accepted thinking, even for Paulsen, who thus plays into Morphy's hands. If White had played 7 N–B3! NxP 8 P–Q4 NxN 9 PxN B–B1 10 B–KB4 P–Q3 11 Q–Q2, the position might have proved disappointing for Morphy.

7 . . .        QPxN
8 B–B4?

The struggle becomes ambiguous. More prudent but sterile is 8 B–K2 NxP 9 NxN RxN 10 P–B3 B–B4 11 B–B3 R–K1 12 P–Q4 B–Q3 13 B–K3 B–K5=. White's bland move 8 B–B4

tries to tempt Black's faulty answer 8 . . . NxP 9 NxN RxN 10 BxPch KxB 11 Q–B3ch. Yet, White's move was inaccurate because it afforded Black the missed opportunity of an aggressive 8 . . . N–N5!; e.g., 9 P–KR3 NxP 10 BxPch K–R1 (10 . . . KxB 11 Q–R5ch and 12 QxB) and Black has the upper hand. In the tournament book, D. W. Fiske suggested 8 . . . N–N5!

8 . . .        P–QN4
9 B–K2

If 9 B–N3 B–KN5 10 Q–K1 P–N5. Already, White has to be on his toes.

9 . . .        NxP
10 NxN       RxN
11 B–B3

The first of a series of misjudgments! 11 P–B3 (to prepare P–Q4) Q–R5 12 B–B3 is in order; or 11 P–Q3 R–K3 12 P–QB3 followed by P–Q4.

11 . . .      R–K3
12 P–B3?      Q–Q6!

Quite logical. What leads Paulsen to underrate the elementary dangers of his "hole" on Q3? He must be counting on a better harvest from his ensuing counterplay than he actually gathers.

13 P–QN4     B–N3
14 P–QR4     PxP
15 QxP       B–Q2?

An inaccuracy which allows 16 Q–R6 Q–B4 17 P–Q4 QR–K1

18 B–K3, almost turning the tables. Black should have played 15 . . . B–N2; but, incomprehensibly for a master like Paulsen, he fails to capitalize on what seems the best chance for counterplay and opens the floodgate of Morphy's first immortal brilliancy.

Paulsen's next move may plan for an alternative 17 Q–B2, but it comes too late. He is getting demoralized.

| 16 R–R2? | QR–K1! |
| 17 Q–R6 | |

Black threatens 17 . . . QxRch and 18 R–R8 mate. At this point, Morphy, an exceptionally fast player, takes twelve minutes to examine fully the impact of his coming shocker. In those days, chess was played without any time limit, although the American game moved at a far quicker pace than the European one.

| 17 . . . | QxB!! |
| 18 PxQ | R–N3ch |
| 19 K–R1 | B–R6 |
| 20 R–Q1 | |

As commonly quoted, if 20 R–N1 B–N7ch 21 RxB R–K8ch 22 Q–B1 RxQch 23 R–N1 RxR mate. But 20 . . . RxRch KxR 21 R–K8ch is quicker! If 20 Q–Q3 P–KB4 21 Q–B4ch K–B1 22 Q–R4 BxR 23 QxP B–N7ch 24 K–N1 R–K8 mate.

| 20 . . . | B–N7ch |
| 21 K–N1 | BxPch. |
| 22 K–B1 | B–N7ch |

Morphy's mating schema is already set in his mind and he need not evaluate other variants as discovered by post-mortems; e.g., 22 . . . R–N7 23 Q–Q3 RxPch 24 K–N1 R–N7ch 25 K any R–N8 mate.

| 23 K–N1 | B–R6ch |

Again, quicker is 23 . . . B–K5ch 24 K–B1 B–KB4 25 Q–K2 B–R6ch 26 K–K1 R–N8 mate.

| 24 K–R1 | BxP |
| 25 Q–B1 | BxQ |
| 26 RxB | R–K7 |
| 27 R–R1 | R–R3 |
| 28 P–Q4 | B–K6 |
| 29 BxB | R/3xPch |
| 30 K–N1 | R/K7–N7 mate |

Paulsen was beaten, but not crushed. Indeed, the defeat stimulated his own ambitions. Strenuously improving all facets of his game, he grew into Europe's leading player and in the post-Morphy era beat the famed A. Anderssen in two matches.

Despite its age, the following game by Morphy is still the most homogeneous example of instruction to be found. It is not only eternally famous, but also exceptionally charming, and was played during a performance of Rossini's *The Barber of Seville*.

## Paris 1858
### *Philidor's Defense*

| P. MORPHY | DUKE OF BRUNS- |
| | WICK AND |
| | COUNT ISOUARD |

| 1 | P-K4 | P-K4 |
| 2 | N-KB3 | P-Q3 |
| 3 | P-Q4 | B-N5 |

An inferior move, dismissed by posterity, but for decades still used by Lasker, Blackburn, and others.

| 4 | PxP | BxN |

Otherwise a pawn is lost, although Black may try to compensate for it by 4 . . . N-Q2 5 PxP BxP 6 B-K2 Q-K2 with an aggressive posture. After the text, White had 5 PxB PxP 6 QxQch KxQ 7 P-KB4 P-KB3 8 R-N1 P-KN3! 9 PxP PxP 10 N-B3 with a superior position. But Morphy continues in his manner.

| 5 | QxB | PxP |
| 6 | B-QB4 | N-KB3? |

White's mating threat is incidental. Basically he is just developing, with two pieces out—and he has a pair of bishops. Black's reply is faulty. He should have played 6 . . . Q-K2 —although it shuts in his bishop —and if 7 Q-QN3 Q-N5ch. If 6 . . . Q-B3 7 Q-QN3 B-B4 8 O-O B-N3 9 N-B3 N-K2 10 P-QR4; or 6 . . . Q-Q2 7 B-K3 N-QB3 8 N-B3 N-B3 9 O-O O-O-O 10 KR-K1 B-K3 with a precarious defense.

| 7 | Q-QN3 | Q-K2 |
| 8 | N-B3! | |

White could have simplified with 8 QxP Q-N5ch 9 QxQ BxQch 10 B-Q2, securing a pawn majority on the queen's side and winning slowly but surely, but Morphy has a more immediate goal. He strengthens his attack, and Black's reply is forced.

| 8 | . . . | P-B3 |
| 9 | B-KN5 | |

White pins Black's only developed piece and it is all over. There is no satisfactory answer.

| 9 | . . . | P-N4 |

No better is 9 . . . P-KR3 10 BxN PxB 11 O-O-O B-N2 12 BxPch QxB 13 R-Q8ch K-K2 14 QxPch K-K3 15 R-Q6 winning; or 9 . . . N-R3 10 B/5xN PxB 11 BxN PxB 12 Q-R4 wins; or 9 . . . Q-B2 10 O-O-O B-Q3 11 BxPch QxB 12 RxB; or 10 . . . B-B4 11 BxPch QxB 12 R-Q8ch.

| 10 | NxP!! | PxN |
| 11 | BxNPch | QN-Q2 |
| 12 | O-O-O!! | R-Q1 |

Black is all tied up. The remainder is exquisitely smooth.

| 13 | RxN! | RxR |
| 14 | R-Q1 | Q-K3 |

Now 15 BxN would win simply; Morphy chooses graceful definitiveness.

15 BxRch!    NxB
16 Q–N8ch!    NxQ
17 R–Q8 mate

Pinning stratagems, similar and equally compelling, often crop up in simple king's pawn openings; e.g., 1 P–K4 P–K4 2 N–KB3 N–QB3 3 B–N5 P–Q3 4 P–Q4 PxP 5 NxP B–Q2 6 BxN BxB (6 . . . PxB!) 7 NxB PxN 8 N–B3 N–B3 9 Q–B3 B–K2 10 P–K5 PxP 11 QxPch N–Q2 12 B–K3 O–O 13 O–O–O B–Q3 14 N–N5 N–N3 15 NxB PxN 16 NxR+ (Korn-Szirmay, Prague Championship preliminaries, 1930).

The next exhibit is intriguing. It is a mailed fist trying to knock out the opponent speedily, although positional prudence would have dictated avoiding any risk, since the position was safely wrapped up already.

The game has had amazing fluctuations. The following encounter had an opening which under modern scrutiny should have given a clear advantage to White; a middlegame filled with continuous tension; and a final phase in which a chance was missed to save the day. It is Morphy at his most daring—or no longer caring.

### London 1858
*Philidor's Defense*

H. E. BIRD                    P. MORPHY

1 P–K4        P–K4
2 N–KB3       P–Q3
3 P–Q4        P–KB4

Philidor's own original follow-up, now known as "Philidor's Counterattack." With more than a century of research into chess openings and principles since Morphy, it is futile to judge the merits of Morphy's choice; but even an amateur would smell danger in the precarious loosening of Black's structure. Still, today's tenets were neither fully known nor accepted by either opponent—and Morphy might even have gambled on it!

4 N–B3!

Stasch Mlotkowski, who provided P. W. Sergeant's *Morphy Gleanings* (New York: McKay, 1932) with much analysis, gives

4 KPxP, or 4 QPxP, or 4 B–QB4
as equally playable.[1]

4 . . .                  BPxP
5 QNxP               P–Q4
6 N–N3

A natural-looking reply, but it
justifies Black's strategy, which
gives him quite good chances.

Since Steinitz, the best an-
swer has been 6 NxP! PxN 7
Q–R5ch P–N3 8 NxP N–KB3
9 Q–K5ch K–B2 10 B–QB4ch
K–N2 11 N–R4 (also 11 NxR)
B–Q3 12 Q–N5ch K–B1 13 Q–
R6ch K–K1 14 N–N6±.

6 . . .                  P–K5
1 N–K5                N–KB3
8 B–KN5             B–Q3

The majority would agree with
8 . . . B–K2 as "safer." Morphy
plays it his way and the sequel
proves him right. He studied
his adversaries' habits well in
advance.

9 N–R5                O–O
10 Q–Q2!?

If 10 BxN PxB 11 N–N4 P–
KB4 12 N–K5 P–B5 13 Q–Q2
Q–N4∓. But 10 P–KB4 or 10
B–K2 was solid.

10 . . .                Q–K1!
11 P–KN4!

11 NxNch PxN 12 BxP RxB 13
Q–N5ch R–N3 14 NxR QxN
15 QxPch K–N2 would have
left Morphy with a dangerous
pair of bishops.

11 . . .                NxP
12 NxN                QxN
13 N–K5               N–B3!?
14 B–K2               Q–R6
15 NxN                PxN
16 B–K3               R–N1

A sound move, seizing the open
file, with a pawn to the better
and a game already won tech-
nically. (Steinitz suggested 13
. . . P–B4!) The attack on the
NP also happens to be the
opener for a combinational
maneuver that could have been
forestalled by 17 P–QB3.

17 O–O–O            RxBP

Steinitz taught a later generation first to be certain that a
combination was sound against
the best defense, but otherwise
to follow the sure positional
path to victory. He thus con-
demned playing for brilliancy
per se or for apparent beauty—
if the core was rotten. But
Morphy did not yet have to
care, and got away by the skin of
his teeth!

[1] Stasch Mlotkowski, originally residing on the West Coast, was a strong
player who, at the age of forty-two, tied Norman T. Whitaker for 1st place in
the U.S. Open Championship in San Francisco in 1923.

18 BxR         Q-R6!!?
19 P-B3!

Forty years later, W. Steinitz, a World Chess Champion, claimed a win for White, with 19 Q-N5 QxPch 20 K-Q2 B-N5ch 21 K-K3, continuing 21 . . . Q-B6ch? 22 B-Q3± instead of 21 . . . Q-R6ch! 22 B-Q3 B-R3 23 KR-N1 B-KB1∓ as found by Maróczy in 1909. It shows that Bird happened to guess right, and that even high-level analysis is bound to be just as fickle as ingenuity. If 19 Q-B3 B-B5ch 20 R-Q2 QxRP 21 Q-QR3 QxQ 22 PxQ P-K6 with Black two pawns ahead. Or 21 P-N3 P-K6 22 BxP BxB 23 R-B1! P-B4! 24 PxP P-Q5 25 Q-B4ch B-K3! 26 QxBch K-R1 wins.

19 . . .        QxP!

Insufficient is 19 . . . P-K6 20 BxP (20 PxQ? BxPch 21 K-B2 B-KB4ch+) B-KB4 21 Q-B2 QxRP 22 B-Q3 BxB! 23 RxB B-R6 24 PxB Q-R8ch 25 K-Q2 QxR 26 P-B4 QxPch 27 K-B3.

20 P-N4!

If 20 Q-B2 RxP! 21 QxR B-QR6 22 QxB QxQch 23 Q-K2

Q-N7ch 24 K-K1 QxPch, winning for Black.

20 . . .        Q-R8ch
21 K-B2        Q-R5ch
22 K-N2?

White is after a win, but hereby loses the chance to draw by 22 K-B1 Q-R8ch with a perpetual (but not 22 . . . BxNP 23 PxB RxP; and 24 Q-N5 Q-R6ch 25 K-Q2 R-N7ch 26 K-K1 RxBch 27 KxR Q-B6ch 28 K-K1 QxKR 29 Q-N1 wins).

22 . . .        BxNP!!
23 PxB         RxPch
24 QxR         QxQch
25 K-B2

Nothing else helps. If 25 K-R2 P-B4! wins in all variations.

25 . . .        P-K6!
26 BxP         B-B4ch
27 R-Q3        Q-B5ch
28 K-Q2        Q-R7ch
29 K-Q1        Q-N8ch

And Black wins. Despite its flaws, the sacrifice of the rook on one wing, followed immediately by an offer of the queen on the other, has captured the imagination.

However, the drive to win a game by beauty rather than by efficiency was epitomized by Adolph Anderssen and not by Morphy the rationalist. Nonetheless, the pursuit of beauty for its own sake can become hollow if not crowned by success—and pure reason followed by a sudden, brilliant exploit can be a truer beauty.

The clash of ideologies came in Paris in 1858, when the un-

crowned king, Adolph Anderssen, succumbed. The match game
score was: Morphy 7, Anderssen 2, and drawn 2. As usual for
Morphy, he started slowly, feeling his ground as he proceeded. He
lost the 1st game, drew the next, and then kept winning. The 9th
game was a brevity, full of punch, but also of substance. The whole
game lasted just half an hour.

## VERSATILITY, MASTERY, INSTINCT

Morphy's challenging sojourn in Europe began with a match against
Loewenthal, who was not unknown to Morphy. In 1850, at the age
of 13, he had beaten Loewenthal in New Orleans 3:0! Then the boy
was already known as a prodigy; but by 1858 Loewenthal had
matured into grandmastership. Yet, Loewenthal served just as a
sparring partner, with a final score Morphy 9, Loewenthal 3, drawn
2. This was the 14th and last game of the match.

### London 1858
*Ruy Lopez*

| P. MORPHY | J. LOEWENTHAL |
|-----------|---------------|
| 1 P–K4    | P–K4          |
| 2 N–KB3   | N–QB3         |
| 3 B–N5    | P–QR3         |
| 4 B–R4    | N–B3          |

The Ruy Lopez was a novel
opening, not yet explored, and
both sides were experimenting.
In addition to his flair for an
early opening of lines, Morphy
was a master of all theory then
known. He enriched his game
by adding new variants whenever the opportunity arose. The
Ruy Lopez as used here already
includes Black's protective . . .
P–QR3; but White does not
continue in the deliberate and
enduring manner of 5 O–O, so
typical for this overture. Instead

once again he opens up with an
early center thrust.

| 5 P–Q4 | PxP |
|--------|-----|

If 5 . . . NxKP? 6 Q–K2 P–B4 7
P–Q5, etc.

| 6 P–K5 | N–K5  |
|--------|-------|
| 7 O–O  | N–B4  |
| 8 BxN  | QPxB  |
| 9 NxP  | N–K3  |

Black's last move restricts his
options. Better would have been
9 . . . B–K2, as adopted by
Morphy against T. P. W.
Barnes in London in 1858. Since
Morphy's day, the whole system
of the Ruy Lopez with 3 . . .
P–QR3 right through the 9th
move, has been defined as "Morphy's." The game Barnes–Morphy continued 10 N–QB3 O–O
11 B–K3 P–B3. With refined
positional treatment, after 12

PxP White can make his pawn majority on the king's wing tell. Modern strategy has turned to *11 ... R–K1 12 R–K1 B–B1 13 P–B4 P–B3* (Alekhine–Keres, Kemeri 1937).

| 10 NxN | BxN |
| 11 Q–K2 | B–QB4 |

A very logical move, even though Morphy found an antidote. Some authorities call *11 . . . B–K2* the safer tactic, but *12 N–B3 O–O 13 B–K3* allows only *13 . . . Q–B1!? 14 N–K4 B–KB4* (*14 . . . B–Q4 15 N–N3 P–QN4 16 P–N3 P–KB4 17 P–KB4±*) *15 N–N3*, with a better game for White. Koenig suggests dynamic counteraction by *11 . . . Q–R5 12 N–Q2 O–O–O or 12 R–Q1 B–K2.*[2]

| 12 N–B3 | Q–K2 |
| 13 N–K4 | P–R3 |
| 14 B–K3 | BxB |
| 15 QxB | B–B4? |
| 16 N–N3 | BxP |
| 17 P–B4 | P–KN3 |

A many-horned dilemma. If (a) *17 . . . Q–N5 18 R–B2 B–R5* (*18 . . . QxNP? 19 QR–QB1*) *19 P–N3±*. Castling is also out; e.g., (b) *17 . . . O–O–O 18 Q–R7* or *17 . . . O–O 18 P–B5*, followed by either *19 P–B6* or *19 KR–B1 B–R5 20 P–N3 B–N4 21 P–QR4*. After (c) *17 . . . P–*

KB4 *18 KR–B1 B–K5 19 NxB PxN 20 QxP*, White stands better. But White's interpolation *17 P–B4*, which foresaw Black's best reply, contained a devilish design.

**18 P–K6!!**

Unmistakably Morphy. Taking the pawn loses the bishop after *19 Q–QB3*. If now *18 . . . O–O 19 P–B5*; if *18 . . . B–R5 19 Q–Q4*; and if *18 . . . O–O–O 19 QR–B1* and *20 Q–R7*, always with a better game.

| 18 . . . | B–B4 |
| 19 NxB | PxN |
| 20 PxPch | KxP |
| 21 Q–KR3 | Q–B3 |
| 22 QR–K1 | KR–K1 |
| 23 R–K5! | |

By minimum means, White has his opponent snared in a maximum grip.

If *23 . . . RxR 24 PxR QxP 25 RxPch* wins and thus Black cannot prevent White from doubling his rooks with even more pressure. Morphy's technique in this game anticipates Capablanca's.

| 23 . . . | K–N3 |
| 24 KR–K1 | RxR |
| 25 RxR | R–Q1 |
| 26 Q–N3ch | K–R2 |
| 27 P–KR3 | |

[2] Imre Koenig, *From Morphy to Botvinnik* (London: Bell & Sons, 1951). Koenig was born in Hungary in 1899, became a Yugoslav subject after 1918, emigrated to England in 1938, and was named an international master in 1951. A British subject since 1949, Koenig moved to the West Coast of the United States in 1953 for reasons of health.

Despite the pawn minority on the queen's wing, White can afford a waiting move.

| 27 . . . | R–Q2 |
| 28 Q–K3 | P–N3 |
| 29 K–R2 | P–B4 |
| 30 Q–K2 | Q–N3 |
| 31 R–K6 | Q–N2 |
| 32 Q–R5 | R–Q4 |
| 33 P–QN3! | |

Black can move no piece without immediate loss, and so is reduced to pawn moves. If 33 . . . P–R4 34 P–QR4 with a complete blockade. If 33 . . . Q–B1 34 Q–N6ch+.

| 33 . . . | P–N4 |
| 34 RxP | R–Q3 |

By giving up his pawn to gain space, Black loses another pawn.

If *34 . . . P–B5 35 PxP PxP 36 R–QB6 P–B6 37 P–R4 R–R4 38 Q–Q1 R–R2 39 Q–Q5++.* The closing part of the game is handled with impeccable skill.

| 35 QxBPch | Q–N3 |
| 36 QxQch | KxQ |
| 37 R–R5 | R–N3 |
| 38 P–KN4 | P–B3 |
| 39 K–N3 | P–R4 |
| 40 R–R7 | PxP |
| 41 PxP | K–B3 |
| 42 P–B5 | K–K4 |
| 43 R–K7ch | K–Q3 |
| 44 P–B6 | R–N1 |
| 45 P–N5 | R–KB1 |
| 46 K–B4 | P–B5 |
| 47 PxP | PxP |
| 48 K–B5 | P–B6 |
| 49 R–K3 | |
| Wins | |

Loewenthal lost the match, but Morphy used the stake to buy a substantial part of the furniture for Loewenthal's newly bought London home.

The next few games help disclose the full spectrum of Morphy's versatility. They embraced all the stylistic trademarks that were later developed in detail by other chess artists. Morphy had an uncanny instinct for technical aspects. He mastered the opening theory of his time and contributed heavily to it with lasting influence. He had a clear insight into positional requirements and was able to switch efficiently from one stratagem to another, depending on the phase of the game or his opponent's psychological makeup.

## FIRST AMERICAN
## CHESS CONGRESS

Round 3, Game 1
New York 1857
*Scotch Gambit (Two Knights'*
*Defense)*

TH. LICHTENHEIN[3]     P. MORPHY

| 1 P–K4 | P–K4 |
|--------|------|
| 2 N–KB3 | N–QB3 |
| 3 P–Q4 | PxP |
| 4 B–QB4 | N–B3 |

The opening started as a Scotch Gambit, nowadays thematically continued with 4 . . . B–B4. With 4 . . . N–B3, Black transposes it into a Two Knights' Defense.

The conventional line is 5 O–O NxP (or 5 . . . B–B4 6 P–K5, the Max Lange Attack) 6 R–K1 P–Q4 7 BxP (or Canal's 7 N–B3?!) QxB 8 N–B3 Q–QR4 9 NxN! B–K3 10 QN–N5 O–O–O 11 NxB PxN 12 RxP B–Q3 (or 12 . . . Q–KB4) with full equality. In the game, White adopts a more impetuous line, which in recent years has shown quite a sting.

| 5 P–K5 | P–Q4 |
|--------|------|
| 6 B–QN5 | N–K5 |
| 7 NxP | B–Q2 |
| 8 NxN? | |

A doubtful move. The right follow-up is 8 BxN.

| 8 . . . | PxN |
|---------|-----|
| 9 B–Q3 | B–QB4 |
| 10 BxN | Q–R5! |

Starting an onslaught, seemingly out of nowhere.

| 11 Q–K2 | PxB |
|---------|-----|
| 12 B–K3 | |

Better would have been 12 O–O.

| 12 . . . | B–N5 |
|----------|------|
| 13 Q–B4 | |

13 Q–Q2 R–Q1 wins for Black. Only 13 P–KN3 was playable.

| 13 . . . | BxB |
|----------|-----|
| 14 P–KN3 | |

14 QxQBPch B–Q2 15 QxRch K–K2 16 P–KN3 Q–N5 17 QxR BxPch 18 KxB Q–B6ch 19 K–N1 B–R6 forces mate after what is called "a brilliant two-rook sacrifice." Also 16 . . . BxPch 17 KxB P–K6ch 18 K–K1 Q–N5ch 19 P–B3 QxP/N7 20 QxR B–N5 wins. 14 O–O B–N3 15 QxQBPch K–K2 leaves Black with a piece to the good.

| 14 . . . | Q–Q1 |
|----------|------|
| 15 PxB | Q–Q8ch |
| 16 K–B2 | Q–B6ch |
| 17 K–N1 | B–R6 |
| 18 QxQBPch | K–B1 |
| 19 QxRch | K–K2 |
| Resigns | |

---

[3] Lichtenhein was also a composer of endgame studies. One of his studies is quoted in W. Korn, *American Chess Art* (New York: Pitman, 1975), diag. 59.

The game depicts some of the early brilliance passed on to us and now part of the arsenal of elementary techniques. But its historic beauty still has its thrill.

Upon his arrival in Paris in 1858, Morphy first challenged "The King of the Café de la Régence," Daniel Harrwitz. Morphy lost the first 2 games, but when he reached the score of 5 to 2, with 2 draws, Harrwitz backed out. With his customary chivalry, Morphy used the prize money to meet A. Anderssen's expenses of coming to Paris, or, with tongue in cheek, he could afford to be generous in order to make certain that his ambition to meet Anderssen was satisfied!

Match Game 4
Paris 1858
*Philidor's Defense*

P. MORPHY   D. HARRWITZ

| | P. MORPHY | D. HARRWITZ |
|---|---|---|
| 1 | P–K4 | P–K4 |
| 2 | N–KB3 | P–Q3 |
| 3 | P–Q4 | PxP |
| 4 | QxP | N–QB3 |
| 5 | B–QN5 | B–Q2 |
| 6 | BxN | BxB |
| 7 | B–N5! | |

A very significant position in the context of the playing style of the day, and also because of Morphy's personal predilections. In the second match game, Harrwitz played 7 . . . N–B3 and Morphy answered 8 N–B3 B–K2 9 O–O–O O–O 10 KR–K1 P–KR3 11 B–R4 N–K1 12 BxB QxB 13 P–K5? with a premature loosening of White's hold, instead of 13 Q–Q2!! followed by N–Q4. Morphy disliked the early exchange of queens after 8 BxN QxN 9 QxQ PxQ 10 N–B3 P–B4! and Black has a pair of bishops against White's knight. Harrwitz was an adherent of the closed game

and of positional play. He might well have feared a Morphy "improvement" on the 2nd match game. Therefore, he switched to

7 . . .   P–B3?

This allows White a minute advantage in space, which is progressively expanded in an exemplary manner. Called for was 7 . . . B–K2! 8 QxNP B–B3! 9 QxR BxQ 10 BxQ BxNP 11 BxP K–Q2=, as analyzed by Hamppe for Bilguer's *Handbuch des Schachspiels*.

| 8 | B–R4 | N–R3 |
|---|---|---|
| 9 | N–B3 | Q–Q2 |

If 9 . . . B–K2 10 Q–B4, threatening the maneuver N to Q4 to K6.

| 10 | O–O | B–K2 |
|---|---|---|
| 11 | QR–Q1 | O–O |
| 12 | Q–B4ch | R–B2 |

Black, feeling uneasy, plays trickily, trying to provoke 13 P–K5. Safer would have been 12 . . . K–R1 or 12 . . . N–B2.

13 N–Q4!

*13* P–K5 is blunted by *13* . . . Q–N5 *14* R–Q4 Q–N3 and *15* P–K6 creates an outpost, but an ever vulnerable one.

| 13 . . . | N–N5 |
|---|---|
| 14 P–KR3 | N–K4 |
| 15 Q–K2! | P–KN4 |

Prevents P–B4 but seriously weakens the king-side.

| 16 B–N3 | R–N2 |
|---|---|
| 17 N–B5 | R–N3 |
| 18 P–B4! | |

The very move that Black's 15th move aimed to forestall.

| 18 . . . | PxP |
|---|---|
| 19 RxBP | K–R1 |
| 20 R–R4! | B–B1 |

Black tries to counter White's aggressive play by equal deployment. But White's knight posted on B5 has more scope than Black's opposite number on K4. White's rooks have command over the bishop's and the rook's open files, whereas Black controls only the knight's file. Thus, in retrospect, *15* . . . P–KN4 is to blame for Black's troubles.

With his next move, White swaps his inactive bishop for Black's only stronghold.

| 21 BxN! | BPxB |
|---|---|
| 22 R–KB1 | Q–K3 |
| 23 N–N5! | Q–N1 |

White threatened *24* NxBP, winning the exchange and preventing the consolidation *23* . . . Q–N1. But Black has to make this move anyway, as there is hardly another choice. If *23* . . . Q–Q2 *24* Q–R5 K–N1 *25* N–B3 or *24* . . . BxN *25* QxR BxR *26* KxB and Black hasn't a good move left. Upon *23* . . . BxN comes *24* QxB with a dominant position, although it requires prolonged play to arrive at the win.

| 24 R–B2! | P–QR3 |
|---|---|
| 25 NxBP | R–B1 |
| 26 N–Q5 | BxN |
| 27 PxB | R–B2 |

Also strategically lost is *27* . . . QxP *28* RxPch KxR *29* Q–R5ch B–R3 *30* NxB! RxN *31* Q–B5ch and *32* QxQR with a pawn to the good in a superior position (Euwe).

| 28 P–B4 | B–K2 |
|---|---|
| 29 R–R5 | Q–K1 |

| 30 P–B5! | RxP |
|---|---|

White was aiming at *31* PxP BxP *32* NxB RxN *33* RxP. White wraps up the game and Black is helpless. *30* . . . PxP *31* QxPch would have lost the rook.

| If *30* . . . R–Q2 *31* PxP BxP | | | **31 RxPch** | **KxR** |
| | | | | |

If *30* . . . R–Q2 *31* PxP BxP
*32* NxB QRxN *33* RxP Q–Q2
*34* R–K8ch R–N1 *35* Q–K5ch
Q–N2 *36* QR–B8+; or *33* . . .
Q–N4 *34* R–K8ch K–N2 *35* Q–
K7ch K–R3 *36* Q–R4ch K–N2
*37* R–K7ch+.

| **31 RxPch** | **KxR** |
|---|---|
| **32 Q–R5ch** | **K–N1** |
| **33 NxBch** | **K–N2** |
| **34 N–B5ch** | **K–N1** |
| **35 NxP** | **Resigns** |

A thoroughly purposeful progress toward the win.

J. W. Schulten was an American expatriate, sleeping and dreaming chess in New York, at the time that Morphy was also in the
city; but mostly he shuttled between the United States and Paris,
and later Berlin. He was one class behind the greatest, losing his
matches to C. H. Stanley and E. Rousseau of the U.S., and against
Saint-Amant and La Bourdonnais of France. Yet, he was not to be
taken lightly, and the defeat that he suffered at Morphy's hand
could have befallen the strongest—and did, as is well known.

### New York 1857
### *King's Gambit Declined*

| J. W. SCHULTEN | P. MORPHY |
|---|---|
| 1  P–K4 | P–K4 |
| 2  P–KB4 | P–Q4 |
| 3  PxQP | P–K5 |
| 4  N–QB3 | N–KB3 |
| 5  P–Q3 | |

Because of his loss of the pres-
ent game, Schulten switched in
a later offhand game to the
more extrovert 5 B–B4 and won
a splendid short gem for him-
self! It went: *5* B–B4 P–B3!
(better than Marshall's *5* . . .
B–QB4 6 KN–K2 O–O 7 P–Q4
PxP e.p. 8 QxP R–K1 9 P–KR3
N–R4 *10* Q–B3 Q–R5ch *11*
K–Q1) *6* P–Q3 B–QN5 *7*
PxKP NxKP 8 B–Q2!! BxN 9
BxB O–O *10* Q–R5 R–K1 *11*
O–O–O!! NxB! (if *11* . . . N–B7

*12* N–R3! B–N5 *13* QxBPch
KxQ *14* PxPch K–N3 *15* RxQ
RxR *16* PxP N–B3 *17* PxR(Q)
RxQ *18* NxN wins) *12* PxN
Q–R4 *13* K–N2 P–KN3 *14* Q–
R6 B–N5 *15* N–B3 BxN *16* PxB
P–QN4 *17* P–B5 PxB *18* P–B6
resigns. Morphy's *17* . . . PxB
was an error, but White had the
far better game at any rate.

In modern times, White
plays first 4 P–Q3, and after 4
. . . N–KB3 retains the option
of either 5 N–QB3 or 5 N–Q2.
This, the Falkbeer variant of
the King's Gambit, with 2 . . .
P–Q4, has had nine lives at
least!

| 5 . . . | B–QN5 |
|---|---|

Or the "overprotection" *5* . . .
B–KB4 6 Q–K2 Q–K2 7 PxP
NxKP 8 NxN QxN 9 QxQ BxQ

10 P–B4 B–QB4 11 B–Q2 P–QB3!

**6 B–Q2        P–K6!**

Morphy's contribution of deep insight into the theory of the Falkbeer Counter Gambit. As he cannot hang on to the pawn, he uses it to retard White's development and to create counter chances on the king's file. Another serious choice is 6 . . . O–O 7 NxP R–K1 8 BxB NxN 9 PxN RxPch 10 B–K2 RxB 11 N–B3 RxBP 12 Q–Q2 Q–Q3 13 O–O–O N–Q2 14 N–Q4 P–QR3 15 P–KN3 R–B3 16 KR–K1 N–K4 17 B–R5 B–Q2 (Spassky-Bronstein, Moscow 1971).

| 7 | BxP | O–O |
|---|-----|-----|
| 8 | B–Q2 | BxN |
| 9 | PxB | R–K1ch |
| 10 | B–K2 | B–N5! |

10 . . . NxP gets one pawn back for Black, but he remains one down and with little hope after 11 N–B3 N–K6 12 BxN RxB 13 Q–Q2 Q–K2 14 K–B2.

However, Morphy never intended to regain material; he gave it up for a poisonous build-up. White can protect his center pawn, but this accelerates Black's attack. Altogether, 10 K–B2 would have been wiser; also, 11 K–B2.

**11 P–B4?        P–B3!**
**12 PxP**

What else? If 12 P–KR3 BxB 13 NxB Q–K2, White cannot castle. But 12 K–B1 may have been worth a try now instead of a move later.

| 12 . . . | NxP |
|----------|-----|
| 13 K–B1 | |

If 13 N–B3 BxN 14 PxB N–Q5 or 13 . . . N–Q5 at once, both winning for Black. Also 13 B–B3 N–Q5 14 BxN QxB 15 N–B3 BxN 16 PxB N–R4 17 R–KB1 NxP 18 R–B2 R–K1∓.

| 13 . . . | RxB! |
|----------|------|
| 14 NxR | N–Q5 |
| 15 Q–N1 | BxNch |
| 16 K–B2 | N–N5ch |
| 17 K–N1 | |

If 17 K–N3 N–B4ch and mate next move. If 17 K–K1 Q–R5ch 18 P–N3 R–K1! and 19 . . . N–N6 mate. After an amazingly rapid deterioration, White is now mated in seven moves.

| 17 . . . | N–B6ch! |
|----------|---------|
| 18 PxN | Q–Q5ch |
| 19 K–N2 | Q–B7ch |
| 20 K–R3 | Q–BPch |
| 21 K–R4 | N–R3 |
| 22 Q–N1 | N–B4ch |
| 23 K–N5 | Q–R4 mate |

If 22 P–KR3 N–B4ch 23 K–N5 Q–R4 mate. A game cast of one solid mold and a classic.

## THE FIRST WORLD CHESS CHAMPION

When the chess world still belonged to refined amateurism, it may not have been appropriate to claim, on one's own, the title of Chess

Champion. Maybe because of modesty, or because of his disdain
for chess being treated as a record-setting sport, Morphy refrained
from attaching any such predicate to his proven deeds. The official
acquisition of the title was left to the dedicated and self-assured
William Steinitz, after his victory over Anderssen in 1866.

Before, and even after, defeating Anderssen, Morphy sought a
match with Staunton, the patriarch of Western chess, just as later
Capablanca insisted on a match with Lasker rather than accept the
latter's offered resignation of the title. But there was no doubt about
the expected outcome, either in the public's mind or in Morphy's.
The recourse Staunton used to evade the issue was to plead greater
commitment to his Shakespearean research. Staunton had high
standing outside the chess world, even though his scholastic authority has since been overtaken by later generations of scholars. He kept
his contact with chess by continuing his column in the *Illustrated
London News* as a hobby, but he no longer practiced the game. He
knew he was past his prime.

In light of Staunton's traditional achievements, the paradox of
Staunton's inability to recognize Morphy's ascendancy and to acknowledge objectively his spontaneous creative gifts is unfortunate.
It was strongly disapproved by many of his contemporaries, and by
later British writers; for example, P. W. Sergeant. Staunton's tournament successes against Cochrane, Saint-Amant, and Harrwitz within
the setting of that period; his well-structured chess compendia; his
taste in endorsing the subsequently famous and still irreplaceable
"Staunton style" chessmen; his evolvement of chess theory, ahead
of his time and ahead of Steinitz; and his organizational feats—all
had gained him his monument in the forum of chess.

Unhappily, his vitriolic attacks on Morphy, and other newcomers,
via his widely circulated chess column, were more harmful to
Staunton than to his victims. The attacks increased in vehemence
as he moved away from actual play. In a well-written book that pays
homage, long overdue, to their countryman, R. D. Keene and R. N.
Coles in *Howard Staunton—The English World Chess Champion*
(*The British Chess Magazine Quarterly,* No. 17, 1975) make a val-
iant effort to defend Staunton's attitude toward Morphy. They
accuse "Morphy's ardent but polemical supporter, F. M. Edge, a
reporter for the American *Herald* [for] exerting biased pressure in
Morphy's behalf." To dispel an ambiguity: Frederic Milne Edge
reported for the *Herald* but was an Englishman. Edge's advocacy of
Morphy may not have been patriotic, but he was apparently aggravated by Staunton's stalling and lack of fair play. (Sergeant calls
Edge biased for Morphy, but not prejudiced against Staunton.)
Staunton had gone through a period when he could have assumed

the championship title, but he didn't; nor did Morphy, who tried his best, however, to induce Staunton to a match. In the absence of Staunton's simply reasoned "no," it does not sound convincing for the above authors to connect this effort to an "American Morphy-Edge syndrome," imposed on "a world [that] was soon to realize that Morphy was an incipient psychopath." We will look at this factor later, but in the present context of an apologia, it is an illogical inference ex post facto. There is much obscurity regarding Staunton's birth and early youth. He had lifted himself up by his own bootstraps. Did he envy Morphy's upper-class upbringing? Had his early obstacles left a scar?

Staunton abandoned practical chess in 1852 (according to Keene and Coles), but vis-à-vis Morphy he made a comeback on the level of dialectics.

Morphy wanted to cement his reputation further, and for the record, but not because of self-doubt. His marginal note, hand-written in 1853, augmented the title page in his copy of Staunton's *Book of the London 1851 Tournament* as "by H. Staunton Esq., author of . . . and some devilish bad games."

Had Morphy wanted to make a nuisance of himself, he could have issued yet another challenge to Staunton before or during his second trip to Europe in 1862, but Morphy was no longer interested. He might have played von Kolisch, had the latter been able to accept the condition of "no stakes" at that time (Morphy would have paid his expenses, though).

Although not self-proclaimed, but still so recognized by popular opinion, Morphy may rightly be considered "the supreme being at chess" of the decade in which he shone; and it is not presumptuous to state that modern world chess championship was first attained by an American from the South. Granting him this title does not take away from his predecessors (Philidor, La Bourdonnais of France, or Staunton of Britain); but between Morphy and Staunton, champions each of two nations, intervened a period of qualitative and quantitative difference: Morphy's chess covered a wider range (note his record in blindfold chess); his personal appeal and the public response provided a more popular resonance than Staunton experienced; and when Morphy, and Anderssen, arrived on the stage, world chess no longer involved merely two great countries, England and France, putting forward their regional best. The "territory" already embraced at least the United States, Britain, France, Germany (and Hungary if we think of Szen and Loewenthal). Russia's Jaenisch and Petrov were absent only by reason of geography.

Staunton never met Morphy solo over the board, although he may have done so clandestinely at Staunton's home, shortly after

Morphy's arrival. It is an unconfirmed rumor. But during one such visit, they played two consultation games, with the second one completed at St. George's Chess Club in London. Both games were won by Morphy and his ally, T. W. Barnes. As the latter was one of Britain's champion players, Staunton could pretend that, unprepared and burdened with work, he actually lost the two games to his own rival Barnes and not to Morphy; but Barnes himself lost almost all his own games against Morphy. Staunton's second, Rev. Owen, was probably the real British champion at that time, as proven by his individual results against Barnes.

## FIRST CONSULTATION GAME

### London 1858
*Philidor's Defense*

| H. STAUNTON AND | P. MORPHY |
| J. OWEN | AND T. W. BARNES |

| 1 P–K4 | P–K4 |
| 2 N–KB3 | P–Q3 |
| 3 P–Q4 | P–KB4 |
| 4 QPxP | BPxP |
| 5 N–N5 | P–Q4 |
| 6 P–K6 | N–KR3! |
| 7 N–QB3! | P–B3 |
| 8 KNxKP | PxN |

This acceptance of White's positional sacrifice is more daring than 8 . . . N–B4 9 N–KN5 Q–B3 10 B–Q3 P–KR3. If 8 . . . BxP 9 BxN.

| 9 Q–R5ch | P–N3 |
| 10 Q–K5 | R–N1 |
| 11 BxN | |

Various analysts, including P. W. Sergeant and Bent Larsen, pointed out White's winning alternative 11 B–KN5 B–N2! 12 P–K7! Q–Q2! 13 Q–B4 N–N4 14 R–Q1, followed by B–

B4; but Black can defend with 13 . . . Q–B4! 14 BxN B–K3 15 O–O–O QxQch 16 BxQ BxN 17 B–KN5 N–Q2 18 PxB P–KR3 19 BxP KxP=. There is also 12 . . . Q–Q4=.

| 11 . . . | BxB |
| 12 R–Q1 | Q–N4 |
| 13 Q–B7 | |

Black shows great confidence in permitting this penetration. It threatens 14 QxBch as well as an immediate mate, but the threats come to naught.

| 13 . . . | BxP |
| 14 QxNP | |

If 14 NxP Q–K2 15 R–Q8ch QxR 16 N–Q6ch QxN, with ample compensation for the queen.

| 14 . . . | P–K6!? |

Even more incisive is 14 . . . Q–K2; e.g., 15 QxR K–B2 16 NxP B–Q4.

| 15 P–B3 | |

15 PxP QxPch 16 B–K2 Q–N3 17 QxKRP has been recom-

mended but is somewhat hazardous. If 15 N–K4 PxPch 16 NxP Q–K2!

| 15 . . . | Q–K2 |
| 16 QxR | K–B2! |
| 17 N–K4 | |

Staunton maintained that 17 R–Q4 would have won him the game, and Maróczy stated that 17 . . . R–QB1 18 B–B4 BxB 19 RxB Q–Q2 would have given Black the upper hand. However, 20 N–K4 R–K1 21 R–B3 would prove Staunton right. Neishtadt suggests 17 R–Q4 P–K7![4]

| 17 . . . | B–KB4 |
| 18 B–K2 | K–N2! |
| 19 O–O | Q–QB2! |
| 20 N–B5 | |

The last four moves exemplify the struggle of White's queen trying to escape its imprisonment, stemming from the impetuous capture of the rook on the one hand, and Black's latent and constant threat to devour the queen by 20 . . . N–Q2 on the other.

20 N–B5 enables the queen to escape, but it leaves White's king vulnerable.

| 20 . . . | BxPch |
| 21 K–R1 | B–B1! |
| 22 R–Q4 | B–N6 |
| 23 R–K4! | K–R1 |
| 24 R–Q1 | Q–KN2 |
| 25 R–KR4 | BxR |
| 26 QxN | B–R3 |
| 27 Q–R2 | |

27 Q–B4 would have promised a longer fight. After 27 . . . BxB 28 R–Q7 B–K2 29 N–K6 B–KN4 30 RxQ BxQ 31 RxRch KxR 32 NxB B–Q8 33 K–N1 BxQBP 34 N–K6 K–B2, the outside pawn secures Black a win. However, 30 NxB QxR 31 Q–B6ch R–N2 32 Q–B8ch R–N1 may allow White a draw. These are the imponderables of over-the-board play.

| 27 . . . | BxB |
| 28 R–Q7 | Q–R3! |
| 29 N–K4! | B–B5! |
| 30 N–B6 | P–K7 |
| 31 R–K7 | Q–B8ch |
| 32 Q–N1 | QxQch |
| 33 KxQ | P–K8(Q)ch |
| 34 RxQ | BxR |
| 35 Resigns | |

Morphy's superiority was so overwhelming—and so obvious to himself as well as to his opponents and spectators—that he was reluctant to continue playing on equal terms any opponent whom he had defeated decisively. With Southern chivalry, he felt obligated to offer handicaps, pawn and move, or even a knight, conceding a

[4] In *Nekoronovannie championy* (*Uncrowned Champions*) (Moscow: 1975). Otherwise meticulous, the author credits Morphy with a composition which actually is one of E. B. Cook's. In his youth, Morphy did indeed compose a two-mover of rather elementary nature, and never repeated that effort.

chance to beat his opponent. Making such offers may also have provided him with the incentive for winning against odds and did, of course, boost his ego. While his attitude was overtly devoid of conceit, a challenge of this nature was not always accepted, or was often derisively rejected by proud adversaries.

## PROWESS AT BLINDFOLD PLAY

One of Morphy's spectacular gifts was his prowess at blindfold play. Whereas Philidor's two simultaneous games *sans voir* in 1783 had created a sensation, Morphy increased the number to eight, and with great ease. Just as Alekhine in later days, Morphy thought little of the value of blindfold chess.[5] As he did not make blindfold play an extravaganza, the limit of his capacity at chess *sans voir* is not known; but surely his capacity would have exceeded eight games. Louis Paulsen used to play up to fifteen games without view of the board. These limits, however, were not governed just by the performer's ability, but also by the necessary limitation of the total time available for the whole "course." And the game was not yet propelled by the gusto revved up by the urge to break records.

Reports of a game or two being played blindfold in Europe go back to mid-thirteenth century, when the Saracen Borzaga toured Italy, playing two games blind and a third game over the board. In later times, Philidor did likewise, in Paris in 1783, shaking the chess world and the scientific community.

Proficiency in visualizing the board and the moves thereon does not necessarily add to the quality of play. It might help advance a player's efficiency to preanalyze his game in over-the-board play and aid his mnemonic faculty and his professional memory. A strong player can indeed conduct at least one game blindfold, without much exertion. An outstanding memory may excel as a gift in itself. A blindfold record may be established by a master without transforming him into a grandmaster merely by virtue of this potential. The functions simply run parallel. Vice versa, a grandmaster may achieve the ability to play one or more simultaneous games blindfold, yet not want to strive to exceed a given, modest limit (in fact, in the Soviet Union blindfold play is frowned upon as being exhibitionist rather than being of qualitative value).

Nevertheless, the combination of both faculties—outstanding qualitative play and playing entirely blindfold—is genuinely daz-

[5] A scholarly survey of Alekhine's attitudes toward blindfold chess, and their general applications, is found in A. Buschke, "Alekhine Blindfold" (*Chess Life & Review*, September 1971).

zling, for the public and connoisseur alike, simply because it is exceptional. However, to give intelligent credit to the creative factors involved and yet retain a sensible rationale, we can draw comparisons to other frameworks. One framework is that of time: the chronological advance of blindfold chess. A second framework is that of parallel performance in other fields, such as music.

Chronologically, Morphy appears to have transformed blindfold chess into a multiple discipline of its own. Philidor, like others before him, played two games blindfold, *but at the same time conducted a third game over the board*—which marks a vast difference from pure blindfold play. The actual presence of a board (with any kind of other configuration on it, which the mind is capable of blotting out), or the scanning of a game score before making the next move, or even holding a blank diagram in front or looking at a checkered wall—any of these conveniently provide an auxiliary mental tool, a crutch, a prop. However, Morphy, and most of his successors, played entirely blind. The comparison does not belittle Philidor's eminence as a Goliath among players. It merely delineates the march of technical advance. Just as the Industrial Revolution progressed universally, Morphy—eighty years after Philidor—played eight games blindfold and simultaneously, without any tool for support.

Morphy had the natural feel for, and was a virtuoso in, the "art and science" of chess. Thus he was able to coordinate strategies, tactics, and themes as played on different "instruments" by, against, and with different players of the chess ensemble attending a séance. Let us compare that product to one from another field, music. We will gain in insight by comparing the magnitude of the blindfold product in both spheres. Unrelated in substance, applying to different senses, and having different effects, they yet have a close affinity.

Between the time of Philidor and Morphy, a man named Ludwig van Beethoven (1770–1827) composed the renowned Ninth (Choral) Symphony. He had become stone-deaf by the age of forty-five. In 1816 he finally realized that he had to give up active performing as a piano virtuoso, and that he was now confined to his own inner world of joy and despair, of fantasy and creation. He began to sketch a few incidental motifs for the symphony which he completed in 1824, at the same time producing several other memorable compositions.

Admittedly, a musical score must be fully transcribed for the orchestra to follow, just as the arbiter in a blindfold chess exhibition calls out the moves to the participants. But the enormous interplay of sounds, tempi, harmony, scales, keys and counterpoint; the tones' absolute value and their combined effect—all had to be conceived entirely in Beethoven's inner ear. When one is deaf, these elements cannot be rechecked against the actual instruments' response and the orchestra players' sensitivity. It is a "blindfold" operation of gigantic scope.

Beethoven's task was more comprehensive than blindfold chess-playing, but he had no time limit. In chess, the task is more confined, but the playing time is restricted.

Beethoven *had* to compose "blindfold" or give up composing, and he had the rare faculty for it. A chess master does not have to do without his tool of vision as long as he is in command of it. Blindfold performers might enjoy the reward, the public attraction, and the fame that goes with the show. It is a talent to be proud of, but not an ingredient of master chess. It can be fun as well—as it was with Morphy, Pillsbury, and Fine; or with Koltanowski, the most entertaining memory artist of all.[6]

It was Morphy's initiative, and both his and L. Paulsen's artistry, that started a fashion and a tendency to rival, and improve on, their output. We will elaborate when we reach Leonard, and Pillsbury.


## MORPHY'S STYLE—AND THE
## ADVENT OF TIME CONTROL

During the First American Chess Congress, Morphy was drawn into a great number of offhand games against all of America's best players, many of whom had congregated in New York during the Congress. His results were so outstanding that he drove all of New York —and all of the United States—to ecstasies of admiration. He drew very few games and lost almost none.

One of these rare defeats was at the hands of a team of three strong New York masters, D. W. Fiske, W. J. Fuller, and F. Perrin. Morphy, as Black, defended with the relatively new Two Knights' Defense 1 P–K4 P–K4 2 N–KB3 N–QB3 3 N–N5 P–Q4! 5 PxP N–QR4; followed by 6 P–Q3, which was the line Morphy preferred when playing White! He must have been flustered by the occasion of facing America's deans of chess, as he fluctuated in his conduct of the game. By the 22nd move Morphy was outplayed by the troika and resigned a losing endgame after White's 50th move. Play had

---

[6] But we also have examples of playing blindfold by necessity. The American master Albert Landrin (1923–) lost his eyesight in younger years. Although blind players can use "Braille type" chessboards, Landrin, at the World Chess Championship for the Blind, Ermelo, 1970, played all his games from memory, without use of a board.

lasted six hours, of which—this time to his detriment—Morphy consumed only one hour.

Despite such rare losses, Morphy mastered most phases of the game and never slavishly adhered to established concept; nor did he veer off for the mere sake of looking original. What seemed to be his forte for attack was simply his confident ability to break away from stale patterns and to conceive a novel plan, with his ruthless drive behind it. Morphy's instincts were so sound that until recently they remained the backbone of the opening structure in the symmetrical kings' pawn games. The velocity and ease of some of Morphy's combinational finishes after positional mastery is amazing.

Moreover, in defiance of the too ponderous chess habits of the day, Morphy never tried, and was mentally too impatient, to outsit his opponents. Their inertia must have been frustrating to his rapid perception.

While European games often lasted an indeterminate time, the slowness did not suit the American temperament with its more youthfully competitive attitude. Americans also took their time rather than lose, but their speed was altogether much faster.

Yet, it was industrial Britain that found the solution to the problem. Until 1861 no time limits at all were imposed, and some big tournament games took sixteen to twenty hours to finish. During the match Anderssen–von Kolisch, London 1861, as an experiment, each player was given an hourglass with a capacity of two hours in each half. Twenty-four moves had to be completed by the time one's hourglass ran out. The project went well because both players, the schoolmaster and the banker, were trained to control themselves.

However, many masters could not adjust to this distracting requirement. They contrasted with Morphy, who, sandglass or not, used up very little time during his portion of any session. He patiently conceded his opponent all the time in the world—or did he dare them with these added odds? Anyhow, he rarely moved away during the opponent's turn, perhaps as a courtesy, but possibly also aware that staying on while the opponent had the move, gave Morphy the added opportunity to think.[7]

Morphy lost his temper once with Paulsen, who was one of the slowest. During the Morphy–Paulsen clashes in 1875, one game of twenty-nine moves took six hours, another one of fifty-three moves dragged on for a record fifteen hours. During a break, a very annoyed

[7] The famous Akiba Rubinstein always walked away after having completed his move, so as not to disturb his opponent and not to benefit from the other player's time on the clock. Changing times, changing mores, changing minds! In later days, no opponent would advise that he had moved, nor would a second dare do so.

Morphy proclaimed that he would never again play Paulsen. Between Morphy and Harrwitz, one session of thirty-four moves lasted five-and-one-half hours and the 9th match game Morphy–Loewenthal took twenty hours to complete sixty-seven moves.

By 1883, the first paired, mechanical chess clocks, invented by T. B. Wilson of Manchester, England, were introduced for use in the 1883 London Tournament. The clock was even fitted with a dial, indicating the number of every move whenever the clock was activated (subsequently, that valuable addition fell by the board). By 1906, the paired chess clocks were fully perfected and generally accepted as an integral feature, doing away with the marathons of bygone times.

However, in the electronic age of later days, these clocks have also become an anachronism, at least where investment in grandmaster chess plays a part. "Handling the clock" and exploiting time pressure or a man's inability to record game scores quickly by hand became subtle weapons in the antagonists' arsenal. Not uncommon were arguments with each other, with the umpires, and with the tournament committees, and disagreements about the clocks' mechanical failures. The pseudolawyers of chess rules were still smugly enjoying a field day when the semimanual, semitechnical chess aids began to appear outdated. It was no longer beyond technical reach to synchronize the board and the men; that is, the moves made, their digital-clock timing, their recording or score-keeping, their projection on a demonstration board, and even their reproduction by magnetic and electronic devices. The matter will be further examined in a special section on chess technology, p. 277. For the moment we turn back from the tool to its operator, the chess player.

## THE SPARK OF INSPIRATION

Watching the increasingly suspenseful progression of a combinational game, even the unusually talented player may ask the question, How does it all come about? However hard the lesser player strives, the final revelation may elude him. The gift of the genius is sensed but cannot be duplicated in its original creativeness. In the following game, White's fatal 14th move offers the opportunity for an admirable double sacrifice that gives birth to another immortal finish by Morphy. Clearly foreseen by Morphy (where is the line between "clearly" and "intuitively"?), it wasn't even suspected by his opponent.

## OFFHAND GAME

### London 1858
*Philidor's Defense*

T. W. BARNES          P. MORPHY

| | |
|---|---|
| 1 P–K4 | P–K4 |
| 2 N–KB3 | P–Q3 |
| 3 P–Q4 | P–KB4 |

This countergambit was the logical follow-up in Philidor's mind when he advocated 2 . . . P–Q3. It intends to uproot White's center, but also weakens Black's position without advancing his development. Yet, the move can cause complications with which Morphy felt familiar; but the risks had not yet been thoroughly analyzed.

| | |
|---|---|
| 4 QPxP | BPxP |
| 5 N–N5 | P–Q4 |
| 6 P–K6! | B–B4 |

In the earlier game Staunton and Owen versus Morphy and Barnes, Black played 6 . . . N–KR3, and the reader may refer to the notes quoted there. Morphy may have varied for reasons of variety and also to avoid any improvements that may have been found for 6 . . . N–KR3. Indeed, a flustered White now elects the riskiest of three avenues, the other two being (a) 7 N–QB3 P–B3 8 N–B7! Q–B3 9 B–K3 P–Q5 10 NxP QxP 11 NxB! QxN 12 QxP; and (b) 7 NxKP PxN 8 Q–R5ch any 9 QxB or 7 . . . B–K2 8 Q–N4, both with a safe game.

| | |
|---|---|
| 7 N–B7 | Q–B3 |
| 8 B–K3 | |

If 8 Q–Q2 BxP 9 NxR N–B3 10 Q–B4 O–O–O 11 QxQ NxQ 12 B–KN5 RxN 13 B–K2 R–B1, with a promising game for Black, but not as promising as White's present move allows!

8 . . .          P–Q5

If 8 . . . BxB 9 PxB QxP 10 NxR N–KB3 11 N–B3 N–B3 12 Q–Q2 B–Q2 13 O–O–O O–O–O∓.

9 B–N5          Q–B4!

9 . . . QxP 10 NxR gives up the exchange without counterplay, whereas the text maintains the strain.

**10 NxR!**

10 B–R4 BxP 11 NxR N–QB3 leaves Black minus the exchange but with an aggressive posture. 10 Q–R5 P–N3 11 Q–R4 BxP 12 NxR N–Q2 would gradually build up a fatal attack.

10 . . .          QxB
**11 B–B4**

Better may have been 11 N–B7 at once, as 11 . . . Q–B3 12 B–B4 BxP 13 BxB QxB 14 Q–R5 maintains a satisfactory game. P. W. Sergeant dismissed 11 N–B7 because of 11 . . . QxP, but Reinfeld refuted this with 12 Q–R5ch P–N3, and 13 QxB wins (so does 13 QxRP!).

11 . . .          N–QB3
**12 N–B7**

If 12 O–O N–R4 13 Q–K2 K–K2∓. Now the clouds gather,

| 12 . . . | QxP |
|---|---|
| 13 R–B1 | N–B3 |
| 14 P–KB3 | N–QN5 |
| 15 N–R3 | |

The imminent sacrifice diverts White's bishop from controlling the square Q3.

| 15 . . . | BxP! |
|---|---|
| 16 BxB | N–Q6ch! |
| 17 QxN | |

If 17 PxN B–N5ch 18 Q–Q2 QxQ mate. White's position falls apart rapidly, despite his rook and knight for the queen and Black's exposed king. It is no match to Black's velocity of blows.

| 17 . . . | PxQ |
|---|---|
| 18 O–O–O | BxN |
| 19 B–N3 | P–Q7ch |
| 20 K–N1 | B–B4 |
| 21 N–K5 | K–B1 |

Making room for the rook to move to K1, as the use of this file is far more effective than . . . O–O–O.

| 22 N–Q3 | R–K1 |
|---|---|
| 23 NxB | QxR |
| 24 N–K6ch | RxN |

And White is finished.

To some, these Morphy gems might be "old chestnuts"; to some, they are the rare, old-vintage wine. With the ongoing accumulation of combinational material devised by masterful players, the treasure trove of fireworks increases. Today's performers are quick to reach back into the past, sense potential dangers, and utilize the winning strategies—but people like Morphy invented them.

## SIGNS OF DECLINE:
## SOLITARY GENIUS OR ECCENTRIC?

After the acute phase of the American Civil War (1860–61) had abated, Morphy set out for a second and last journey to Europe during 1862–63. However, he played no more tournament chess. His potential as the reigning chess power still remained. His string of successes against the strongest competition should have sustained his supreme confidence. Then too, his gain in sheer technical experience might have ensured swift and infallible handling of any contest from beginning to end. Yet, some of his Paris games, almost exclusively with de Riviére, betray crucial moments of inattention. Perhaps it was due to lack of sustained tourney competition and to fading interest, or possibly to the intangible onset of sometimes defective thought processes.

The chess enthusiast will be familiar with the chess phenomenon called Morphy; but, for the not-so-ardent novice, an overview is in order of the lightning rise, the glorious zenith, and drastic disintegration (or, at least, disappearance) of the genius Morphy.

Reportedly, Paul Morphy learned the moves at the age of ten and became addicted at once. However, he wasn't allowed time for chess at the expense of other studies, and so entered the international limelight at the "late" age of twenty. In 1859, after returning from his foreign tour de force, he accepted some editorial work on chess. He was heavily imposed upon with challenges and social obligations. He became fatigued and irritated, feeling that his hobby was becoming a distracting burden. After his New Orleans homecoming, Morphy's involvement in chess kept decreasing and it practically halted in 1867, with the exception of occasional games at knight odds, with his old schoolmate Charles A. Maurian. Maurian grew too strong for odds, and in 1869 their private get-togethers ceased.[8] It is curious that Morphy always refused to give up odds once given, instead of reverting to even terms once they seemed called for. In a way, it meant denying the opponent a fair chance while sitting on a reputation.

Morphy's general withdrawal from social life—or "melancholia," as it was called—might today be diagnosed as paranoid. Did chess genius affect his mental health, or was his skill at the game of no psychological consequence? We cannot easily pinpoint what "genius" is, where it lies, or how long its effects will last. The making of any champion can be restructured from his or her tangible career; and while the champion may have been a prodigy, or ingenious, in a conversational or journalistic context, he may not have possessed the insights characteristic of a genius in its strictly encyclopedic definition. A genius might, but more often might not, be overtly *sympatique*. Actually, genius is often forced into isolation, even madness —through an abnormal predominance of sensibility and of irritability over reproductive power, or through exhaustion derived from an unending drive toward expression. It is one of the ingredients of the Greek genius, the demon, and a component of Greek tragedy.

Mastery of a specialty neither includes nor excludes the *idiot savant*, or dementia. It may be proof of a high intelligence quotient ("I.Q."), whatever its meaning; but, likewise, it may not, and rather sidetrack the proof of universal ability. Different again is the early manifestation, such as in a "prodigy," of signs of outstanding

---

[8] Maurian remained a pioneering power and a strong player. Together with A. E. Blackmar and C. F. Buck, he founded the New Orleans Chess Club in 1880, and also contributed to the appendix, edited by J. W. Miller, to the *Synopsis of the Chess Openings*, to which we will refer later in this book.

ability in certain fields, be it mathematic, or chess, or speed calculation, or rapid sensory perception and recall. Superiority due to over-
training is again a different matter altogether. Some people may be
born with highly retentive memories and with a heightened capabil-
ity to organize their experience, and their natural gifts may be
pushed along by the occasion, by practice, by persuasion or pressure,
or by instruction.

A gifted child may show rare ability, develop it to some substantial
degree, but after a while lose interest and switch to other activities.
It is the duration of each influence which determines if and how
one's behavior toward chess is altered, if ever—whether one bends
normally to strains, however severe, or instead breaks away from
normative reality into personality disorders. As to Morphy's own
feelings about his chess "career" (and the atmosphere of chess
clubs!), we append this extract from a letter he wrote from Paris
early in 1863 to his scholarly mentor and friend D. W. Fiske: "We
are following the conflict [the Civil War] for upon the issue depends
everything in our life. . . . I feel little disposed to engage in the
objectless strife of the chess board . . . the time devoted to chess is
literally frittered away. . . . I never patronize Le Café de la Régance;
it is a low, ill frequented establishment. . . ."

I have not been vainly elaborating in this section. Morphy's decline was a predictive omen of some replicas a century later. Let us
now turn to the concluding phase of Morphy's life—and what has
been conjectured about it.


## THE TWILIGHT OF A GENTLEMAN

Paranoia, as attributed to Morphy by Reuben Fine quoting Ernest
Jones, is a type of mental disorder or psychosis, commonly classified
as one of the less violent types of schizophrenia with manic-depres-
sive manifestations.[9] It mostly occurs in the withdrawn, seclusive
type. The introvert nature of chess-playing and the individual pairing of opponents point to a certain compatibility of chess with this
temperament.

No evidence exists for pathological causes of paranoia. There may
be an organic basis for it in some portion of the front lobes (the
cortex). Here is the center for certain aptitudes such as: (1) memory

[9] R. Fine, *The Psychology of a Chess Player* (New York: Dover, 1956;
reprint 1976); and E. Jones, *The Problem of Paul Morphy: A Contribution to
the Psychoanalysis of Chess* (London: London Institute of Psychoanalysis,
1930–31).

(in the case of Morphy, prodigious indeed), abstract reasoning, including philosophical thought, and extrasensory perception; (2) musical interest (which Morphy had to a high degree, at least as a listener); and (3) mathematical perception (Morphy's less prominent discipline, probably because his school and home atmosphere was geared more to humanistic study).

Under favorable circumstances, these aptitudes, as also a gift for chess, reveal themselves in early childhood or infancy. In philosophy, Descartes', Spinoza's, Comte's, Hume's, Berkeley's, and Schopenhauer's ideas of the universe were forged before they were twenty-five. Pascal's revolutionizing mathematical theories were formed at the age of eleven. On the other hand, early development is not a prerequisite, once a latent predisposition toward chess exists. Em. Lasker, Tarrasch, and other masters developed quite "normally"; Rubinstein (b. 1882), a quiet, orthodox, poor Talmudist, learned the game at the late age of twenty and reached his peak between 1906 to 1914, when a first denial of a match with Lasker and the outbreak of World War I shattered his hopes. Rubinstein professionally lived from chess only. His disappointment may have directly led to his subsequent mild-mannered and inoffensive agorophobia, with more justification than has been advanced in the case of Morphy.

Whereas mathematics in various forms are applied to many human activities; and whereas musical arts, from folk songs to polyphony, appeal to the multifaceted senses of many people, chess is restricted to a specific kind of abstract understanding. It is a construed simulation of conquest, and its pretense of power play—and its particular gift for "formal exercise"—has its limitations. Therefore, chess does not primarily appeal to large audiences, and, in the United States, has never commanded such general resonance.

The psychoanalyst E. Jones first fixed interest on Morphy's mental profile. He applied the conventional tools of the Freudian workshop, to analyze Morphy's assumed father-hate, and the transference of this feeling, among others, to "father-substitute" Staunton. It was he whom Morphy wanted to beat and was refused the chance, an occasion that may have triggered a neurosis. A similar mechanism was supposed to have been at work in a later demonstration of persecution mania, when Morphy brought an unjustified lawsuit against his brother-in-law. But these diagnoses were based in a distant past and partly on symbolic interpretations.[10] They do not help

---

[10] While Morphy tried hard to meet and beat the "past" master Staunton, the result of such a match was too predictable to cause a mental crisis for Morphy. Nor is there any other corroborating proof of "father antagonism."

distinguish between intense but still realistic motivations, and purely psychotic, irrational reactions. Nor does the thesis determine the definite onset of an abnormality which overrules rational function.

Paranoia is characterized by persistent, logically reasoned delusions (possibly appearing side by side with bizarre actions), commonly delusions of persecution or of grandeur, expressed in a very pronounced manner. In the former case, the paranoiac may do violence to the imaginary persecutor (as Morphy tried to do to his brother-in-law by legal means) or feel otherwise threatened (he is said to have accepted food only from his mother or sister). In the latter case, the paranoiac may see himself as an exalted person with a mission of great importance to accomplish.

As said before, once Morphy had defeated an opponent, he insisted on playing at odds only. This insistence may have been motivated by feelings of grandeur, by his incentive, or by feelings of chivalry.

Morphy's complete retirement from chess may have had quite natural roots. One can no longer give odds?—then call it quits! The man was a sophisticate with proper upbringing. Chess was merely his extravagant recreation. He was hardly impressed by the idea of chess as an independent discipline of socioeconomic importance. His father's restraints—allowing chess only once a week—did not emotionally block Morphy's full application to the study of law. It was reputed that he could recite from memory all of Louisiana's legal code; he graduated *summa cum laude* in 1855 and was admitted to the bar at nineteen, with the sole condition not to practice until coming of age at twenty. He took out a year to "find himself" at chess. For Morphy, chess must have been the pursuit of an esoteric, and glorified, ideal.

However, when he first came into contact with the chess crowd, both the cream and the tyro, and with the chessomaniacs and the chessocracy, his idealism, or his naivety, or his illusions must have started to crack. He became disenchanted with some of his opponents' too human shortcomings when they tried to win with no holds barred or to evade defeat by stalling. Both the Parisian circus air and the domestic patriotic frenzy repelled him—as must have Staunton's attitude. Perhaps he was too delicately balanced to bear the roughness of life. He began to take exception to being espoused as the foremost craftsman of an activity which he did not consider a profession, or perhaps perceived as irrelevant. He did not cherish the prospect of being idolized by men below his stature and, possibly, themselves desirous of status. Morphy distrusted their motives. He publicly declared his divorce from chess as early as 1861. However, to add aggravation to injury, his fame persisted and even became a handicap when he returned to New Orleans in 1864 and tried to set up a law practice. He experienced that in the public eye he remained "The Chess Player," and in the players' eye he emphatically became "The Pride and Sorrow of Chess."

Instead of a personality, with its foibles, he became a "character."

It has been rumored that the same situation prevailed in his pursuit of a lady whom he wanted to marry. It is not the place here to discuss what came first, the chicken or the egg; that is to say— whether Morphy's fame as a player was the only obstacle to his professional success, or whether it was already clouded by some other attitudes that discouraged clients; whether any quest of his for female love (of which very little, nay, almost nothing, is known) was impeded by his fame, or had other physiological or psychological undercurrents.

His public playing dried up, and when he could not secure diplomatic assignment, despite his legal background and fluency in languages, perhaps being considered too lukewarm about slavery, he stopped playing chess altogether, even privately.

There remains, of course, the irrelevant question as to how competent Morphy really was or would have been in activities other than chess; and whether his linguistics or his mnemonic acquisition of legal codes would have made him a successful diplomat or lawyer. Circumstances, or he himself, did not allow the chance of transition nor the possibility to find the answer. His hypersensitive temperament reacted with sharp disappointment, and his latent predisposition toward mental imbalance weakened his defenses; it readied him for neurosis, or for a later psychosis which passed from a latent to a more acute state.

A dormant inability to maintain interpersonal relationships—a situation which may also affect one's sex life—became more evident. Thus even his famed courtesy and brevity of expression might have been Janus-faced: Was it courtesy? Or shyness? Or arrogance? Or contempt? The tendency to live in an inner world became more pronounced, and added to his boredom and sadness. His feelings of failure might have been further accentuated by the reality that the Confederacy was the loser. His economic situation also suffered, as an aftermath of the War and because of the lack of professional income.

Despite all this, however, there are no signs of true mental disintegration at the time of his death, when he suffered a sudden cerebral stroke at the age of forty-eight. His father Alonzo apparently died from the same cause, at the age of fifty-eight, possibly a genetic coincidence. Morphy's uncle and father were fairly strong players, soon beaten by Paul. The same happened to Capablanca's

father, and it must have helped both sons to overcome any sup-
pressed patricidal desires!


## AN IMMORTAL LEGEND

Morphy became a legend, not because of any infallibility, but because of his pioneering vision. He forcefully introduced the mid-
nineteenth century to new conceptions and independent thought in
chess. He had an innate chess sense and was self-trained, as most
great individuals were in isolated early America. He single-handedly
surpassed his peers and inspired future generations. He was able to
add the spectacular ingredient of blindfold prowess, and he had the
public-relations advantage of being young, learned, and handsome.
In manners he was sometimes impetuous, but appeared to be open
and natural. He helped put America on the map culturally—via
chess. Like Gene Tunney, who withdrew from boxing in 1928 while
still champion, Morphy went offstage unbeaten.

It remains unresolved to what extent any champion's mannerisms
are the cause or effect of his chess skill. But it must be doubted that
Morphy's active involvement in the game *per se* caused his hard-
ships. To quote Philip W. Sergeant: "After all, being a genius,
Morphy could not be expected to escape from the penalty of genius
—which is not madness, but a capacity for suffering which the
eminently sane, but otherwise not eminent, do not possess." Some
of the hardship and psychic stresses he underwent may also have
been due to the violence inherent in the dynamic climate of
Morphy's America.

Ultimately, the query lingers, but the answer is Delphic: What
further progress and fulfillment would Morphy have achieved by
remaining active in chess and obliging his public? He would have
perpetuated what he already had proven to himself and others—
that he was a champion in chess.

# 3.

# Vignettes of Post-Morphy Chess

Many things may follow in a great man's wake: inspiration, nostalgia, and desolation; consolidation of gains; or search for further truth.

All these things occurred with Morphy's passing. We give one inspired game.

**Philadelphia 1860**
*Giuoco Piano*

| J. SMITH | G. DERRICKSON |
|----------|---------------|
| 1 P–K4 | P–K4 |
| 2 B–B4 | N–KB3 |
| 3 N–KB3 | N–B3 |
| 4 O–O | B–B4 |
| 5 P–Q3 | P–Q3 |
| 6 B–KN5 | B–KN5 |

Nowadays, these simple strategies are no longer used, as they have become stereotyped and sterile. Now 6 . . . N–QR4 would be the best move, breaking a symmetry that does not favor Black; for instance, 6 . . . B–KN5 7 N–Q5! N–Q5 8 P–B3! BxN 9 PxB N–K3 10 B–R4±.

In times past, this variation was unknown, and in this game,

Black succeeds with his old brand of vigor.

**7 P–KR3?    P–KR4!**

7 QN–Q2 N–Q5 8 P–B3 NxNch 9 NxN Q–Q2 10 P–Q4 would have been safer.

**8 PxB    PxP**

Take first, think later. 8 QN–Q2 N–Q5 9 P–B3 NxNch 10 NxN would have forced Black's QB to retreat or take. Now White's QN remains frozen.

| 9 N–R2 | P–N6 |
|--------|------|
| 10 N–KB3 | N–KN5! |

A queen sacrifice that recurs in many similar positions in the latter half of the 19th century.

| 11 BxQ | BxPch |
|--------|-------|
| 12 RxB | PxRch |

A futile gesture is 12 . . . R–R8ch 13 KxR NxRch 14 K–N1 NxQ 15 B–R4+.

| 13 K–B1 | R–R8ch |
|---------|--------|
| 14 K–K2 | RxQ |
| 15 KN–Q2 | |

To prevent 16 P–B8(Q) and save the rook. If 15 N–R2 R–K8ch+.

| 15 . . . | N–Q5ch |
|----------|--------|
| 16 KxR | N–K6ch |
| 17 K–B1 | N–K7 mate! |

Demonstrating the "choke," shown in the diagram.

This sparkling play was introduced by European players, and its American appearance is gratifying. In a profoundly artistic and sophisticated form it was reenacted shortly afterwards in a game played by the American chess magician Samuel Loyd (1841–1911), although he hardly needed prior indoctrination.

## SAM LOYD: PROBLEMIST AND PUZZLE KING

Sam Loyd's, the "Puzzle King's," chess constructions are not just a sequel, but a complement to Morphy's marvelous games. They complete the picture of American chess at its peak. Sam Loyd was America's most talented chess problemist. His inventiveness, daring, and unexpected themes are outstanding.

Born in 1841, he was a prolific composer, and much of his best work was done between 1857 and 1861, before he was twenty years old. After this spurt, Loyd stopped devoting time to chess problems, although he resumed some of this activity during later years. He never gave up chess, though.

Loyd's fame spread across the world, and in 1857 he became problem editor of Fiske's new *The Chess Monthly*, the world's best chess organ at that time. It was during the same year that Morphy placed first in the First American Chess Congress. To quote Alain C. White in *Sam Loyd and His Chess Problems*: "Thus in a single year America has made her meteoric appearance as the leading nation in the chess world, in periodical literature, in chess play, and in problems" (New York: Dover, 1962).

Loyd did not disdain practical play. Problemists and study composers are usually strong players, but may lack the "killer instinct" and prefer the quiet, formal exercise instead. Loyd was strong indeed, but was always on the lookout for something unusual or spectacular, which hurt his positional soundness and combative success, but these were not this artist's primary motives in chess.

In 1867, the exuberant young man of twenty-six decided to test himself in grandmaster play. He set out for Paris and entered an International Grandmaster Tournament, attended by the contemporary luminaries Kolisch, Winawer, Steinitz, de Riviére, the French champion S. Rosenthal, and others.

## PARIS INTERNATIONAL TOURNAMENT 1867

*Giuoco Piano*

S. LOYD       S. ROSENTHAL

| | | |
|---|---|---|
| 1 | P–K4 | P–K4 |
| 2 | N–KB3 | N–QB3 |
| 3 | B–B4 | B–B4 |
| 4 | P–Q3 | P–Q3 |
| 5 | N–B3 | N–B3 |
| 6 | B–K3 | B–N3 |

No comment about the openings played more than a century ago!

| | | |
|---|---|---|
| 7 | P–KR3 | N–QR4 |
| 8 | B–N3 | NxB |
| 9 | RPxN | B–K3 |
| 10 | N–QN5? | |

10 BxB would have secured White a lasting command of the open rook's file.

| | | |
|---|---|---|
| 10 | . . . | BxB |
| 11 | PxB | P–B3 |
| 12 | N–B3 | Q–B2 |

| | | |
|---|---|---|
| 13 | P–KN4 | P–QR3 |
| 14 | P–Q4 | O–O–O |
| 15 | P–Q5 | B–Q2 |
| 16 | P–N5 | N–K1 |
| 17 | N–Q2 | P–QB4 |
| 18 | N–B4 | P–R3 |
| 19 | Q–R5 | R–B1 |
| 20 | PxP | R–R1 |
| 21 | PxP | RxQ |

These skirmishes are finely drawn. Black cleverly aims at 21 QxBP RxP! 22 Q–B3 (to protect the RP) N–B3! and after . . . R/Q–R1 and . . . B–K1 Black gains crushing pressure on king-side. Loyd's maneuvers must be circumspect.

| | | |
|---|---|---|
| 22 | P–N8(Q) | RxP |
| 23 | RxR | BxR |
| 24 | N–N5!! | Q–K2 |
| 25 | Q–R7 | B–N5 |
| 26 | N–R7ch | K–N1 |
| 27 | RxP!! | N–B2 |
| 28 | R–R5 | Q–B3 |

Preparing the counterattack, 29 . . . Q–B6. So far, Rosenthal

has no inkling of what did or
was going to hit him.

| 29 Q–R1 | R–R1 |
| 30 Q–B1! | B–B6 |
| 31 N–N6 | Q–R5ch |
| 32 K–Q2 | Q–N5 |

Black prevents 33 N–Q7ch and
threatens the devastating 33 . . .
R–R8.

| 33 QxB!! | QxQ |
| 34 N–Q7ch | K–R1 |
| 35 N–B6 dbl. ch | N–R3 |
| 36 N–N6 mate | |

White artistically chokes his adversary with a problem master's
grand brilliancy.

The next game is not grandmasterly, as Loyd's physician-friend
Dr. Moore was rather a dilettante at practical chess, although he
was a talented problemist. However, it is the outcome of this game
that matters.

### Elizabeth, New Jersey 1876
### *King's Gambit*

S. LOYD                    C. C. MOORE

| 1 P–K4 | P–K4 |
| 2 P–KB4 | PxP |
| 3 P–Q4 | P–Q4 |
| 4 B–Q3 | N–KB3 |
| 5 BxP | P–B4 |

If one wants to comment on
the ancient treatment, 5 . . .
PxP might have been more
natural.

| 6 B–N5 | PxKP |
| 7 BxP | PxP |
| 8 BxN | QxB |
| 9 N–KB3 | B–QB4 |
| 10 O–O | O–O |
| 11 QN–Q2 | P–Q6ch |
| 12 K–R1 | PxP |
| 13 BxPch | KxB |
| 14 QxPch | Q–N3 |
| 15 QxB | N–R3! |

A crafty offering of a rook.
After 16 QxR B–R6! 17 N–R4
BxPch 18 K–N1 Q–N3ch wins.

| 16 Q–QN5 | N–B2 |
| 17 Q–B4 | Q–N3 |
| 18 N–KR4 | P–R4 |
| 19 N/2–B3 | R–R3? |
| 20 N–K5 | P–B3 |
| 21 R–B3 | QxP |
| 22 R–K1 | P–B4 |
| 23 R–KR3 | P–B5 |

Black's bishop attacks the dangerous rook, but because of Black's slowness, he could now succumb to 24 N–B5ch R–R3 25 RxRch PxR 26 QxNch B–Q2 27 QxBch R–B2 28 QxRch and mate in the next move. This pragmatic mate in six would be any practical player's obvious and safe course—but not Loyd's! The problemist in him intuitively and by choice employs a beautiful device in composition called the "Novotny theme," which transforms the finale into a three-move brilliancy.

**24 Q–K6!!**

A quiet, sacrificial, key move. The object is to cut Black's bishop off KR6 and Black's rook off KR3. The capture of the queen by any of the two pieces will create mutual interference.

If 24 . . . RxQ 25 N–B5ch K–N1 26 N–K7 mate and likewise after 24 . . . NxQ. If 24 . . . BxQ 25 N–N6ch K–N1 26 R–R8 mate. Again, if 24 . . . Q–B6 25 N/4–B3 mate or 24 . . . QxPch NxQ mate.

Black resigns.

Loyd's influence as an originator has had a lasting effect throughout. He is also one of the few American composers/players who rated a special issue in his honor by Rafael Kofman: *Izbrannyie Zadachi S. Loyda (Selected Problems of S. Loyd)* (Moscow: 1960). On the ninety-one pages of his monograph, Kofman gives a biographical overview and a selection of Loyd's production, showing his influence on the compositions of later composers. Loyd is also one of the godfathers of "unorthodox" problems (they are now classed as "heterodox" or as "fairy chess"), a category frowned upon for a while in official chess circles in the USSR, but by now tacitly pursued by its composers.

## THE FIRST SPROUTING

The young tradition started by Morphy, Loyd, and others, gave rise to a number of prominently endowed chess centers in Baltimore, Philadelphia, Pittsburgh, New Orleans, and elsewhere. They began to compete with New York, which had held an undisputed lead, with New England following closely behind. They all produced strong players and theoreticians; for example: J. M. Hanham, of the Philidor Defense variant, which bears his name and is still its mainstay; C. S. Howell, whose variation of the Ruy Lopez has stayed legitimate; Professor Isaac Rice who fervently sponsored analysis and events devoted to his, not quite sound, Rice Gambit. (His Rice trophy was carried to and fought for during the Anglo-American Universities Cable Matches); D. M. Martinez of Philadelphia, who won a match against J. Mason 3:1 and another one against G. H. Mackenzie 3:2—the amateur casually defeating both U.S. Champions; P. Ware, Jr., of Boston, of the "Meadow Hay" opening *1 P–QR4–5–6*, of the Stonewall opening *1 P–Q4 P–Q4 2 P–KB4*, and partner with H. N. Stone in the Stone–Ware variation of the Evans Gambit; and the Vermonter A. Blackmar (1826–88), who introduced the still hotly dissected and potent Blackmar Gambit, and later moved to New Orleans.

The president of the Pennsylvania Chess Federation, J. L. McCutcheon employed the move *1 P–K4 P–K3 2 P–Q4 P–Q4 3 N–QB3 N–KB3 4 B–KN5 B–N5* in his game against W. Steinitz during the latter's simultaneous exhibition in New York, December 1885, and he used it locally before or after; thus the variation has since been named after McCutcheon. The sequence was first employed in international master chess in the game Karl Pitschel–Josef Héral, Vienna International Tournament 1873 (*see* le Lionnais, *La Partie Française*, 1936); incidentally, White won in both cases. However, McCutcheon, not a mean player, picked up this move and forged it into a system, testing it out between 1880 and 1890 in a number of correspondence games against international masters, including Em. Lasker and Amos Burn of Britain. After 1895, Burn, Marshall, Showalter, and others often employed it successfully.[1]

Similarly, "E. Delmar in Philadelphia in 1865" is the credit given in *Modern Chess Openings*, 5th edition (1932), to the assumed originator of the "Metger Unpin" (*8 . . . Q–K2*) in the Four Knights' Game. But I have not found this move recorded before 1893, when it occurred in von Bardeleben–Metger at Kiel. It then fell into disuse, was revived by Rubinstein, and is now passé.

Turning from symbols back to players, P. Ware, Jr., was just a strong local amateur; and when he went to Vienna to play in the 1882 International (Grandmaster) Tournament, he landed at 16th place—but he won a protracted game against the then World Champion W. Steinitz (who placed first) and also beat Max Weiss! The story of Gustavus Reichhelm of Philadelphia will follow later in this book; but his latent strength, without international practice, already showed in his match results against Mackenzie (in 1864, 1:1; in 1865; 4½:1½; in 1875; 3½:2½; and in 1876 and 1880, no win, no loss, but three draws) and against Mason, whom he defeated in 1874 3½:2½. Thus one may wonder who the champions

---

[1] See William Cook, *The Chess Player's Compendium*, 5th ed., with a new supplement by Alfred Emery (Philadelphia: McKay, 1910). Also M. Morgan, *Chess Digest* (Philadelphia 1901–5).

were: Martinez? Reichhelm? Or the Masons and Mackenzies, simply because they lived off chess? Was the static mind getting the better of the peripatetic one?

Reichhelm was the chess editor of the Philadelphia *Evening Bulletin* from 1861 to 1870, and of the *Chess Record* till 1873, two of Philadelphia's seven, and of America's eighty-seven, chess columns during that period.

Some games considered significant then were compiled by Miron J. Hazeltine, a close friend of Sam Loyd, in his *Brevity and Brilliancy in Chess* (New York: 1866). It is a curious medley of domestic and foreign games without dates or places of playing, written in the informal style of the day. He also edited the chess column in the *New York Clipper* from 1856 till his death in 1907, the second longest uninterrupted duration of a chess column under the same authorship (H. Helms' in the *Brooklyn Daily Eagle* lasted sixty-two years).

Hazeltine's anthology contains several games of Fiske, Loyd, Mackenzie (whom he spells McKenzie), Marache, Montgomery, Morphy, L. Paulsen, Perrin, Reichhelm, Stanley, F. Thompson, and others. He also quotes a game by a "Herr Suhle" (Berthold Suhle, 1837–1904), as one of eight games played blindfold in Germany in the early 1860s; which was shortly after the Morphy (and Paulsen) séances had caught on. Then, without giving a date, Hazeltine also mentions a James A. Leonard "playing eight opponents blindfold at once" at the New York Chess Club, winning 2, losing 1, and drawing the remaining 5 "because of the late hour." This brief notice does not tell the full story of another post-Morphy loss. Leonard played these games early in 1862, at the age of nineteen. The year before, he had visited the Philadelphia Chess Club to play some matches, and, in Reichhelm's words, he "was, after Morphy, the most promising player America ever produced. He died several years after this date." Leonard was killed early in the Civil War, in Winter 1862.

Aside from Delmar and Hanham (and Hodges), who in the 1880s and 1890s kept battling each other for domestic primacy, Judge Max Judd (1852–1906) also was an occasional but menacing contender. He entered the fray by placing 4th (with 10 points) out of nine contestants in the 2nd (double-round) American Congress in Cleveland in 1871; came in 1st in the American 1872 contest; and landed respectably in 3rd place (behind Mackenzie 10½ and H. Hosmer 10) at the 3rd American Congress in Chicago in 1874. At the 4th Congress in Philadelphia in 1876, he was runner-up (9½) to Mason's 10½ points. In the 1890s, Judd was U.S. Consul General in Vienna, Austria; but after his return to the States, he still placed

1st—3rd in a tie with J. Johnson and L. Uedemann (14½ each) in the 4th Western Chess Association Tournament, Chicago 1903 (actually, the 3rd U.S. "Open" Tournament). In St. Louis 1904, Marshall took the honors with 8½ points, followed by Judd with 7, with Uedemann, E. Kemeny, Jaffe, Mlotkowski, and others trailing behind.

A contemporary who died young, just as Leonard, was Alexander G. Sellman (b. 1856) of Baltimore, who at the age of twenty-four attended the 5th American Chess Congress in New York in 1880. He placed 3rd, with 12½ points out of 18 possible, in front of Judd, Delmar, and Ware (Mackenzie was first, and C. Mohle second). Thus encouraged, Sellman followed Morphy's example and embarked for the double-round Grandmaster Tournament in London in 1883. Alas, he scored only 6½ points out of 26 possible, finishing in 12th place; but he maintained an even score against the winner, the formidable Zukertort. He took ill after his return and died in Spring 1888.

In the same tourney, the 13th–14th (and last) place was taken by Skipworth and Mortimer with 3 points each; but again, two of Mortimer's points consisted of one win each against Zukertort and Chigorin, who had shared 3rd–4th place with Blackburn; Steinitz placed second.

James Mortimer was born in Richmond, Virginia, in 1833; graduated from Virginia University; joined the U.S. diplomatic service; and was stationed in Paris from 1855 till 1860 as U.S. Attaché. He possessed a volatile temperament which influenced his chess style and his turbulent career, although his disposition was mellowed by an outgoing nature. While no games of his against Morphy seem to be recorded, he kept up contact with the fellow-Southerner during the latter's second sojourn to Paris. Torn between loyalties to his Federal employer and the Southern Confederacy, Mortimer quit his political post in 1860 and turned journalist. He departed for London in 1870, became a popular playwright, and, after the exile of Napoleon III to London, founded the London *Figaro*, Napoleon's official, government-in-exile organ.

Both Napoleon's asylum and the *Figaro* were short-lived, but for different reasons. Napoleon died in London in 1873; the newspaper died over a dispute on freedom-of-the-press reporting. The newspaper—representing the views of the former monarch—was often embroiled in controversy, and in one instance Mortimer was directed by the British judicial courts to disclose the name of a contributor who had written an article which was allegedly subject to criminal libel. Mortimer refused to disclose his source and went to prison, and in the process the *Figaro* folded. With it folded a good chess column which had been run by Loewenthal, and later by Steinitz.

Still, Mortimer's energy did not suffer, nor did his prestige, which, on the contrary, gained in esteem. He played chess vigorously in order to win, mostly overdoing it and ending up with a loss! At seventy-four years of age he took part in the Master Tournament in Ostend in 1907, and beat Tartakover, Znosko-Borovsky, and Blackburne. At the BCA International Congress in London in 1886 he overcame Taubenhaus, Mason, Pollock, and Schallopp, and finished in front of Hanham, who had come there from New York.

James Mortimer wrote two best-selling little chess books, published in London, and was the father of the Mortimer Defense to the Ruy Lopez, and the Mortimer–Frazer Attack in the Evans Gambit; but these contributions of an American player are shared by his adopted Britain, which had become his real home.

Altogether, these were the days when chess laurels were shared by professionals and by strong amateurs alike, when players combined chess with other pursuits in life. Often affluent chess patronage provided the financial support for illustrious visiting players, some of them temporary, some of them staying on permanently. In the second category, one of the most influential bore the name Wilhelm Steinitz!

## THE STEINITZ INTERREGNUM

Morphy's true successor to Caïssa's throne was Wilhelm Steinitz, a strikingly brilliant player who was originally a disciple of the school of brilliancy at any price. Soon, however, his dissecting mind found the flaws in that reckless style.

Steinitz witnessed the results of Morphy's attacking principles—the need for development, logically prepared and meticulously carried out. He concluded that such awesome aggressive power functioned best in face of inadequate defense. Consequently, Steinitz became the architect of sound defensive play. His theories had a profound effect on the chess strategies of generations to come, and he made important additions to Philidor's theses. He also beneficially drew on, and enlarged, the principles of closed play and defense as advocated by H. Staunton. It would do injustice to this towering champion's self-professed loyalties to America, and to his host's admiration and hospitality, to omit the "New American" Wilhelm Steinitz from a proper pedestal in America's Chess Hall of Fame.

Steinitz presided over the chess world for twenty-eight years after defeating Anderssen in 1866 (and Zukertort in 1872). He also reigned by virtue of his original and innovative theories on the game. A Bohemian Jew, born in Prague (then in the Austrian crownland of Bohemia) in 1836, he "made his home first in England and later in the United States; he was the first player to use the title of champion of the world. . . . He successfully defended the title from 1866 until 1894, when Emanuel Lasker (b. 1868), a Prussian Jew, defeated him in a match for the championship by 10 wins to 5, with four draws."[2]

Though the chroniclers differ about Steinitz's birth date, it was May 14, 1836. His playing career was a checkered one. He suffered from very bad health after 1872 and didn't play tournament chess for ten years thereafter, using the intervening decade to formulate his main chess principles. Even after he had acquired the title, he derived a secure but hardly more than modest salary from his chess column in *The Field*. Only in 1882 did he again enter a leading event in Vienna. Despite lack of practice, and thus a disastrous start, he tied for 1st place among eighteen grandmasters.

But his outlook may have grown too professional for British amateur attitudes, and also too systematic. Controversies were sharpening. A change of venue was in the cards. By 1882, "Steinitz's relations in England, where, though naturalized, he had remained a 'foreigner for 20 years,' grew more unpleasant than ever. Having previously resigned from 'The Field,' Steinitz gladly accepted an invitation by Mr. David Thompson of Philadelphia, to fulfill an engagement at the Franklin Chess Club. Like the great Roman, the Bohemian Caesar came, saw, and vanquished. . . . His reception was so cordial that he resolved to make this country his permanent home."[3]

However, Britain did not cast off Steinitz, nor was he forgetful. He maintained his British ties and took part in the London Tournament of 1883. It was a disappointment for him that he did not place 1st but 2nd only, 3 points behind Zukertort, who, together with his followers, especially the Hungarian-born Leopold Hoffer, started a strong challenge to Steinitz's precepts and position. Relentlessly, Steinitz gathered his own sponsors, who backed him in a match against Zukertort in 1886, with the locations shared between New York, St. Louis, and New Orelans. Steinitz crushed his opponent 10 to 5, with 5 draws. Zukertort, broken in health, returned to England, where he died in 1888.

---

[2] H. J. R. Murray, *A History of Chess*, p. 889.
[3] Ch. Devide; *A Memorial to William Steinitz* (New York: Putnam, 1901).

Between 1885 and 1891, Steinitz founded, edited, and contributed to the *International Chess Magazine,* the perfect prototype of a chess periodical.[4] In 1889 Steinitz began the first of two volumes of the *Modern Chess Instructor,* which summarized his theories. He also collated the tournament book of the 6th American Chess Congress, New York, 1889 (published in 1891).

In the same year he defeated Mikhail Chigorin of Russia, in a chess duel sponsored by the prestigious Havana (Cuba) Chess Club. It proved that he was still one of the strongest over-the-board players. Their practical encounter also tended to test some of Steinitz's firmly founded opening ideas against Chigorin's more dynamic, neoromantic concepts, but here Steinitz did not convince. Nevertheless, he won the match!

In 1892, Steinitz lost his first wife and his 18-year-old daughter. From then on, Steinitz's fortunes began to wane. Missing some promising chances, he lost the World Championship match to Lasker in 1894 and fared even worse in a fierce but tragic return match in Moscow in 1896. He began to show symptoms of mental disorientation, partly schizophrenic (challenging God to a match), partly hallucinatory. He is said to have imagined to draw energy from the earth, or be or become able to make chess pieces move on the board by mere exercise of brain power. Psycho-Telepatho-Kinesis? Steinitz today may not have been considered a paranoiac, but a psychic maverick in search of . . .

While returning to the States from Moscow in 1897, Steinitz made a slow trip through Europe. He made some improvements in his tournament standing, but ended up without a prize at London 1899, although he is said to have badly needed the money. His fame had disappeared, and so had his ambition and subsistence. His second mate, struggling hard to make frugal ends meet, had to place him in the East River Sanatorium on New York's Ward Island. There the man who had lived—and enlivened—the world of chess, died destitute on August 12, 1900, and was buried in a pauper's grave like Kieseritzky before, and others after him.

---

[4] It also contains some unique endings, reproduced in W. Korn, *American Chess Art: 250 Portraits of Endgame Study* (New York: Pitman, 1975). A fate equal to that of Steinitz's periodical befell *Lasker's Chess Magazine,* a world leader in quality founded in 1904 when Lasker stayed on in this country after tying for 2nd at Cambridge Springs in 1904. The journal folded in 1909 when Lasker went back to Europe and its tournament activities. He returned to the United States in 1937 and died in New York in 1941.

## THE BRITISH-AMERICAN LEND-LEASE

The vacuum of the official U.S. Championship was formally filled by a dashing personality—not one of Morphy's striking chess caliber, but nevertheless of imposing presence and an adventurous and daring disposition.

George Henry Mackenzie, born in 1837 in Scotland, purchased a commission in the British Army at nineteen, served till 1861, resigned from the tedium to become a chess professional, beat the strongest British amateur, Dublin-born Rev. G. A. MacDonnell, and emigrated to the United States in 1863. There he rejoined the armed forces by accepting a commission in the Federals, and rose to the rank of captain. After the war, he settled in New York and won the 2nd (1871), 3rd (1874), and 5th (1880) American Chess Congresses.[5] He yielded first place to J. Mason in the 4th (1876) Congress. This interval was only a small consolation to Mason, who afforded Mackenzie an opportunity to produce one of the best games of his career at the International Tournament in Paris in 1878, which was attended by both men as U.S. representatives. The loss of the game might have contributed to Mason's return to his native Britain. If so, it did not improve his playing luck. Mason used to start his tournaments well, but, probably because of his drinking habit, finished them disastrously. This pattern held true regardless of the tournament's length or the quality of competition (the sole exception being in London in 1892, when he placed 2nd to Em. Lasker).

Mason was a talented writer and made a living in later years by his pen. Mackenzie, however, shared the fate of many other players, and died in near-poverty of angina pectoris in 1891 in New York— "near" because he at least had an army pension, meager though it was.

Young America accepted Mackenzie as one of its own, because of his success, his service, and his adoption of the United States as his home. He and Mason were neither barred from flying the Stars and Stripes in Paris of 1878, nor delegated for the sake of carrying it. They were emissaries of chess enthusiasm as such, bred on the country's strength and convictions. Mackenzie made it to 4th place among Europe's best, and also did not spare his countryman Mason. The following was the "Scottish-Irish" skirmish in magical Paris.

[5] As something old and ever new: At the 5th Congress, G. H. Mackenzie and W. Grundy tied for 1st with 13½ points each, but Grundy was disqualified when he purportedly "purchased" a few of his wins! Mackenzie reaffirmed his chess supremacy by insisting on and winning two tie-breaking games.

## INTERNATIONAL TOURNAMENT

### Paris 1878
*French Defense*

G. H. MACKENZIE    J. MASON

| | |
|---|---|
| 1 P–K4 | P–K3 |
| 2 P–Q4 | P–Q4 |
| 3 N–QB3 | N–KB3 |
| 4 PxP | PxP |
| 5 N–B3 | B–Q3 |
| 6 B–Q3 | O–O |
| 7 O–O | N–B3 |
| 8 B–KN5 | N–K2 |
| 9 BxN | PxB |
| 10 N–KR4 | K–N2 |
| 11 Q–R5 | R–R1 |
| 12 P–B4 | P–B3 |
| 13 R–B3 | N–N3 |
| 14 QR–KB1 | Q–B2 |
| 15 N–K2 | B–Q2 |
| 16 N–N3 | QR–KN1 |

Black, sheltered behind an impregnable stronghold, has skillfully regrouped all his men for an all-out assault against White's king-side and after . . . K–B1 the fun may start—or is his vision wrong?

17 Q–R6!!ch    KxQ

The king is sucked into a cul-de-sac.

| | |
|---|---|
| 18 N/4–B5ch | BxN |
| 19 NxBch | K–R4 |
| 20 P–N4ch | KxP |
| 21 R–N3ch | K–R4 |
| 22 B–K2 mate | |

A treasure trove. The Irish clearly played already then the same impressive role in the States as in England.

## THE GREENING OF AMERICAN CHESS

In the coming period, American chess quietly absorbed the achievements of the Morphy and Steinitz eras. The sporadic encounters with Europeans were surprisingly successful, which was remarkable, considering that domestic chess was and remained an amateur's pursuit. With few exceptions, its peaks were achieved during a master's spare time. This is in contrast to the practice of future decades, when chess in other countries, particularly in the USSR, became a specialized, full-time profession.

With Morphy's premature demise and no heroic idol around to succeed him, Chess America receded from feverish enthusiasm to recreational pastime. No one thought chess was worth institution-alization. It wasn't an irreplaceable national treasure.

## SHIPLEY, HODGES, AND OTHERS

One of our strong gentlemen-players was W. P. Shipley (1860–1942), several times Philadelphia's chess champion. He also assisted in the publication of Gustavus C. Reichhelm's *Chess in Philadelphia*, a work which sheds much light on American chess (Philadelphia: 1898).

The 6th American Chess Congress was staged in New York in 1889 and was jointly won by Max Weiss of Austria and Mikhail Chigorin of Russia. Paying a visit to Philadelphia, Weiss non-chalantly played the local yokel.

### Philadelphia 1889
### *Scotch Game*

W. P. SHIPLEY       M. WEISS

| | | |
|---|---|---|
| 1 | P–K4 | P–K4 |
| 2 | N–KB3 | N–QB3 |
| 3 | P–Q4 | PxP |
| 4 | NxP | N–B3 |
| 5 | NxN | NPxN |
| 6 | B–Q3 | P–Q4 |
| 7 | P–K5 | N–N5 |
| 8 | O–O | B–QB4 |
| 9 | B–KB4 | P–KN4 |
| 10 | B–Q2 | NxKP |
| 11 | Q–R5 | P–KR3 |
| 12 | R–K1 | B–Q3? |

One might ask why Black did not play positionally 11 ... B–K2! 12 R–K1 NxB 13 PxN B–K3, but as an international play-er, Black wants to keep up the state of anxiety, planning ... K–B1. All his pieces will then quickly swing into action. But his plan fails.

| | | |
|---|---|---|
| 13 | P–KB4 | B–K3 |
| 14 | PxN | B–B4ch |
| 15 | K–R1 | Q–Q2 |
| 16 | BxP | B–B7 |

White now carries his advan-tage to a vigorous conclusion. 16 Q–B3 would have consoli-dated the gains conservatively.

| | | |
|---|---|---|
| 17 | R–K2! | B–N5 |
| 18 | P–K6! | BxQ |
| 19 | PxQch | KxP |
| 20 | B–B5ch | K–K3 |
| 21 | B–K7 **mate** | |

As late as January 5, 1924, W. P. Shipley, in consultation with S. T. Sharp, strongly and stubbornly defended a difficult game against Alekhine in Philadelphia, before going under on the 53rd move. The game is given as No. 6 in A. Alekhine, *Auf dem Weg zur Welt-meisterschaft* (Berlin: 1932).

After an interlude during which Samuel Lipschuetz and the

"Kentucky Chess Lion," Jackson W. Showalter, may have been considered at least the American Champions extraordinary, Albert S. Hodges played two matches against Showalter in New York in 1894, losing the first one 8:6:4, and winning the second match with a score of 5 wins, 3 losses, and 1 draw. With the second match having counted as the title match, Hodges became the official title claimant, although the combined score would have been 11:11 with 5 draws.

The authenticity of the U.S. Champion title was rather vague at that time, with the players' strength judged by often varying results, and the public playing it by ear. The returns in prestige or money were not hotly contested and were based, rather, on the "credits" of the time. A first, semiofficial tabulation in the *Official Blue Book and Encyclopaedia of the United States Chess Federation* (New York: McKay, 1956; rev. ed., 1973) attempted a determination in the following order:

1865—Paul Morphy
1871—G. H. Mackenzie
1890—Jackson W. Showalter
1892—Samuel Lipschuetz
1894—Albert Hodges
1897—H. N. Pillsbury
1906—Jackson W. Showalter
1909—Frank J. Marshall

The chart is in some respects contradictory, as the Blue Book admits that, "prior to 1936, the title of the U.S. Chess Champion was decided in match play exclusively," that "Morphy was recognized as the strongest player." Morphy's successor, Captain Mackenzie, was referred to as "the national champion," but the title did not become official until 1890, when it was won by Jackson W. Showalter. Apparently match results and congress wins were intermixed in these evaluations. Mackenzie won the 2nd, 3rd, and 5th American Congresses in 1871, 1874, and 1880. But then, Mason interposed in 1876. Recognizing the titles as assumed by match results, the picture is blurred, yet allows a glimpse at who was who.

Showalter won at the Congress in St. Louis in 1890, in front of Pollock and Lipschuetz, with Max Judd not taking part in the tourney. As it happened, Showalter, late in the same year, lost an individual match to Max Judd by a crushing 7:3, no draws, but Judd did not lay claim to a title! (Showalter revenged himself against the older Judd in 1892, winning 7:4:3.)

The next championship round was not decided by winning in any congress match, but by a duel against Showalter in 1892, won by Samuel Lipschuetz with 7:1:7—quite a margin. Samuel Lipschuetz (born in Hungary in 1863) arrived in the U.S. in 1887, took part in the well-attended 6th American Congress in New York in 1889, and ended in 6th place. However, this was the first placing by an American resident in front of Mason, Judd, Delmar, and Showalter. In addition, Lipschuetz beat Chigorin and Gunsberg among the leaders. Thus, Lipschuetz had a fair claim to championship, if unspoken custom was to apply. Just the same, Lipschuetz nailed down his claim in 1892. Subsequently, Lipschuetz, by narrow margins, lost two nontitle matches to Showalter, in 1895 and 1896, but clinched first prize in the Manhattan Chess Club Tournament in New York in 1900, ahead of Showalter and Hodges.

Soon thereafter, he returned to Europe, left chess, and died in Hamburg in 1905.

It has not been established whether Lipschuetz stayed in the United States simply as a resident, or if he ever took out citizenship. The fact remains that he made his mark on the U.S. atlas, even if only as the editor of the *Columbia Chess Chronicle* (1887–1890).

Albert B. Hodges staged a match in 1894, basing his candidacy on homegrown Showalter's reputation and readiness for battle. I already mentioned the results of that match. Thereafter he maintained a better-than-average record against all comers. He took part in all Anglo-American cable matches, never losing a game.

CABLE MATCHES

The thirteen Anglo-American cable matches staged between 1896 and 1911 generated as much passion among chess players, as any World Series among followers of baseball. The final match score was 6 wins apiece per team and 1 draw. Leading American and British players were recruited, with ten to twelve players in each match. Several times Blackburne played first board for England, and Pillsbury did likewise for the United States. So did Marshall and C. S. Howell.

A one-time event in a similar genre was the Parliamentary Cable Chess Match in 1897 between the British House of Commons and the U.S. House of Representatives. The score was 2½:2½.

Another duel, this one of Ivy League type, consisted of eleven Anglo-American University (Intercollegiate) matches, between 1899 and 1922, with the trophy donated by Professor Rice. Their total was also even: 4 wins each, 3 draws. In 1907, Capablanca sat at board one for Columbia University, and eked out a draw. Board three was occupied by team captain Louis Julius Wolff (Columbia), who won against L. Illingworth (Cambridge). In 1908, Julius Wolff held board two, winning again. (Julius, born in 1886, had dinner with me in 1978 and proved that not just the Armenians reach a healthy old age.) Harlow B. Daly, another old-timer still alive in 1977, was a frequent stalwart in the Anglo-American cable matches, and so was William A. Ruth, who played in the 1909 match; he was born in 1886 and lived to 1975. He made a name for himself in early-American opening theory by popularizing the Ruth Opening 1 P–Q4 N–KB3 2 B–N5, which in later epochs of unlimited means of publicity was "adopted" as the Trompovsky or the Veressov Opening.

A brilliant participant in the same matches was Albert W. Fox (b. 1881), who was dreaded for his razor-sharp rapier, as seen, for example, in his game versus T. F. Lawrence of the U.K. in the 13th, and last, match on April 21–22, 1911. In 1904, Fox won the Brooklyn Chess Club Championship and was invited into the Cambridge Springs 1904 tournament, where he defeated Chigorin, Janowski, Schlechter, and Teichmann, and drew with Showalter. In 1905–06 he became the flagbearer of the Manhattan Chess Club, ahead of Johner, Marshall, and others, bringing off a multitude of brilliancies.

Another participant in the International Intercollegiate matches, or rather one of its active organizers, was Harold M. Phillips, born in 1874 in Lithuania. He arrived in the United States in 1887, entered City College of New York in 1892, and was the undisputed junior and senior chess champion of this city-financed seat of learning which, with its tough criteria, produced outstanding alumni, descendants of the poor. Phillips entered Columbia University Law School in 1896 and participated in its chess matches, being instrumental in the later adoption (1941) of U.S. Intercollegiate chess as a regular fixture. In 1902, Phillips consolidated his domestic reputation by winning the Manhattan Chess Club championship and always lent organizational, administrative, and monetary support to the cause of chess. Phillips was a one-time New York State champion, and a member of the U.S. Olympic Team of 1930, covering third board. He passed away in January 1967.

UEDEMANN, ELLIOTT, AND "THE MANDARINS"

Another player who left a lasting legacy was "Old-New American" Louis Uedemann, who arrived from Germany in 1866 at the age of twelve, headed for Chicago, and stayed and died there in 1912. He topped the 1st and the 3rd U.S. Open Championship in Excelsior, Minnesota, in 1900 and 1902 respectively, and functioned as the chess editor for the *Chicago Tribune*. He won a match with Chajes 5 to 4, with 3 draws.

His lasting achievement is the invention of the "Udemann Code," as it is now spelled, a telecommunication notation first suggested by him in the *Brentano Chess Monthly* in 1882. With each of the sixty-four squares of the board carrying a separate two-letter designation, his code became part of the (International) Laws of Chess, and was recognized as an official system for the transmission of moves, with each move requiring no more than, and exactly, four letters of the Latin alphabet (it should not be confused with the four-digit numerical notation, used in correspondence chess).

Many years younger than Uedemann, but for a while competing on the same home base, was E. P. Elliott. He came 2nd in the 2nd Western Chess Association Tournament in Excelsior, in 1901, trailing M. N. MacLeod's 13 points by only ½ point, and coming 2nd again in Excelsior in 1902 with 14½ points against Uedemann's 16½ out of 18. In Chicago in 1903, S. P. Johnston was 1st, Max Judd 2nd, Uedemann 3rd, and Elliot placed 4th–5th with 13 out of 17 possible points. In Excelsior in 1905, Elliott still missed the highest placing, landing in 3rd to 5th position with 12½ out of 17 (still, and always, a most impressive percentage); but again in Excelsior, both in 1908 and 1912, Elliott came out on top. Elliott became Minnesota champion in 1903, but in the 1920s moved to Los Angeles.

Another homespun offspring was the Bostonian lawyer Franklin Knowles Young (1857–1931), who invented the so-called "Synthetic Method of Chessplay."[6] His numerous writings were designed to prove that scientific chess play is the imitation of methodical warfare. Thus the maneuvers employed by chess masters are supposedly identical with the movements, grand strategies, and high tactics of army marshals. Young formulated an intricate nomenclature which prompted a caustic comment in *Chess Review* that graduation from military academy was needed before taking a course in chess.[7] While such analogies as Young's were amply discredited, "His Generalship" Young was just the same a very respected, imaginative, and feared practitioner who beat H. B. Daly in the U.S. Postal League Tournament in 1910–11.

Franklin Young's games were pretty ones, but he played another significant role as well. He was a member of the Boston group of chess enthusiasts, consisting of J. F. Barry, C. F. Burille, L. Dore, H. N. Stone, P. Ware, Jr., and others, who called themselves "The

---

[6] Not to be confused with J. W. Young, a very active chess contender using Philadelphia as his home base.

[7] Or, to quote Gerald Abrahams, *Not Only Chess* (London: George Allen and Unwin, 1974, p. 41): "Chess is described as a war game: and both activities have evolved into objective sciences. Should we, then, expect the generals to be good at chess? That, I suggest, would be *non sequitur*, if only because few of them are good at war. . . ."

Mandarins of the Yellow Button," a minute allusion to the German seven-master group, "The Pleiades," of the 1850s.[8]

It was uplifting for the chess enthusiasts of the post-Morphy era to watch the jolly fighters happily carrying on for the fun of a fulfilling recreation. Before Steinitz's maxims penetrated deeper, brilliant chess was carried on by its own momentum. It was somehow supported by the opponents' cooperation, for it seemed standard practice to disdain the "positionally" safest defense. The answers were deliberately risky, played in decorative, chivalrous fashion— even when, or perhaps because, the scales were already tilted, and restraint might have come too late.

Chess does not operate in a vacuum. The eras of brilliancy, of positional principles and precaution, and later of modernism and experimentation—all in due course created a social convention. Also, imperceptibly began the shift from sheer, lofty, amateurish but also good-quality enjoyment toward the increasingly marked rift between a hobby and a profession. Later on, chess was getting near that no-man's-land of giving in too early and compulsively to the pressures of organized instruction, with the concomitant loss of easygoing exuberance. I remember an aphorism coined by David L. D. Levy, the Scottish champion and chess writer also well known in the United States: he said that he had reached the peak of his ability, and "would *never play that well enough to lose getting fun out of the game*" (italics mine—W. K.).

[8] Barry won a masterpiece of a game against the budding master Harry Nelson Pillsbury in Boston in 1889, when Pillsbury was just starting his career. It wasn't until New York, 1893, that Pillsbury began to move to the foreground.

The game Barry–Pillsbury, and a host of other games from the American "middle ages," is found in the extensive and valuable anthology by Francis J. Wellmuth, *The Golden Treasury of Chess* (Philadelphia: McKay, 1943).

# 4.

# Pillsbury: The Epic and
# the Tragedy

With a life span of just thirty-four years, Pillsbury, like Morphy, left an indelible mark on global chess. He was a solid virtuoso, and an intense, but flickering, flame.

## TRIUMPHAL ASCENT

The Yankee from New England started playing chess slowly, at first without an inkling of his real power. He consolidated his East Coast fame roughly between the years 1890 and 1894, and became the best of New York's players in 1894 and 1895. He thus encouraged his sponsors in the Brooklyn Chess Club to raise money to enter him as the American representative in the outstandingly attended First International Tournament in Hastings in 1895. Pillsbury, a twenty-two-year-old unknown, crossed the ocean in pursuit of fame. He was without European or world prestige, simply confident of his ability. Hastings had arraigned twenty-two of the strongest masters, including the World Champion (Lasker), the ex-Champion (Steinitz), and the national champions of Austria, England, France, Germany, Italy, and Russia. In one great leap forward, Pillsbury emerged as the tournament winner. He virtually duplicated Morphy's precedent. It was the victory of an untrammeled youngster from a developing country; once more sheer talent and genius triumphed over established reputations. Pillsbury, "The Hero of Hastings," became Morphy's heir. At Hastings, Pillsbury lost to World Champion Em. Lasker, but defeated his most dreaded adversary and mentor, W. Steinitz. Early in the tournament, Pillsbury met the somewhat upright Praeceptor Germaniae, Dr. Siegbert Tarrasch, for decades everyone's most enduring challenger. Tarrasch was of short stature, nearsighted, touchy. But he made up by his fortitude at the chessboard, and by his immense didactic ability. He was a leading theoretician, and propagator of the Queen's Pawn Openings. Yet it was Pillsbury who, together with the then American champion Showalter, forged some of the more formidable systems of the Queen's Gambit.

### Hastings 1895
*Queen's Gambit Declined*

H. N. PILLSBURY    S. TARRASCH

| 1 P–Q4 | P–Q4 |
| 2 P–QB4 | P–K3 |
| 3 N–QB3 | N–KB3 |
| 4 B–N5 | |

Pillsbury's favorite weapon, and the start of a complete system perfected by him and Showalter.

| 4 . . . | B–K2 |
| 5 N–B3 | QN–Q2 |
| 6 R–B1 | O–O |
| 7 P–K3 | P–QN3 |
| 8 PxP | PxP |

In general outline, the last few moves contain strategical alternatives which bore fruit in later decades. In one of them, White can develop 6 Q–B2 and move his queen's rook to Q1. Black can maintain a stronger defensive wall by 7 . . . P–B3 rather than the fianchetto. On the other hand, the defender can strengthen his fianchetto formation by moving sooner or later . . . N–K5 with . . . BxB and . . . QxB to follow. Pillsbury's exchange of pawns temporarily closes Black's diagonal. White's next move is preferable to 9 B–N5 or 9 Q–R4,

| 9 B–Q3 | B–N2 |
| 10 O–O | P–B4 |

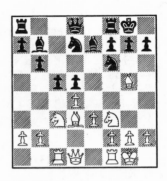

**11 R–K1**

The way the game proceeded, the rook should have stayed on the KB file to support the recurring pawn push to B4–B5. White can adopt various strategies according to personal taste; e.g., 11 N–K5 or 11 PxP (to create hanging pawns) or 11 B–B5 (to prevent 11 . . . N–K5 12 BxB QxB 13 BxN QxB 14 PxP, with a weak Black's center pawn).

In a later round against Schlechter, Pillsbury chose 11 B–N1 (which probably should have been preceded by 11 PxP PxP and now 12 B–N1), with the sequel 11 . . . N–K5 12 B–B4 NxN 13 RxN (better 13 PxN) P–B5! But 12 BxB QxB 13 PxP NxN 14 RxN PxP 15 P–QN4 would have supplied an initiative. Steinitz recommended (11 B–N1) P–B5 at once.

Good prospects face *11 Q–K2 N–K5 12 B–KB4 NxN 13 PxN P–B5 14 B–B5 P–N3 15 BxN QxB 16 N–K5 Q–K3 17 B–R6.*

**11 . . .                    P–B5**

At this point it is again worth looking into the maneuver *11 . . . N–K5 12 B–KB4 NxN 13 PxN P–B5 14 B–N1 P–QN4 15 P–K4 PxP 16 BxP BxB 17 RxB N–B3,* while *12 BxB QxB 13 PxP?!* makes for complications.

**12 B–N1                  P–QR3**
**13 N–K5                  P–N4**

Black tries to forestall the strong buildup of White's center, as he is left cramped after *13 . . . NxN 14 PxN N–Q2! 15 B–B4 N–B4 16 Q–Q2 P–QN4 17 QR–Q1±.*
White's next pawn move is typical of the "Pillsbury Setup," a stonewall allowing slow but sure deployment of all attacking forces and an eventual BP thrust forward.

| | |
|---|---|
| 14 P–B4 | R–K1 |
| 15 Q–B3 | N–B1 |
| 16 N–K2 | N–K5 |
| 17 BxB | RxB |
| 18 BxN | PxB |
| 19 Q–N3 | P–B3 |
| 20 N–N4 | K–R1 |
| 21 P–B5! | Q–Q2 |
| 22 R–B1 | R–Q1 |
| 23 R–B4 | Q–Q3 |
| 24 Q–R4 | QR–K1 |
| 25 N–B3 | B–Q4 |

| | |
|---|---|
| 26 N–B2 | Q–B3 |
| 27 R–B1!! | P–N5 |
| 28 N–K2 | Q–R5 |
| 29 N–N4 | N–Q2 |

Both sides have developed their full offensive and defensive potential. After *29 . . . QxP* White would have won at once with *30 NxP PxN 31 QxBPch R–N2 32 R–N4;* or *30 . . . R–Q1 31 NxB.* Black's last move prevents this sacrifice.

**30 R/4–B2!     K–N1!**

With the inventive finesse of his 30th move, which vacates the square KB4, White aims at *30 . . . QxP? 31 N–B4 B–B2 32 P–Q5!* (not *32 N–N6ch BxN 33 PxB P–R3 34 RxP NxR 35 RxN P–B5∓*) *N–K4 33 NxP PxN 34 QxBPch K–N1 35 P–Q6 R–Q2 36 N–K6±.*
After Black's reply, White must take time to preserve his rook's pawn, else the advanced pawns will turn into steamrollers.

| | |
|---|---|
| 31 N–B1 | P–B6 |
| 32 P–QN3 | Q–B3 |
| 33 P–KR3 | P–QR4 |
| 34 N–R2 | P–R5 |
| 35 P–N4 | PxP |
| 36 PxP | R–R1 |
| 37 P–N5 | R–R6 |
| 38 N–N4 | BxP |

White has stalled Black's counterattack long enough. White regroups for the final onslaught on the king's wing. Black's queen-side becomes irresistible

—but too late! Actually, it was Black's turn to temporize with 38 . . . K–R1! or rather give up the exchange by 38 . . . RxP! 39 NxR BxN with more immediate counterthreats.

| 39 R–KN2 | K–R1 |
|----------|------|
| 40 PxP   | PxP  |
| 41 NxB!  | RxN  |
| 42 N–R6  | R–N2 |
| 43 RxR   | KxR  |
| 44 Q–N3ch! | KxN |

It is a moot question if Black ever anticipated this knight sacrifice. It must be accepted,

else 44 . . . K–B1 45 Q–KN8ch K–K2 46 QxR wins.

Possibly Black relied on 45 R–B4 R–N8ch, with a beneficial perpetual check. But White has an unexpected waiting move in store. Black, a piece up, is helpless.

| 45 K–R1!   | Q–Q4  |
|------------|-------|
| 46 R–KN1   | QxBP  |
| 47 Q–R4ch  | Q–R4  |
| 48 Q–B4ch  | Q–N4  |
| 49 RxQ     | PxR   |
| 50 Q–Q6ch  | K–R4  |
| 51 QxN     | P–B7  |
| 52 QxP mate |      |

With the 21st and last round approaching, Pillsbury led by ½ point, and thus needed another crucial ½ point in order to share first place, and a full point to keep abreast of Chigorin and Lasker, who were close behind. Pillsbury's opponent was Isidor Gunsberg, who was an erratic man (because of ill health) but quite capable of causing a last-round upset. Moreover, Gunsberg was trailing Burn, Janowski, Mason, and Bird by only ½ point, and a win over Pillsbury would have gained him fivefold better placing. Gunsberg was no overawed "drawing master," and reporters' commentaries state that Pillsbury fell into, and Gunsberg bypassed, some clearly drawish opening lines with the 11th–13th moves. However, any comments are rather academic in the context of the ensuing bitter battle.

### Hastings 1895
### Queen's Gambit

H. N. PILLSBURY          I. GUNSBERG

| 1 P–Q4  | P–Q4    |
|---------|---------|
| 2 P–QB4 | P–QB3   |
| 3 P–K3  | P–KN3?! |
| 4 N–QB3 | B–N2    |
| 5 N–B3  | N–B3    |

A profoundly hypermodern fianchetto design, conceived more than thirty years before the full development of the Gruenfeld Defense. While Black is not yet fully aware of all its exactitudes, he employs some of the principal strategies (moves 7, 10) and slips only when well into the middlegame.

| 6 B–Q3 | O–O!  |
|--------|-------|
| 7 N–K5 | PxP   |

A timely diversion which forestalls (7 . . . QN–Q2) 8 P–B4.

| 8 | BxBP | N–Q4 |
|---|------|------|
| 9 | P–B4 | B–K3 |

Contains the venom 10 . . . BxN 11 BPxP? NxN! winning the bishop.

**10 Q–N3**

A move that was criticized because it allows Black to simplify by substantial exchanges of material. 10 B–Q3, followed by P–KR4, was suggested by P. W. Sergeant as more aggressive. But Pillsbury's selection of 10 Q–N3 was based on the presumption that the move would gain important space and mobility in the forthcoming endgame.

| 10 | . . . | P–QN4 |
|----|-------|-------|
| 11 | BxN | BxB |
| 12 | NxB | QxN |
| 13 | QxQ | PxQ |
| 14 | N–Q3 | N–Q2 |
| 15 | B–Q2 | KR–B1 |
| 16 | K–K2 | P–K3 |
| 17 | KR–QB1 | B–B1 |
| 18 | RxR | RxR |
| 19 | R–QB1 | RxR |
| 20 | BxR | B–Q3 |
| 21 | B–Q2 | K–B1 |
| 22 | B–N4 | |

Suddenly a window opens on some secrets of White's position. Perhaps when he played 10 Q–N3, he intuitively or by sheer power of rapid calculation, foresaw the whole chain of exchanges.

In broad outline, Black's weak squares (and White's possible points of occupation) are QB4 and K5; Black's knight can post itself on QB5 or K5, but from QB5 the knight can be dislodged by P–QN3 and on K5 the knight has no effective future. Upon 22 . . . BxB 23 NxB N–N1 24 P–N4 K–K2 25 K–Q2 P–QR4 26 N–Q3 N–Q2 27 N–B5! exerts commanding pressure.

| 22 | . . . | K–K2 |
|----|-------|------|
| 23 | B–B5 | P–QR3 |
| 24 | P–QN4! | P–B3 |
| 25 | P–N4 | BxB |

If 25 . . . N–N1 26 P–KR4, with a threatened breakthrough on the king-side. So far Gunsberg has always found the right answer. It is at the next critical move that he falters, missing the last and only chance to withstand the relentless assault.

**26 NPxB      N–N1?**

A natural defensive move relying on equilibrium on the king-side and in a leisurely way preparing for . . . K–Q2 and . . . P–QR4 with a deadlock.

But an immediate 26 . . . P–QR4 was called for; e.g., 27 P–B6 N–N3 28 N–B5 K–Q3 or 27 P–B5 P–N4 28 P–B6 N–N3 29 N–B5 PxP 30 PxP K–Q3 31 N–N7ch KxP 32 NxPch K–B2 and . . . N–B5. After the text, White designs one of the most beautiful practical endgame studies in chess history.

**27 P–B5!!**

Literally, a smashing conception. The menace is 28 PxKP KxP 29 N–B4ch, winning the QP and the game; and 27 . . . NPxP 28 PxP PxP 29 N–B4 leads to the same result, just as 27 . . . KPxP 28 PxP P–N4 29 N–N4! shifting the attack to the queen-side just as in the game. If 27 . . . P–QR4 28 N–B4 (28 PxKP P–N4!).

| 27 . . . | P–N4 |
| 28 N–N4! | P–QR4 |
| 29 P–B6!! | K–Q3 |

Clearly, if 29 . . . PxN 30 P–B7!

| 30 PxP | NxP |

Again, if 30 . . . PxN 31 P–K7 KxKP 32 P–B7 and queens.

| 31 NxN | KxN |
| 32 P–K4! | |

The crowning surprise.

| 32 . . . | PxP |
| 33 P–Q5ch! | K–Q3 |
| 34 K–K3 | P–N5 |
| 35 KxP | P–R5 |
| 36 K–Q4 | |

Black has a pawn majority on each wing, but cannot offset the center pawns.

| 36 . . . | P–R4 |

All variations are precision-tooled by White; e.g., (a) 36 . . . P–B4 37 PxP P–N6 (if 37 . . . K–K2 38 K–B5 P–N6 39 P–Q6ch K–Q1 40 P–B6 PxP 41 P–B7+; and if 37 . . . P–N5 38 P–B6 P–R4 39 P–B7 K–K2 40 P–Q6ch K–B1 41 P–Q7+) 38 PxP PxP (or 38 . . . P–R6 39 K–B3 K–K2 40 P–N4 P–N5 41 P–N5+) 39 K–B3 K–K2 40 KxP P–N5 41 K–B4 P–R4 42 K–B5 P–R5 43 P–Q6ch K–Q1 44 P–B6 and wins. (b) 36 . . . K–K2 37 K–B4 P–N6 38 PxP PxP (38 . . . P–R6 39 K–B3 P–B4 40 PxP P–R4 41 P–N4 P–R7 42 K–N2 P–R8(Q)ch 43 KxQ P–N5 44 P–N5 P–R5 45 P–N6 P–N6 46 PxP PxP 47 P–Q6ch KxP 48 P–N7, etc. queening with check) 39 KxP P–B4 40 PxP P–N5 41 K–B4 P–R4 42 K–B5 P–R5 43 P–Q6ch K–Q1 44 P–B6 wins.

| 37 PxP | P–R6 |
| 38 K–B4 | P–B4 |
| 39 P–R6 | P–B5 |
| 40 P–R7 | Resigns |

While Hastings marked Pillsbury's ascent, it also signaled the partial decline of Britain's dominance, which from then on shifted to the European continent, although a few talents—e.g., O' D. Alexander, Sir George Thomas, and the professional F. D. Yates— tried to hold the fort. Its elite aged, without replacement in sight until 1972, when an English financier-patron, James D. Slater, who also supported the Fischer–Spassky match generously, offered size- able incentives to British players, and the game experienced a native rejuvenation. In the area of problems, Great Britain had remained very active, with imposing figures like G. Heathcote, T. R. Dawson, and many others.

Pillsbury's return from Hastings was topped by a triumphal recep- tion at the Pouch Gallery in Brooklyn. He made his entrance in true American fashion: with a ticker-tape parade through a chess crowd's cordon.

Within a short time, he had run the gamut of apprenticeship to mastery of contemporary chess knowledge. Built into Pillsbury's astounding chess consciousness were Morphy's clear and economic concepts of rapid development along open lines; a heritage of classi- cal styles as evidenced by Pillsbury's beautiful combinations; full command over positional play and defense as propagated by W. Steinitz and S. Tarrasch; superior handling of middlegame tactics and endgame technique; and a profound sense of opening analysis and strategy that enabled him to understand, employ, and perfect many impressive innovations, notably in the Queen's Gambit. His proficiency was the smooth road to his success; it would become an example to later generations of American players.

He seemed to be without discernable idiosyncrasies; no emotional flaws impeded his play. He tackled all opponents without hesitation. The only trouble he had was with Steinitz—the man, coincidentally, whose theories Pillsbury respected most. Young Harry had a decisive minus score against Steinitz in St. Petersburg in 1895–96. The stout, garrulous, and stubborn elder Steinitz dug in most deeply against this shining knight of light. The confrontation was similar to Reshevsky–Fischer in their short-lived, inconclusive match in Los Angeles in 1961.

When Pillsbury completed Hastings, he was World Champion timber. He had good looks, a gentle and composed attitude, dignified and elegant manners, and an easygoing, trustful disposition. Yet, he never made it to that pinnacle, the chess throne. The reason was tragic; and while a definite explanation was neither given nor recog- nized, a probable one is now feasible, lifting the veil off an enigma. The public beginning of the drama was at the St. Petersburg Tour- nament in 1895–96.

That gala was under the aegis of Czar Nicholas II, an admirer of chess, which had become a favorite among the Russian nobility and upper middle class; the masses had not enough leisure time available to indulge. The patron's choice was elitist: just Russia's best, Chigorin; Lasker and Steinitz, the present and recent World Champions; and Pillsbury, the young star from the New World, who had overtaken all at Hastings. With only Tarrasch unable to attend, the tourney was meant to be the first one of "grandmasters" exclusively. At the St. Petersburg Tournament of 1914, Czar Nicholas II proclaimed the grandmaster title official for the five finalists, Marshall, Capablanca, Lasker, Tarrasch, and Alekhine (two Americans, two Central Europeans, one Russian).

## THE FALTERING COLOSSUS

Pillsbury was a dynamo from the New World, and his astonishing success at Hastings jolted the international chess organizers into a rapid succession of invitations, the first one being from Russia. Pillsbury was asked to enter a match tournament of six games each between Em. Lasker, Pillsbury, Steinitz, and Chigorin, during the period of December 13 to January 28.

The contest was highly exacting. Pillsbury—a not-yet-seasoned novice in a faraway land—not only had to prepare for his encounters, but also had to send home journalistic reports. This function was expected of him by his American audience and sponsors, in return for financial patronage. (By the way, there were no coaches or seconds in the chess armory of that time.)[1]

In his first game, Pillsbury was paired with Em. Lasker, the world's best, who must have been taken by surprise by the way he was blockaded and strangled in pre-Nimzowitsch style.

| St. Petersburg 1895 | | In Pillsbury's hand the knight |
| --- | --- | --- |
| *Petrov's Defense* | | will prove amazingly mobile. |

His defense is both elastic and aggressive. According to theory, there is no flaw in the variation as adopted, although 5 Q–K2 is also favored by some grandmasters.

| EM. LASKER | H. N. PILLSBURY |
| --- | --- |
| 1 P–K4 | P–K4 |
| 2 N–KB3 | N–KB3 |
| 3 NxP | P–Q3 |
| 4 N–KB3 | NxP |

---

[1] The concession of using seconds to help in preparation and during adjournments began with the Alekhine–Euwe championship match in 1935. It was meant as a compromise: to reconcile the prohibition, in Laws of Chess, to consult others during the game, and the undeniable fact of the widespread practice.

| 5 | P–Q4 | P–Q4 |
|---|------|------|
| 6 | B–Q3 | B–K2 |
| 7 | O–O  | N–QB3! |
| 8 | R–K1 | |

For 8 P–B4 see Browne–Bisguier, given on p. 243.

| 8 | . . . | B–KN5 |
|---|-------|-------|
| 9 | P–B3  | |

9 BxN? PxB 10 RxP P–B4 11
R–K1 BxN 12 QxB NxP; or 11
QxB NxP 12 Q–Q3 N–K3; or
11 PxB? P–B4 12 R–B4 O–O is
good for Black.

9 P–B4 N–B3! 10 PxP is refuted by Pillsbury's suggested
answer 10 . . . QxP 11 N–B3
BxN 12 NxQ BxQ 13 NxB NxN
14 RxB O–O–O!

The text 9 P–B3 underpins
White's QP and threatens 10
BxN; therefore, Black's answer
is forced and to some degree
weakens his king-side. But
White does not follow up consequentially and thus concedes
the initiative.

| 9 | . . . | P–B4! |
|---|-------|-------|

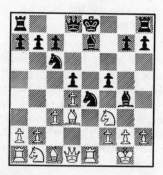

**10 Q–N3?!**

A commonsensical move if followed up as suggested by theory

during the next eighty years.
White might also have moved a
man twice now, in a dynamic
manner; i.e., 10 P–B4!—a move
found by Krause in 1895, but
not widely known then. Or did
Lasker know and not play it because he had already foreseen a
refutation published by Maróczy
seven years later? It runs 10 . . .
B–R4! 11 P–KN3 BxN 12 QxB
NxP 13 Q–K3 B–K3 14 PxP
O–O 15 BxN R–K1∓. One
may imagine that Lasker, a practical player throughout, did not
indulge in dissecting theory in
essays, but had found the answer to 10 P–B4 and had kept it
to himself in case anyone would
play it against him. But he was
beaten to the punch when
Maróczy pointed out the de-
cidedly better 10 . . . B–R4 after
the game Maróczy–Pillsbury,
Monte Carlo 1902, when Pillsbury played 10 . . . O–O and
lost.

| 10 | . . . | O–O |
|----|-------|-----|
| 11 | B–KB4 | |

The opponents know that 11
QxP would hasten Black's king-
side attack by 11 . . . R–B3 12
Q–N3 R–N1 13 Q–B2 R–KN3
14 B–K2 B–Q3. White's 10th
move intended to build pressure on the queen-side, vacate
the square Q1 for White's QR,
and at the right moment push
P–QB4. White therefore develops his QB now, to prevent
it from being shut in by an immediate QN–Q2 or KN–Q2.

However, White's last three moves prove too slow and they favor Black's attack. White believed that his side was safe from an attack despite the coming doubling of his KB pawns. The question is whether White has convincing alternatives, mainly to prevent Black from doubling White's KBPs; e.g., (a) *11 KN–Q2 NxKBP 12 KxN B–R5ch 13 P–N3 P–B5 14 K–N2 PxP 15 PxP Q–Q3* (as old as Schlechter); or (b) *11 QN–Q2 K–R1 12 QxNP R–B3 13 Q–N3 R–N3* (Showalter–Pillsbury, Cambridge Springs 1904), both variants being considered level throughout, with Black's attack to compensate for the pawn minus.

Seventy years later, in the 6th match game Karpov–Korchnoi 1974, White played the more insistent *12 P–KR3*, whereupon *12 . . . BxN 13 NxB R–N1* retains the equilibrium. After Korchnoi's *12 . . . B–R4*, White could take *13 QxNP R–B3 14 Q–N3 R–N3*, and after *15 B–K2!* was a pawn up with a consolidated formation. E. Mednis, in *How Karpov Wins* (New York: McKay, 1975), calls *11 QN–Q2* a Karpov innovation, which is not so; but it may be called novel in conjunction with *12 P–KR3!* (c) *11 BxN PxP 12 RxP BxN 13 PxB RxB* is good for Black.

| 11 . . . | BxN |
| 12 PxB | N–N4 |
| 13 K–N2 | |

*13 BxN? BxB 14 QxP R–B3 15 Q–N3 B–B5!* does not look hopeful.

| 13 . . . | Q–K2 |
| 14 Q–B2 | N–K3 |
| 15 B–QB1 | B–Q3 |
| 16 N–Q2 | QR–K1 |
| 17 N–B1 | N/K3xP!! |

White has been constantly retreating, with Black nonchalantly placing his forces into strategically favorable spots. He now reaps the harvest.

| 18 Q–Q1 | RxR |
| 19 QxR | NxP!! |
| 20 KxN | P–B5! |

The start of a blockading stranglehold. White's next move refutes *21 . . . Q–R6ch 22 K–K2 R–K1ch*, winning the queen, and also provides an escape hatch for the harassed king. But in the process White must give up a piece.

| 21 Q–Q1 | N–K4ch |
| 22 K–K2 | |

*22 K–N2 P–B6ch 23 K–R1 Q–R6 24 N–K3 N–N5! 25 Q–N1 NxP wins.*

| 22 . . . | Q–N5ch |
| 23 K–Q2 | QxQch |
| 24 KxQ | NxB |
| 25 K–K2 | N–K4 |

Black is two pawns up and has a superior position. The remaining part of the game is a demonstration of how to wind up quickly and securely. Nowadays the game would be terminated

at this stage, allowing the contestants a rest—unless the loser
is in a spiteful mood, or hopes
that the spectators will go
home before he has to give up.

| 26 | P–B3 | R–K1 |
| 27 | P–N3 | N–N5ch |
| 28 | K–Q2 | N–K6 |
| 29 | B–N2 | N–N7 |
| 30 | P–KR3 | B–B4 |
| 31 | N–R2 | B–B7 |
| 32 | P–QB4 | PxP |
| 33 | PxP | P–KR4 |
| | Resigns | |

In the same round, Steinitz took revenge for his loss at Hastings.
He acted as Pillsbury's particular nemesis in the games to come, although in the first half of the tourney, Pillsbury resisted the spell by
drawing in the 2nd round, and fighting to an inspired standoff as
Black in the 3rd round.

As known from dispatches, and from reports in Russia's *Novoye
Vremya* (translated by "La Stratégie"), Pillsbury, who had arrived
in St. Petersburg on December 6, "played without visible effort, with
assurance and ease. The endgame especially [against Lasker] was
rapidly played by Mr. Pillsbury."

Pillsbury, who was the embodiment of chess knowledge supreme,
controlled his exuberant drive for brilliancy where it was not war-
ranted. In this he was a disciple of Steinitz, and followed the teaching of the man whom he admired and feared—and against whom he
fared the worst!

In the first half of the tournament, Pillsbury beat Lasker a second
time, after Lasker's ill-timed effort to squeeze a win out of a level
position. The third game produced a deadlock. Halfway through the
tourney, with 3 wins against Chigorin to his credit, with three
triple-rounds down and three to go at the start of the New Year
1896, Pillsbury was leading with 6 points against Lasker 5½, Steinitz
4½, and Chigorin 1½. The American was not the sort to let go.
On January 2 the 4th round commenced, and two days later Pillsbury was pitted against Lasker, who seemed to be back in form. But
this time medical disaster struck Pillsbury—suddenly, acutely, and
savagely. And as time went on, it ironically instigated a fiction. Pillsbury, the undisputed leader after the first half of the tournament,
suddenly floundered in the second, scoring a mere 1½ points out
of 9; only to recover slowly and too late, when he drew three out of
the last four games. What caused the unpredictable collapse of this
tower of strength?

Years later, the grapevine had it that in St. Petersburg, Pillsbury
"contracted an illness which seriously impaired his health, and
ultimately proved fatal to him." (P. W. Sergeant and W. H. Watts,

*Pillsbury's Chess Career* [New York: McKay, 1937; Dover, 1966].)
The conjecture was repeated by B. F. Winkelman in 1935 as "the
malady contracted at St. Petersburg [which] manifested itself in
insomnia and restlessness" *Modern Chess* [Philadelphia: McKay,
1935] ; and was again repeated by P. Wenman in 1948 in his *H. N.
Pillsbury* [London: Mitre Press, 1948]. However, it slowly became
an "open secret" that "in St. Petersburg Pillsbury contracted the
syphilis that was responsible for his early death" H. C. Schonberg,
*Grandmasters of Chess* [New York: Lippincott, 1972].[2]

The same opinion had by then been expressed as a fact in A. D.
de Groot: *Thought and Choice in Chess* (The Hague: Mouton,
1965, p. 355): "Pillsbury did decline appreciably before he was
thirty, but this was primarily due to the physical and mental consequences of the then incurable infectious disease that was also
responsible for his early death in 1906."

The curious fact remains that neither Pillsbury's contemporaries,
nor the obituaries and biographies issued soon after, or even a considerable time after his death, pointed to syphilis as the culprit.
Syphilis was not often recognized in those days, because of its ability
to disguise itself under the symptoms of many other diseases. Hence,
it is still called "The Great Mimic"; but there is a possibility that
the mimicking process also reverses. We will now look at the symptoms, the purported causes, and the written and oral transmission of
the story by witnesses near the scene.

Reports before and at the time of Pillsbury's death merely speak
of "an illness contracted through overexertion of his memory cells,"
or of

> Pillsbury's mental overstrain, aggravated by heavy smoking; or of his
> compulsive blindfold productions which adversely affected his com-
> petitive tournament record and only served as a means to attract a
> wide audience; his subsequent nervous breakdown caused by phe-
> nomenally excessive feats of memory and irregular living habits which
> supported psychiatrists' opinion of the period that the multiple blind-
> fold séances were the principal reason for Pillsbury's exhaustion (L.
> Bachmann, 1914).

Aside from Bachmann's dubious speculations on the harmful
consequences of blindfold play, he describes "Pillsbury's sudden onset of attacks of delusion, especially in Philadelphia on March 1,
1905, when he was taken to hospital and attempted to throw him-

---

[2] The author, for decades the music critic for the *New York Times*, applied
his impeccable prose not only to this book, but also to many sporadic articles
on chess in the *N. Y. Times Magazine* and elsewhere. He also covered the
Fischer–Spassky match in Reykjavik.

self out of the window." "He recovered just as abruptly, scored a number of triumphs in May, but his nerves began to fail again."[3] As is well known, in January 1906 in Bermuda, he suffered a stroke that left him partially paralyzed, and survived a second one in March in Philadelphia. He passed away in June 1906.

Six years after the happenings in St. Petersburg, well-informed L. Hoffer wrote in *The Field* (September 1902): "How far Pillsbury damages his chances by exhibition play is difficult to say; the constant effort must affect his nerves 'though he is not conscious of it as yet." This supposition is devoid of any allusions to other suspected reasons for Pillsbury's collapse, and so is Marshall's comment: "Unfortunately, he took little care of his health and constant blindfold play left its mark on him" (Frank C. Marshall, *My Fifty Years of Chess* [In *Chess Review*, 1942; and New York: Dover, 1960]).

Working from the premise that Pillsbury contracted syphilis in Russia, a timetable of events would be useful. He arrived in Russia on December 6, with a week to spare before the first game. If Pillsbury did indeed contract syphilis shortly after his arrival, he could have evidenced symptoms about two to three weeks later (between December 27 and January 2). A prompt diagnosis could have caused a mental shock which might not have worn off for two to three weeks; but during that time his game began to improve. Within a few months, some secondary symptoms involving joints, eyes, and the nervous system could have affected him. We note that he played somewhat unsteadily in the Nuremberg tournament in July–August 1896. His affliction may then have remained dormant until it remanifested itself neurologically. Progressive brain damage may have been accompanied, or preceded, by (cerebral) aneurysms and creeping paralysis.[4] Thus, assuming the diagnosis of syphilis to be true, the pattern is set and no medical authority would dispute the possibility. We might observe, however, that the speed of development of the disease was extreme, and that his would have been a most exceptionally severe case.

No records are available, however, because Frankford Hospital (now a borough of Philadelphia) didn't keep patient records before 1908. Nor did a search at the Bermuda health facilities produce a chronicle of the apoplectic stroke he suffered there. The diagnostic "Wassermann Test" was not even invented until 1908. As was dis-

---

[3] For the record, these press reports were strongly denied by W. P. Shipley in *The American Chess Bulletin*, 1905, p. 164.

[4] Aneurysm is a blood-filled dilation of a blood vessel resulting from disease of the vessel wall. If the dilated, weakened area of a cerebral artery bursts, blood seeps out and presses on delicate brain tissue, producing a stroke or strokelike symptoms.

closed to me by Pyotr Romanovsky in 1952, Pillsbury "was not choosy about his female companions and chess followers—which might be the basis for the fact or just the belief that he caught a disease; neither [Romanovsky's older friend] Duz-Khotimirsky ever attributed to Pillsbury the acquisition of such a sickness in St. Petersburg, nor anyone else professed knowledge of any such fact or rumor."

The question remains: Why the continued silence—both by Pillsbury and his contemporaries—over such cause of his illness? Citing a Victorian tendency to hush it up seems insufficient. Pillsbury did not desist from marriage in the face of an incident which would have dealt him such a shock to his playing strength. He was neither dishonest, nor naive.

As told by A. Horowitz, William Napier related to him some of his own recollections. Napier, for many years Pillsbury's second, said, "Pillsbury tried to explain his failure against Lasker on violent attacks of headaches, drowsiness, heavy sleep, and imbalance during the middle of the tournament, which he was unable to shake off" (a state of mind he referred to as late as 1905, in a letter from Bermuda to the *American Chess Bulletin*), and that "Pillsbury had mentioned his bad physical condition in one of his newspaper releases from St. Petersburg, but this must be buried somewhere."

Equally revealing—or inconclusive—were Dr. Tartakover's "insider's" comments during World War II, when he was stationed in London as Lt. Xavier Cartier of the Free French Forces. We often met at Lommer's Mandrake Chess and Social Club in the Soho.[5] Tartakover remembered Dr. Tarrasch's revelations of Pillsbury's ailments. In 1902 or 1903, Pillsbury complained to Dr. Tarrasch about the "troubles his nervous system was giving him." Tarrasch considered all eventualities: Pillsbury did not show any eczemas that could point to a chronic blood condition, nor did he manifest any movements that would indicate some other pathological problems. His fingers trembled, due to heavy smoking. Pillsbury described a state of recurring haziness that cleared only upon concentration, but left him at times weak and irritable, depriving him of sleep. He showed no defects of vision or speech, but suffered from headaches and wondered if "he had some troublesome growth in his head" (Pillsbury's own supposed words) that since St. Petersburg kept bothering him to an unsettling degree. Trying to quieten him by psychotherapy, Tarrasch also applied hypnotic treatment but was

[5] Harold M. Lommer, international master of chess composition and author of *1234 Modern Endgame Studies* (New York: Dover, 1968) and of *1357 End-Game Studies* (New York: Pitman, 1975), lives in retirement in Valencia, Spain.

not sure that he succeeded, perhaps due to linguistic barriers. He never ruled out the possibility that purely biological effects of some blood clots or burst veins, perhaps induced by nicotine or memory stress, may have played a part in the patient's discomfitures. Modern research on nicotine's potential effect on the brain may augment this observation.

Inasmuch as the reports by Napier and Tartakover are less hearsay than those of various other authors theorizing about a social disease contracted in St. Petersburg, we can perhaps use them to form another hypothesis; namely that Pillsbury suffered from either acute or chronic aneurysm, whose first occurrence was at St. Petersburg. It then abated to some degree, and thus enabled him to continue functioning. Soon, however, his condition worsened, to the point where he suffered cerebral tumors and hemorrhages of varying impact. He probably suffered other acute attacks in Nuremberg in 1896, and later.

The pressures caused by these erosions were ultimately fatal, but they need not have been caused by syphilis. Undoubtedly, an earlier infection of venereal disease can neither be ruled out nor proven. It is interesting to refer to Pillsbury's letter from Bermuda, wherein he describes the pains following his stroke as being similar to those suffered in Nuremberg back in 1896! This supports the theory of an aneurysm, a circulatory defect which periodically affected his well-being but was situated in an area of the brain not vital for abstract thinking. His condition was not constant, for he had the continued, though episodic, ability to play exceptionally well (for instance, against Lasker, and against Marshall in 1904). If, instead, a venereal disease were to blame, then progressive syphilitic decay should have caused a steady deterioration of his faculties.

The encounter with Lasker on January 4th, 1896, illustrates Pillsbury's sudden instability of play, probably due to his state of health. In the first half of the tourney, Pillsbury had won 2 games from Lasker, and drawn 1, all in an impeccable manner.

In this game, Pillsbury springs an important innovation in the opening, but fails to carry it through properly, and is duly being outplayed. Then Black fails to follow up correctly (22 . . . R–B2?) and reaps victory only because White overlooks a saving clause on move 26.

Lasker's victory after 18 . . . R–QR6!! was well deserved, but Pillsbury's weak handling of the game discloses his apparent indisposition.

St. Petersburg 1896
*Queen's Gambit Declined*

H. N. PILLSBURY     EM. LASKER

| | |
|---|---|
| 1 P–Q4 | P–Q4 |
| 2 P–QB4 | P–K3 |
| 3 N–QB3 | N–KB3 |
| 4 N–KB3 | P–B4! |

A counterthrust with no risk of Black's being left with an isolated center pawn, as contrasted to the Tarrasch Variation *1 P–Q4 P–Q4 2 P–QB4 P–K3 3 N–QB3 P–B4 4 PxQP KPxP* and the option *5 PxP.* However, even Black's isolated QP may turn into a spearhead in some lines. The consensus varies.

In this game, White has a choice of the solid *5 BPxP NxP 6 P–K3 N–QB3 7 B–Q3 B–K2 8 O–O O–O=*; or *5 P–K3 N–B3 6 P–QR3 N–K5 7 Q–B2 NxN 8 PxN B–K2 9 B–N2 O–O 10 B–Q3 P–KR3 11 O–O N–R4 12 N–Q2 QPxP 13 NxP NxN 14 BxN P–QN3=* (Petrosian–Fischer 1971). Pillsbury chooses a line which is double-edged and novel. It raised eyebrows with his contemporaries.

| | |
|---|---|
| 5 B–N5! | BPxP |
| 6 QxP!? | N–B3 |
| 7 Q–R4? | |

But here White slips, which proves that he did not play a prepared variation, but went through his last two moves impulsively. He fails to think of the better alternative, which he

employed more than eight years later against the same opponent (see p. 83). For a person whose firm grip showed in Hastings, and even during the first half of the present tourney, the looseness at this early stage is a curious symptom; and Lasker truly seizes the initiative.

| | |
|---|---|
| 7 . . . | B–K2 |
| 8 O–O–O | Q–R4 |
| 9 P–K3 | B–Q2 |
| 10 K–N1 | P–KR3! |
| 11 PxP | PxP |
| 12 N–Q4 | O–O |
| 13 BxN | BxB |

Black remains with a pair of bishops which pose a latent danger. White's most prudent reply would have been either 14 Q–B4 or 14 Q–N3. Pillsbury continues with rational attacking moves, but is stormed from the opposite direction.

| | |
|---|---|
| 14 Q–R5 | NxN |
| 15 PxN | B–K3 |
| 16 P–B4 | QR–B1 |
| 17 P–B5!? | RxN!! |

As reported by W. E. Napier, Pillsbury called this "the only startling and utterly diabolical surprise he suffered in all his career abroad." Indeed, the way that Black quietly forces the 18th move hardly has a rival in master practice.

**18 PxB**

Pillsbury says "show me"; but even if he no longer likes the looks of his position, he also thinks there is nothing else to be done, because *18 PxR QxP 19 Q–B3 Q–N5ch 20 Q–N3 BxPch 21 B–Q3 QxQch 22 PxQ B–N5* leaves Black with a formidable attack. But, with hindsight, this alternative is also worth consideration.

| 18 . . . | R–QR6!! |
|---|---|

Terrific! If now *19 PxR Q–N3ch 20 K–R1 BxPch 21 RxB QxRch 22 K–N1 PxP* wins; or *19 P–K7 R–K1 20 PxR Q–N3ch 21 K–B2 R–B1ch 22 K–Q2 BxQP 23 P–K8(Q)ch RxQ 24 B–Q3 Q–R4ch 25 K–B1 QxPch*, and mate next move.

| 19 PxPch | RxP |
|---|---|
| 20 PxR | Q–N3ch |
| 21 B–N5 | QxBch |
| 22 K–R1 | R–B2? |

A world chess champion (Lasker) should not be forgiven his errors—more proof that Pillsbury played this game listlessly. He was below his usual strength, as will be apparent on the 26th move. Playing *22 . . . Q–B5* at once would have been necessary.

| 23 R–Q2 | R–B5 |
|---|---|
| 24 KR–Q1 | R–B6 |
| 25 Q–B5 | Q–B5 |
| 26 K–N2? | |

White fails to seize the draw allowed by Black's *22 . . . R–B2.* White should have leveled after *26 Q–N1 RxP 27 Q–N2,* but now he is moribund.

| 26 . . . | RxP |
|---|---|
| 27 Q–K6ch | K–R2 |
| 28 KxR | Q–B6ch |

And Black mates in four.

## THE HERCULEAN INTERIM

After St. Petersburg, Pillsbury attended the Nuremberg International Tournament in 1896. The best players of the period, nineteen in all, competed, with Maróczy landing in 2nd place, and Pillsbury and Tarrasch sharing 3rd and 4th place.

Emanuel Lasker emerged as the winner, but Pillsbury won their individual encounter and, for his splendid victory, was awarded the brilliancy prize donated by Vienna's Baron Albert de Rothschild.

## INTERNATIONAL TOURNAMENT

**Nuremberg 1896**
*French Defense*

H. N. PILLSBURY          EM. LASKER

| 1 P–K4 | P–K3 |
|--------|------|
| 2 P–Q4 | P–Q4 |
| 3 N–QB3 | N–KB3 |
| 4 P–K5 | KN–Q2 |
| 5 P–B4 | P–QB4 |
| 6 PxP | N–QB3 |
| 7 P–QR3! | NxBP |

An aggressive line is 7 . . . BxP 8 Q–N4 0–0 9 N–B3 N–Q5.

| 8 P–QN4 | N–Q2 |
|---------|------|

Lasker's postmortem preferred the more active 8 . . . P–Q5 9 QN–K2 P–Q6! 10 N–N3 Q–Q5, and he may have been right.

| 9 B–Q3 | P–QR4 |
|--------|-------|

Black tries to regain control of his square QB4, but the strategy is too slow; 9 . . . P–B4 may have been better.

| 10 P–N5 | QN–N1 |
|---------|-------|
| 11 N–B3 | N–B4 |
| 12 B–K3 | QN–Q2 |
| 13 O–O | P–KN3 |
| 14 N–K2 | B–K2 |

Black's 13th move was played to prevent the breakthrough P–B4–B5; but now 14 . . . B–N2 and 15 . . . O–O would have been a better defense.

| 15 Q–K1 | N–N3 |
|---------|------|

Commentators dismiss 15 . . . NxB 16 PxN as strengthening White's center after P–Q4, but actually P–Q4 would only fossilize White's pawn structure and keep his pieces hemmed in. 16 . . . N–B4 17 P–Q4 N–K5 18 P–N4 (mounting a dubious king-side attack) B–Q2 19 P–QR4 B–N5 or similar turns may prove that the conservative strategies do not tally with modern fluid tactics.

| 16 KN–Q4 | B–Q2 |
|----------|------|
| 17 Q–B2 | |

Threatening 18 NxP and then to win back one of Black's knights.

Black has at his disposal either 17 . . . QR–B1 or 17 . . . Q–B2, followed by 18 . . . N/4–R5 and 19 . . . N–B5.

| 17 . . . | N/3–R5 |
|----------|--------|
| 18 QR–N1! | P–R4 |

White's last move prevented 18 . . . N–N7, but it also contains a hidden point, as will be seen later. Black's answer, designed to stop 19 P–N4, does not turn out well. Incorrect is 18 . . . NxB 19 PxN BxRP? 20 R–R1! Q–K2 21 N–B2. But 18 . . . O–O 19 P–N4 P–B4 was playable.

**19 P–N6!**

The outline of a vision. White vacates square QN5, clearing it for use by his bishop, threatening 20 B–B5; and White's RP or NP serve as a come-on. If 19 . . . NxP? 20 NxP!! PxN 21 BxN.

19 . . .          NxB
20 PxN          BxP!?

Now the pawn can be taken, as 21 R–R1 achieves nothing. A rational view has Black a pawn up on the queen-side, with White's QNP about to fall after . . . R–R3. Preparation for a White king-side attack—with P–N3, P–R3 followed by P–N4 —is slow and allows Black counterchances after . . . PxP.

But Pillsbury does not stoop to mere logic—he uses miraculous imagination, culminating in the sacrifice of the exchange on move 24. With Black's forces dislocated, we witness a Pillsburian eruption followed by tremors.

**21 P–B5!!**

A quite unexpected offer of White's QNP is followed by another one on the king-side, which clears KB4 for the knight. If 21 . . . KPxP 22 N–B4 NxP 23 N–B2 or 22 . . . B–B3 23 R–R1 Q–K2 24 NxB PxN 25 Q–R2, winning a piece, or also 23 NxB PxN 24 P–N7 R–QN1 25 B–R7, winning the exchange.

21 . . .          NPxP
22 N–B4          P–R5

To prevent 23 Q–N3 and 24 Q–N7 or 23 Q–B3 P–R5 24 NxBP PxN 25 NxP, all bringing devastation. But now another sacrificial streak enters. It's on both wings at the same time, and is more decisive than 23 NxBP PxN 24 NxP.

23 R–R1!          B–K2
24 RxN!          BxR
25 N(Q4)xKP PxN
26 NxKP

After five strokes the debacle is over. Black loses swiftly after 26 . . . Q–B1 27 QxBP (to be followed by 28 B–N5) with (a) 27 . . . R–KN1 28 Q–B7ch K–Q2 29 N–B5ch; or 28 N–B7ch K–Q1 29 P–K6 B–B3 30 Q–B7 R–K1 31 Q–N7; or (b) 27 . . . Q–B3 28 B–N5! QxPch 29 P–Q4 Q–N5 30 Q–B7ch K–Q2 31 BxB QxB 32 N–B5ch K–Q1 33 NxPch K–Q2 34 P–K6ch, etc., both winning.

Black elects to prolong the struggle positionally by giving up the queen for rook and bishop; but his pawns are too weak and scattered to allow true resistance.

26 . . .          B–Q2
27 NxQ          RxN
28 B–B5          R–QB1
29 BxB          KxB
30 Q–K3          R–B3
31 Q–N5ch

On the 50th move Black's agony ends.

## PRODIGIOUS MEMORY BANK

Pillsbury's outstanding ability at blindfold chess is well known. It's a pastime he enjoyed partly because of its exceptional publicity value, partly because of the challenge: He genuinely went all out to establish an "unbeatable" record of opponents played blindfold. He possessed a miraculous memory, with a fantastic ability for instant photographic retention, almost computerlike rapidity of calculation, and great power of visualization.[6] At the start of an exhibition in London in 1899, Pillsbury was handed a list of twenty-eight difficult words. Glancing at it for fifteen seconds before laying it aside, he rattled off the row of words and then did it again backwards. The next day he repeated the same words from memory.

Prior to Pillsbury's blindfold chess séances, the record for games played simultaneously stood at fifteen, but not always against opponents of high caliber. His intention was not just to top that figure, but to go to an extreme unlikely to be matched by others. He reached his peak in Germany in 1902, taking on twenty-one opponents of master strength, winning 3, drawing 11, and losing 7 games. It exceeded, by one, the number of participants at the Franklin Chess Club of Philadelphia on April 28, 1900. In Philadelphia, facing an array of strong players, he had lost 1, drawn 5, and won 14. (Later, Alekhine exceeded Pillsbury's record.) Here is one of Pillsbury's *sans voir* victories.

**Brooklyn, New York 1900**
*Vienna Game*

H. N. PILLSBURY     C. S. HOWELL
(BLINDFOLD)

| 1 P–K4 | P–K4 |
|--------|------|
| 2 N–QB3 | N–QB3 |

Another effective answer to the Vienna Game is 2 . . . N–KB3, and if 3 B–B4 NxP! or 3 P–B4 P–Q4 4 PxKP NxP 5 N–B3 B–K2!

After 2 . . . N–QB3, the game may maintain the character of, and have a steady chance to transpose into, the King's Gambit proper, with the authorities still divided in their preferences for White's or Black's position.

| 3 P–B4 | PxP |
|--------|-----|
| 4 N–B3 | P–KN4 |
| 5 P–KR4 | P–N5 |
| 6 N–KN5 | |

[6] *Everybody's Magazine* of September 5, 1904, gave a vivid description, as related by Pillsbury himself, of his breakdown of the game into groups, and into styles of openings, to facilitate quick play in the opening stages; then memory had to take over.

And here duly arrives the Hamppe–Allgaier line of the King's Gambit Accepted. It is out of date and might not be sound, but it eminently suits an attacking spirit who likes to disinter unexpectedly some ever old, yet ever new, KP gambit. The next two moves play themselves.

| | |
|---|---|
| 6 . . . | P–KR3 |
| 7 NxP | KxN |
| 8 P–Q4 | P–Q4 |

Nowadays 8 . . . P–B6 9 PxP B–K2! or 9 B–B4ch P–Q4 10 BxPch K–N2 has come to the fore.

**9 BxP!?          B–N2**

At the time, the Vienna Gambit was not mentioned in the classical Bilguer except for 3 . . . P–Q4, which was believed to be the convincing refutation, and therefore any cross-referencing to the Hamppe–Allgaier was omitted. Actually, C. S. Howell had his doubts (and so apparently had Pillsbury), and he selected this sequence of the Hamppe–Allgaier with the initial 2 . . . N–QB3 instead of 2 . . . N–KB3 because at this point it allowed him the option of 9 . . . N–B3 or 9 . . . KN–K2; or 9 . . . QN–K2; or 9 . . . PxP?— or his actual choice 9 . . . B–N2.[7]

Later exploration discovered

9 BxP B–N5! stabilizing Black's QP; e.g., 10 B–QN5 KN–K2 or 10 P–K5 B–K3. Therefore, 9 PxP might be best.

A game W. W. Adams–H. Steiner, Hollywood 1944, ran 9 PxP QN–K2 10 BxP N–N3 (10 . . . NxP 11 B–B4 P–B3 12 O–O±) 11 B–K5 B–Q3 12 B–QB4 NxB 13 PxN BxP 14 Q–Q3!! N–B3 15 O–O–O P–N4 16 NxP K–N2 (this move might have been more useful one move earlier) 17 P–R5 B–B5ch 18 K–N1 R–B1 19 P–KN3 B–N4 20 P–Q6 (of course!) P–B3 21 N–B7 R–QN1 22 QR–K1 N–K1 23 Q–N6ch K–R1 24 B–Q3 N–B3 25 R–K7 QxR 26 PxQ R–N1 27 P–K8(Q) resigns.

**10 B–K3          B–B3**

A waste of time, helping White consolidate and create a brilliancy. Possibly, Black wanted to forestall 10 . . . KN–K2 11 PxP KNxP 12 B–QB4 B–K3 13 O–Och.

**11 P–KN3          PxP?**

The game might have been tenable after 11 . . . KN–K2 12 P–K5 B–N2 13 B–K2 B–B4 14 Q–Q2 Q–Q2, at least against someone other than Pillsbury.

| | |
|---|---|
| 12 B–B4ch | K–N2 |
| 13 O–O | BxQP? |
| 14 R–B7ch | K–N3 |
| 15 P–R5ch | KxP |
| 16 R–N7!! | |

[7] Howell was a noted analyst of master strength, and coauthor, with K. F. Young, of *The Minor Tactics of Chess* (Boston: 1894; reprinted Little Brown, 1920).

A sudden, fatal blow to the exposed king. An early mate is
unavoidable—the method is a
showpiece. If 16 . . . BxBch 17
K–N2, with the double threat
18 Q–R1ch or 18 B–B7 mate.

| 16 . . . | N–K4 |
|----------|------|
| 17 BxB | N–N3 |
| 18 K–N2 | R–R2 |
| 19 Q–R1ch | N–R5ch |
| 20 QxNch | QxQ |
| 21 B–B7 mate | |

The kaleidoscopic shifts in Pillsbury's next blindfold game illus-
trate the precision of his deep and fast calculations. His achievement is even more impressive when one realizes that this was just
one of twenty simultaneously played sightless games, all of which
required complex analysis.

### Philadelphia 1900[8]
#### Ruy Lopez

H. N. PILLSBURY     S. L. BAMPTON
(BLINDFOLD)

Franklin Chess Club cham-
pion. Bampton played first
board.

| 1 P–K4 | P–K4 |
|--------|------|
| 2 N–KB3 | N–QB3 |
| 3 B–N5 | N–B3 |
| 4 O–O | NxP |
| 5 P–Q4 | N–Q3 |
| 6 B–R4 | P–K5 |

Shortly afterwards, 6 BxN or 6
PxP became customary.

| 7 R–K1 | B–K2 |
|--------|------|
| 8 N–K5 | O–O |
| 9 N–QB3 | B–B3 |
| 10 B–B4 | R–K1 |

Gives up a second pawn for
quick development. 10 . . . N–
B4 might have been safer.

| 11 N–N4 | BxP |
|---------|------|
| 12 N–Q5 | B–K4 |
| 13 NxB | NxN |
| 14 Q–R5 | P–KB3 |
| 15 B–QN3 | K–R1 |
| 16 R–K3 | P–KN3 |
| 17 Q–R4 | R–K3 |

Protects the KBP. If 17 . . .
P–KN4 18 BxN PxQ 19 BxPch,
or 18 . . . RxB (or PxB) 19
Q–R6.

| 18 R–R3 | P–KR4 |
|---------|-------|
| 19 NxKBP | |

Sergeant and Watts remark
here, "quite a brilliant conception and one which seems per-
fectly sound." But the author's
next comment is perplexing—
that with correct defense White
would have no winning line! Do
the conflicting views reflect
merely confused semantics?
Capturing the knight, 19 . . .

---

[8] P. W. Sergeant and W. H. Watts, in *Pillsbury's Chess Career* (*American
Chess Bulletin*, 1922; New York: Dover, 1966), erroneously give the date as
1897.

QxN 20 QxQch RxQ 21 BxN
or 19 . . . RxN 20 BxN loses
the exchange.

| 19 . . . | N–B4 |
| 20 Q–N5 | N–B2 |
| 21 QxNP | QxN |
| 22 RxPch | N(2)–R3?! |

Black's last move is criticized
by Sergeant and Watts (and
other commentators) as inferior to "22 . . . N/4–R3?! 23
QxQ RxQ 24 BxN/B7 RxB5
25 RxNch K–N2 and Black retains his piece." They thus
neutralize their aforementioned
praise. But as discovered by I.
Chernev (in *The Chess Companion* [New York: Simon &
Schuster, 1968], 22 . . . N/4–
R3 also wins for White forcibly
after 23 B–K5!! QxB (not

23 . . . NxB 24 RxN mate,
or 23 . . . RxB 24 QxQch wins)
24 QxN/7 Q–N2 (preventing
25 RxNch RxR 26 Q–N8 mate)
25 BxR PxB 26 RxNch QxR 27
R–Q1 Q–N4 (or 27 . . . Q–R5
28 P–KN3 Q–N4 29 P–KR4
Q–N2 30 R–Q8ch K–R2 31
Q–R5ch Q–R3 32 R–R8ch and
White wins) 28 P–KR4 QxRP
29 P–KN3 Q–N4 30 K–N2, followed by *31* R–R1ch and mate.

| 23 QxQch | RxQ |
| 24 B–K5 | K–N2 |
| 25 P–KN4 | NxP |
| 26 R–N5ch | K–R3 |
| 27 BxR | NxB |
| 28 RxN | K–N3 |

If 29 R–B4? K–N4 would win
the exchange. Maybe the blindfold player will overlook it?

| 29 R–K5! | P–Q3 |
| 30 R–K7 | B–R6 |
| 31 K–R1 | R–KB1 |
| 32 R–N1ch | N–N5 |
| 33 RxKP | K–B4 |
| 34 R–K2 | R–K1! |
| 35 R/1–K1! | N–K4 |
| 36 P–KB4! | KxP |
| 37 R–B2ch | |

Wins in another five moves.

## SAMSONIAN INTERLUDE

Pillsbury's final exertion, near the termination of his life, was at the
big American event, the International Master Tournament in Cambridge Springs, Pennsylvania, in 1904. With the exception of
Tarrasch and Maróczy, the world's leading masters took part. Even
the sometimes elusive Emanuel Lasker was there, tying Janowski

for 2nd and 3rd place. Lasker's game with Marshall ended in a draw. The tournament turned into a national triumph with Frank J. Marshall fighting his way to 1st place. But equally important was Pillsbury's subjugation of the World Chess Champion, Em. Lasker. The American's massed force erupted here in one last upheaval.

**Cambridge Springs,**
**Pennsylvania 1904**
*Queen's Gambit Declined*

H. N. PILLSBURY          EM. LASKER

| | |
|---|---|
| 1 P–Q4 | P–Q4 |
| 2 P–QB4 | P–K3 |
| 3 N–QB3 | N–KB3 |
| 4 N–KB3 | P–B4 |
| 5 B–N5 | BPxP |
| 6 QxP | N–B3 |
| 7 BxN! | |

A surprise departure from St. Petersburg 1896, where Pillsbury had played, and lost out, with 7 Q–R4. It also proves that Lasker, confident of the soundness of the defense, had not analyzed the line since 1896. Otherwise he might have played 6 . . . B–K2.

Moreover, Lasker knew that Pillsbury had not employed this variation since 1896—neither at Nuremberg 1896 (see P. 77), nor London 1899. On both occasions, Pillsbury had chosen 1 P–K4. But eight years later, Pillsbury was ready with a surprise. Those were the days when secret weapons were one's own, and weren't derived by group analyses to benefit team play. This meeting thus becomes a fierce echo of the St. Petersburg encounter, with the attackers

reversed. Black's reply is forced. If 7 . . . NxQ 8 BxQ N–B7ch 9 K–Q2 NxR 10 B–R4 or 7 . . . QxB 8 QxQ PxQ 9 PxP, with material advantage for White.

| | |
|---|---|
| 7 . . . | PxB |
| 8 Q–R4 | PxP! |
| 9 R–Q1! | |

Best play on both sides, almost a century ago. Pillsbury maintains the grip on the KBP. If instead (a) 9 P–K3 P–B4! 10 QxBP B–N2 11 B–K2 B–Q2 12 O–O Q–B2 13 KR–Q1 O–O 14 P–K4 PxP 15 NxP P–K4, with a good game for Black (Bogolyubov–Alekhine, Munich 1942); or (b) 9 QxQBP Q–N3 10 Q–N5 B–B4 11 P–K3 B–Q2 12 O–O–O QxQ 13 BxQ P–QR3 14 B–Q3 R–B1∓ (Olexa–Bečák, Bratislava 1952).

| | |
|---|---|
| 9 . . . | B–Q2! |
| 10 P–K3 | N–K4 |

Two years later, in the All-Russian Championship in 1906, F. I. Duz-Khotimirsky, against E. Znosko-Borovsky, played 10 . . . P–B4 11 QxBP B–N2 12 Q–N3 BxNch 13 QxB Q–R4 with equality, which prompted the venerable Bilguer to prefer the system 5 P–K3 to 5 B–N5. But by then, Pillsbury had had his revenge.

Euwe's recommendation *10 ... B–K2* is shaky, because of *11 BxP Q–N3 12 O–O N–K4 13 NxN PxP 14 Q–R5* with pressure.

| 11 NxN | PxN |
| 12 QxBP | Q–N3 |
| 13 B–K2 | QxNP |

Confident of his superior development, White offers a pawn and Lasker takes the bait, lacking a better choice.

If *13 ... R–B1 14 Q–Q3±.* If *13 ... Q–N5 14 Q–B7±.* If *13 ... B–B3 14 O–O R–KN1 15 N–K4 B–K2 16 B–R5 B–Q4 17 RxB PxR 18 QxP R–KB1 19 QxKP±.* If *13 ... B–K2 14 O–O B–KB3* (Sergeant) *15 N–N4+.*

| 14 O–O | R–B1 |
| 15 Q–Q3 | R–B2 |
| 16 N–K4 | B–K2 |
| 17 N–Q6ch | K–B1 |

Black is already strapped. White's attack becomes irresistible after *17 ... BxN 18 QxB K–Q1 19 R–Q2 Q–N3 20 QxP/K5.*

| 18 N–B4 | Q–N5 |
| 19 P–B4 | PxP |

If *19 ... P–K5 20 Q–Q4! R–N1 21 QxRP B–B4 22 Q–N8ch R–B1 23 Q–K5* winning. But even after the text, Pillsbury's attack gathers momentum.

| 20 Q–Q4! | P–B3 |
| 21 QxBP | Q–QB4 |
| 22 N–K5 | B–K1 |
| 23 N–N4 | P–B4 |
| 24 Q–R6ch | K–B2 |
| 25 B–B4! | |

Clearly, *25 ... QxB* cannot be played, because of *26 N–K5ch.* Pillsbury is finishing splendidly.

| 25 ... | R–B3 |

*25 ... B–Q2 26 RxB RxR 27 QxKPch K–K1 28 N–B6ch* and mate next move.

| 26 RxPch | QxR |
| 27 R--KB1 | QxRch |
| 28 KxQ | B–Q2 |
| 29 Q–R5ch! | K–N1 |

If *29 ... K–N2 30 Q–K5ch K–N1 31 N–R6ch K–B1 32 QxR* mate.

| 30 N–K5 | Resigns |

## SHOWALTER, PILLSBURY, AND MODERN CHESS THEORY

The next U.S. Champion, the "Kentuckian Chess Lion," Jackson W. Showalter (1860–1935), was a solid pillar of American chess. He was, however, not well known, being first overshadowed by Pillsbury's prominence and then by Frank Marshall's greater verve. In addition, he led an insular life, removed from frequent European chess activity.

Showalter was ex-officio champion before Pillsbury won their individual match in 1897, and official U.S. Champion from 1906 to 1909. He held Pillsbury at bay with two draws at the Paris International Tourney in 1900, defeating Marshall there as well. As late as 1915, he came 1st in the Western Association (later known as the "U.S. Open") championship at Excelsior, Minnesota, for many years the official locality for these contests. Showalter also occupied second board in the Anglo-American cable matches.

Showalter's most penetrating influence was in the openings, especially the Queen's Gambit—at any side of the board! Here, he developed strong defensive ideas that took much of the danger out of this slow, but persistent and pernicious, steamroller. Pillsbury was a newcomer to this system; but he employed his mentor's methods creatively throughout, and enriched them with tactical surprises as shown in the next game between mentor and pupil. It is the embodiment of modern concepts, conceived at the turn of the century.

Both sides' handling of the opening is profound. Aware of Showalter's thorough mastery of "his own" method, Pillsbury varies on move 7. The strategy of the minority attack on the queen-side is a novel discovery; and the shift of tactics from one wing to another exemplifies a mastery comparable to the highest level of contemporary technique, with Pillsbury at his best. On the other hand, Showalter also performs supremely, and the loss is to his credit.

**New York 1898**
**Match Game 5**
*Queen's Gambit Declined*

H. N. PILLSBURY    J. SHOWALTER

| | |
|---|---|
| 1 P–Q4 | P–Q4 |
| 2 P–QB4 | P–K3 |
| 3 N–QB3 | N–KB3 |
| 4 B–N5 | B–K2 |
| 5 P–K3 | O–O |
| 6 N–B3 | QN–Q2 |

Known to all as the Orthodox Defense, with its manifold ramifications. In 1898, many of its advanced concepts had already been tried, adopted, or for a while discarded.

In this position, four months later in Vienna, Schiffers against Pillsbury sprung the more unusual 6 . . . P–QN3, with the continuation 7 PxP PxP 8 B–Q3 B–N2 9 N–K5—a favorite stronghold of Pillsbury, who plays it here before castling, and also foregoes the "thematic" move QR–B1, which serves no purpose in this system.

Nevertheless, 6 . . . P–QN3 (or rather 6 . . . P–KR3 7 B–R4 7 P–QN3) later on grew into the prolific Tartakover Variation, preferably with 7 PxP NxP! But 7 PxP PxP 8 B–Q3 is quite satisfactory, if Black unexpectedly and profitably switches away from the fianchetto and into 8 . . . P–KR3 9 B–R4 9 . . . B–K3 with a solid center, using 6 . . . P–QN3 to support a subsequent . . . P–QB4. Only change is constant!

**7 PxP**

A deviation from Pillsbury's pet move, 7 R–B1. The unexpected is typical of important match play, when standard lines and prepared variations are shunned, if possible, and surprises are sprung upon the opponent. After 7 R–B1, the logical follow-up then as today is 7 . . . P–B3 8 B–Q3 PxP 9 BxBP N–Q4 10 BxB QxB 11 O–O NxN 12 RxN P–K4 13 P–K4 PxP 14 QxP P–QN4! 15 B–K2 P–QB4 with equality, quoted in the Bilguer without source, but actually introduced by Showalter. Also 14 . . . N–N3 15 B–N3 B–K3 is good, and therefore 13 P–K4 went out of fashion. Showalter's other lucid idea was 9 . . . P–QN4, to develop the QB to N2.[9]

| 7 . . . | PxP |
|---------|-----|
| 8 B–Q3 | P–B3 |
| 9 Q–B2 | R–K1 |
| 10 O–O | N–B1 |
| 11 N–K5 | N–N5 |
| 12 BxB | QxB |
| 13 NxN | BxN |

White loses his pivotal knight, as 13 P–B4 is not playable in

this position; but he is seeking other compensation.

| 14 QR–K1 | Q–B3 |
|----------|------|
| 15 P–QR4! | |

Starting a hitherto unsystematized maneuver—the minority attack, which neutralizes Black's pawn majority on the queen-side. White does not even need to keep his pieces on the queen's wing to carry out this stratagem, nor does it help Black to keep the rook there. Instead, Black hopes to gain time for a king-side attack.

| 15 . . . | R–K2 |
|----------|------|
| 16 P–N4 | QR–Q1 |
| 17 P–N5 | Q–N4! |
| 18 P–B4! | |

Black intends to regroup; i.e., . . . R–K3 and . . . R–R3, so White takes precautions.

| 18 . . . | Q–B3 |
|----------|------|
| 19 Q–Q2 | B–B4 |
| 20 P–R5! | Q–N3 |
| 21 BxB | QxB |
| 22 P–R6 | BPxP |
| 23 NxNP | Q–Q2 |

Black might have played 23 . . . Q–K3, but apparently prefers to keep White's backward king's pawn under observation. The characteristic of the position is that sooner or later White can apply pressure on Black's rook's pawn by doubling

[9] West Coast international master I. Koenig in *Chess from Morphy to Botvinnik* (London: Bell, 1951).

rooks on the queen's rook file
(keeping the KP protected by
his queen, and moving K–B2).
Black's isolated queen's pawn is
another weakness.

| 24 PxP! | P–QR3 |

If 24 . . . QxN? 25 R–N1!

| 25 N–B3 | QxP |
| 26 R–N1 | Q–B3 |
| 27 KR–B1 | Q–Q3 |

Another subtlety—if 27 . . .
RxP 28 N–K4!

| 28 N–Q1 | N–N3 |
| 29 P–N3 | P–KR4 |
| 30 Q–K2 | P–R5 |
| 31 Q–R5 | PxP |
| 32 PxP | N–B1 |
| 33 R–B5 | R–Q1 |

Black's 32 . . . N–B1 aims at
getting the knight back into
play. Meanwhile, Pillsbury
operates admirably on both
wings, tightening a positional
noose. Every move is a threat.
The next move prepares to attack the queen and the RP.

| 34 QR–B1 | P–N3 |
| 35 Q–B3 | N–K3 |

| 36 R–B8! | K–N2 |
| 37 RxR | NxR |

If 37 . . . QxR 38 R–B6! R–R2
39 N–B3! or 38 . . . N–B2 39
P–B5! But now the noose becomes a garrotte and a pawn
falls.

| 38 R–B5! | N–K3 |
| 39 QxP | Q–N1 |
| 40 R–B1 | Q–N5 |
| 41 N–B2 | Q–Q7 |
| 42 Q–K5ch | P–B3 |
| 43 QxPch!! | |

Mastery of simplification, con-
verting the middlegame into a
won ending.

| 43 . . . | KxQ |
| 44 N–K4ch | K–B4 |
| 45 NxQ | P–N4 |
| 46 P–Q5 | PxP |
| 47 NPxP | NxP |

Then come:

| 48 PxN | KxP |
| 49 R–B5 | R–Q2 |
| 50 N–B4 | K–K5 |
| 51 P–Q6 | K–Q5 |
| 52 R–B7 | |

And White wins. A positional
*zugzwang* game.[10]

Here, Showalter produces a polished gem in smashing style with
the 8th match game in 1897.

[10] *Zugzwang* is a German expression for the simple "tied up," "under duress,"
"in a squeeze," "bound to move, losing." The term can be, and is being,
stretched so loosely as to lose its precise technical meaning except in situations
as in this game, and even more so in endgames, where the position is so sewn
up; or where the ensuing opposition play in an ending is so clear that any
move loses. The term is often confused with "winning the tempo (or the opposition)" in endgames and should be used with discretion.

New York 1897
Match Game 8
*Ruy Lopez*

J. SHOWALTER    H. N. PILLSBURY

| | |
|---|---|
| 1 P-K4 | P-K4 |
| 2 N-KB3 | N-QB3 |
| 3 B-N5 | N-B3 |
| 4 O-O | NxP |
| 5 P-Q4 | N-Q3 |
| 6 B-R4 | PxP |
| 7 P-B3 | PxP |
| 8 NxP | B-K2 |
| 9 N-Q5 | O-O |
| 10 R-K1 | B-B3 |
| 11 B-B4 | N-K1 |

With this knight's retreat, Pillsbury seems to consolidate his defense admirably. The knight intends to prevent NxP, prepares to retake after NxBch, and clears the square Q3 for an impending . . . P-Q3. Thereafter, Black's position would be a fortress, with White two pawns down. Can this be an illusion?

**12 RxN!**

Giving up the exchange, to remove the palace guard. If *12 . . . RxR 13 BxP* wins Black's queen. Soon White recovers the exchange—and then some.

| | |
|---|---|
| 12 . . . | QxR |
| 13 NxP | Q-K5 |
| 14 B-Q6 | R-N1 |
| 15 B-B2! | Q-KN5 |
| 16 BxR | KxB |
| 17 Q-Q6ch | B-K2 |
| 18 R-K1! | |

Almost every move is a massive hit.

| | |
|---|---|
| 18 . . . | P-KN3 |
| 19 Q-Q2 | Q-R4 |
| 20 N-Q5 | B-Q1 |
| 21 Q-B3 | P-B3 |
| 22 NxP | B-R4 |
| 23 NxQPch | |

White mates in five moves.

## NAPIER AND PILLSBURY

William Ewart Napier (1881–1952) came to the United States from Great Britain at the age of five. Later, he went to Europe to study music, but actually spent a good part of his time on chess. After his return to the States in 1905, he acquired U.S. citizenship in 1908 and became a top-flight insurance executive and actuary.

At the age of sixteen, Napier beat Steinitz in the 2nd game out of 2. Napier won a brilliancy prize against Chigorin at Monte Carlo 1902 and against Bardeleben at Hanover 1902. He beat Marshall in two individual matches. He lost a game to World Champion Em. Lasker at Cambridge Springs 1904, yet it is often quoted in praise of Napier because of his extraordinarily exacting resistance.

Here is Napier's game with Chigorin that won him a brilliancy prize.

## Monte Carlo 1902
*Evans Gambit*

W. E. NAPIER          M. CHIGORIN

| | |
|---|---|
| 1 P-K4 | P-K4 |
| 2 N-KB3 | N-QB3 |
| 3 B-B4 | B-B4 |
| 4 P-QN4 | BxP |
| 5 P-B3 | B-R4 |

Pillsbury called 5 . . . B-B4 less risky, and it was the preference of the day, but it all peters out after 6 P-Q4 PxP 7 O-O P-Q3 8 PxP B-N3 9 N-B3 N-R4 10 B-KN5 N-K2 11 BxPch KxB 12 N-Q5 R-K1 13 BxN RxB 14 N-N5ch K-N1 15 Q-R5 P-KR3 16 Q-N6 PxN 17 N-B6ch with a perpetual (Chigorin); or 9 . . . B-KN5 10 B-QN5 K-B1 11 B-K3 KN-K2 12 P-QR4 P-QR4 13 B-QB4 B-R4 14 K-R1 N-N5 15 P-Q5 N-N3 also with equality (Pachman), whereas Black naturally tries to refute a gambit.

In the text, the same variations arise because Black by-passes a stronger reply on move 6.

| | |
|---|---|
| 6 P-Q4 | PxP |

Black could have well diverged with 6 . . . P-Q3 7 Q-N3 Q-Q2 8 PxP B-N3!

| | |
|---|---|
| 7 O-O | P-Q3 |

Black has an alternative in 7 . . . KN-K2 8 PxP P-Q4 9 PxP KNxP 10 B-R3 B-K3 11 B-N5 B-QN5 12 BxNch PxB 13 BxB NxB 14 Q-R4 Q-Q3= (Pachman).

| | |
|---|---|
| 8 PxP | B-N3 |
| 9 N-B3 | N-R4 |
| 10 B-N2 | N-K2 |

Better would have been 10 . . . NxB 11 Q-R4ch P-B3 12 QxN N-K2. As further shown, the QN will remain offside and White's bishops will become agile. 10 B-KN5 would transpose into the first subvariation of 5 . . . B-B4. Actually, Black allowed himself to be fooled.

| | |
|---|---|
| 11 B-Q3 | O-O |
| 12 P-Q5 | N-N3 |
| 13 N-K2 | P-QB4 |
| 14 Q-Q2 | B-N5 |
| 15 N-N3 | BxN |
| 16 PxB | N-R5 |

Pillsbury gives 16 . . . B-B2 first, freeing the QNP for advance and counterplay on the queen-side. White's answer exposes Black's maneuver as a waste of time.

| | |
|---|---|
| 17 Q-B4 | N-N3 |

If 17 . . . Q-N4 18 QxQ NxPch 19 K-N2 NxQ 20 P-KR4 wins the piece!

| | |
|---|---|
| 18 Q-B5 | R-B1 |
| 19 B-B3 | |

To prevent its being shut out by . . . P to B5 to B6.

| 19 . . . | R–B2 |
|---|---|
| 20 K–R1 | P–B3 |
| 21 R–KN1! | R/2–B2 |
| 22 B–B1 | P–B5 |
| 23 B–R3 | BxP |
| 24 N–K2 | N–K4 |

When White made his 21st move, he must have reckoned with the unacceptable offer of an exchange. After 24 . . . BxR 25 RxB N–K4 26 N–Q4, White recoups his lost material with momentum. If 25 . . . P–QN4 26 RxN PxR 27 QxP R–K1 28 N–B4! Black's loose knight on QR4 is another sore point. From here, White's pressure soon becomes unbearable.

| 25 R–N2 | B–K6 |
|---|---|
| 26 N–B4 | BxN |
| 27 QxB | P–KN4 |

27 . . . K–R1 would have been better, but White still prevails.

| 28 B–K6 | K–R1 |
|---|---|
| 29 Q–Q2 | P–N3 |
| 30 BxR | RxB |
| 31 P–B4 | PxP |
| 32 QxP | N–N2 |
| 33 QR–KN1 | N–B4 |
| 34 BxN | QPxB |
| 35 Q–N4 | P–KR3 |
| 36 Q–R5 | Q–KB1 |
| 37 R–N6 | K–R2 |
| 38 RxPch | Resigns |

Napier smoothly and mercilessly deposes the czar of the all-Russian players, who committed just one early carelessness: 10 . . . N–K2. Chigorin was enormously strong, but had far less occasion to sharpen his international experience than the more centralized Europeans had.

Pillsbury, who had a congenial friendship with Napier, in chess and in life, was always pleased with Napier's successes. Napier also established ties with Pillsbury's family by marrying Pillsbury's niece, Florence Gillespie.[11]

In London in 1904, Napier finished first in a field of 17, ahead of Teichmann, Blackburne, Gunsberg, Leonhardt, and others. In that same year he tied with H. E. Atkins for the British championship and won the play-off against Britain's powerful first player. Atkins, who wrote the introduction to the first (1911), second, and third editions of *Modern Chess Openings* was "potentially perhaps the most talented of British masters."[12]

Napier produced three witty brochures between 1934 and 1935 under the heading *Amenities and Background of Chess-play*. Many

---

[11] By the way, the family never subscribed to the rumor that Pillsbury was a victim of general paresis (see Chapter 4).

[12] Harry Golombek, A *History of Chess* (London: Routledge & Kegan Paul, 1976), p. 172.

of his reminiscences were edited by A. I. Horowitz and reissued under the title *Paul Morphy and the Golden Age of Chess* by W. E. and E. J. Napier (New York: McKay, 1957). Actually Napier's three "units" did not begin and end with Morphy, but summarized many chess events up to Napier's time.

# 5.

# "Go for Broke" Marshall

Just as Morphy, Frank J. Marshall learned chess at ten. He started eating, breathing, and dreaming chess at the age of sixteen, similarly to his predecessor Pillsbury. Although they were about the same age, Marshall outlived Pillsbury by thirty-eight years. He was one of the last to mix professional chess with fun.

Frank J. Marshall (1877–1944) was the incarnation of an ever-optimistic poker-chess player. He had a sure intuition for the right tactical requirements in off-balance positions, and he could create those positions—but only if his opponent was of a similar breed. He was a hazard-loving schemer who failed against the stubborn match-player. When he played against Lasker in a grandmaster tournament, Marshall fell to him; but he brilliantly defeated World Champion Lasker in the immensely strong International Master Tournament in Cambridge Springs in 1904. On stimulating home ground, Marshall placed 1st, with 13 points out of 15 and a margin of 2 points between himself and Lasker and Janowski, who shared 2nd and 3rd prize with 11 points each. Chess America was delighted.

Marshall's extroverted and happy-go-lucky audacity brought him popularity and fame—and a little more money than was earned by the introspective types. Marshall went everywhere for chess, always going all-out for a win, as well as for his own inner satisfaction in playing. He ate chess, but it never ate him. He simply enjoyed chess with joie de vivre, without getting manic over it. His temperament is reflected in his openings—innovations which bespeak adventurous vision, coupled with a daring and enterprising will.

## THE EARLY YEARS

To start, we witness Marshall's win, at the 1900 Paris International Tournament, over Pillsbury, his mentor, who finished 2nd. Marshall also beat the 1st-prize winner, Lasker. In this tournament, Marshall and Maróczy placed 3rd and 4th in a field of seventeen, twelve of them front-runners.

**Paris International Tournament**
**1900**
*Petrov's Defense*

H. N. PILLSBURY  F. J. MARSHALL

| 1 P–K4 | P–K4 |
|---|---|
| 2 N–KB3 | N–KB3 |
| 3 P–Q4 | P–Q4 |
| 4 KPxP | PxP |
| 5 B–QB4 | B–N5ch |

Pillsbury is confident that victory will be his, as his young disciple is inexperienced in international competition. He tries to force a win at any cost, but plays right into Marshall's forte—the risky position. 3 . . . P–Q4 was a novelty, typical of Marshall's style. Pillsbury's counter was not the best. 5 B–N5ch P–B3 6 PxP PxP 7 B–K2 B–QB4 8 P–B3 (or even 5 QxP) would have been better.

| 6 P–B3 | Q–K2ch |
|---|---|
| 7 B–K2? | PxP |

7 Q–K2 would have quickly equalized, but Pillsbury wants variety.

| 8 PxP | B–QB4 |
|---|---|
| 9 O–O | O–O |
| 10 P–B4 | R–K1 |
| 11 B–Q3 | B–KN5 |
| 12 B–N2 | N–K5 |
| 13 QN–Q2? | NxP! |

Cashing in on White's misjudgments. 13 BxN QxB 14 QN–Q2 would have been pref-

erable, and best would have been 12 QN–Q2.

| 14 RxN | BxRch |
|---|---|
| 15 KxB | Q–K6ch |
| 16 K–N3 | |

16 K–B1 KxBch loses the piece without compensation; but walking into the open will prove unhealthy.

| 16 . . . | QxB |
|---|---|
| 17 KxB | R–K7! |
| 18 K–R3 | N–Q2 |

This is more precise than an immediate 18 . . . P–KR4 (to be followed by . . . Q–B4ch) because of 19 QxR! QxQ 20 R–K1 Q–Q6 21 R–K8ch, with a stranglehold.

| 19 R–B1 | P–KR4 |
|---|---|
| 20 Q–B2 | N–B4 |

White had to prevent the deadly . . . Q–B4ch, but cannot exchange queens without getting into an outright lost position.

21 P–N3

This and the next move mean hanging on without hope. If *21* QxQ NxQ 22 R–B2 P–KN4; and now 23 K–N3 P–N5 24 N–R4 N–K8 25 R–B1 RxN 26 B–B3 R–QB7! wins; or 23 NxP N–K8 24 R–B1 RxN 25 B–B3 R–Q6ch; or 23 P–N4? N–B5ch 24 K–N3 R–N7 mate (analysis from *Marshall's Best Games of Chess* [New York: Dover, 1960].

| 21 . . . | P–KN4 |
|----------|-------|
| 22 P–N4  | RxN   |
| 23 QxQ   | RxQ   |
| 24 R–B3  | P–B4  |
| 25 K–N2  | BPxP  |
| 26 NxP   | R–Q7ch |
| 27 K–N3  | RxB   |
| 28 P–KR3 | R–KB1 |
| 29 PxP   | PxP   |
| 30 KxP   | R/1–B7 |

White resigned at last. He could have resigned after Black's 22nd move, and he should have after the 26th.

## MARSHALL AND CAPABLANCA

The next game shows Marshall for once holding his own against the invincible chess machine, José Raúl Capablanca. While "Capa" was not anxious to look for innovations in the openings, Marshall again invents an aggressive, but very sound, novelty; and the middlegame becomes a marvel of intricate maneuvers. The outcome does honor to both players of this match in 1909, despite its lopsided score: Capablanca, 8 wins; Marshall, 1 win, 14 draws.

Capablanca did not really distrust opening innovations, but he did not attach primary importance to originality in this phase. He rather waited for his opponents to look for them, and for him to refute them. The most celebrated example of this kind, both ways, might be Capablanca–Marshall, New York 1918. Marshall sprang his fascinating surprise, the Marshall (Counter) Attack in the Ruy Lopez. Capablanca, unprepared and extempore, accepted an offered sacrifice instead of turning away from it, defended cooly, repulsed Black's ensuing attack, and won the game. But this outcome applied only to the particular, first version of Marshall's line. It still is very much alive and on the agenda of contemporary opening play, although the analysis of its ramifications has considerably progressed since its inception in 1918.

New York 1909
Match Game 14
*Ruy Lopez*

J. R. CAPABLANCA   F. J. MARSHALL

| 1 P–K4 | P–K4 |
|--------|------|
| 2 N–KB3 | N–QB3 |
| 3 B–N5 | P–QR3 |
| 4 B–R4 | P–Q3 |
| 5 P–B3! | P–B4 |
| 6 PxP | |

The strongest reply to, but not a refutation of, Black's natural strategy. White's 5th and 6th moves are now known as the "Siesta" variation, which leads to equality. It has been so christened since Budapest 1928! Some circles prefer 5 NxBch as a more ambitious line of play. This opening line continued dormant from 1909 to 1928, although it was occasionally tried in the intervening years. 5 . . . P–B4 is reminiscent of the Schliemann Attack, but without its risks; it is sharper than 5 . . . B–Q2 or 5 . . . N–B3.

Instead of 6 PxP, Réti tried to undermine Black's center by 6 P–Q4 BPxP 7 N–N5! PxP (Znosko–Borovsky suggested . . . P–Q4) 8 NxKP N–B3 9 B–N5 B–K2, and Black stood better in Réti–Capablanca, Berlin 1928, a game inspired by the preceding "Siesta" tournament. However, the mistake was 8 NxKP in place of the better 8 BxN.

| 6 . . . | BxP |
|---------|-----|
| 7 P–Q4 | P–K5! |
| 8 Q–K2 | |

A solid, quiet line, but it lets Marshall have his play. Capablanca is not rattled by Marshall's aggressive response—so aggressive that Capablanca himself used it twenty years later! A. Steiner–Capablanca, Budapest 1928, continued 8 B–KN5 B–K2 9 N–R4 B–K3! with a fully consolidated and yet flexible game for Black. Livelier would have been 8 N–N5 P–Q4 9 P–B3 P–K6 10 P–KB4 N–KB3, with many sidelines, but analyzed into oblivion. 8 . . . N–B3 9 P–B3 PxP 10 QxP is intriguing.

| 8 . . . | B–K2 |
|---------|------|

Also 8 . . . N–B3 9 B–B2 B–K2 10 N–N5 P–Q4.

| 9 KN–Q2 | N–B3 |
|---------|------|
| 10 P–KR3 | P–Q4 |
| 11 N–B1 | P–QN4 |
| 12 B–B2 | N–QR4 |
| 13 N–K3 | B–N3 |
| 14 N–Q2 | O–O |
| 15 P–QN4 | N–B5 |
| 16 QNxN | QPxN |

If 16 . . . NPxN 17 P–QR4, with a potentially dangerous pawn majority. By slow, careful, and deft play, White has taken the sting out of Black's early initiative. Black has an isolated center pawn and seemingly backward queen-side pawns, whereas White's QRP and QP may be dynamic, if Black isn't on the alert. However, he is.

| 17 P–QR4 | N–Q4! |
|----------|-------|
| 18 NxN | QxN |
| 19 PxP | |

If *19* B–K3 P–QR4! and Black becomes very mobile. There is a lot of poison ivy in these innocuous-looking patches.

| 19 . . . | P–K6 |
| 20 O–O | RxP |
| 21 RxR | PxRch |
| 22 QxP | R–KB |
| 23 Q–K2 | BxB |
| 24 QxB/2 | |

24 QxB/7 PxP 25 QxP B–Q6 would leave White dangerously constricted.

| 24 . . . | PxP |
| 25 B–K3 | B–Q3 |
| 26 B–B2 | Q–N4 |
| 27 Q–K4 | |

It is necessary to ward off 27 . . . Q–B5, but otherwise the game has leveled out. 27 . . . Q–Q7 is answered by 28 Q–K3 with an exchange of queens, favorable for White.

| 27 . . . | P–R3 |
| 28 R–K1 | |

Anti-positional is 28 R–R8 Q–B8ch 29 B–K1 RxR 30 QxRch K–R2 *31* Q–K4ch P–N3! with a promising endgame for Black. After the text, Black decides to call it a day.

| 28 . . . | RxB! |
| 29 KxR | B–N6ch |
| 30 K–N1 | BxR |
| *31* QxB | Draw |

The match Capablanca–Marshall seemingly kept the U.S. Championship rights in abeyance, with Capablanca sometimes claiming seniority; that was before he assumed a stronger international pedestal after winning the tournament in San Sebastian in 1911.

Within the protocol of these challenges, however, Showalter had been the "sitting" champion. Marshall challenged him, and at Lexington, Kentucky, in September 1909, won the title with a score of 7 wins, 2 losses, and 3 draws. Marshall officially retained his position till 1936, when he retired undefeated. Thereupon, the machinery of regular annual championship tournaments was set in motion and Reshevsky won the first U.S. Championship in New York in 1936.

Frank J. Marshall's trophy became the U.S. Championship emblem of the national title.

Considering the shock of the 1909 match between the two, Marshall later stood up very well to Capablanca. In an intranational tournament in New York in January 1911 (Swiss master P. Johner was also invited), Marshall scored 10 points out of 12 possible, drawing with Capablanca 9½. Two years later, in January 1913, the result was reversed: Capablanca 11, Marshall 10½ out of 13 possible; and again they drew their individual game. In July 1913, Capablanca made a clean sweep of 13 points out of 13 possible (a

100% score, repeated by Fischer in 1961) in the New York Rice
Chess Championship Tournament, but Marshall was not in it.
Czech grandmaster Duras was, placing 2nd with 10½ points.

As a consequence of the January tourney, six of the highest placed
participants (Marshall, Capablanca, Jaffe, Janowski, Chajes, and
Kupchik, replacing Stapfer) went to Havana's tropical heat. The
turbulent tournament, despite fierce acclamations for native Capablanca, left Marshall in first place with 10½ points, and Capablanca
following with 10. It was a double-rounder, with Cuba's Blanco and
Corzo added to the list locally.

However, the individual outcome Capablanca–Marshall was
1½:½. Back in New York in an intimate tourney, Capablanca won
5 points out of 5, Marshall 4, with only one loss to Capa. At San
Sebastian 1911 they had drawn; at New York 1915 and 1924, they
drew all four games; at Lake Hopatcong 1926, Kissingen 1928, and
Budapest 1928, it was always a draw! Marshall also drew the game in
the first part, the main tourney, at St. Petersburg 1914 (Marshall
lost, though, 2:0, at New York 1918, and was worn out at New York
1927, losing 3½:½, and New York 1931).

## THE "MARSHALL SWINDLES"

Marshall's next game recalls the golden age of combination. It
solidified his reputation as the most successful aggressive player of
his day. This brilliancy is only one of many.

### Breslau 1912
#### French Defense

S. M. LEVITSKY    F. J. MARSHALL

| 1 | P–Q4 | P–K3 |
| 2 | P–K4 | P–Q4 |
| 3 | N–QB3 | P–QB4 |

Again, a typical Marshall challenge.

### 4 N–B3

White plays it safe. The coun-
terchallenge would be 4 KPxP
KPxP 5 PxP BK3?! but not 5
. . . P–Q5 6 B–N5ch N–B3 7

BxNch PxB 8 QN–Q2 with a
positional plus. White's QPxP
is called for, thus isolating
Black's QP. It could have been
played as late as the 6th or even
the 8th move.

| 4 . . . | N–QB3 |
| 5 KPxP | KPxP |
| 6 B–K2 | N–B3 |
| 7 O–O | B–K2 |
| 8 B–KN5 | O–O |
| 9 PxP | B–K3 |

If 9 . . . P–Q5 10 BxN BxB 11
N–K4, holding on to the pawn.

After the text, if *10* N–QR4
N–K5!

| 10 N–Q4 | BxP |
| 11 NxB? | |

Nowadays nobody would choose
to exchange and thus reinstate
Black's pawn center. One would
select the more flexible *11*
B–K3.

| 11 . . . | PxN |
| 12 B–N4 | Q–Q3 |
| 13 B–R3 | QR–K1 |
| 14 Q–Q2? | B–N5! |

*14* P–R3 might have prevented
the pin, and *14* Q–Q3 also was
better. *15* . . . P–Q5 now threatens.

| 15 BxN | RxB |
| 16 QR–Q1 | Q–B4 |
| 17 Q–K2 | |

White gives up the pawn on
QB3, expecting to recapture on
Q5, as Black's KP will be
pinned. But in the ensuing
melee, Marshall towers head
and shoulders over his opponent. White could have had
*17* P–R3 BxN *18* QxB QxQ *19*
PxQ, but with a bad endgame.

| 17 . . . | BxN |
| 18 PxB | QxP |
| 19 RxP | N–Q5! |
| 20 Q–R5? | |

If *20* Q–K5 N–B6ch! *21* PxN
R–N3ch wins. White would

have been left with some fight
after *20* Q–K4 R–B5! *21* Q–K5
Q–Q7! *22* R–QB5 N–K7ch *23*
K–R1 RxP! *24* Q–R1!

| 20 . . . | QR–KB1 |
| 21 R–K5 | R–R3! |
| 22 Q–N5 | |

If *22* Q–N4 (or *22* Q–Q1) N–
B6ch and *23* . . . QxR wins.

| 22 . . . | RxB! |
| 23 R–QB5?! | |

If *23* PxR N–B6ch. White's
sideswipe seems to create
trouble for Black and possible
salvation for White, but in fact,
hell breaks loose.

| 23 . . . | Q–KN6!! |
| Resigns | |

If *24* BPxQ N–K7ch and mate
next; if *24* RPxQ N–K7 and
mate. If *24* QxQ N–K7ch *25*
K–R1 NxQch *26* K–N1 NxR,
with a piece ahead.

The finale is so utterly captivating that Marshall was reported to
have been showered with gold pieces by the spectators. The legend

has met with much skepticism. I. A. Horowitz carefully discounts it and Harold C. Schonberg says, "it should have been," but declares the story "apocryphal." These remarks contradict Marshall's own direct statement, in his *My Fifty Years of Chess*, in answer to the question whether the incident really happened: "Yes, that is what happened, literally."[1]

The official record in the tournament book of Round 6, played on July 20, merely states "Marshall being Black, played one of the most elegant games of the tournament. In Morphy style, he brought off a piece of brilliant pyrotechnics, putting up his queen for capture in three different ways."[2] No mention is made of a shower of gold.

Eyewitness reports, as circulated in Europe in the 1920s, come close to corroborating Marshall's story. Two of the Czech participants at Breslau, Oldrich Duras, who had shared 1st prize with A. Rubinstein, and K. Treybal, both senior master members of the Dobrusky Chess Club in Prague, often took pleasure in recounting this and other episodes to the junior members, including myself. As corroborated by their compatriots Dobiáš, Hromádka, Pokorný, Thelen, and other Czechs who had also been to Breslau, what really happened was the paying of a bet. As the story was told, the Leningrad master Levitsky was accompanied by another Russian, P. P. Saburov, a well-to-do patron of the game. Another visitor was Alexander Alekhine, a dapper, prosperous aristocrat who was on his way from Stockholm (where he had won 1st prize) to a tournament in Vilna. Saburov, Alekhine, and a few other Russian guests made it their duty to place a wager on Levitsky's win over the "played-out American." However, Marshall upset their patriotic predictions and the bettors tossed over their pledges. Rubles, marks, Austrian crowns, and similar coinage of the period were minted partly or fully in gold. As related by Zidlicky, even two silver Maria Theresa thalers came in the "shower," something not mentioned in the respectable accounts of the tournament book.

As concerns Marshall's striking combination in his game against Levitsky, the idea was in simpler form inseminated before him, and utilized also in later games; but rarely in such sparkling shape. To mention some examples, many a book on Morphy and many chess anthologies include the game N. Marache–P. Morphy, New York 1857, where Black's knight-sacrifice on KN6 creates an unusual coda. W. Korn's *The Brilliant Touch in Chess* (New York: Dover, 1966)

---

[1] Later reprinted as *Marshall's Best Games of Chess*.
[2] XVIIIth Congress of the German Schachbund (Breslau: 1912), p. 71; translation of the German text mine.

contains the Marshall, the Morphy, and two more examples of such technique (diagrams 163–166).

The next virtuoso performance is a rebirth of the very first game quoted in this volume, that of Paulsen–Morphy, but with half a century of technical refinement added. Both opponents, Janowski and Marshall, enjoyed the friendship of an identical sponsor, Leo Nardus, a wealthy resident of French Tunis. As Marshall conveys in his autobiography, during Nardus' visit to New York in 1899, he insisted that Marshall enter the London Tournament that same year, and that Nardus gave generously toward the fund raised for his expenses. Marshall played in the single-round "master" contest; Janowski, nine years his elder, in the double-round international masters tournament. For a long time, Nardus supported Janowski's attendances and the tournament prize funds. He had a liking for adventurous chess and remained loyal to both Marshall and Janowski. In Janowski's best period—during Hastings 1895, Nuremberg 1896, Budapest 1896, Vienna 1898, and London 1899 (where he placed second, after Lasker)—he chalked up plus scores against Steinitz, Em. Lasker, Pillsbury, and Chigorin. In 1913, he beat Capablanca, and Alekhine suffered at his hands at Scheveningen 1913 and Mannheim 1914—after Alekhine had won first prize in Stockholm, and Janowski was a worn-out dandy (he was often needled about his infatuation with immaculate dress).

David Janowski resided in the United States from 1915 to 1924, among others placing 2nd at New York 1916, 1st at Atlantic City 1921, and 3rd at Lake Hopatcong 1923. He finished last at New York 1924, but drew one of his games with Capablanca. In 1925 he retired to his old European haunts to invest his prize money in losing at roulette.

**Biarritz 1912**
**Match Game 3**
*Petrov's Defense*

D. JANOWSKI     F. J. MARSHALL

| | |
|---|---|
| 1 P–K4 | P–K4 |
| 2 N–KB3 | N–KB3 |
| 3 NxP | P–Q3 |
| 4 N–KB3 | NxP |
| 5 P–Q4 | P–Q4 |
| 6 B–Q3 | B–Q3 |
| 7 P–B4 | |

On Black's 6th move, 6 . . . B–N5 is weak, but 6 . . . B–K2 is an equalizer. The text, 6 . . . B–Q3, looks active, and is vindicated by 7 P–B4. But the correct continuation is 7 O–O! B–KN5 8 P–B4 O–O 9 PxP P–KB4 10 N–B3 N–Q2 11 P–KR3 B–R4 12 NxN PxN 13 BxP N–B3 14 B–B5 K–R1 15 P–KN4 NxQP, as in Spielmann–Marshall, Hamburg 1910, which

went *16 Q–Q3?* instead of *16
B–K6! B–B2 17 N–N5 BxB 18
NxB Q–R5 19 Q–N3!* (C.
Alexander–Mallison, Brighton
1938).

| 7 . . . | **B–N5ch** |
| 8 **K–B1?** | |

*8 QN–Q2 O–O 9 O–O BxN 10
BxB B–N5=* was called for.

| 8 . . . | **O–O** |
| 9 **PxP** | **QxP** |
| 10 **Q–B2** | **R–K1** |
| 11 **N–B3** | **NxN** |
| 12 **PxN** | |

White's king is dislocated, but
Black does not seem to be fully
developed. Both his bishop and
the rook's pawn are under fire,
and after *12 . . . B–R4 13 R–
QN1 P–QB3 14 P–KR4*, White
mounts a potentially nasty attack.

It is, therefore, most unexpected that Black can turn the
tables with one sudden stroke.

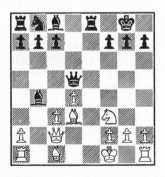

| 12 . . . | **QxN!!** |
| 13 **PxB** | |

The same magnificent resource
as employed in Morphy's aforementioned game, but here the
strategic adroitness is even
more marked.

Obviously *13 PxQ? B–R6ch
14 K–N1 R–K8ch* leads to mate;
thus White employs a safe positional defense. But now Black's
pieces suddenly become strong.
Therefore, White's best would
have been the interpolation *13
P–KR3! Q–Q4 14 PxB! QxP
15 B–N2 QxP 16 BxPch K–R1
17 B–Q3*, with rightfully even
chances.

After the text, Marshall's war
of nerves started as his ingenious
sacrifice won out.

| 13 . . . | **N–B3!** |
| 14 **B–N2** | |

Not *14 B–K3 B–R6 15 KR–N1
RxB* (Marshall).

Tartakover and DuMont in
*500 Mastergames of Chess*
(London: Bell, 1952; New York:
McKay, 1954) misjudge the
situation by suggesting *14 P–
KR3* or *14 B–Q2*, but *14 P–KR3
Q–R4* leaves Black with the
superior game; whereas *14 B–
Q2 NxQP! 15 Q–B4* (*15 PxQ
B–R6ch* and mate next move)
*B–R6! 16 R–KN1 P–QN4 17
QxN QR–Q1* and similar
tactical threats are very favor-
able for Black.

| 14 . . . | **NxNP!** |
| 15 **BxPch** | **K–R1** |
| 16 **PxQ** | |

16 Q–B4 B–R6 17 R–KN1 KxB 18 PxB N–Q6 19 Q–B2 QxRPch 20 R–N2 R–K5! 21 K–N1 QR–K1 winning. Black's attack goes into high gear.

| 16 . . . | B–R6ch |
|---|---|
| 17 K–N1 | NxQ |
| 18 BxN | R–K7! |
| 19 R–QB1 | QR–K1 |
| 20 B–B3 | R/1–K6 |

A flamboyant move. Pragmatic was 20 . . . RxB 21 RxR R–K3 and mate next move.

**21 B–N4**

If 21 PxR R–N7ch 22 K–B1 RxBch, etc.; or 21 B–K4 RxQB.

| 21 . . . | R/6xP |
|---|---|
| 22 B–Q1 | R–B3 |
| Resigns | |

In *My Fifty Years of Chess*, Marshall himself comments that after his 12th move a disbelieving Janowski muttered "swindle," the popular epithet heard about Marshall whenever he snatched victory from defeat. This is another example of the making of a myth, and a disservice to Marshall's uncanny ability to squeeze the last ounce of resistance from a seemingly hopeless loss. Marshall himself used the term "swindle" in a lighthearted fashion, often saying that he "swindled" his opponents. Though joking, he was basically modest —and honest. Unfortunately, his opponents used his statement as an alibi for their loss, insinuating that Marshall had never won any game "honestly." The unjust appellation of a "Marshall Swindle" has been indiscriminately attached, by opponents and commentators alike, to almost all of his victories. His miraculous escape against Yates, from a lost into a drawn-pawn ending—which was based entirely on his superb grasp of endgame finesse that had escaped Yates—was dubbed "swindle" by an American author! With hindsight, Marshall might have avoided the title *Marshall's Chess "Swindles"* (New York: The American Chess Bulletin, 1914), his first book.

The thought of swindling at chess may, in fact, hold a hefty dash of absurd truth, despite the success of the game being grounded, as is believed, in accuracy and inescapable logic. One might be clever in business, but one cannot cheat at chess. Whether an accountant is dead honest or the crookedest crook, he cannot transform, on his balance sheet, the loss of even one penny into profit by a penny. Chess provides no psychological mechanism for a trickster. However, the player may employ a lot of twists and tricks in conducting a chess game—sometimes crudely, sometimes subtly, depending on his and the opponent's class. Though the game begins with an even division of forces, one of the players often is the winner—merely showing that, to quote Sherlock Holmes, to excel at chess is the mark of a scheming mind.

While we digressed into the area of chess "psychology," we stopped short of going deeply into its "ethics." Incalculable are the incidents and arguments of players' "j'adoubing" techniques; tapping and twisting; blowing smoke; noisily moving about—right up to using the washroom for quiet analysis while the game is in progress; and stopping and starting clocks with or without justification, while lodging protests and arguing with the umpires.

It's all part of the game!

## GETTING AWAY WITH MURDER

The next encounter sheds light on the popular creed that the great ones are often lucky in getting away with murder; whereas those who are a class below rarely meet such fortune. Although the maxim is somewhat fallacious (simply, more attention is paid to the vicissitudes of the master players, the others are said merely to blunder), it almost holds true in this instance.

In the formidable New York 1924 tournament, both American participants, Frank Marshall and Edward Lasker, put in a glamorous performance. Marshall placed 4th after Em. Lasker, Capablanca, and Alekhine—the former, current, and future world champions.

Several times in his game with Emanuel Lasker, Marshall had a win within his grasp, yet let the game slip into a draw. Lasker's "electromagnetic brain waves" must have been more powerful and he escaped into a draw. Incidentally, neither Lasker's nor Marshall's final standing would have been affected had Marshall won—the game was not decisive! But they did not know that in the 9th, out of 24, rounds.

**New York 1924**
*Queen's Gambit*

F. MARSHALL        EM. LASKER

| 1 | P-Q4 | P-Q4 |
|---|------|------|
| 2 | P-QB4 | P-QB3 |
| 3 | PxP | PxP |
| 4 | N-QB3 | N-KB3 |
| 5 | Q-N3 | P-K3 |

More aggressive is 5 . . . N-B3 6 N-B3 N-QR4 7 Q-B2 B-Q2 8 B-B4 R-B1 and Black is fully

developed. Even after the text, Black achieves equality and therefore 3 N-KB3! N-KB3 4 PxP PxP 5 N-QB3 is more solid than the queen's early excursion. If 3 N-QB3 PxP is the accepted version.

| 6 | B-B4 | N-B3 |
|---|------|------|
| 7 | N-B3 | B-K2 |
| 8 | P-K3 | N-KR4 |
| 9 | B-N3 | O-O |
| 10 | B-Q3 | P-B4 |
| 11 | B-K5 | |

The threat is . . . N to B3 to K5, with a strong stonewall. Therefore White aims for an exchange. If 11 . . . NxB 12 NxN, with White's stonewall after P–B4.

| 11 . . . | N–B3 |
| 12 BxN | RxB |
| 13 R–QB1 | B–Q3 |
| 14 N–QR4 | Q–R4ch |

Active play! If 14 O–O Q–K1! and . . . Q–R4, with a buildup on the king-side. Now Black's queen is diverted to the queenside and he is misled into believing that he has the initiative.

| 15 N–B3 | R–N1!? |

15 . . . Q–Q1 16 N–QR4 would have made it an early draw by perpetual! As it is certain that neither Lasker nor Marshall intended to play it safe, it might have been good psychology for Lasker to retreat the queen and bank on Marshall's forcing an inferior alternative! (The grandmaster draw is a modern play-safe scourge—excepting drawing master Karl Schlechter. In his case, the recipient was lucky.) Instead, Lasker drifts into a sluggish situation and Marshall's "loss of tempo" proves beneficial.

| 16 O–O | P–QR3 |

To prevent 17 N–QN5 and 18 N–K5.

| 17 N–QR4 | B–Q2 |
| 18 N–B5 | Q–B2 |

"A lamentable necessity, as 18 . . . B–K1 would be met by 19 NxNP Q–B2 20 NxB! RxQ 21 NxB, followed by NxRch and PxR" Alekhine in the tournament book).

| 19 N–K5! | B–K1 |

The game is getting complex. If 19 . . . BxN/K4 20 PxB KR–B1 21 R–B2, with enormous pressure; if 20 . . . R–N3 21 NxB QxN 22 Q–N6; and if 19 . . . NxN 20 PxN BxP 21 P–B4, with 22 N–K4 to follow.

| 20 P–B4 | Q–K2 |
| 21 P–QR3 | R–R3 |
| 22 R–KB2 | P–KN4 |
| 23 P–N3 | K–R1 |
| 24 Q–Q1 | PxP |
| 25 NxN | PxN |
| 26 KPxP | Q–KN2? |

Losing an important pawn. It is unclear why Lasker did not pick 26 . . . P–R4.

| 27 BxRP | B–R4 |
| 28 Q–Q2 | R–N1 |
| 29 B–K2 | B–K1 |
| 30 Q–K3! | R–B3 |
| 31 B–B1 | Q–K2 |
| 32 P–QR4! | P–KR4 |
| 33 R–N2? | P–R5 |
| 34 N–Q3? | Q–QR2 |

White was overcautious and hesitated pushing the QRP vigorously. Now Black gains some respite, although it should not count heavily.

| 35 P–N3 | R–N2 |
|---------|------|
| 36 N–K5 | PxP |
| 37 PxP | Q–N3 |
| 38 P–R5! | |

White regains force by giving up the dormant pawn, so as to open up a new file for attack.

| 38 . . . | QxRP |
|----------|------|
| 39 NxP | Q–N3 |
| 40 N–K5 | R–QB2 |
| 41 RxR | QxR |
| 42 P–KN4! | PxP |
| 43 NxP! | RxP |
| 44 QxP? | |

The momentum of the last few moves should have been climaxed by 44 B–Q3! B–R4 45 N–R6 R–B1 46 Q–N5 and 47 Q–N8ch winning. White's move contains a loophole, which Lasker detects and slips through.

| 44 . . . | RxBch! |
|----------|--------|
| 45 KxR | B–N4ch! |

This is it. Marshall reckoned only with 45 . . . Q–B8ch 46 Q–K1 B–N4ch 47 K–B2 Q–B5ch 48 K–N1 QxPch 49 K–R1 Q–N2ch 50 N–K5! BxN 51 RxQ BxR 52 Q–R4ch, etc. and Black loses. Now White's efforts should come to naught. Although Lasker is still trapped, he pays no great penalty.

| 46 R–K2 | BxRch |
|---------|-------|
| 47 QxB | Q–B2ch |

| 48 Q–B2 | K–N2 |
|---------|------|
| 49 N–K3 | B–B5? |

49 . . . B–R6! 50 QxQch KxQ 51 NxP B–N7 (Ed. Lasker) would have clinched the draw, whereas the move played should have lost. Marshall overlooked his last chance to cash in on previous excellence, and again Black gets away with it.

| 50 K–K2! | Q–B2 |
|----------|------|
| 51 Q–N2ch! | K–B1 |
| 52 NxP?? | |

52 QxQP BxN 53 KxB would have forced Black's resignation. He who hesitates falls to Lasker's spell.

| 52 . . . | Q–B7ch |
|----------|--------|
| 53 K–B3 | B–Q7! |
| 54 Q–B1 | QxPch |
| 55 K–K2ch | K–K1 |
| 56 Q–B5 | |

Alekhine believes that even the winning of a piece by 56 N–B6ch K–K2 57 KxB no longer wins; e.g., 57 . . . Q–N7ch 58 K–K3 Q–B6ch 59 K–K4 Q–B7ch 60 K–K5 Q–B2ch 61 K–B5 Q–B7ch 62 K–N5 Q–Q7ch and 63 QxP. After the text move White also loses his pawn (from the tournament book).

| 57 KxB | QxPch |
|--------|-------|

A draw is agreed upon after a few more moves.

It is noteworthy that in the very same tournament, Em. Lasker contrived another exceptional draw. His sole knight stymied his namesake Ed. Lasker's rook and pawn. The event has since made history and is recorded in many manuals and game collections, especially those of Edward Lasker.

## BRILLIANCY PRIZE

In 1928, masterfully mixing tactical surprise with positional solidity, Marshall as Black prevailed over Aaron Nimzowitsch, the father of the "Hypermoderns." The triumph earned him the First Brilliancy Prize over Nimzowitsch, who a year before had almost beaten Alekhine out of challenging Capablanca for the World Chess Championship.

### Bad Kissingen 1928
*Queen's Indian Defense*

A. NIMZOWITSCH    F. J. MARSHALL

| | |
|---|---|
| 1 P–Q4 | N–KB3 |
| 2 P–QB4 | P–QN3 |

After decades of orthodoxy, the mature Marshall challenges the Nimzowitsch of "My System," using the author's own theses of modernity. This fianchetto is usually deferred till after; e.g., 2 . . . P–K3 3 N–KB3 P–QN3 or accelerated by *1* . . . P–QN3.

| | |
|---|---|
| 3 N–QB3 | B–N2 |
| 4 B–N5 | |

Trying to prove that Marshall isn't being eccentric enough, Nimzowitsch starts a wrong experimentation. *4* P–B3 is a better method to contain Black, *4* Q–B2 another, but after *4* . . . P–K3 5 B–N5 leads back into the main column.

| | |
|---|---|
| 4 . . . | P–K3 |
| 5 Q–B2 | P–KR3! |
| 6 B–R4 | B–K2 |

The natural answer. White should have played 6 BxN QxB 7 P–K3 B–N5 8 N–B3, when 8 . . . BxN? 9 PxB QxBP 10 R–KN1! would have brought on disaster. In the position on the board White still had the solid 7 P–K3, but instead continues with misconceived pawn moves which weaken his center.

| | |
|---|---|
| 7 P–K4? | O–O |
| 8 P–K5 | N–Q4! |

This must have come as a great surprise, although the Baltic master mistakenly believes that Black's knight is going to be in trouble. He therefore avoids the safe exchange 9 BxB NxB 10 N–B3 N–R3.

| | |
|---|---|
| 9 B–N3? | N–N5 |
| 10 Q–N3? | P–Q4! |

Not now *11* P–QR3? PxP! *12* BxP (*12* QxP N–B7ch) BxP∓.

| | |
|---|---|
| 11 PxP e.p. | BxQP |
| 12 O–O–O | N/1–QB3! |

The gathering storm. If 13 P–QR3 N–R4 14 Q–R4 B–B3 15 N–N5 N–R7ch 16 K–N1 BxB 17 RxB P–R3 18 KxN PxN 19 PxP B–Q4ch 20 K–N1 B–N6 wins. Thus White exchanges bishops first and sees a rosy picture, instead of the looming catastrophy.

**13 BxB          QxB**
**14 P–QR3**

If 14 N–B3 N–R4; if 14 N–N5 Q–B5ch 15 Q–K3 QxQch 16 PxQ NxPch 17 K–N1 KN–N5 18 NxBP N–R4 winning.

**14 . . .          NxP!**

A positional sacrifice, with a powerhouse of tactical threats in its wake. Upon 15 QxN P–QB4 16 Q–R4 B–B3 17 Q–R6 Q–B5ch 18 K–N1 QxBP 19 KN–N2 KR–Q1, White succumbs.

| | |
|---|---|
| **15 RxN** | **QxR** |
| **16 PxN** | **QxKBP** |
| **17 Q–Q1** | **KR–Q1** |
| **18 Q–K2** | **Q–B5ch** |
| **19 K–B2** | **P–QR4!!** |
| **20 PxP** | **RxP** |
| **21 N–B3** | **R–R8** |
| **22 K–N3** | |

White is in a bind. He wants to answer 22 . . . Q–B8 with 23 Q–QB2, but Black doesn't do him that favor.

| | |
|---|---|
| **22 . . .** | **P–QN4!** |
| **23 Q–K5** | |

If 23 PxP B–Q4ch 24 NxB Q–R5ch 25 K–B3 RxN; or 23 NxP B–K5.

| | |
|---|---|
| **23 . . .** | **PxPch** |
| **24 K–N4** | **Q–B8** |
| **25 N–QN5** | **P–B4ch** |
| **26 QxP** | **QxPch** |
| **27 KxP** | **R–B8ch** |

Actually, White resigned before the 26th move.

Apart from his biography *My Fifty Years of Chess*, Marshall sporadically wrote a few titles, to pick up a little money on the side; such as: *Marshall's Chess "Swindles"* (New York: The American Chess Bulletin, 1914), containing 125 of his games; then *Chess Masterpieces* (New York: Simon & Schuster, 1928), a collection of other masters' annotated games; also, *Comparative Chess* (New York: McKay, 1932), an anthology of masters' games, and a mixture of short essays.

Marshall was foremost an exuberant player, always ready with advice, and he played a stimulating role in the 1933, 1935, and 1937 U.S. Olympic teams.

Sadly, even a national champion's, and international grandmaster's, life was not secure enough to establish a home and a firm professional domicile by one's own means. It thus was a deserved blessing when a group of devotees, among them Thomas Emery, C.

Kelly, A. H. Mann, and G. A. Pfeiffer, joined up in 1914 to form the "Marshall Chess Divan" of New York at 35th Street; and after the war purchased the building at 23 West 10th Street, which has since then been housing the "Marshall Chess Club." After Marshall's death in 1944, the premises were administered by his widow Caroline ("Carrie") and then by Kathryn Slater, a woman chess master in her own right. The club has counted many distinguished names among its board and club members; and many of the Manhattan C. C. versus Marshall C. C. team tournaments have been of a high caliber. The club's president for many years was Ed. Lasker, succeeded in 1970 by Walter Goldwater, who had been a New York chess bookseller for forty-five years.

# 6.

# Hemispheric Capablanca

The person who became the embodiment of chess in everyone's mind throughout the world, Capablanca, belongs among these pages—even though some may claim that in calling him an American chess master, we are construing a double national identity for him, both Cuban and American. Not so; as a person, he was a Cuban.

## DOUBLE HERITAGE

José Raúl Capablanca y Graupera was born into a colonial Spanish army captain's family in Havana, Cuba, in 1888, ten years before Cuba's political independence from Spain was declared, and forty-six years before the nearby U.S.' rights of intervention were abrogated in 1934. In 1905, he was sent to New York to continue his education at Columbia University. His residence there coincided with an increased frequency of chess events in the area, and only one year after he had begun his studies, Capa had practically made a fulltime activity of chess. Besides, as the parents' purse strings tightened, Capablanca found a happy reason to play chess for a stake. Thus, Capablanca spent the latter part of his formative years in America. He became to a great extent an American player, within the larger forum of the United States. His most permanent residence was New York. He conducted his championship affairs from there, published his original manuscripts on chess there, spent his final years there, and died there, leaving behind a Russian-born widow who acted as an executive in a large American shipping firm.

Just the same, it would be an affront to ignore Cuba's support of, and pride in, their talented offspring, support which has paid dividends to the self-esteem of independent Cuba's chess talents and chess supporters, who have staged many international events in

Havana. Capablanca remained a Cuban national throughout his life, and his native land proudly accorded him diplomatic status. Europe sometimes excluded Capablanca from an all-American count, just as it often did with "Neo-Americans." But Capa may as justifiably be included in the U.S. contingent of that era as Paul Keres was in the Soviet one after the annexation of Estonia. When at his peak, Capablanca found it insignificant to enter a national U.S. event (just as Fischer refrained from doing after 1967); but Capa did briefly claim U.S. Championship after his defeat of Marshall in 1909, although it had not been an official title match. He also participated in some of the earlier Anglo-American cable matches.

J. duMont's memoir in H. Golombek's *Capablanca's Hundred Best Games of Chess* (London: Bell, 1970, p. 1), states that, "Capablanca has frequently been compared with Morphy, and not without good reasons. Both were of Latin descent, became masters at the age of twelve. They beat every contemporary American [sic!] player at the age of twenty, following this up immediately by a visit to Europe, where they beat the foremost European masters with consummate ease." Reading this, we could think of many more such parallels among prodigies. However, duMont's comparison of "Latin descent" is a first—vague—pitfall. Such a term could embrace any nation of Romance linguistic stock be it French, Italian, Portuguese, Romanian, Spanish; be biologically meaningless; and ultimately differentiate between, or give credit to, none. Morphy's mixed parentage happened to be predominantly Irish, at least as to the continued patronym, and thereafter Iberian-French-Creole (as applied to Spanish/French mixture). While Capablanca was trilingual, in Spanish, French, and English, often preferring the latter two to his "native idiom," his ancestry shows neither Morphy's bimixtures, nor prior intermarriages with the indigenous Cuban population. The Spaniard Pablo Moran, in *Agonia de un genio*, A. *Alekhine* (Madrid: Edit. Aguileras, 1972), p. 55, hints at Capablanca's family having left Spain for Cuba—shortly after its discovery by Columbus in 1492—due to the expulsion of Sephardic Jews from Spain, and the latest persecution there of baptized Jewish "Marranos." Moran thus emphasizes the ongoing contribution to chess by players of Spanish cultural heritage, regardless of past ideologies.

## THE CHESS MACHINE

The astonishing margin of Capablanca's victory (8:1 with 14 draws) in his match with Marshall in New York in 1909, coupled with

Marshall's own recommendation and his willingness to step aside in Capa's favor, secured Capablanca a U.S.-backed invitation to attend the international tournament in San Sebastian, Spain, in 1911, as the U.S. representative.[1] Marshall may have started his match against Capablanca optimistically unprepared, and not quite aware of the prodigy's clout. But he soon realized the potential of the Cuban gate-crasher.

Capablanca's entry at San Sebastian was first treated with some reserve and even derision by critics and by the chess clan. Youthful upstarts who crash the select party had more than once been unwelcome: they were looked upon as still unproven and immature; brazen, as Robert J. Fischer of a later period; and obtrusive, as an earlier Morphy had looked to Staunton. The attitude quickly changed when Capablanca beat everyone out of first place; but then the reserved attitude was reciprocated by the victor. The nonchalant winner was enthusiastic about, but not intoxicated with, chess, which he called "not an intellectual game." Capa's factual contribution was in the nature of an effortless abstraction of pure technique. That skill, plus his inborn genius, kept him champion until 1927, when to his own astonishment he was toppled by Alekine's indomitable will power, and lost the suffix "the unbeatable."

After a meteoric career; after gaining, losing, and trying to recover the chess crown, and after a brief revival of his former power in 1936, Capablanca began to be more concerned with his diplomatic duties and his home life. His second wife, Olga, did not want him to turn away from their newly established social life, to the extent by then required by high-caliber chess. Still, he remained very attached to the game, as also to the United States and to the chess of New York, the city which had become his new diplomatic assignment just before war broke out. Whether Capa's failure to get a rematch contributed to his early angina pectoris, or whether his abstention from continuous exertion gave him a few more years to live, is an unanswerable question. He was seized by a fatal heart attack while watching a game at the Manhattan Chess Club in 1942.

It may be surmised that, at a given time, Capablanca was so unyielding in his confidence in his own game that he simply could not fathom ever losing at chess. In this respect, he was the victim of his own too aloof self-confidence. He also deftly circumvented

[1] Marshall's action was similar to the one that enabled Fischer to play in the 1970 Interzonal, after Benko dropped out in his favor and Lombardy did likewise. In the end, both Marshall and Capablanca were invited to the San Sebastian tournament.

the idea of an unpalatable loss by accepting many draws from opponents under the spell of his aura, when an uncertain position
required an intensive effort at winning; Capablanca did not like
chess to become labor. He had absorbed chess by sight at the age of
four and hardly ever lost a game until much later. With him, chess
was in his genes. Believing that he would easily prevail, and with a
considerable purse at stake, he could not really stall Alekhine's
challenge so soon after he had won Lasker's crown three years
earlier. Why wait and hang on, and let the money go down the
drain?

Capablanca also enjoyed another rare and solid asset among chess
players. Coming from an established middle class, well groomed and
polished, his livelihood was secured and his job as a diplomat a
permanent one. He basically was a gentleman-player at leisure, a
semiprofessional. It was easy for him to throw out challenges,
frustrating to bargain, and embarrassing to seek (and be denied) the
substantial backing that would have tempted Alekhine before 1935.
His brusqueness vis-à-vis Alekhine may also be explained by his sense
of civic propriety as a diplomat. Yet, Alekhine, an aristocrat, flaunted
these rules in a Thorstein Veblen manner. Alekhine had a real, and
only, income and aim: living for chess and nothing else. The Cuban
and the Russian were diametrically opposed.

Capablanca's widow Olga allowed a glimpse into the private
side of Capa in a touching essay "The Young Manhood of José
Raoul Capablanca" (*Chess World*, May/June 1964). It is a true
biography, something rarely found in chess books, despite their
frequent claim to be biographical.[2] In view of the many excellent
collections of Capablanca's games on the market, we refer readers
to them rather than append a game here.

---

[2] The Russian-born Princess Olga Chagondayev, whose lingua franca was
French, a language frequently employed by Capablanca in his profession, uses
the frenchified spelling "Raoul," the pronunciation of which has the same
effect as that of the correct original, "Raúl."

# Shaping an American Image

# 7.

# Toward Utility and Pragmatism

The era of Morphy, Pillsbury, and Marshall saw the last of the solitary chess troubadors—players who pursued chess in search of beauty and who devoted their hours to the game for its own sake. They retreated from life's realities and submerged themselves into the abstract world of obsession. But they did it unselfishly; that is, they cared little for more lucrative occupations, and cast aside their other interests so that the demands of chess could be met.

## BEGINNINGS OF A NEW ERA

Because in America chess was not an ideal medium for mass entertainment, it lacked real financial rewards. It was not universally considered an admirable profession, but rather an introversion, a lamentable weakness.

Indisputably, chess virtuosos are showered with the praise and admiration of connoisseurs. At rare times, their skill is lucratively rewarded. However, it is important to remember that the reward is not for the chess master's contribution to the cultural life of the populace. Instead, it is a demonstration of appreciation of one man's utterly individual effort, and of the manifestation and triumph of one ego over another.

We like to see the fighter. We like to speak of a human being's indomitable will. But, no matter how voluble the praise, how humbling the genius, or how impressive the prize, the relationship between sponsor and chess master was always that of donor and recipient, never of compensation between equals. Thus, it was always the patron/sponsor who initiated a project, never the audience, which contributed little financially. The result was that no matter how articulate and well-meant the admiration, its components often were frenzy without financial sacrifice, or support mixed with con-descension. The "commercial" paid for the show if the product was profitable—which it rarely was in the market place.

Perhaps it is not surprising, then, that the next generation of chess enthusiasts drew a line between the potential of chess as a satis-fying hobby and its limitations as an occupation. Still, during these turn-of-the-century years, American chess stayed at a generally high level. Masters sporadically took time from work and with a hobby-ist's zeal threw themselves into their recreation. In this way, the American amateur achieved success for quite a long time. In fact, when compared to the number of full-time European chess profes-sionals who flourished or languished in the continent's coffeehouses, hectically touring clubs and shopping for tournaments, the Ameri-cans' success is out of all proportion.

A look at the socioeconomic history of the chess players of that time might give a clue to the particular nature of the American player. Most of the old guard, shortly before and after World War I, came from recent European immigrant stock, especially of Jewish heritage. We can speculate that there was an inherent trend toward intellectual outlets, one of which was chess. Furthermore, these peo-ple had no prior standing in the established middle or upper class, a standing that would have conferred economic professional benefits. The "art"-isanship of chess was one of very few ways to gain limited (or perhaps universal) acclaim. It was a way to satisfy ambition. Somehow, it was also part of the entertainment business—but on a lower pay scale! This stratum had not yet broken out of the barriers into which it might sometimes be confined.

Chess-playing was nostalgically mixed with the particular flavor of the vernacular of the old country and with an animated lower-middle-class humor: the "kibitzer" was the meddlesome, interfering onlooker; the "patzer" or "potzer," or "duffer" (a term already some-what assimilated) described the dilettante or woodpusher; "sac-over-the-head" was another name for the sacrifice. There was also the killing "zwischenzug" and the taunting "make the opponent eat his pieces," a saying which is said to have originated during the De-pression, when players resorted to forming the chessmen out of pieces of stale bread!

In the New York area, there were plenty of social chess rooms open long hours: Fursa's chess rooms near Times Square; the Man-hattan, the Marshall, the Brooklyn, and other chess clubs. From spring through autumn the crowds congregated in Greenwich Village's Washington Square (or in a corner of Central Park). The Chess Divan in Washington, D.C., the Hermann Steiner Chess Club in Los Angeles, and the Chicago Chess Club were open all year round. But outside these centers, chess-playing had a meager role—or was not found lucrative enough.

Yet, the picture was not entirely gloomy, as there was a corps of affluent or untiring admirers of chess who lent steady support. Alexander Bisno, Walter Fried, Morris Kasper, Harold Phillips, Rosser Reeves, Julius and Lessing Rosenwald, Jerry Spann, Morris Steinberg, Maurice Wertheim, and many more could be counted on the U.S. "board of chess promotion" during the second third of the century, supporting chess by their intellectual know-how, their connections, and their experience in fundraising. Most of them acted, and many still do, as genuine, unselfish devotees in the furthering of the wonderful game, constantly recruiting new disciples.

This old guard drew its motivation from chess tradition, but there wasn't a great enough reward or opportunity for full-time play. Hence they remained amateurs, pursuing a livelihood elsewhere. The truly aspiring players found chess to be a harsh mistress. Success could not be based on abstract, idealized beauty at any risk. Their playing style became hardfisted, realistic. What counted was the result. Therefore, the strategy was for sound and effective play. The point-count replaced beauty, and the old idols were discarded. Combinative sparkle—perhaps sound, often unsound, but always risky—was reappraised. The ingredient of American drive and method also made for change. Dilettantish chivalry, or brilliancy with a flaw, could not stand up to the precepts of Western technology.

Also in the newly established Chess Olympics, the playing style became one of utility, concentration, and pragmatism. In 1927, after an informal beginning in 1924, the International Team Tournaments or Chess Olympics or Olympiads became official.[1] Since training had to be compact to be effective, most of the teams came from the Northeast coast, where the "old guard" had mostly settled. New York was the center, as behooved the dimensions and the explosive tempo of the metropolis. The new generation clearly embraced the modern style, which combined a highly effective game strategy with the team's goal of solid victory. The result was clear and impressive: U.S. teams swept to the top in five successive International Team Tournaments. After flexing their muscles for the first time at The Hague 1928, when Americans placed 2nd, the U.S. teams finished 1st at Prague 1931, Folkestone 1933, Warsaw 1935, and Stockholm 1937. The leading representatives on the U.S. teams

---

[1] "Chess Olympiads" is British usage, and "Chess Olympics" American. "Olympiad" is actually a term borrowed from the athletic Olympic games with their four-year cycle.

during the years 1931–37 were Dake, Fine, Horowitz, Kashdan, Kupchik, Marshall, Reshevsky, Simonson, and H. Steiner.

Although the USSR participated in these Olympics, its organized chess machine was not yet in gear. In addition, strong Estonia, Lithuania, and Latvia were individual participants not yet absorbed in the Soviet contingent, leaving them an outlet for expression of individual and ethnic identity. The United States slipped in standings after the war (Dubrovnik 1950—4th place, Munich 1958—4th place, Varna 1962—4th place), when state-supported East European teams became strong. True, America finished second at Leipzig 1960 and at Havana 1966, but at this juncture, semiamateur devotion could no longer compete with the round-the-clock involvement and financial security of the Soviet chess emissaries. In the United States another change was also occurring: R. Byrne, Bisguier, Evans, and others had arrived, replacing the old guard.

## AVANT-GARDISTS AND SCOUTMASTERS

In the vein of such high-spirited freelancers as Napier and others who treated chess as a diversion, and in order to introduce the fore-runners of the successful vanguard which enters the coming chapter, we relate a few short suspense stories from that transitional period.

### EDWARD LASKER

First among the greats of this transitional period was Edward Lasker. He was born in 1885 in Berlin, and was a very distant relative of the great Emanuel Lasker. His mother was American, and he came to the United States in 1914 to stay. He settled into a job with Sears Roebuck and Company in Chicago.

Along with his employer, Julius Rosenwald, he was instrumental in spreading interest in chess in the Midwest.[2] Ed. Lasker's *Chess Strategy*, later retitled *Modern Chess Strategy* (New York: McKay, 1968), was a best-seller, as were some of his subsequent, entertainingly written books.[3] He also was an official Master of the Japanese board game Go.

Edward Lasker did not score heavily in international events because such success became, increasingly so, restricted to professionals

[2] The Manhattan Chess Club Championship and the U.S. Championship, which used to be held mostly in New York, were often subtitled "Julius Rosenwald Tournament."

[3] E.g., *The Adventure of Chess* (New York: Doubleday, 1950) and *Chess for Fun and Chess for Blood* (New York: McKay, 1942), both reprinted by Dover Publications, New York.

who ate, drank, and lived for chess only. They studied the latest wrinkles of extended opening theory and related tactics, as well as intensely investigating a prospective foe's psychology and strategic idiosyncrasies—not by getting the feel during opening play over the board, but well ahead of time. Such research cannot easily be afforded by even the strongest amateur.

Among 16 participants, Edward Lasker came first in the Metropolitan Chess League Individual Championship in New York 1914–15. This success was followed by his topping the 17th Western Chess Association Tournament (the leading annual national contest). With a ½ point ahead of Showalter, he collected 16½ points out of 19 possible.

In 1923, Lasker barely lost his match against Marshall with a close score of 8½ to 9½, and he played very creditably in the illustrious New York 1924 International Tournament.

Before going to New York, Edward Lasker sent a calling card, cosigned by Britain's champion and later international master, Sir George Thomas, winner of the City of London Chess Club Championship 1913–14. Caught off guard, Thomas suffered a stunning defeat at Ed. Lasker's hands at their first meeting, a five-minute clock game.[4]

### CITY OF LONDON
### CHESS CLUB 1911
*Dutch Defense*

ED. LASKER          G. A. THOMAS

| | |
|---|---|
| 1 P–Q4 | P–KB4 |
| 2 P–K4 | PxP |
| 3 N–QB3 | N–KB3 |
| 4 B–KN5 | P–K3 |
| 5 NxP | B–K2 |
| 6 BxN | BxB |
| 7 N–KB3 | O–O |
| 8 B–Q3 | P–QN3 |
| 9 N–K5 | B–N2 |

Black did not choose the best available defense. 4 . . . N–B3

or 4 . . . P–B3 are considered safer; whereas 4 . . . P–K3, followed by the slow 8 . . . P–QN3, leaves Black constricted. Even 9 . . . BxN 10 PxB Q–R5 11 P–KN3 Q–K2 12 Q–Q2 B–N2 13 O–O–O N–B3 14 P–KB4 provides no relief. There is, of course, a difference between mere pressure and sudden death, but with Black supplying the hammer, Lasker drives the nail into the coffin.

10 Q–R5          Q–K2?

Correct is 10 . . . KBxN 11 PxB R–B4! or 11 QxB N–B3.

[4] In due course, Sir George's caliber grew to the point of tying Euwe and Flohr for joint 1st–3rd prize at Hastings 1934–35, beating Capablanca and Botvinnik in the process!

11 QxPch!          KxQ
12 NxB dbl. ch. K–R3

Obviously, if 12 . . . K–R1 13
N–N6 mate.

13 N/5–N4ch   K–N4
14 P–R4ch     K–B5

A swifter deathblow is from 14
P–B4ch K–R5 (14 . . . KxP 15
P–N3ch K–B6 15 O–O mate or
15 . . . K–N4 16 P–R4 mate)
15 P–N3ch K–R6 16 B–B1ch
B–N7 17 N–B2 mate. But
Lasker was already hooked by
the prettier sequence:

15 P–N3ch      K–B3
16 B–K2ch      K–N7

17 R–R2ch     K–N8
18 O–O–O mate

It is a picture-postcard mate,
often quoted in chess breviaries.
Marginally, from a perfectionist
composer's artistic viewpoint,
the final mate is not pure but
impure; i.e., it is dual in its
nature, as 18 K–Q2 also mates,
but 18 O–O–O has more ex-
pressive éclat. Thus the practitioner would hit upon the
pragmatic 14 P–B4ch, and not
even think of seeking fleeting
beauty in glamor which might
be flawed.

Edward Lasker made a name for himself with quite a few of such
brilliant smashes. At Scheveningen 1913, he suddenly shattered
F. Englund's illusions by sacrificing his queen for a solid-looking
pawn, forcing a most elegant diagonal two-bishop mate. It seeded
the germ for an almost identical conclusion by Peru's Esteban Canal
in a simultaneous exhibition at Budapest 1933.

He also has been one of the first who, both as a chess master and
an electrical engineer, studied, and reported on the beginnings and
the progress of, computer chess programming.

HERMANN HELMS AND BLITZ CHESS

Hermann Helms was a trailblazer with a similar animus as possessed by a Mortimer, a Marshall, or a Napier, playing an out-and-
out temperamental game on a joyful instrument. Helms was born
on January 5, 1870 in Brooklyn, New York, was brought to Germany
at the age of three, and then to Halifax, Nova Scotia, in 1880. In
1887 he moved back to Brooklyn, to stay. While in Canada, he
learned to be a crack cricket and soccer player and remained a
player and reporter of these sports throughout his future life. Joining the then "Brooklyn Chess and Checkers Club," he made chess
another one of his favorites; and the first tournament table carrying his name was "Buffalo 1894," scene of the New York State
Chess Association Tournament. (At the same location, he placed
1st in 1925.) In the Brooklyn Chess Club (double-round) Cham-

pionship 1897, he came in 2nd, with 7 points to Napier's 8, but in front of Marshall 6½. He drew both games against Napier and won both against Marshall. In the same club's Rice Tournament 1904, Helms went to the top with 7 points out of 10 possible, with C. S. Howell 2nd. Theory right or wrong, the "Rice" was just to his liking.

Known in later years as the "Dean of American Chess," Helms founded the *American Chess Bulletin* in 1904 and edited it until his death on January 6th, 1963—beating the Grim Reaper by one full day, to complete his ninety-third year of age. During the magazine's last two decades, its game section was tended by Anthony Santasiere.

While many modern magazines, saturated with overwhelming projections of the death struggles and ratings' violence of the chess tournaments, might be a fitting reflection of what is likewise prominent in the main pages of the tabloids, Helms' reportages were truly versatile. Over a long time his periodical was the first and foremost showcase, in even balance, for games, problems, studies, essays, and strictly objective and always pertinent national and foreign news. Helms also directed the chess column in the *Brooklyn Daily Eagle* from 1893 to 1955, when the paper closed down. Over a span of sixty-two years it presented the longest period of uninterrupted editorship of a column.

Helms was the type who, á la Mortimer, would rather go to jail than betray truth or principle, regardless of favored friend or shunted foe; and he edited other chess publications, often at a financial risk to himself. He was a very cordial person while at the same time keeping both a respectful and respected distance. I remember how he, many years my senior, first called me "Mr.," later "Walter," just as, I later realized, Mr. Reshevsky, Mr. Evans, and many others were no "Sammy" or "Larry" to him. He considered instant familiarity by diminutive to be somewhat demeaning to the other person—perhaps in European tradition.

In 1951, Helms was instrumental in directing a youngster, "Master Bobby," to the Brooklyn Chess Club ("Master," especially in British usage, is applied to a youth too young to be called "Mister").

Helms also shared the privilege of playing in five of the annual Anglo-American cable matches between 1896 and 1910. He was an excellent analyst, but had no *sitzfleisch* for protracted tournament play and excelled instead at speed chess.[5] Up to his venerable age,

---

[5] *Sitzfleisch*, literally, "buttock meat" or "sitting flesh," means to be glued to one's chair or to sit it out, as contrasted to moving around between moves, perhaps to see how other players' games are developing. The term also implies having done one's homework. F. V. Morley defines *Sitzfleisch* as the habit of

he turned up at any rapid transit of note within the New York metropolitan area, remained a menace to any player, and always ended near the top.

The following short entries—which depict Helms' blitz-chess technique, but also incorporate other prominent antecedents— exemplify touch-and-go skittles of ten or five seconds per move. In a common variant of a speed-chess game, the adversaries' chess clocks were set at five, seven, or ten minutes before "midnight"; then either side had a chance to score a win before the flag fell, or could lose by overstepping the time limit—even with a winning position. The improvisations; the dynamism; the chance to get a lot of practice under one's belt; the gamble; the compression of many games into a limited period of leisure; the training toward quick comprehension of the secrets of a position—all helped carve out a useful niche for this mode of play.

The next two examples are from "speed tournaments"—ten-seconds-a-move games, with the turns to move controlled by a gong. This particular handling of a blitz was going out of favor because it did not allow allotting a greater share of the total time to the in-dividual needs of specific moves, and also because any hesitation to move exactly when the gong sounded caused controversies among players and problems for umpires.[6]

## SPEED TOURNEY

### New York 1942
*Evans Gambit*

H. HELMS          O. TENNER

| 1 | P–K4 | P–K4 |
|---|------|------|
| 2 | N–KB3 | N–QB3 |
| 3 | B–B4 | B–B4 |
| 4 | P–QN4 | B–N3 |

Positional play in a rapid transit is a matter of special circum-stance. The nature of the event does not usually lend itself to

this approach, except as a wait-ing game—waiting for the op-ponent to make a speedy blunder! Helms chooses ad-venture and continues in this vein.

| 5 | P–QR4 | P–QR3 |
|---|-------|-------|
| 6 | P–R5 | B–R2 |
| 7 | P–N5 | PxP |
| 8 | BxP | N–B3 |
| 9 | B–R3! | NxKP |
| 10 | Q–K2 | NxBP |

10 . . . N–Q3 would have been the last resort.

---

remaining stolid in one's seat hour by hour, making moves that are sound but uninspired, until one's opponent blunders through boredom. Psychoanalysts have their own interpretation.

[6] The method is still used in large-scale Lightning Tourneys, with the added proviso that a king, left in check when the gong sounds, is "taken"—and his game is lost.

| 11 NxP | N–Q5 |
|---|---|
| 12 NxQPch!! | NxQ |
| 13 N–B6 mate | |

The gamble paid off. It needed a lot of foresight, and at breakneck speed.

MANY GAMES, MANY PLAYERS

OSKAR TENNER (1886–1948), though long past his prime when he succumbed to Helms at speed chess in 1942, was no small fry. He had taken part in the Major Premier Section of the Breslau Chess Congress 1912, became a Czech National Master in 1913, and played in the Major Premier at Mannheim 1914, ranking 2nd, before the outbreak of World War I cut the tournament short. A cosmopolitan in every sense, Tenner emigrated to the United States in 1922 and was runner-up in the hectic Rapid Transit Tournament Final Section, New York 1924: 1st, Capablanca 4; 2nd, Tenner 3½; 3rd, Maróczy 2½; 4th–5th, Schapiro and Tartakover 3 each; 6th, Meyer 1.

Tenner lit the following sparkler against his Manhattan Chess Club comember in 1923:

## MANHATTAN CHESS
## CLUB 1923

O. W. FIELD            O. TENNER

1 . . .            Q–R6
  Resigns

OSCAR CHAJES, who came from the same area as Tenner, was born in Brody, Austria, in 1873. He arrived in the States as a young man, just in time to finish first in the Tenth Western Chess Association Tournament 1909. He secured 2nd place in the same event in 1910, trailing G. H. Wolbrecht. At New York 1911 and 1915, he won 3rd prize behind Marshall (1st) and Capablanca (2nd), and also finished very respectably in various New York tournaments in 1913, 1914, 1915, 1916, and 1918. At Rye Beach, New York 1918, he was runner-up to A. Kupchik, overtook him to place first in the 1919–20 Manhattan Chess Championship and in the "Rice Progressive" tourney of the same year, and also came first at Rochester, New York 1917.

But the feathers in his cap were his victory over Capablanca at New York 1916, and his brilliancy prizes against Tartakover and Perlis at the International Grandmaster Tourney at Carlsbad 1911, which was attended by the cream of the decade.

### INTERNATIONAL GRANDMASTER TOURNAMENT

#### Carlsbad 1911

O. CHAJES                    J. PERLIS

**34 P–R8(Q)!!**

A sacrificial decoy which becomes meaningful after White's next, utterly amazing, sacrifice.

The element of brilliancy is enhanced by the particular setting: Black is superficially quite safe, with two advanced center pawns, of which one is bound to queen in short order.

| 34 . . . | RxQ |
|----------|-----|
| 35 RxP!! | |

By diverting Black's rook, White threatens 36 B–K6 mate and 35 . . . PxR 36 B–K6ch K–R1 37 N–N6 also mates. Therefore the rook returns to the king's file.

| 35 . . . | QR–K1 |
|----------|-------|
| 36 Q–N3ch | R–B2 |
| 37 R–K6! | RxR |
| 38 BxR | PxP |
| 39 BxRch | Resigns |

O. Chajes died in Berlin in 1928.

CHARLES JAFFE (1883–1941), one of Chajes' contemporaries, did not aspire to professional laurels, yet finished astoundingly well even against the fiercest players. He placed 4th in the New York International Tournament 1911 (Marshall 10, Capablanca 9½, Chajes 9) and 3rd at New York 1913 (Capablanca 11, Marshall 10½, Jaffe 9½ out of 13). At New York 1922, Jaffe's standing was Ed. Lasker, Jaffe 3, and Reshevsky 2½ points.

Jaffe's great moment was Carlsbad 1911. He was last, out of 26; but still, he took 8½ points away from the strongest European assembly, winning a brilliancy prize against Spielmann, beating Leonhardt, Cohn, Levenfish, Burn, Johner, Alapin, and Fahrni, and drawing with Salwe.

ABRAHAM KUPCHIK (1892–1970) was in his teens when he came to the United States from Poland. He was active in American chess between 1910 and 1940. His games have been rather ignored in our anthologies, although he was an ever-dangerous opponent and a reliable mainstay in team matches. Apart from coming in 1st in the New York State Championships of 1918 and 1919; in the 1925 Western Chess Association Tourney in Cedar Point, Ohio; in the 1926 New York Rice Memorial; at Lake Hopatcong 1923 (tying with Marshall); at Bradley Beach 1928 and the Manhattan Chess Club Championship 1927–28, he also secured 2nd prize at the strong Pan-American meet at Lake Hopatcong, 1926 (Capablanca first, Maróczy and Marshall 3rd and 4th) and, together with Kashdan, at the 1926 Manhattan Chess Club Championship (Maróczy 1st). At Bradley Beach 1929 the foreign masters Alekhine and Lajos Steiner pocketed 1st and 2nd prizes, with Kupchik and I. S. Turover placing 3rd–4th. During the Warsaw Chess Olympics of 1935, Kupchik occupied board three, scoring 71.1 percent.

S. D. FACTOR of Chicago (1884–1949) made a good showing at Cedar Point, Ohio 1925, coming in 2nd, with 11 points out of 13 possible. He took part in the Olympics at The Hague in 1928, seated at board three and scoring 71.3 percent among 17 participants.

H. HAHLBOOM was another brightly lit comet, but of short stay. He fought himself into 1st place in the Western Chess Association Championship in St. Louis, Missouri, 1929, scoring 8 points, ahead of J. Anderson's, H. Steiner's, and N. Whitaker's 7½ each.

WEAVER W. ADAMS (1901–1963), a rather individualistic personality, was a principled and polished New Englander. Untiringly, W. W. Adams maintained that 1 P–K4, coupled with the fact that White is half a tempo ahead, guarantees victory for the first player. He must, of course, play faultlessly. Adams' publication *White to Move and Win* (1934) for a while provided a catch phrase almost as popular as Capablanca's *Remistod*. Later, Adams issued two more monographs: *Simple Chess* (1946, revised 1958) and *Absolute*

*Chess* (1959), stressing the factors of power, mobility, options, and weaknesses to be observed in the planning and judgment of a game.

In the strong Pan-American Tournament, Hollywood 1945, Adams scored better than 50 percent, but his intransigence impaired his immense natural ability. His last overt success was in winning the 49th U.S. Open Championship in Baltimore in 1948, a 12-round Swiss knockout.

In later years Adams failed in both health and wealth, and for some time was a guest at the New Jersey home of E. Forry Laucks, a wealthy chess patron. When I visited with Adams at the estate in the 1950s, he often sat at the large concert piano there, improvising —and we talked beaux arts rather than chess.

E. LAUCKS maintained a country home fondly known as the "Log Cabin Chess Club." The basement was crammed with bunks, ready for use by Laucks' chessomanic friends during sporadically held rallies.

Laucks also held spectacular "chess junkets." He would call at any time and pack several of his favorite chess experts into airplanes or cars, defraying all expenses of extended trips to Canada, Europe, or Mexico. In 1959 Laucks financed the Log Cabin Invitational Tournament in honor of the club's Twenty-fifth (Silver) Anniversary. The event and the stakes, considerable by 1959 standards, were won by Lombardy, with Benko 2nd, Evans 3rd, and Bisguier and R. Byrne 4th–5th. A note of discord occurred when a majority of players voted Reshevsky out of the tournament. They did not acceed to his—admittedly controversial—request to postpone games falling on his Sabbath—but the courtesy was often accorded to him in national and big international tournaments. Arnold Denker, the 1944–46 U.S. Champion, had pleaded Reshevsky's case and dropped out in protest.

NORMAN TWEED WHITAKER (1890–1975) was a frequent member of the Log Cabin troupe. He was a colorful man of turbulent background and versatile talents. At the 8th American Chess Congress, Atlantic City 1921, he placed 2nd after Janowski, who, as a resident but a French national, took part *hors concours de titre* only. Whitaker tied for the U.S. Open Championship in 1923, when he was cochampion with Mlotkowski (another steady and impressive contender in American chess, as was already noted in the chapter on Morphy and again in 1930, when he was cochampion with S. D. Factor). In partnership with Glenn Hartleb, Whitaker published *Selected Endings* (Heidelberg: 1960). The book is a casual potpourri of 365 endgames chosen at random, yet it is a first because it was produced bilingually, in English and in German (by

Dr. Werner Lauterbach). Whitaker also functioned on various occasions as the organizer and umpire in regional tournaments.

FRED REINFELD was the most prolific American chess author,
known to patrons of the most prestigious as well as the most humble
bookstores. His tournament activities were limited to the New York
area (Intercollegiate chess champion, New York State chess champion, Marshall and Manhattan Chess Club champion), but he
published about sixty titles. Reinfeld's best output appeared in the
1930s and 1940s. His annotations to the games of Alekhine, Botvinnik, Capablanca, Colle, Keres, Lasker, Nimzowitsch, and of British
chess masterpieces are of prime value. Together with Irving Chernev
he produced some very readable compendia; e.g., *The Fireside Book
of Chess* (New York: Simon & Schuster, 1949), an early leader in
its genre.

His writing was aided by a phenomenal memory for master games,
and by intensive adherence to a work schedule which enabled him
to pour out his stream of books in quick succession. Too often,
though, his pace made it impossible to sustain the excellence of his
earlier titles, and he became repetitious. After his death, many
sections from his books were over and again reprinted by various
paperback publishers, often under changed titles.

When I spoke to Reinfeld in 1950, I questioned him about the
contrasting quality of his early and late writing. He said: "In those
days I played and wrote seriously—but got nothing for it. When I
pour out the mass-produced trash, the royalties come rolling in."
Reinfeld agreed when I asked, "But you lost a pastime?"

ANTHONY SANTASIERE (1904–77), Reinfeld's contemporary, casually intermixed music, painting and poetry of sorts, with dogged
promotion, since 1936, of his own "futuristic" opening, Santasiere's
Folly—1 N–KB3, followed by 2 P–QN4, a refinement of 1 P–QN4,
the "Orang-Utan" opening.[7]

---

[7] The origin of the term "Orang-Utan" is another example of a chess myth.
Its promoters took the credit away from the originator! Tartakover employed 1
P–QN4 against Maróczy at New York 1924, and is purported to have been
inspired by a visit to the Bronx Zoological Gardens the day before the game.
In fact, the term was coined by Réti after the 5th match game Tartakover–
Réti, Vienna 1919, which started 1 P–QN4 P–K4 2 B–N2 P–KB3! (Earlier
examples were Fleissig-Schlechter, Vienna 1895, and a game by Berthold
Englisch as White, London 1883.) *Modern Chess Openings*, 5th ed. (1932),
called it the Polish Opening, apparently in reverse to the Polish Defense 1
P–Q4 P–QN4, and the name stuck. The first comprehensive Western use dates
from Leonhardt Schiffler's *Orang Utan Eroeffnung* 1.b2–b4 (East Berlin:
Sportverlag, 1953), published under the auspices of the interconnected Eastern
bloc. In the USSR, A. P. Sokolsky experimented with the move since 1936,
but it did not really grow into a system until the late 1960s, and *MCO*, 10th
ed., and *MCO*, 11th ed., duly acknowledge his contribution.

The point is illustrative of the relentless Eastern chess propagation designed to minimize other regional contributions. In 1952, an active New York chess and Union organizer called to berate me for not giving proper credit in *MCO* to Sokolsky for 1 b2–b4; for calling Rauzer's attack in the Sicilian as being Richter's; for attributing Ufimtsev's Defense to Pirć; and so on. A. Kotov and M. Yudovich's *Sovyetskaya Shakhmatnaya Shkola* (Moscow: 1954) contains a similar, vitriolic attack on *MCO*, 7th ed. (1946) and it is still found in their English translation, *The Soviet School of Chess* (New York: Dover, 1961), p. 81.

Santasiere won the U.S. Open Championship in Peoria, Illinois, in 1945. Eccentric Anthony definitely had a gift for fantasy. In New York in 1926, he won a game against W. W. Adams with a bishop and rook mate on the 19th move, which has entered almost any anthology on combinations and brilliancies. In March 1977, *Chess Life & Review* reprinted a selection of Tony's best "capriccios."

T. A. DUNST, R. DURKIN, A. KEVITZ, W. RUTH, and O. ULVESTAD all left original contributions. While the former four added to unusual and irregular openings and defenses, Olaf Ulvestad enriched the Two Knights' Defense. He became a hero when he beat David Bronstein in the U.S.–USSR match, Moscow 1946. (In the same event, Kevitz defeated grandmaster Bondarevsky 1½:½.) Olaf Ulvestad went into retirement in Northern Spain, and in 1970 turned up at first board on Andorra's Olympic team, scoring a very good 47½ percent.

NEWELL BANKS of Detroit, Michigan (1878–1977), functioned exceedingly well both as chess master and as world checkers champion. I never so much as drew with him at checkers. In the Master's Invitational Tournament at Chicago 1926, Banks beat Isaac Kashdan and U.S. Champion Frank Marshall, drawing with S. D. Factor, ex-champion H. W. Showalter, and O. Chajes.

In the preliminary section of the U.S. Open Championship, held in Chicago at the same time, first place in the preliminary section was secured by Herman Steiner, the dominant West Coast master, and second was won by Leon Stolzenberg of Detroit. In the final section, however, the roles were reversed, with Leon holding the title.

HERMAN STEINER (1905–55), born in Slovakia, then part of Hungary, and emigrating to the States at sixteen years of age, was one of the Hungarian Triumvirate of Steiners, the other two being Andreas (Endre) who remained homebound, and Lajos, who went to Australia after World War I.

While his namesakes achieved more international prominence than he, Herman made up for it with pleasant exuberance, successfully employed in the teaching and promotion of chess, especially on the West Coast. Yet, he also had his very high peaks in tournament play: State of New York champion in 1929; U.S. Open champion in 1946 and cochampion (with Yanofsky) in 1942; U.S. Olympic team member in 1928, 1930, 1931, and 1950; 1st at London 1946, with 9 points out of 11 possible and ahead of O. Bernstein, Tartakover, and Golombek; and, to crown it all, U.S. Champion 1948.

LEON STOLZENBERG (1895–1974) had entered the United States after World War I. He was to become one of the country's leading national and international correspondence chess players. He won the Michigan State championship several times and was the U.S. Open champion twice, in 1926 and in 1928 (the U.S. Open was then known as Western Chess Association Tournament).[8]

H. E. JENNINGS was another American championship competitor, though of sporadic participation. He came 1st at Buffalo 1917, and joint 1st and 2nd with Carlos Torre at Rochester 1924, both very strong New York State Association events.

[8] Leon, who had been a medic in the hospital at Tarnopol in World War I, corrected an error, traceable to a collection of games by Alekhine (Berlin: 1922): A blindfold game, quoted therein as Alekhine–Von Feldt, was actually played against Dr. Martin Fischer, the intern; and it occurred in 1916, not in 1917. In 1975, *Michigan Chess* published some of Stolzenberg's best games.

# 8.

# Storming Olympus and
# Other Heights

## THE VANGUARD

Frank J. Marshall, along with other spirited Americans, was the
seasoned flagbearer who entered the Olympic staging ground after
its inception in 1927. Those early Olympic chess games matched
contestants from all over the globe, players who often had not
known of each other until they met personally.

Participation in the Olympic contests required fresh approaches.
Research into an opponent's mentality, careful avoidance of prepared
analysis, adaptation to an opponent's predilections, preservation of
strength through intermittent play for a draw—all these considerations of match or tournament play were of little use when faced
with the intense speed and pressure of the Olympics' then very
hectic timetables.[1] Under these conditions, sophisticated baggage

---

[1] The so-called "Swiss Systems" reflect a similar atmosphere, and so do the
"thirty moves in thirty minutes" weekend contests, which have become ad-
missible for participants' grading within the U.S. Federation's rating tables.
The narrow time limits employed at the earlier Olympics changed after
World War II. The regulations, in effect through 1975, generally allowed for
one round a day, starting in the afternoon, with six participants in each team
of four boards alternating at the team captain's discretion. The rate of play was
three and one-half hours for the first forty moves; and adjourned games were to
be finished the next morning. With the Haifa 1976 Olympics, a turnabout was
instituted in order to cope with the increasing number of teams participating
in the Olympics. The round-robin team meets (and their subsequent subdivi-
sion into first and secondary groups) were replaced by a Controlled Swiss
System Pairing and Scoring Method applied to the larger groups, keeping the
length of the event down to a reasonable period. Thus the round-robin system
was practically abolished for the sake of greater participation. An even more
concentrated Swiss knockout system was introduced at the Masters-Plus Tourney,
Lone Pine 1977, with two and one-half hours for forty-two moves (i.e., five
hours of play) and the resumption of adjourned games after a two-hour break,
up to another four hours of continued play (unfinished games declared drawn).
Whatever the set-back of the system, the decrease in adjournment time also reduced the chance (and risk) of outsiders' advice and consultation.

became surplus and was discarded in favor of natural instinct. Stamina was also needed, plus a bit of luck, as no surprise was ever ruled out.

One important element that had helped to sharpen the Americans' play was the intense training many players had received in the course of New York's exacting chess-club activities. They provided a plethora of splendid sparring partners for sharpening one's game. Also, the Americans' preference for speed chess, or rapid transit, helped immensely in stimulating their perceptions, and was a great boon in Olympic tourneys, with their fast tempo and restricted time limits.

Of immense aid in stimulating Americans' Olympic proficiency was Capablanca's residence in New York. His presence was a great instructional asset and enhanced the technical perfection achieved and maintained by his disciples. As might be imagined, Marshall, as team captain at times, fit in well with the Olympic environment, and the freshness of youth supplied by his teammates provided another resource.

The invasion of Europe by the U.S. Olympic players must have been traumatic. That it has remained so may be judged from the slow and grudging acknowledgment accorded Americans in European chess literature. Chroniclers of the Olympic games have reproduced only a minute percentage of games played by the American contingent, and in many cases those they lost. From their narrations, one almost gains the impression that all Olympic matches won by the American teams were won on the basis of *Schlagschach,* an eccentric variant of chess, wherein the game is won by the side which is quickest in giving up material, and the opponent is under obligation to capture whenever possible, and lose!

The insufficient bibliographical support of the true record may be a reflection of the lingering resentment against the uncivilized cowboys who drove in to shatter the respected traditions of the Old World. It shows ambivalence in realizing that a New World chess immigrant is indeed a full American. This impression of inaccurate acknowledgment is confirmed by statistics: In the 1928, 1931, 1933, 1935, and 1937 Olympics, the United States played 340 games with a score of 235 points, or a winning average of 68 percent—about 7 games out of 10. One of the first chroniclers, A. Foeldeak in his *Schach-Olympiaden (The Chess Olympiades)* (Amsterdam: Ten Have, 1971) gave 81 sample games from these five events, including 12 American games, of which 7 are losses, 1 a draw, and only 4 are wins! Most of the credit went to the losing teams. Božidar M. Kažić's *International Championship Chess* (New York: Putman, 1974), on the whole a first-class compilation, extracted 40 games from the same

Olympics. Of these 9 are American, with a score of 5 losses, 1 draw, and 3 wins.

In all fairness, I must add here that the U.S. percentages at the Hamburg 1930 Olympics were low—the United States placed 6th only. The Depression discouraged costly trips. Included in the team were H. M. Phillips, who paid his own way, and the internationally untested J. F. Anderson.[2] Nevertheless, the United States scored 41½ points out of 68 games played, a good average compared to Poland's (1st place) 48½ points. This success is more favorably reflected by Foeldeak, who gives 21 games from Hamburg, of which 6 are American—2 losses and 4 wins. The recognition is mainly due to the performance of I. Kashdan, whose meteoric impact drew much attention.

## KASHDAN: THE LOGICIAN

At The Hague 1928, Isaac Kashdan, one of America's brightest lights and still very active, scored 13 points out of 16 possible on board one, winning a gold medal. At Hamburg 1930, the young star (b. 1905) beat grandmaster Gideon Ståhlberg in this historic battle.

### HAMBURG OLYMPICS 1930

*Nimzo-Indian Defense*

G. STAHLBERG          I. KASHDAN
(SWEDEN)              (U.S.)

| 1 | P–Q4  | N–KB3 |
| 2 | P–QB4 | P–K3  |
| 3 | N–QB3 | B–N5  |
| 4 | Q–N3  | P–B4  |
| 5 | PxP   | N–B3  |

In 1955, Ståhlberg suggested 5 . . . N–R3 6 P–QR3 BxP 7 N–B3 P–QN3 8 B–N5 B–N2 9 P–K3 B–K2= (Botvinnik–Eliskases, Moscow 1936) as better, but the text regained popularity in later years.

| 6 | N–B3 | N–K5   |
| 7 | B–Q2 | NxQBP  |
| 8 | Q–B2 | O–O    |

At these crossroads, 8 . . . P–B4, followed by . . . BxN and . . . N–K5 is the preferred sequence.

9 P–K4

Tempted to refute Black's temporizing, and to prevent . . .

---

[2] J. F. Anderson had finished a very creditable 2nd–4th in the 30th Western Association Tournament, San Louis 1929, in a tie with H. Steiner and N. T. Whitaker (H. Hahlbohm came first). But Hamburg 1930 had an unsavory aftereffect: the discrediting of America's international chess prestige. The U.S. team leaders undertook to organize the 1933 Chess Olympics in Chicago, but they did not; Folkestone 1933 had to step into the breach.

P–B4, White stumbles. He should have continued 9 P–QR3 BxN 10 BxB P–B4 11 P–QN4! N–K5 12 B–N2! As proven by techniques developed here and by other players later on, White's KP turns into a liability.

9 . . .         Q–B3

Threatens 10 BxN Q–N3!

**10 O–O–O    P–QN3!**

Upon 10 . . . BxN 11 BxB Q–B5ch 12 N–Q2! QxBP? comes 13 P–QN4! N–R3 14 P–N5. The text provides an escape for the knight if needed, and opens a line for the bishop.

**11 B–Q3       P–QR4
12 K–N1       Q–N3**

12 P–QR3 is answered by 12 . . . P–R5 and if 13 PxB NxNP 14 Q–N1 N–N6 mate. Obviously, these turns don't usually arise in master practice, but their hidden presence proves how many subtle pitfalls are contained in positions that seem innocuous to the naked eye.

**13 KR–N1      B–R3
14 B–K3**

White had to counter 14 . . . P–Q4, with a resulting loss of a pawn.

**14 . . .        NxB
15 QxN        BxN
16 PxB        P–Q4!**

Typical of Kashdan's forcefully simple style. He visualizes that after the coming simplification which removes the risk of complications, White's positional weaknesses make an even more distinct target.

**17 KPxP       QxQch
18 RxQ        BxP
19 R–Q2       BxP
20 BxP**

Hobson's choice. Not taking leaves White behind in material, but taking means a vulnerable open file.

**20 . . .        KR–N1
21 R–N2       P–R5
22 B–B7**

Black's straightforward challenge was 22 . . . P–R6 23 R–N5 B–B5 and there is no truly satisfactory answer. If 22 K–R1 P–R6 23 R/2–N1 B–K5 24 R–N3 B–N7 25 R–N5 R–R3 26 R–QB1 B–Q6 wins; or 22 P–QR3 BxN 23 PxB N–K4 24 B–Q4 B–B5! 25 RxRch RxR 26 K–R2 P–K4 with a winning endgame.

**22 . . .        R–QB1
23 B–B4       N–R4
24 R–QB1**

Apparently sound, yet the pawn will fall. If 24 B–K5 P–B3 25 B–Q4 P–K4; or 24 B–Q2 N–B5.

**24 . . .        B–K5ch
25 K–R1       N–N6ch!!
26 PxN        PxPch
27 R–R2       RxR mate**

Actually, White resigned after Black's combinational 25th move.

The whole game had proceeded with the apparent ease reminiscent of Capablanca and of Morphy. This technocratic pragmatism, free of an unnecessary quest for embellishments, bore Kashdan's imprimatur. In the same tourney and in a similar manner, Kashdan triumphed over another strong protagonist of the solid school, Salo Flohr of Czechoslovakia, who later developed into a potential World Champion contender. Like any true grandmaster, Kashdan was very much at home in the endgame and won a special prize for his conduct of this one.

### HAMBURG OLYMPICS
### 1930

*Nimzowitsch Defense*

| I. KASHDAN | S. FLOHR |
|---|---|
| (U.S.) | (CZECHOSLOVAKIA) |

| 1 | P–K4 | N–QB3 |
|---|---|---|
| 2 | P–Q4 | P–Q4 |
| 3 | P–K5 | B–B4 |

The defense is to very few people's liking, but if played at all, the variants with 2 . . . P–K4 3 PxP NxP 4 N–KB3 B–N5ch 5 P–B3 B–Q3; or 3 P–Q5 QN–Q2 4 B–Q3 P–Q3 are preferable. Instead of the text, 3 . . . P–B3 4 P–KB4 B–B4 5 N–K2 P–K3 6 N–N3 PxP 7 BPxP B–N3 is playable.

| 4 | P–QB3 | P–K3 |
|---|---|---|
| 5 | N–K2 | KN–K2 |
| 6 | N–N3 | B–N3 |
| 7 | B–Q3 | Q–Q2 |
| 8 | Q–B3 | P–N3 |
| 9 | N–Q2 | N–R4 |
| 10 | P–KR4 | BxB |
| 11 | QxB | P–QB4 |
| 12 | P–N4 | PxNP |

This option is more promising than 12 . . . P–B5 13 Q–B2 N/4–B3 14 B–B4!

| 13 | PxP | N–B5 |
|---|---|---|
| 14 | P–R5 | R–B1 |

Fortune would have turned in Black's favor after *14* NxN PxN *15* QxB R–B1 and *16* . . . N–N3. But Kashdan took care.

| 15 | P–R6! | P–N3 |
|---|---|---|
| 16 | N–B3 | N–B4 |
| 17 | P–R3 | Q–R5 |
| 18 | R–QN1 | P–R4 |
| 19 | N–K2 | PxP |
| 20 | P–N4!? | PxP!? |

Black gives up the knight in exchange for two passed pawns, which he considers more than sufficient compensation. But this might have been one of the rare wrong assessments by the twenty-two-year-old Flohr, who at that time "floored" almost anybody—at least in rapid-transit play. After 20 . . . N–K2 21 PxP N–B3 (or even 21 . . . P–QN4), White still has to show if and how to win.

| 21 | PxN | NPxP |
|---|---|---|
| 22 | R–N1 | P–N4 |
| 23 | N–Q2! | NxN |

To prevent *24* N–N3, blockading the pawns. And if Black

grabs the pawn, he loses both passed pawns after 23 . . . BxP 24 N–B3.

| 24 BxN | P–N5 |
| 25 R–KN3! | R–B5 |

24 . . . P–R7? 25 R–QR1 is useless, whereas 25 N–B1 RxNch and 26 . . . P–N6 would have proven Black's point. Now comes a battle of wits and cool maneuvers.

| 26 N–B1 | Q–R2 |
| 27 N–N3 | Q–B2 |
| 28 K–K2 | K–Q2 |
| 29 R/1–N1! | R–B7 |
| 30 R–N8 | RxR |
| 31 RxR | B–K2 |

If 31 . . . BxP 32 K–Q1! With his 29th move White remarkably ignores any threat of Black's pawns marching, as . . . P–R7 would soon end in the pawns' containment and capture. With White's rook on the 8th rank, White will develop dynamic counterplay.

| 32 Q–N5ch | Q–B3 |
| 33 Q–N8 | Q–R3ch |
| 34 K–Q1 | R–B1 |

Black must simplify to stem White's effective counterattack.

| 35 RxR | QxR |
| 36 QxQch | KxQ |
| 37 K–B2 | K–N2 |
| 38 N–B1 | K–B3 |
| 39 K–N3 | K–N4 |
| 40 N–R2 | B–R5 |

Black tries to balance the loss of the queen-side pawns by

winning Black's center pawns. White offsets the attempt very precisely.

| 41 B–K1 | P–B3 |
| 42 NxP | PxP |
| 43 PxP | B–N4 |
| 44 N–B2 | K–B3 |
| 45 N–Q4ch | K–Q2 |
| 46 KxP | BxP |

As his queen-side pawns are doomed, Black's king hurries back to protect his king's pawn.

With Black's two minor pieces facing White's piece and two pawns, there is always hope for a win, but also hope for the defender that the opponent might commit an inaccuracy.

The decks are clear, but they need a thorough mop-up—and Black's two passed pawns can still become active.

| 47 K–N3 | B–B5 |
| 48 N–B3 | P–R4 |
| 49 B–B3 | B–R3 |
| 50 B–N4 | B–N2 |
| 51 B–Q6 | B–R3 |
| 52 K–B3 | B–N2 |
| 53 K–Q3 | B–R3 |
| 54 K–K2 | B–B8 |

| | |
|---|---|
| 55 K–B1 | B–N7 |
| 56 B–B5 | K–B3 |
| 57 B–Q4 | B–B8 |
| 58 K–N2 | B–B5 |

58 . . . B–R3 would prevent the coming exchange of bishops, but enables White to penetrate the king-side. If 59 K–R3 K–N4! 60 K–R4 K–B5 61 B–N2 K–Q6 62 KxP K–K5.

| | |
|---|---|
| 59 B–K3! | BxB |
| 60 PxB | P–Q5! |

A sacrifice that increases Black's mobility, allows his king the command of the center, and almost secures him a draw; e.g., 61 NxPch R–Q4 62 N–B3 K–K5 63 K–B2 P–B5=.

| | |
|---|---|
| 61 PxP | K–Q4 |
| 62 K–N3 | K–K5 |
| 63 N–N5ch | |

An ingenious finesse, giving up material for space as a short-cut to victory.

| | |
|---|---|
| 63 . . . | KxP |
| 64 K–B4 | K–Q4 |
| 65 N–B3 | K–B5 |
| 66 K–N5 | K–Q4 |
| 67 K–B6 | P–B5 |

Or 67 . . . K–K5 68 N–N5ch K–K6 69 NxP P–B5 70 NxP KxN 71 P–K6 P–R5 72 P–K7, etc., winning by one tempo.

**68 N–R4**

Also 68 N–N5 P–R5 69 NxP P–B6 70 N–B4ch K–K5 71 N–R3 K–K6 72 K–N5 wins. As it happens, White's choice creates beautifully accurate endplay.

| | |
|---|---|
| 68 . . . | K–K5 |
| 69 KxP | P–B6 |
| 70 NxP | KxN |
| 71 K–B5! | P–R5 |
| 72 P–K6 | P–R6 |
| 73 P–K7 | P–R7 |
| 74 P–K8(Q) | K–N7 |
| 75 K–N5 | P–R8(Q) |
| 76 Q–K2ch | K–N8 |
| 77 K–N3 | Resigns |

I picked a victory of Kashdan over Flohr, because of the latter's exceptional prominence—but I do it with a pang of conscience, as Salo Flohr and I used to share many escapades. Against his chess, I held my own for a while, but later became a mere observer.[3]

After Hamburg 1930, Kashdan stayed on for a short while to participate in the *Meisterturnier*, Frankfurt 1930, where he met

[3] Flohr was often invited to "Villa Tereza" to play international master A. F. Ilyin-Zhenevsky, who served as a counsellor to the Soviet Embassy in Prague. Young Ilyin was expelled from school in St. Petersburg in 1912 and sent by his affluent parents to Geneva to study. There he annexed the town's chess championship in 1914. He returned to Russia in 1917, to become Soviet Military Commissar. He and N. V. Krylenko, Soviet Chief State Prosecutor and later USSR Commissar of Justice and Chairman of the All-Russian chess section were the force behind the powerful drive to make Soviet chess dominant. We will take up this—for the United States, very important—topic in a later chapter.

Nimzowitsch, who had not participated in any Olympics. Kashdan drew his game with Nimzowitsch but came in only 2nd in the tournament, ½ point behind Nimzowitsch's 9½, out of 11 possible.

Kashdan composed a few exquisite endgame studies in partnership with I. A. Horowitz, with whom he founded *Chess Review*, coediting it during its first years. He subsequently moved to Los Angeles, retired in 1970, but remained active as an International Arbiter to various Olympics; as tournament organizer in the States; as author; as chess columnist to the *Los Angeles Times*, and as a frequent Board member of the U.S. Chess Federation.

## HOROWITZ: THE ENTREPRENEUR

Israel Albert Horowitz (b. 1907) was a shrewd businessman, a first-class chess editor, a sparkling writer and conversationalist, and an agile and well-informed journalist. But first and always he was a passionate connoisseur of chess. Whenever a chess fan, expert or beginner, stepped up to his crowded desk, Horowitz would interrupt his work, set up a board, and dive into the game.

His magazine, *Chess Review*, presented a selective mixture for both the tyro and the gourmet: national and recent international news; games and postal chess; compositions; quality essays; and opinionated letters to the editors, provided they showed some perspective. During a period when chess magazines had hard going, Horowitz made his journal into a flawless, exemplary publication of international repute by personal energy and effort, without any organization to back or sustain him. Editorial assistance was provided by a group of well-chosen contributors, and part of his income came from a well-assorted stock of literature and good merchandise. My own connection with the magazine lasted from 1956 to 1969, during which time Horowitz had two pages a month available for me. The first series ran as "Spotlights on the Openings," the second, as "The Finishing Touch."

Al was the Marco Polo of chess, and the whole United States was his turf. For many years he single-handedly spread the word throughout the Midwest and the West, delighting his audiences with lectures and simultaneous displays, successfully handling the sale of subscriptions, books, and equipment even against the membership-subsidized competition of the U.S. Chess Federation's discounted merchandise, advertised in its mouthpiece, *Chess Life*.

Notwithstanding some old chestnuts and skittles, produced at the spur of the moment, Horowitz was really a formidable chess personage. In the first postwar radio match against the Soviet Union in 1945, he overwhelmed Salo Flohr in an encounter that gained him a brilliancy prize.

## U.S.–USSR RADIO MATCH
### 1945

*Caro-Kann Defense*

I. A. HOROWITZ      S. FLOHR

| 1 P–K4 | P–QB3 |
|---|---|
| 2 P–Q4 | P–Q4 |
| 3 N–QB3 | PxP |
| 4 NxP | N–B3 |
| 5 NxN | NPxN |

4 . . . P–K3 is too passive and 4 . . . B–B4 5 N–N3 B–N3 was only then starting to be explored. Black's 4th and 5th moves form a distinct idea which has had its ups and downs. It has never been refuted, merely exhausted!

| 6 N–K2?! | B–B4? |
|---|---|

A reply which plays into White's hands. Instead of provoking the very formation anticipated by White, Black also has (a) 6 . . . B–N5 7 P–KB3 B–R4 8 P–QB3 N–Q2 9 N–N3 Q–N3 10 P–KR4 P–KR4 or (b) 6 . . . P–KR4 7 P–KR4 B–N5 or (c) 6 . . . R–N1.

| 7 N–N3 | B–N3 |
|---|---|
| 8 P–KR4 | P–KR3 |

Now the difference becomes clear between this line and the subvariation 6 . . . B–N5, where Black's 10 . . . P–KR4 blocks the advance of White's RP, but keeps the option of developing

his black-squared bishop to N2 or R3; or, after . . . P–K3, to K2. But now 8 . . . P–KR5 9 P–QB3 and 10 B–K2 would lose Black his KRP. Yet Flohr was no newcomer to this development, and actually it is White's forthcoming novelty (at his 11th move) that discredits the strategy.

| 9 P–R5 | B–R2 |
|---|---|
| 10 P–QB3 | Q–N3 |
| 11 B–QB4! | |

Hitherto the established sequel was 11 B–Q3 BxB 12 QxB, with ensuing counterplay by Black. The text is infinitely more suspenseful.

| 11 . . . | N–Q2 |
|---|---|
| 12 P–R4 | P–R4 |

A move that Horowitz, Fine, and others called routine, but 12 . . . P–K3 13 P–R5 Q–B2 14 Q–B3 is no better than the main line in the text, which is clear and consistent. Its restrictions can be blamed on Black's immovable pawn position.

| 13 Q–B3 | P–K3 |
|---|---|
| 14 O–O | B–B7 |
| 15 B–B4!! | B–N6 |

The purpose of Black's last two moves—to exchange, and castle queens. But White's bishop turns aside and Black's pieces are somewhat off-side. Of course not 15 . . . QxNP 16 R–R2, winning the bishop.

**16 B–Q3!          P–K4?**

The first crack in the wall. 16 . . . O–O–O 17 N–K4 P–QB4!? 18 N–Q2 B–Q4 19 B–K4 BxB 20 NxB P–B4 21 NxP BxN! 22 PxB NxP might have left Black with more fight.

**17 B–K3          B–Q4**
**18 B–K4          Q–N6**
**19 PxP          PxP**
**20 QR–Q1          BxB**

White already commands the field. Also 20 BxB QxB 21 QxQ PxQ 22 QR–Q1 N–B3 23 KR–K1 B–K2 24 N–B5 reduces the problem to a won ending with a pawn up (the way Kashdan might have treated Flohr), but Horowitz wants to hook a goldfish if he can.

**21 QxB          Q–K3**

21 . . . QxNP? 22 RxN! wins outright.

**22 R–Q2          N–B3**

Inadequate are (a) 22 . . . B–B4 23 R/1–Q1; or (b) 22 . . . O–O–O 23 R/1–Q1 B–B4 24 N–B5 BxB 25 N–Q6ch K–B2 26 QxB N–N3 27 Q–B5 with relentless pressure; or (c) 22 . . . N–B4 23 BxN BxB 24 R–K1 P–B3 25 N–B5.

**23 Q–B3          R–KN1**

If 23 . . . N–Q4 24 R/1–Q1 B–K2 25 P–B4 NxB 26 QxN and 27 . . . Q–N6 is decisive (Horowitz in *Chess Review*).

**24 R/1–Q1          R–N5**
**25 N–B5?!          P–K5!?**

While 25 N–B5 looked like a blunder, losing a piece, it actually forces the win of the exchange.

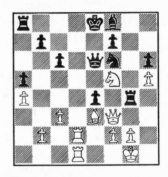

**26 B–N6!**

The hat trick. If 26 . . . PxQ 27 R–Q8ch, with a textbook mate next move.

Black continued the irretrievably lost game with 26 . . . RxPch (if 26 . . . B–K2 27 QxR NxQ 28 N–N7ch+) 27 QxR QxN 28 R–Q8ch RxR 29 RxRch K–K2 30 Q–N3 N–Q2 31 B–B7 Q–Q4 32 P–QB4 Q–KN4 33 QxQ and Black resigned soon after.

The next collision is with another one of the perennial U.S. Championship contenders, A. Denker.

## U.S. CHAMPIONSHIP

### New York 1946–47
*Queen's Indian Defense*

I. A. HOROWITZ        A. DENKER

| | |
|---|---|
| 1 P–Q4 | N–KB3 |
| 2 P–QB4 | P–K3 |
| 3 N–KB3 | P–QN3 |

With this move, and Black's answer, we enter the modern phase of the closed Indian, fianchetto, formations, which call for delicate timing; for alertness to possibly favorable or unfavorable transposition; for alternative play on both wings; and for a watchful eye for breakthroughs in the center, which is not directly occupied, but kept under control from the diagonals. They contain less fireworks; the jockeying for advantage is more subtle. The pressure is insidious. But if a maneuver proves inaccurate, the punishment can either be as swift as in the olden days, or the ending may turn out to be a slowly killing vise.

| | |
|---|---|
| 4 P–KN3 | B–N2 |
| 5 B–N2 | B–N5ch |

A "close" defense calls for keeping pieces closer to home; hence, 5 . . . B–K2 6 O–O O–O would ensure a tighter control; e.g., 7 N–B3 N–K5! 8 Q–B2! NxN 9 QxN P–Q3 10 Q–B2 P–KB4 11 N–K1 Q–B1=.

| | |
|---|---|
| 6 QN–Q2 | N–K5 |

In the present setup, this advance post on K5 does not have

reserves to sustain it. White's center pawn would be better contained by 6 . . . O–O and . . . P–Q4! White's reply releases the pin promptly, and Black must declare.

| | |
|---|---|
| 7 O–O! | NxN |

The underpinning 7 . . . P–KB4 8 P–QR3 B–K2 (8 . . . BxN 9 NxB) 9 N–K5 proves ineffective.

| | |
|---|---|
| 8 BxN | BxB |
| 9 QxB | O–O |
| 10 Q–B2 | N–B3 |

10 . . . P–Q3 11 N–N5! QxN 12 BxB is a primitive trap, but it tactically allows White a finesse that keeps Black away from the better square Q2.

| | |
|---|---|
| 11 QR–Q1 | P–Q3 |

The strategy 11 . . . P–Q4 no longer works; e.g., 12 PxP PxP 13 R–B1! Q–B1 (13 . . . Q–Q2 14 N–K5! or 13 . . . R–B1 14 B–R3!) 14 KR–Q1 and Black is immobilized.

| | |
|---|---|
| 12 P–Q5! | PxP |

Borrowing an expression of Capablanca's, *la petite combinaison,* 12 . . . N–N1? 13 PxP PxP 14 N–N5!! has become a reality. Thus, the exchange of pawns is forced.

| | |
|---|---|
| 13 PxP | N–N5 |
| 14 Q–B4 | P–QR4 |
| 15 P–QR3 | N–R3 |
| 16 P–QN4 | Q–Q2 |
| 17 R–Q4! | KR–K1 |
| 18 P–K3 | PxP |

| 19 PxP | P–QN4 |
|--------|-------|
| 20 Q–Q3 | B–B1 |

Black tries to regroup his bogged-down forces, but is hopelessly hemmed in wherever he turns.

| 21 R–B1 | R–N1 |
|---------|------|
| 22 R–KB4 | Q–Q1 |
| 23 P–R4 | P–R3 |
| 24 Q–B3 | B–Q2 |
| 25 R–R1 | Q–B1 |
| 26 K–R2 | R–N3 |
| 27 N–Q4 | N–N1 |
| 28 R–QB1 | Q–R3!? |

If White is tempted to take the pawn by 29 QxP R–QB1 wins the queen. But White simply waits for the ripe fruit to drop.

| 29 P–N4 | B–B1 |
|---------|------|

If 29 ... R–QB1, Black remains a helpless onlooker. If 29 ... Q–B1 30 K–N3 (or 30 B–B3) P–N4 31 PxP PxP 32 R–B6 Q–Q1 33 N–B5 and White turns into a boa constrictor. Black gives up the blockaded QBP to gain lines for his heavies, and to transfer his tied-down knight.

| 30 QxP | R–N2 |
|--------|------|
| 31 Q–B3 | N–Q2 |
| 32 QxB!! | RxQ |
| 33 RxRch | N–B1 |

After 3 ... K–R2 White mates in a few moves. White's few pieces are all actively poised for the kill while Black's general staff is out of touch.

| 34 N–K6!! | P–N3 |
|-----------|------|

Total futility. And after 34 ... PxN 35 R/4xNch K–R2 36 R–R8ch K–N3 37 B–K4ch, White also has an abundance of wins.

| 35 RxNch | K–R2 |
|----------|------|
| 36 R/4xPch | RxR |
| 37 RxRch | K–R1 |
| 38 B–K4 | Q–R8 |
| 39 BxP | Resigns |

If 39 ... Q–K4ch 40 P–B4 and the rook mates on B8.

Apart from publishing books written in an easy style, Horowitz ran several chess columns; e.g., in the *Saturday Review* and the *New York Times*. His *The Complete Book of Chess* (originally *The Personality of Chess*; New York: Macmillan, 1963; Collier, 1969) lovingly compiled in coauthorship with problemist P. L. Rothenberg, contained a fascinating overview of the fringe benefits of chess.

In 1969, Al arranged a merger of his *Chess Review* (including its popular postal-chess section) with the U.S. Chess Federation's *Chess Life*, and since September 1969 the combined magazine has been known as *Chess Life & Review*.

While covering the Fischer–Spassky match at Reykjavik 1972 for television and his columns, Horowitz fell ill, and at the age of sixty-five passed away after his precipitous return to New York.

After Hamburg 1930, the next Olympic event, the Folkestone Olympiad (1933), was narrowly won by the United States with 39 points, to runner-up Czechoslovakia's 37½. In the last dramatic round against the Czechs, Kashdan and Simonson had lost their games, and Fine had a bad position, when Marshall decided that he had to beat K. Treybal by hook or by crook, and did so, heroically. Kashdan's last-round loss was, incidentally, against Salo Flohr, who this time got his own back. Albert C. Simonson was only nineteen years old when he joined this team as "backstop," filling the reserve board. He was a rising star of New York's Met League, a very promising chess player, and represented "a sound mind in a sound body." Simonson posed a real threat to Reshevsky in the 1st U.S. Championship 1936 (Reshevsky 11½; Simonson 11; Fine and Treysman 10½; Kashdan 10; Dake and Kupchik 9; Kevitz 8; Horowitz 7; Factor 6½; H. Steiner and Denker 6; S. Bernstein 5; Hanauer 4½; W. W. Adams and Morton 3). This tournament table might serve as useful roster depicting the leading players of the period on the American scene. In the 2nd U.S. Championship in New York 1938, Simonson scored 11 points out of 16, placing 3rd in a strong field (Reshevsky 13; Fine 12½). He subsequently opted out of public chess competition.

The Folkestone tournament book was compiled and annotated by Kashdan, and alongside Fiske's record of the First American Chess Congress, remains one of the showpieces of chess journalism. Kashdan applied the same strictness to his editions of the 1st and 2nd Piatigorsky Cup tournament books (Los Angeles 1963 and 1966); and his weekly column in the *Los Angeles Times* is exemplary for the massed brevity, accuracy, and richness of news.

The Warsaw Olympics of 1935 were fought with the winning contingent of Fine, Horowitz, Kupchik (replacing Kashdan), Marshall, and Dake. Dake's win over O. Cranston of Ireland, a miniature lasting just nineteen moves, has remained a multiquoted classic.[4]

## DAKE: THE DURABLE

Arthur Dake was born in Portland, Oregon, in 1910, learned chess at seventeen, and remained an Oregonian throughout; but when dwelling in New York, the sailor from Oregon usurped the Marshall Chess Club championship in 1930–31, at the club's height of

[4] "Miniature" is a game won within about twenty-odd moves; also known as a "Quickie," but mainly in rapid transit. In problems and studies, "miniature" applies to a composition containing no more than seven men, including kings.

strength. It secured him an invitation, both on this count and as a West Coast resident, to the Pan-American tournament at Pasadena 1932. This was the tournament that gave cause to the aforementioned negotiations with Alekhine when he demanded a separate honorarium in case Capablanca would be invited to participate as well. Perhaps Alekhine (whose only domestic engagement hitherto had been at Bradley Beach, New Jersey, in 1929) did after all know of the hidden strength of the American players; he did indeed draw against young Rueben Fine, and lost the following fine game.

### Pasadena 1932
### *Caro-Kann Defense*

A. DAKE                    A. A. ALEKHINE

| 1 | P–K4 | P–QB3 |
| 2 | P–Q4 | P–Q4 |
| 3 | PxP | PxP |
| 4 | P–QB4 | |

A move prominently used for the first time in Réti–Duras, Vienna 1908.

| 4 | . . . | N–KB3 |
| 5 | N–QB3 | N–B3 |

5 . . . P–K3 seems the most prudent answer, but due to overexploration, other variants have been tried as well. 5 . . . PxP is premature as long as White has not played B–Q3. Playable but somewhat restrictive is 5 . . . P–KN3 6 Q–N3! B–N2 7 PxP O–O 8 B–K2 QN–Q2 9 B–B3 N–N3 10 B–N5 P–QR4! 11 P–QR4 B–B4 12 QR–Q1 Q–Q3.

### 6 N–B3

Both this, and 6 B–N5 were scrutinized by the Danish analyst Dr. Krause in 1911. In the 1930s, Panov concentrated on the text move, whereas later on, Botvinnik chose the more aggressive 6 B–N5. Again, 6 . . . P–K3 is Black's most solid reply and details of the many sidelines of the (Réti–) Panov–Botvinnik Variation are found in many specialized openings books. In the 1930s, the system was still in a highly experimental stage.

| 6 . . . | B–K3!? |

An exclamation mark for novelty, but a question mark for value. Upon 6 . . . P–K3 7 P–B5 N–K5 8 B–QN5 B–Q2 (8 . . . Q–R4 9 Q–N3+) 9 O–O B–K2 10 R–K1 NxN levels. 6 . . . PxP 7 BxP P–K3 again is a waste of tempo if played before White's B–Q3, and it allows White's isolated center pawn to become a battering ram rather than a fixed target. 6 . . . B–N5 7 PxP NxP 8 Q–N3 BxN 9 PxB P–K3 10 QxP allows White more freedom.

Alekhine's dubious choice of 6 . . . B–K3 signals his intention to lure a possibly bookish novice into the unknown—but it boomerangs. White's riposte is logical and thematic, and

Black's QB loses its raison d'être on K3.

| | |
|---|---|
| 7 | P–B5! | P–KN3 |
| 8 | B–QN5 | B–N2 |
| 9 | N–K5 | Q–B1 |
| 10 | Q–R4 | B–Q2 |

This forced retreat proves Black's 6th move futile.

| | |
|---|---|
| 11 | O–O | O–O |
| 12 | B–KB4 | P–QR3 |

Black's last tactical chance to free his game would have been 12 . . . N–KR4 with many complications; but they all end in equality.

| | |
|---|---|
| 13 | BxN | PxB |
| 14 | KR–K1 | N–R4 |
| 15 | B–Q2 | |

Threatening N x QP and maintaining his grip.

15 . . .          R–R2

A natural-looking defense, but its defect appears nine moves later!

| | |
|---|---|
| 16 | R–K2 | B–K1 |
| 17 | QR–K1 | P–B4 |
| 18 | N–B3 | N–B3!? |

If 18 . . . B–B3 19 B–N5. With the sacrificial text, Black plans to cut off White's far-flung rook and then win it. But he also needs to sacrifice a second pawn and is left with insufficient compensation after his strategy has been discredited.

| | |
|---|---|
| 19 | RxP | RxR |
| 20 | RxR | P–B5!? |

If 20 . . . N–K5 at once, then 21 B–B4 is murderous. The text tries for counter chances.

| | |
|---|---|
| 21 | BxP | N–K5 |
| 22 | B–K5 | B–R3 |
| 23 | NxN | PxN |
| 24 | N–N5!! | |

Due to a tactical quirk, the knight need not retreat lamely as expected by Black, but actively joins in White's assault. If 24 . . . BxN 25 R–N7ch K–R1 26 R–QB7ch wins the queen.

| | |
|---|---|
| 24 . . . | Q–B4 |
| 25 | Q–N3ch | B–B2 |
| 26 | NxB | RxN |
| 27 | RxR | QxR |
| 28 | Q–N8ch! | Q–B1 |

After 28 . . . B–B1 29 B–Q6, White exchanges all pieces and remains with two pawns up; whereas by 28 . . . Q–B1 29 QxQch KxQ followed by . . . K to K2 to K3 and to Q4, Black hopes to prevent a breakthrough.

| | |
|---|---|
| 29 | P–Q5! | P–K6 |
| 30 | P–B4 | QxQ |
| 31 | BxQ | K–B2 |
| 32 | PxP | K–K1 |
| 33 | P–QN4 | K–Q1 |
| 34 | P–QR4 | |

And Black resigns after a few more hopeless moves.

Arthur Dake played in the 1931, 1933, and 1935 Olympics, the last one at Warsaw, where he achieved a score of 86.1 percent on board four. B. M. Kažić relates that Dake did not take part in the Poland—U.S. encounter there because he was of Polish origin (Dakowski).[5] As Dake told me, however, the reason for his "abstinence" was a message that two days before the match, one of his parents had died back home in the States and he was mourning!

During the U.S.–USSR match 1946, Dake drew both games with grandmaster Lilienthal.

All this might have been enough of a successful activity, but in 1974 Dake waded back into high-class chess at Lone Pine, California, beating Norman Weinstein of the brimful young generation, and grandmaster L. Lengyel of Hungary. At Lone Pine 1975, he drew his games with Bisguier, Saidy, and Biyiasas, and in 1977 he still drew there with N. Weinstein, Biyiasas, Denker, and others.

Having retired from the continuous tournament circuit before the institution of the treadmill of ratingdom, Dake made it only to international master when the title was conferred on him in 1954 in belated recognition of his contribution to U.S. chess; the failure to recognize him as a grandmaster reflected on the system, not on the person.


## RESHEVSKY: THE STEADY ROCK

The 7th Olympiad, at Stockholm 1937, included a new, powerful personality who would remain in the forefront for a long time, almost two-score years, and remain a power always to be reckoned with even after: "Sammy" Reshevsky, a former prodigy.

During Reshevsky's debut as team member at the 1937 Stockholm Olympics, he was, among others, paired with Savielly Grigorievich Tartakover of the Polish team.[6] The Stockholm encounter spotlighted Reshevsky's sure ability to ward off many assaults calmly, hang on to a small plus in material, and then imperceptibly increase his hold until the opponent's resources are exhausted.

[5] *International Championship Chess*; a complete record of FIDE events, with a Foreword by the President, Dr. M. Euwe (New York: Pitman, 1974).

[6] Tartakover (or, also: Tartakower) has been mentioned in these pages before. He was an inventive and seasoned grandmaster, born in 1889 at Rostov-on-Don, of Khazar-Jewish parentage. He had Swiss and Viennese schooling, and later was a Free French War volunteer under the name of Lt. Xavier Cartier. He became one of the most brilliant writers on chess.

## STOCKHOLM OLYMPICS
### 1937

*Center Game*

S. G. TARTAKOVER     S. RESHEVSKY

| | |
|---|---|
| 1 P–K4 | P–K4 |
| 2 P–Q4 | PxP |
| 3 QxP | N–QB3 |

While opening up lines might be logical, it is here premature and simplistic. Black's attacking move fully offsets White's advantage of the first move.

Why Tartakover chose an opening which dissipates the initiative is not explained in his own commentaries, nor is the opening mentioned in Tartakover's gigantic *Die Hypermoderne Schachpartie* (Vienna: 1925).[7] Perhaps the obscurity of the opening is the reason for Tartakover's eccentric preference against Reshevsky, who was known to rely on the "book."

| | |
|---|---|
| 4 Q–K3 | N–B3 |
| 5 N–QB3 | B–N5 |

As against the restrained 5 . . . B–K2, the text, together with 7 . . . R–K1, exposes White's KP to pressure and Black, castling queens, prepares the ground for a lively king-side pawns' attack.

| | |
|---|---|
| 6 B–Q2 | O–O |
| 7 O–O–O | R–K1 |
| 8 B–B4 | P–Q3 |

Being careful rather than heeding Steinitz' rule that a sacrifice is refuted by its acceptance; e.g., 8 . . . BxN 9 BxB NxP 10 Q–B4 N–B3 11 N–B3 P–Q3 12 N–N5 B–K3 13 B–Q3 P–KR3 14 P–KR4! N–Q4 15 B–R7ch K–R1 16 RxN BxR 17 B–K4, as played riskily in Winawer–Steinitz, Nuremberg 1896. Black continued 17 . . . P–B3 and after 18 BxB BPxN 19 PxP N–K4 20 P–N6 pleaded nolo contendere to the threat 21 RxPch PxR 22 QxP mate, a backhanded way of proving the center game sound!

Keres commented that Steinitz might have returned the exchange by 17 . . . RxB 18 NxR N–K4 with equality. But 19 NxP QxN 20 BxN Q–QB3 21 R–Q1 B–K5 22 P–QB3 still leaves White with a powerful potential. As an afterthought, but without further analysis, Reshevsky hinted at 8 . . . N–QR4 as the most active defense, and 9 B–Q3 P–Q4 10 Q–N3 PxP 11 NxP NxN 12 BxN BxBch 13 RxB Q–K2 indeed leaves Black in good shape. So does 9 B–K2 P–Q4 10 NxP NxN 11 Q–Q3 Q–B3! 12 PxN B–KB4 13 Q–KB3 BxBch 14 RxB N–B5 15 BxN R–K8ch 16 R–Q1 Q–N4ch 17 K–N1 Q–Q7!—as in Jacobsen–Urzica, Groningen 1969–70.

| | |
|---|---|
| 9 N–B3 | B–K3 |
| 10 BxB | RxB |

---

[7] It took him two years to write this unique classic, and netted him 500 Austrian Schillings—then about $500!

**11 N–KN5        R–K1**
**12 P–B4**

If *12 P–B3 P–Q4*; whereas now *12 . . . P–Q4* fails for *13 P–K5 P–Q5 14 Q–R3 PxN 15 BxP*, with a strong attack. Now Tartakover heats up the game.

**12 . . .        P–KR3**
**13 P–KR4?!        Q–B1**

Black declines to take the piece, because *13 . . . PxN 14 RPxP BxN 15 BxB NxP 16 Q–R3 K–B1 17 BxPch K–K2 18 KR–K1* wins for White. The text foresees and prevents *16 Q–R3!* Neither *14 . . . N–Q2 15 Q–R3 K–B1 16 N–Q5*, nor *14 . . . N–R2 15 Q–R3* saves the day.

**14 Q–B3        K–B1!**

Black must refrain from either *14 . . . PxN? 15 RPxP BxN 16 BxB NxP 17 Q–R5+* or *14 . . . Q–N5 15 N–Q5 QxQ 16 NxQ NxN 17 PxN*, whereas the text threatens to capture the king's knight.

**15 N–Q5**

White creates great complications, and it needs Reshevsky's

defensive stubbornness to handle them coolly.

Interestingly, Tartakover might have retained a safe edge by *15 QR–K1! PxN 16 RPxP N–N1 17 R–R8*, with a mounting attack. Tartakover gave *15 KR–K1 PxN 16 RPxP N–N1 17 Q–R5*, with a serious attack, but *17 . . . Q–Q2* stops it all and Black's king escapes via K2–Q1 if necessary.

**15 . . .        NxN!**

According to Tartakover, *15 . . . BxBch 16 RxB PxN* would allow White to maintain his momentum; but the assessment is superficial, as was shown by Blumenfeld's deeper analysis in 1938, when he proved that *16 KxB* was essential so as to leave White the later option of doubling rooks on the KR file.

After *15 . . . BxBch 16 KxB PxN*, White has one satisfactory alternative out of two: (a) *17 RPxP NxN! 18 R–R8ch K–K2 19 RxRch KxR 20 R–KR1 N–Q5 21 Q–B2 Q–N5! 22 R–R8ch K–Q2 23 RxR NxKBP 24 QxQN QxPch and Black wins*. But White can draw by: (b) *17 NxN! PxN 18 RPxP PxP! 19 PxP Q–K3 20 Q–B6 QxQ 21 PxQ K–N1 22 R–R3 N–K4 23 QR–KR1 N–N3 24 R–R7 R–K3 25 R–N7ch K–B1 26 RxN!=*.

Thus Reshevsky's choice, which will net him a pawn, was instinctively best.

**16 PxN        N–Q5**
**17 Q–Q3**

Useless are 17 Q–R5 PxN 18 RPxP Q–B4∓ or 17 Q–B2 B–B4∓.

| 17 . . . | N–K7ch |
|---|---|
| 18 K–N1 | BxB |
| 19 RxB | |

If 19 QxB PxN 20 RPxP Q–N5 21 R–K1 K–N1 and Black wins (Reshevsky).

| 19 . . . | NxP |
|---|---|
| 20 N–R7ch | K–N1 |
| 21 N–B6ch | PxN |
| 22 Q–N3ch | N–N3 |
| 23 P–R5 | Q–B4 |

Better than 23 . . . K–N2 24 PxN PxP 25 Q–B4, with good pull.

| 24 PxN | PxP |
|---|---|
| 25 R–B2 | Q–N4 |
| 26 Q–QB3 | Q–K4 |

Forcing the queens off the board helps Black to make his pawn plus tell. If 27 Q–Q3? Q–K8ch; if 27 QxP Q–K8ch; and if 27 Q–Q2 Q–K6 or 27 . . . P–KR4.

| 27 RxBP | QxQ |
|---|---|
| 28 PxQ | K–N2 |
| 29 R–B2 | R–KB1 |
| 30 R–K2 | QR–K1 |
| 31 R/1–K1 | RxR |
| 32 RxR | R–B8ch |

Inaccurate is 32 . . . K–B2 33 R–B2ch K–K2 34 R–K2ch K–Q2 35 R–K6 R–KN1 36 R–B6, and Black's progress is arrested.

| 33 K–N2 | K–B2 |
|---|---|
| 34 P–B4 | P–KR4 |

| 35 K–B3 | P–KN4 |
|---|---|
| 36 P–B5 | |

The only way to create compensatory play.

| 36 . . . | PxP |
|---|---|
| 37 K–B4 | P–N5! |

White maintains equilibrium after 37 . . . P–N3 38 K–N5 R–B3 39 R–K5 R–N3 40 K–R6 P–B3 41 PxP RxP 42 RxNP.

| 38 KxP | P–N6 |
|---|---|
| 39 K–Q4 | P–R5 |

Not 39 . . . R–B7 40 K–K3 RxRch 41 KxR K–B3 42 K–B3=.

| 40 P–B4 | P–N3 |
|---|---|

Threatens 41 . . . R–B7 42 K–K3 RxR 43 KxR K–B3 44 K–B3 K–B4 with a win.

| 41 P–R4 | R–B7 |
|---|---|
| 42 R–K4 | RxP |

White puts up a subtle defense. Black could go astray here with 42 . . . P–R6 43 PxP P–N7 44 R–N4 (Reshevsky).

| 43 RxP | R–QR7 |
|---|---|
| 44 R–N4 | P–N7 |

After 44 . . . RxP 45 RxP P–N4 46 K–B5 RxPch 47 KxP, White might salvage the game. But after the text, White is strapped for an answer. If 45 K–K3 RxP or 45 K–Q3 K–B3, and Black's king enters decisively.

| 45 P–R5 | PxP? |
|---|---|

More incisive is 45 . . . P–N4!; e.g., 46 PxP? R–R5ch! or R–

QB7! Reshevsky, as usual, was getting into time trouble and thus made the win harder for himself.

| 46 K–B3 | P–R5 |
| 47 P–B5 | K–B3 |
| 48 R–N8! | K–K4 |
| 49 R–N5ch | |

After 49 P–Q6 PxP 50 P–B6 R–R8 51 RxP R–QB8ch 52 R–QB2 RxRch 53 KxR K–K3! 54 K–B3 P–Q4 55 K–N4 K–Q3 56 KxP KxP, Black wins.

| 49 . . . | K–B3! |

Avoiding the stumbling block 49 . . . K–B5 50 P–Q6! PxP 51 PxP KxR 52 P–Q7 P–N8(Q) 53 P–Q8(Q)ch K–B5 54 Q–B6ch K–N6 55 Q–N7ch K–R7 56 Q–R8ch K–N7 57 Q–N8ch, with a draw.

| 50 R–N8 | |

But if now 50 P–Q6 PxP 51 PxP P–R4! 52 P–Q7 K–K2 53 R–N7ch K–Q1 54 K–B4 R–Q7 55 K–B5 P–R6 56 K–B6 P–R7 and Black wins; whereas 51 . . . KxR? 52 P–Q7, or 51 . . . K–K3? 52 R–N6ch K–Q2 53 K–N4 P–

R4ch 54 KxP P–R6 55 K–R4 only draws.

| 50 . . . | K–B2 |
| 51 R–N4 | P–R4 |
| 52 P–B6 | K–K2 |
| 53 R–N6 | K–B2 |
| 54 R–N4 | R–B7! |

Black is out of time trouble and enters the final phase of a race to queen.

| 55 P–Q6 | P–R6! |
| 56 PxP | P–R7 |
| 57 P–B8(Q) | P–R8(Q)ch |
| 58 K–B4 | R–B7ch |
| 59 K–N5 | |

59 K–Q5 Q–Q8ch 60 K–K5 R–B4ch 61 K–B4 R–B5ch loses the rook.

| 59 . . . | Q–B8ch |
| 60 K–R4 | |

If 60 KxP R–B4ch 61 K–N6 Q–N4ch 62 K–R7 Q–R4ch 63 Q–R6 Q–B2ch 64 K–R8 R–QR4 wins.

| 60 . . . | R–R7ch |
| 61 K–N3 | Q–N8ch |
| 62 K–B3 | R–B7ch |
| 63 K–Q4 | P–N8(Q)ch |
| 64 Resigns | |

### THE NEAR-CHAMPION

Despite a somewhat introspective disposition, Reshevsky became by all standards an American chess pioneer who made an immense contribution. Born in 1911 in Poland as Schmul Rzeszewski, he left there at the age of nine and arrived in the United States the same year. After a spectacular series of simultaneous displays and of matches with leading masters, Reshevsky settled in the Midwest to complete his education, obtaining a degree in accounting in 1931. The funds for his schooling came from the indomitable Julius

Rosenwald of Chicago, and room and board was offered by chess patron Morris Steinberg, who at that time resided in Detroit.

Faced with the choice of neglecting competitive chess altogether, so as to concentrate solely on a career, or of staying with a safe livelihood, but devoting time to chess as well, Reshevsky chose the latter course after he had reasserted his supremacy at the International Tournament at Syracuse 1934 by not losing any games. He ranked among the world's top players, coming out first, or at least among the first three, at Margate 1935, Yarmouth 1935, Kemeri 1937, Hastings 1937–38, Leningrad–Moscow 1939, Hollywood 1945, the New York International 1951, the New York Rosenwald Tournament 1954, and the Dallas International 1957. He won or shared in the leading places of the U.S. Championship in 1936, 1938, 1940, 1942, 1946, and as late as 1969 and 1972—quite a stretch. Reshevsky created no theories or opening systems as such. His forte was defensive sturdiness, coupled with tactical skill, which enabled him to rebound whenever the opponent relaxed his hold. "Sammy's" winning record against the best (Alekhine, Botvinnik, Capablanca, Dake, Denker, Fine, Flohr, Kashdan, Em. Lasker) is impeccable. But he never reached the cherished summit. Several factors may be at the root of this regrettable failure.

First, Reshevsky's religious orthodoxy may have been a deterrent. It may have provided an ideological backbone, but it was very rigid in scope. His upbringing may have allowed him little leeway when practical circumstances called for some flair and flexibility. Religious strictures often proved a hindrance to more frequent tournament invitations. Organizers felt that the general schedule should not be upset by Reshevsky's obligatory Sabbath interruptions, often necessitating rescheduling of games. At that time there was no "Fischer impact" to force the impressarios into concessions for the stars, or to stretch time and financing to accommodate them.

Second, while Reshevsky had endless perseverance and ambition to win, his habitus lacked that adventurous luster which inspires the audience and in turn reinforces the champion's dash and confidence. Sometimes his nimbus worked wonders; e.g., in the U.S. Championship 1946, but it did not carry him to the top in the international forum. Reshevsky's handling of the game was somewhat passive—it was a counterattack on the opponent. His playing pattern may have been influenced by the ghetto commandment to lie low in a hostile world. He did not have the nonchalance that a less stringent environment allows.

Third, his lack of early systematic schooling and unavailability of literature in his original tongue, may be to blame for the late, perhaps too late, efforts to fully absorb the theory of openings and thus incorporate them into his play as a selective weapon right from the start. (Of course, Capablanca never studied the openings either, but that was long before Sammy; and then, for Sammy, came time out for school first.) Instead, Reshevsky played White "with a move in hand." Later, Petrosian had a similar style, but without the same handicaps. Significantly, Reshevsky's natural genius shone through when an opening was unusual, and the players were on their own. But in grandmaster chess, opponents do not readily allow the game to veer away from their own prior preparation.

Fourth, World War II erupted during Reshevsky's most formative years, and between 1939 and 1946 he had no proper sparring partners. Here Reshevsky suffered a misfortune similar to Akiba Rubinstein's, whose championship prospects were cruelly shattered by World War I and whose broken hopes hastened his psychosis.

Finally, one wonders to what extent Reshevsky's schooling interfered with his preoccupation with chess. Might it have inhibited his rise to the top? Discoveries and inventions in music, mathematics, chess, and many other fields often occur during adolescence or early youth. In 1922 Reshevsky was at the beginning of a rising chess curve, but was artificially kept dormant. The pros and cons of chess versus imitative education aside, we could hypothesize that a prodigious Reshevsky might thus have been denied the "ultimate" achievement in chess and the hypertensions of a genius—in favor of a balanced diet and social normalcy. He retained the strength and fervor.

By the time Reshevsky regained his full power, he was running against the Russian hegemony. His staying power remained his most remarkable feature, only wavering when the fifth hour of play took its gerontological toll of an old trooper.

Among other titles, Reshevsky published collections of his games; e.g., *How Chess Games Are Won* (New York: Pitman, 1962), traversing 1951–60. His chess column in *Chess Life & Review* contributed the title to his *The Art of Positional Play* (New York: McKay, 1967); and a Dover paperback (New York: 1960), *Reshevsky's Best Games of Chess*, covered the time to 1946 (originally issued by *Chess Review* in 1948 as *Reshevsky on Chess*).

In the following game, we see Reshevsky locking horns with a former World Chess Champion (against whom Reshevsky shows a plus score, when one totals up all the games they played against each other).

## AVRO TOURNAMENT

### Amsterdam 1938
*Gruenfeld Defense*

M. EUWE          S. RESHEVSKY

| 1 P–Q4 | N–KB3 |
| 2 P–QB4 | P–KN3 |
| 3 P–B3 | P–Q4 |

Aborting White's attempt to avoid the regular Gruenfeld Defense. If 3 . . . B–N2 4 P–K4 P–Q3 5 B–K3 O–O 6 N–K2 P–K4 7 QN–B3, with a strong grip. As played, Black allows White a pawn majority in the center, but his pieces become active.

| 4 PxP | NxP |
| 5 P–K4 | N–N3 |
| 6 N–B3 | B–N2 |
| 7 B–K3 | O–O |

Stronger than 7 . . . N–B3 8 B–N5, followed by 9 KN–K2. Now threatens 8 . . . P–K4 9 P–Q5 P–B3, with total mobility for Black. Also 8 . . . P–QB3, followed by 9 . . . P–K4 may be considered.

### 8 P–B4!

The power of undogmatic thinking. At the cost of a tempo, White shifts his strategy and vacates KB3 for the knight; he also reinforces the hold on the center— . . . P–K4 is no longer possible.

8 Q–Q2 N–B3 9 O–O–O P–K4 10 P–Q5 N–Q5 equalizes. But now Black forces the pawn advance just the same and subsequently breaks up White's pawn center, giving him an isolated pawn.

The whole opening strategy was developed and perfected by the "Hypermoderns" and later became standard.

### 8 . . .          N–B3!

Now the cautious 8 . . . P–QB3 would vindicate White's treatment after 9 N–B3 B–K3 10 Q–Q2 N–N5 11 BxN BxB 12 P–B5! with good attacking chances.

After the text, 9 N–B3 is countered by 9 . . . B–N5 10 P–Q5 N–N1 11 B–K2 P–QB3 12 Q–N3 PxP 13 PxP N/1–Q2 14 O–O P–K3! Hence the advance is forced.

### 9 P–Q5          N–N1

Preferable to 9 . . . N–R4 10 BxN RPxB 11 R–B1 and 12 P–QN4. Now White is at the crossroads, but slightly slips and never recovers. From here on, Reshevsky increases his advantage with an iron will.

### 10 N–B3?

A sound-looking move, which abides by several good rules: Morphy's, to develop; Lasker's, to develop knights before bishops; and Euwe's, to follow up logically on the purpose of 8 P–B4. Yet, White should have been more energetic in counteracting Black's pawn-wrecking plans. Better would have been (a) to take the sting out of

Black's poisonous king's bishop by *10* B–Q4 BxB *11* QxB P–QB3 *12* N–KB3 O–O–O and there would no longer be the danger of being left with a vulnerable "isolani" on Q5; or *10* . . . P–QB3 *11* BxB KxB *12* Q–Q4ch P–B3 with a balanced game. (b) *10* P–QR4 P–QB3 *11* P–R5 N/3–Q2 *12* P–K5 PxP *13* QxP N–QB3=; or *10* . . . P–K4 *11* P–R5 N/3–Q2 *12* N–B3 PxP *13* BxP R–K1=.

*10* . . .            **P–QB3**
*11* **Q–N3**

Reshevsky suggested *11* PxP but after *11* . . . NxP and *12* . . . B–N5; Black retains the better position.

*11* . . .            **PxP**

No better is *11* . . . BxNch *12* PxB PxP *13* BxN PxB *14* PxP±.

*12* **NxP**

Black wins a pawn after *12* PxP BxNch *13* PxB QxP! *14* BxN Q–K5ch.

*12* . . .            **NxN**
*13* **PxN**          **N–Q2**

Euwe's strategy has failed; he has no initiative and an exposed center pawn. Black's coming check is very timely, just before White castles, and it secures a decisive advantage for Black.

*14* **B–K2**        **Q–R4ch!**

If *15* K–B2 N–B3 *16* KR–Q1 N–N5ch *17* K–N1 NxB *18*

QxN BxP∓. If *15* N–Q2 N–B3 *16* B–B3 R–Q1, winning the pawn. This leaves White only one move.

*15* **B–Q2**        **Q–N3!**

White still cannot castle into safety and if *16* QxQ NxQ, winning either White's queen's or knight's pawn. Besides, there is the latent threat *16* . . . QxQ *17* PxQ BxP; e.g., *16* O–O–O QxQ *17* PxQ N–B4 *18* B–B4 P–QN4 *19* BxP NxPch *20* K–B2 R–N1∓. Therefore:

*16* **B–B3**        **BxBch**
*17* **PxB**         **Q–K6!**

Winning a pawn. If *18* P–N3 N–B4 *19* Q–B2 N–K5 or *18* Q–B4 N–B3 and *19* . . . N–K5. During the next phase, Euwe tries to put together a counterattack to regain the material lost, while Black concentrates on defense. White's 18th move is about the only logical one.

*18* **P–B4**        **QxP**
*19* **O–O**         **Q–B2**
*20* **K–R1**        **N–B3**
*21* **Q–K3**        **B–N5!**

White's *20* K–R1 was designed to prevent an exchange of the queen by . . . Q–N3. White needs all his men to retaliate and cannot afford simplifications. But *21* . . . B–N5 achieves a favorable exchange of pieces, especially as Black's bishop is not so active as the knight. White's reply creates some problems, but Reshevsky can handle them.

| 22 | Q–R6 | BxN |
| 23 | RxB | P–QN4! |

White had planned QR–KB1 and R–KR3, threatening RxN. But Black's timely and powerful thrust prevents 24 R–KR3 because of 24 . . . Q–K4 25 R–K1 PxP, etc. If 24 QR–KB1 Q–K4 25 B–Q1 PxP and White is lost.

| 24 | PxP | Q–K4 |
| 25 | R–K1 | NxP |
| 26 | R–KR3 | Q–N2 |
| 27 | Q–Q2 | P–K3 |
| 28 | R–Q3 | QR–N1 |
| 29 | P–QR4 | N–N3 |
| 30 | Q–N4? | |

This final positional misjudgment causes the waste of an important tempo two moves later. White should have pushed immediately 30 P–R5 N–Q4! 31 R–QN3 KR–B1 (31 . . . R–N2 32 B–B3!) 32 B–B1 (32 KR–QN1 N–B6!) N–B2 33 KR–QN1 Q–K4 34 Q–N2 QxQ 35 R/3xQ R–N2; or 33 P–N6 PxP 34 PxP N–Q4 35 P–N7 R–B2 36 KR–QN1 P–B4 37 B–R6, besetting Black with more difficulties and tactical threats. Probably 37 . . . Q–K4 is most active, although combinational turns like 37 . . . N–B6?! 38 R–B1!? N–K5!? disclose how quickly Black can take over.

| 30 . . . | QR–B1! |

Possibly White reckoned with 30 . . . KR–Q1. White does not push 31 P–R5 as follows in the game, but plays 31 Q–R5 R–B2 (31 . . . N–Q4 32 B–B3! or 31 . . . P–B4 32 B–B3) 32 KR–Q1 or 32 B/B3 with a sudden initiative, as Black's officers are blocked in on the queen-side without enough mobility.

| 31 | P–R5 | N–Q4 |
| 32 | Q–N3 | R–B4 |

Black's strategic superiority is now striking as compared to the earlier 30 P–R5 missed by White. However, Reshevsky was now in time trouble, and it persisted until his 40th move was completed.

32 . . . Q–K4 is also tactically strong. White's rook is threatening to uncover a triple attack on pawn and bishop by . . . N–B3, and even threatening 33 . . . QxB! 34 RxQ? R–B8 mate! But the text 32 . . . R–B4 is good enough. It prevents 33 P–N6 RxP! 34 P–N7 R–N1 35 Q–B4 Q–B1 or 35 R–QB1 R–R8!∓.

| 33 | B–B3 | R–N1 |
| 34 | BxN | R/4xP! |

34 . . . R/1xP? 35 BxP RxQ 36 R–Q8!ch Q–B1 37 RxQch KxR 38 BxR wins.

| 35 | Q–R2 | PxB |
| 36 | RxP | Q–B6 |
| 37 | R–KB1 | R–N7 |
| 38 | Q–R4 | R–N8 |
| 39 | R/5–Q1 | RxR |

39 R/1–Q1 was suggested as better; e.g., 39 . . . RxRch; 40 QxR. Yet, Black has the situation under control and can select a suitable winning procedure according to the book. Only the time trouble is still worrisome.

| 40 RxR | P–QR3! |
|---|---|

The crucial and crushing blow, which literally seals White's fate just at the time of Black's time control—the 40th move. It freezes White's QRP, which now remains under constant observation while Black will be free to maneuver on the kingside and utilize his plus pawn.

| 41 P–R3 | R–N4 |
|---|---|
| 42 R–R1 | K–N2 |
| 43 Q–R2 | Q–N7 |
| 44 Q–R4 | R–N4! |

After an exchange of the only mobile piece left, Black's win

would become even more certain. But now Black's plan is taking shape—hammering away at White's king. White, on the other hand, will keep Black tied to defending the pawn. One or the other will have to give way.

| 45 R–R2 | Q–B6 |
|---|---|
| 46 R–R1 | P–R4 |
| 47 Q–R2 | R–KB4 |
| 48 K–R2 | P–N4! |
| 49 Q–R4 | R–B5 |
| 50 Q–R2 | P–N5 |
| 51 PxP | Q–K4 |

A neat interpolation. If 52 K–R1 (or N1) PxP and . . . P–N6 winning. The reason is self-evident.

| 52 P–N3 | R–K5 |
|---|---|
| 53 Q–N1 | R–K7ch |
| 54 K–R3 | PxPch |
| 55 K–R4 | |

If 55 KxP R–K5ch 56 K–R3 Q–R4ch, etc. If 56 K–B3 R–K6ch.

| 55 . . . | R–R7ch |
|---|---|
| 56 KxP | Q–K7ch |
| 57 Resigns | |

51 K–N5 P–B3ch and mate next move; or 57 K–B5 R–B7ch and mate in 3; or 57 K–B4 R–B7ch 58 K–N5 P–B3ch 59 K–R4 R–R7 mate.

Time trouble was always Reshevsky's hallmark, and often his undoing. Although the forced rapidity of his moves sometimes had an unnerving effect on his opponents, this certainly was not intended, but was merely a by-product. Reshevsky spent inordinate time on the basic elements of a position as it developed from its early stages. His concerns were in choosing the right move and strategy, and conceiving the future course of the game. He often absorbed these factors to such an extent that he could rattle off a string of correct moves, winning the final endplay.

Some players perform better under compulsion. But just as often, time pressure works the other way. A masterly neoromantic strategy need not conform to any predictable pattern of methodology; it relies on flexibility. Thus some energy and time must be kept in reserve to meet contingencies. To rattle the opponent by deliberate casualness may easily boomerang. True, Capablanca once gave up 52 minutes on the clock against Edward Lasker, in order to win in another 45; and Fischer conceded Reshevsky 55 minutes of "odds" at Sousse, 1976. But the mechanism is not foolproof!

SOLID PERSEVERANCE

In 1938, the AVRO Tournament was sponsored by the Dutch Broadcasting Corporation to determine a potential challenger to Alekhine for the World Chess Championship. The tourney comprised the world's eight best players. Fine and Keres shared 1st–2nd prize, Botvinnik came 3rd and Alekhine, Euwe, and Reshevsky tied for 4th–6th, followed by Capablanca and then Flohr.

While Reshevsky's result did not qualify him as an immediate contender, he maintained his reputation as one of the stronger masters. He kept it through the next ten years, and was once more called upon to assert his claim in the World Chess Championship sponsored by FIDE in 1948, three years after Alekhine's demise. So high was Reshevsky's rating and his demands at that time, that he was granted an honorarium of $2,000 as against $250 each for the others. Alas, trying to win in drawn positions, and suffering again from underpreparedness for such stiff competition, Reshevsky tied for 3rd with Keres, with 10½ points each. Botvinnik amassed 14 points, far ahead of Smyslov's 11. Euwe scored only 4 points out of a possible 20.

Although Reshevsky's standing was most creditable, it showed that, for all practical purposes, he had lost the race to the top for good. A different generation was on the march, whose zest, tempo, intensity, and teamwork made up for experience, tradition, and priority. They absorbed the large reservoir of past knowledge and added their youth. We will look at their accomplishments later.

How subtle the differences were in the playing strength of the four top contenders and how dangerous Reshevsky could be—anywhere at any time—is demonstrated by one of his five games against the emerging champion.

## WORLD CHESS CHAMPIONSHIP

### The Hague 1948
*Nimzo-Indian Defense*

H. BOTVINNIK          S. RESHEVSKY

| 1 | P–Q4 | N–KB3 |
|---|------|-------|
| 2 | P–QB4 | P–K3 |
| 3 | N–QB3 | B–N5 |
| 4 | P–K3 | |

The Nimzo-Indian Defense may have become one of the most explored and therefore conventional of variants of the Indian Defenses, but it is also one of the first comprehensive systems invented by the Hypermoderns, and the most solid one. 4 P–K3 may be considered White's stablest and most flexible choice. Other possibilities are (a) 4 B–N5 P–KR3! 5 B–R4 P–B4 6 P–Q5 BxNch 7 PxB P–K4 (1) 8 P–Q6 O–O 9 P–K3 R–K1 10 B–K2 N–B3 11 N–R3 P–QN3=; or (2) 8 P–K3 P–Q3 9 Q–B2 QN–Q2 10 N–B3 Q–K2=. (b) 4 Q–B2 P–B4! 5 PxP O–O 6 B–B4 BxP 7 N–B3 P–QN3 8 P–K3 B–N2 9 B–K2 N–B3 10 O–O R–B1 11 QR–Q1 B–K2 12 R–Q2 N–QR4 13 N–K5 P–Q4=. (c) 4 P–QR3 BxNch 5 PxB, with the aggressive and logical reply 5 . . . P–B4! White attempts to build up a center bastion and later make use of the B-pair. Black tries to block any such advance (. . . P–QB4 and . . . P–QN3) or bust it (. . . P–Q4) with greater mobility for his knights; e.g., (1) 6 P–B3 P–Q4! 7 PxQP NxP 8 PxP P–B4 9 Q–B2 O–O 10 P–K4 PxP 11 PxP N–B5=; or (2) 6 P–K3, transposing into the present game.

| 4 . . . | | P–B4 |
|---------|--|------|

These are the crossroads that prove the viability of the Nimzo-Indian as a tactical and psychological weapon. Black can deviate with 4 . . . P–Q4; with a Queen's Gambit without 4 B–N5 or 4 . . . P–QN3, a Nimzo-Queens Indian; or 4 . . . O–O, which leaves Black all options. The possibility of varying one's strategy from one tourney to the next and thus avoiding prepared analysis is an important consideration in the choice of openings. Actually, Reshevsky used each of these three variants on three different occasions against Botvinnik.

| 5 | P–QR3 | BxNch |
|---|-------|-------|

White also has 5 B–Q3 O–O 6 N–B3 P–Q4 7 O–O PxBP 8 BxP QN–Q2 9 Q–K2 PxP 10 PxP P–QN3, with a wide-open game for both sides. Actually, 5 P–QR3 is strategically called for against 4 . . . P–Q4; but it is a misconception here—Botvinnik's first in this game.

| 6 | PxB | N–B3 |
|---|-----|------|

Present practice points to 6 . . . P–QN3! 7 B–Q3 B–N2 as Black's best counter.

| 7 | B–Q3 | O–O? |
|---|------|------|
| 8 | N–K2!? | P–QN3 |

A position typical of this overture for generations. It illustrates how Black focuses on White's pawn on QB4. In turn, White will try to set his pawns going for a king-side attack. But, with even deeper insight, we can already discern nuances with the apparently innocuous transposition from first 7 . . . P–N3! 8 N–K2 O–O! or first 7 . . . O–O, which might, and probably should have been, replied by 8 PxP!—e.g., 8 . . . Q–R4 9 N–K2 QxBP! (not 9 . . . N–K4 10 P–QR4 R–K1 11 B–R3 NxBch 12 QxN QxRP 13 N–Q4+) 10 P–QR4 R–Q1! 11 B–R3 Q–QR4 12 P–B5±, never allowing Black's developing siege.

**9 P–K4      N–K1**
**10 B–K3**

Another transfer point. Playable are also 10 O–O B–R3 (10 . . . P–Q3 11 P–K5!) 11 Q–R4 (or 11 P–B4—Bronstein) Q–B1! 12 B–K3; or 10 P–K5 P–B4 11 PxP e.p. NxP 12 B–K3 B–R3. Black's 9 . . . N–K1 prepares the riposte . . . P–B4, to stop an advance of White's pawns, recalling a stratagem of Capablanca against Johner as White, Carlsbad 1929, which went: 1 P–Q4 N–KB3 2 P–B4 P–K3 3 N–QB3 B–N5 4 P–K3 O–O 5 B–Q3 P–B4! 6 N–K2 N–B3 7 P–QR3? BxNch 8 PxB P–QN3! 9 O–O B–R3 10 P–K4 N–K1 11 B–K3 P–Q3 12 Q–R4 N–QR4 13 KR–Q1 Q–B2 14 QR–

B1; and now 14 . . . QR–Q1 would have achieved full equality, although Capablanca's less precise 14 . . . Q–B3 still won him the game after a few of White's inaccuracies.

**10 . . .      P–Q3**

To answer PxP with QPxP, and also to protect the BP. But Black can ignore the attack and move at once 10 . . . B–R3 11 N–N3 (11 PxP? N–K4!) N–R4 12 Q–K2 R–B1 13 R–QB1 N–Q3! 14 P–K5 PxP 15 BxP N–B4= (Polugayevsky–Furman, USSR Championship 1958).

**11 O–O**

Through experience with this game, the theory of this opening has advanced. It prefers 11 N–N3! Q–Q2 (11 . . . B–R3 12 P–B4! and the key move . . . P–B4 is not possible) 12 O–O B–R3 13 P–B4 P–B4 14 Q–R4 PxKP 15 BxP B–N2 16 P–Q5±.

**11 . . .      N–R4**
**12 N–N3      B–R3**

Black refrains from the immediate 12 . . . P–B4 because he expects it to be more effective after White logically continues (13 Q–K2 Q–Q2) 14 P–B4. Intriguingly, White need not routinely play 14 P–B4 as he did in the game, whereas after 12 . . . P–B4 13 KPxP KPxP 14 B–B4 P–N3 15 Q–K2 N–KB3 16 KR–K1 KR–K1 17 Q–R2 Q–Q2 18 N–B1 Q–R5 19 N–Q2, or 17 Q–B1 Q–Q2

*18* P–QR4 N–N6 *19* R–R2, White's bishops have more scope.

**13 Q–K2          Q–Q2!**
**14 P–B4!?**

A most complex situation. Faulty is *14* P–QR4 PxP *15* PxP R–B1 *16* QR–B1 N–N6. Also wrong is *14* P–K5 P–B4! *15* P–B4 P–N3 (akin to the game as played) or *15* PxP e.p. NxP, with advantage for Black.

But promising might have been the tripling of pawns by *14* PxP NPxP (*14* . . . QPxP *15* P–K5 Q–B2 *16* B–N5; or *15* . . . R–Q1 *16* KR–Q1; or *15* . . . P–B4 *16* PxP e.p. NxP *17* B–B4) *15* P–K5 P–B4 *16* B–B4 PxP *17* QxP BxP (*17* . . . QxB *18* QxKPch R–B2 *19* QxB+) *18* BxB NxB *19* QxBP R–B1 *20* Q–Q4 QxQ *21* PxQ N–B3 with equality. The omission of this move vindicates Black.

**14 . . .           P–B4!**

Regardless of the foregoing variants, this now remains the cornerstone of Black's plan: stopping the dreaded four-pawn formation and keeping White's bishops imprisoned behind their own pawn barrier. It is instructive to note that to continue the counterattack with the logical *14* . . . Q–R5 wins here for White by a ferocious onslaught, gaining momentum precisely at this crucial moment; e.g., *14* . . . Q–R5 *15* P–B5 BxP *16* PxP BxP *17* B–QN5 Q–N6 *18* P–Q5 B–B1 *19* BxN RxB *20* RxP! KxR! *21* Q–R5ch K–K2 *22* B–N5ch K–Q2 *23* Q–B7ch R–K2 *24* QxR mate. If *20* . . . QxBP *21* QR–KB1 and *22* Q–KB2+; also *16* . . . BxB *17* PxPch RxP *18* QxB±. After *14* . . . Q–R5 *15* P–B5 NxP *16* KR–N1 PxP *17* NxP N–B3 *18* B–N5, the threat *19* N–K3 is deadly, and if *17* . . . P–QN4 *18* B–N5 P–B3 *19* B–R4 N–B2 *20* P–K5±.

**15 QR–K1**

Aiming at *16* P–Q5 P–N3 *17* PxKP QxP *18* PxP PxP *19* NxP RxN *20* Q–N4ch N–N2 *21* B–Q4 R–K4 *22* Q–N3! PxB *23* PxR BxP! *24* KPxP Q–R3 *25* BxBch NxB *26* Q–B3 wins. If *15* P–Q5 P–N3 *16* QxP QxP *17* PxP PxP∓. It all goes to show how much subtle foresight, how many pitfalls, and how many forced sequences are contained in a position that still seems to be in the realm of opening analysis. It also highlights the delicate problems of proper transition into a balanced middlegame.

Actually, as Black's next move stifles White's strategy at once, the immediate *15* QR–Q1 and *16* KR–K1 would have been preferable.

**15 . . .          P–N3!**
**16 R–Q1          Q–KB2**

Botvinnik realizes too late that *16* P–Q5 is met by *16* . . . N–N2, and at the loss of a tempo changes his strategy. Black, on the other hand, finds it now expedient to move away from the queen's file so that 17 QPxP can be answered by 17 . . . QPxP, without danger of discovering a *gardez* by 18 BxP.[8] Still useless is 16 . . . Q–R5 17 P–Q5 BxP 18 PxKP BxP 19 PxP BxP (19 . . . PxP 20 BxQBP) 20 NxB PxN 21 P–N4 with a vehement attack. If 17 . . . NxP 18 PxP NxB 19 QxN BxB 20 QxB PxP 21 NxP Q–B3 22 N–N5±.

| 17 P–K5 | R–B1 |
| 18 KR–K1 | QPxP! |

Another possible course is 18 . . . PxQP 19 BxQP NxP 20 PxP N/1xP 21 QxP KR–K1 22 QxQch KxQ 23 K–B2 B–N2, and Black has a won ending. Now, White's center has been put out of action.

| 19 QPxKP | N–KN2 |
| 20 N–B1 | KR–Q1 |

Black controls the open queen's file, while both White's queen and bishop are tied to the defense of the QBP. White's knight moves to KB7 to support the QBP by N–Q2 (or N–K3 when the bishop vacates the square); but White's men are in each other's way.

| 21 B–KB2 | N–R4! |
| 22 B–N3 | Q–K1 |

Now 22 . . . Q–R5 becomes reality.

| 23 N–K3 | Q–R5 |
| 24 Q–R2 | NxB |

24 . . . P–N4 is even more forcing.

| 25 PxN | P–R4? |

A slip, as it allows 26 B–B2! but is missed by White; e.g., 26 . . . Q–B3 27 P–R4, with a somewhat better defense. More exact is 25 . . . Q–N6! 26 QxQ NxQ 27 P–N4 PxN 28 NxP N–R4 29 N–K3 K–B2!

| 26 B–K2 | K–B2 |
| 27 K–B2 | Q–N6 |

With two rows of double pawns and an isolated KRP, White faces a lost endgame and, therefore, Black exchanges the only active pieces.

| 28 QxQ | NxQ |
| 29 B–Q3 | K–K2 |
| 30 K–K2 | N–R4 |
| 31 R–Q2 | R–B2? |

Again, more accurate is 31 . . . K–B2.

---

[8] "Gardez," French for "guard," or "watch (your queen)," —now obsolete and no longer required, just as to say "check" is not obligatory.

**32 P–N4!?**

White's *31 R–Q2* was in preparation for transferring the king via Q1 to B2, but the plan fails, for 32 K–Q1 R/2–Q2 33 K–B2 NxP! Now White, facing strangulation, resorts to desperate means. A standoff might have succeeded with 32 R–KR1 R/2–Q2 33 R/2–Q1 N–N6 34 P–N4! RPxP (34 . . . BPxP 35 BxP N–Q7 36 RxP NxP 37 R–R7ch K–B1 38 RxR RxR 39 RxR NxKPch 40 B–Q3±) 35 R–R6 RxB 36 R–R7ch= (analysis by J. Soudakoff and S. Goodman in their tournament book).

The idea of P–N4 was right, the timing was wrong. With Black's next move, he again threatens to take the QBP and foils 33 P–N5.

| 32 . . . | R/2–Q2 |
|---|---|
| 33 PxBP | NPxP |
| 34 R/1–Q1 | |

It has become too late for 34 R–KR1 NxP 35 R/2–Q1 RxB! More complex is 34 R/2–Q1 K–B2! 35 K–KR1 K–N3 36 KR–N1 (36 P–N4? RPxP 37 NxP RxB!) K–R3 37 R–KR1 B–N2 38 R–R2 K–N3!! 39 R/1–KR1 RxB 40 RxP RxNch 41 KxR! NxPch 42 K–K2 R–Q7ch 43 K–K1 RxP 44 R–R7 R–N8ch winning. In here, if 38 KR–N1 N–N6 39 R–KR1 N–B8ch 40 RxN RxB 41 R/R–Q1 RxR 42 RxR RxR 43 KxR P–R5 44 K–K2 BxP 45 NxB P–R6 46 K–B2 P–R7 wins. There remains 39 P–N3 B–B6ch 40 KxB RxB 41 K–K2 RxR 42 RxR RxR 43 NxR N–R4 44 K–Q3 P–R5 45 PxP K–R4 46 N–N2 KxP 47 K–K2 K–N5 48 K–K3 K–N6!; or 47 K–K2 K–N6 48 K–K3 K–N5! with winning opposition play.

The course of the game as continued speaks for itself.

| 34 . . . | P–R5! |
|---|---|
| 35 K–K1 | N–N6 |
| 36 N–Q5ch | PxN |
| 37 BxP | NxR |
| 38 RxN | PxP |
| 39 BxR | RxB |
| 40 R–KB2 | K–K3 |
| 41 R–B3 | R–Q6 |
| Resigns | |

There is a curious lesson to be learned from the foregoing encounter. It concerns the relative depth of prepared analysis and the meaning of opening theory in general. At the time of the game, the redoubtable system of the late Nimzowitsch was well established. The interconnection or the divergencies of White's P–QR3 or P–K3 and K2, and of Black's . . . P–Q4 or . . . P–QB4 and . . . P–QN3 were already under thorough investigation and tried in tournaments by 1948.

While the ramifications of these overlapping systems are clearer with hindsight, they are also logical and comprehensible enough to have been explored in all detail during home preparation by tournament players. Yet, it was left to the heat of battle to examine the consequences of some distinct opening moves. As no one doubts the overwhelming credentials of these players, we may assume that much of the apparent depth of theory is ephemeral—or, during a confrontation, subject to amnesia or to stage fright.

The chess elite of those days, though at the top of professional chess, were semiprofessionals only, pursuing another occupation alongside. Thus, they used their "feel for chess," not having had time to memorize by rote. This development came later, when the volume of theory seemed to demand full-time devotion—whether successfully remains a puzzle which we will meet again later on.

At any rate, by the time this game was played, Reshevsky was at the steady high level of his power and mastered most all aspects of chess. Although he did not rival Fine's sovereignty at rapid transit (i.e., lightning or speed chess, or blitz), he ranked among the first in such events.

Reshevsky was also adroit at blindfold chess, although he abandoned such performances when he had matured into master competition. At the early age of eight, during his *wunderkind* séance at London 1920, Reshevsky already conducted himself as an accomplished craftsman. He won a high-quality game, given in his *Reshevsky on Chess*, against the former British Champion (1912) R. C. Griffiths—and in an opening in which the top analyst Griffiths was an undisputed specialist. He was among the first compilers of *Modern Chess Openings* (the rights to which he passed on to me in 1947—W.K.).

## FINE: THE GREAT PROMISE

"American chess has come of age. It is no longer a bizarre affectation of the longhairs; it has finally become a popular game, played by everybody, at home, in chess clubs, in barber shops, on the street, everywhere. Even women in Hollywood play chess and we used to say that when that happened, the revolution would be here." Were these words written after Robert J. Fischer's advent? After the beginning of Women's Liberation? No. They are quoted from Reuben Fine's *The World Is a Chess Board* (New York: McKay, 1948), one of Fine's many books that helped put chess on the library shelves.

Fine was born in New York City in 1914, learned the game at the age of eight, and at eighteen was champion of the Marshall Chess Club. In the same year he also won the Western Open in Minne-

apolis, an official national event. He also won at Detroit 1933 and
tied Reshevsky for 1st and 2nd at Chicago 1934.

Rapidly surging upwards, he joined the U.S. team for the 1933
Olympics, and undoubtedly liked the intellectual incentive of the
changing panorama in Europe's chess. After returning to home base
from his first European encounter, Fine entered the International
Tournament at Syracuse 1934, and as a nineteen-year-old, freshly
baked international master, he captured the brilliancy prize for his
win over the seasoned Italian, Mario Monticelli.

The game is full of beautiful sacrifices, not brought about by a
weak, substandard defense, but as a scientifically handled culmina-
tion of superior tactics. Also the defense contains some vitriol: It
seems so dull that it almost provokes Black into taking action and
into overreaching himself. At that phase, Black may effectively
react!

### INTERNATIONAL
### TOURNAMENT

**Syracuse, New York 1934**
*Caro-Kann Defense*

M. MONTICELLI          R. FINE

| | |
|---|---|
| 1 P–K4 | P–QB3 |
| 2 P–Q4 | P–Q4 |
| 3 N–QB3 | PxP |
| 4 NxP | B–B4 |

This line allows development
for Black's QB, which otherwise
remains shut in. On the other
hand, Black has less of a center.

| | |
|---|---|
| 5 N–N3 | B–N3 |
| 6 N–B3 | |

Dynamic is 6 P–KR4 P–KR3
7 N–B3 N–Q2 8 P–R5 B–R2
9 B–Q3 BxB 10 QxB Q–B2 11
B–Q2 P–K3 12 Q–K2! KN–B3
13 O–O–O O–O–O 14 N–K5
NxN 15 PxN N–Q2 16 P–KB4
B–K2 17 N–K4 N–B4 18 N–
B3 P–B3 19 PxP BxP 20 Q–B4

Q–N3= (Spassky–Petrosian,
World Championship 1966).
If 6 B–QB4 P–K3 7 KN–K2
N–B3 8 N–B4 B–Q3.

6 . . .          P–K3

Casually played, as it allows the
choice 7 N–K5, which can be
prevented by playing first 6 . . .
N–Q2. As Black must put up
with an initial congestion in
any line of the Caro-Kann, this
transposition is not lethal, but
it needlessly allows the opponent a choice.

7 B–QB4

7 P–KR4 P–KR3 8 N–K5 would
take better advantage of the
omission . . . N–Q2. The text
also neglects the need for 7
B–Q3 N–Q2! 8 O–O KN–B3 9
P–B4 B–K2 10 BxB RPxB 11
Q–K2 Q–B2 12 R–Q1 O–O=
(MCO, 10th ed.). To leave
Black's bishop unopposed
creates future trouble.

7 . . .            N–B3
8 Q–K2            QN–Q2
9 N–K5

9 B–B4 and 10 O–O–O was imperative. The imposing centralization 9 N–K5 is deflated by Fine, who gains a very mobile bishop pair. 10 QxN BxP loses a clear pawn.

9 . . .            NxN
10 PxN            N–Q2
11 P–B4

Black's threat was . . . Q–R4ch, winning the KP, but the text weakens White's power base.

11 . . .           B–QB4
12 B–N3

If 12 B–Q2 BxP. If 12 B–K3 Q–N3! 13 BxB QxP! 14 R–Q1 NxB∓. The enterprising 12 P–B5 PxP 13 P–K6 fails after 13 . . . O–O! 14 PxN QxP, and White is lost. More auspicious is 12 P–B3 Q–N3 13 P–N4, dislodging the troublesome bishop; or 12 . . . P–N4 13 B–Q3 BxB 14 QxB Q–N3 15 N–K4 with some hopes.

12 . . .           P–QR4
13 P–QR4

White might try to simplify by 13 P–B3, but 13 . . . P–N4 14 B–B2 Q–R5! or 13 . . . Q–R5 ties him up. If 13 B–Q2 P–R5 14 B–B4 BxP.

13 . . .           Q–N3!

Fine resists the temptation of 13 . . . B–N5ch 14 P–B3 N–B4

15 B–B2 N–Q6ch 16 K–B1 B–QB4 17 P–B5!!

14 B–Q2           O–O–O
15 N–B1           B–N5!

If 15 O–O–O B–Q5, followed by 16 . . . N–B4, which is even more forceful than Tartakover's suggestion 15 . . . B–N5.

16 O–O–O

16 BxB was suggested as an alternative, but 16 . . . QxQch 17 Q–Q2 N–B4 18 QxQ PxQ leaves White's setup full of weak holes. If 16 P–B3 BxP 17 BxB QxB, Black's threats are taking menacing shape.

16 . . .           N–B4
17 Q–K3

Allowing an inferno to break loose. But neither 17 BxB RxRch 18 QxR NxBch 19 PxN QxB, nor 17 K–N1 NxB, nor 17 B–K3 NxBch 18 PxN P–QB4 19 N–Q2 BxNch 20 BxB (20 . . . Q–K5 is threatened) B–Q6 21 Q–B3 (else 21 . . . P–B5) Q–N3 helps in the long run.

White is altogether too cramped.

17 . . .           R–Q6!

With grandmasterly perception, Black activates his power decisively, deflecting the pawn which protects White's bishop.

If 18 Q–K2 RxB/3 19 PxR NxP mate.

18 PxR            NxBch
19 K–B2

| | | |
|---|---|---|
| 19 K–N1 NxBch 20 RxN QxQ | 19 . . . | B–QB4 |
| 21 NxQ BxR leaves Black a | 20 Q–R3 | N–Q5ch |
| piece up. The finish needs no | 21 K–B1 | Q–N6 |
| comment. | 22 N–K3 | QxQP |
| | 23 Resigns | |

In 1935 Fine clinched 1st prize in Milwaukee, ahead of Dake and Kashdan, and later sat at first board for the United States in the Warsaw Olympics. Staying behind in Europe, he again placed 1st in the prestigious Hastings Christmas Tournament 1935–36. In Amsterdam in 1936, Fine shared 1st prize with the then World Champion M. Euwe, ahead of Alekhine.

There followed Nottingham 1936, where Botvinnik and Capablanca shared 1st and 2nd prize with 10 points each, and Euwe, Fine, and Reshevsky were just ½ point behind, in front of Alekhin, Flohr, and Em. Lasker. At Zandvoort 1936, Fine settled in 1st place, out of twelve participants, ahead of Euwe and Keres, and without losing a game. It was deplorable that the surety and swiftness of Fine's 1936 successes was not accompanied by a performance at Moscow the same year, which would have given him the chance of a preliminary encounter with Capablanca and Botvinnik.

The chain of successes continued through Hastings 1936–37 (2nd prize, 7½ points, just behind Alekhine's 8 points); Moscow 1937 (1st prize); Ostend 1937 (1st–3rd, Fine, Grob, and Keres); Stockholm 1937 (1st prize); Margate 1937 (1st–2nd, Fine and Keres, 7½ points each; 3rd Alekhine, 6 points). Fine's win against Alekhine was one of his finest ever, although Alekhine got his own back the same year at Kemeri, whereupon Fine gained the upper hand again the following year in the AVRO tournament!

At the 1937 Stockholm Olympics, Fine occupied board two in deference to Reshevsky, who had beaten him for 1st position at New York 1936, where the results had been: Reshevsky 11½, Simonson 11, Fine and Treysman 10½ each, Kashdan 10, Dake and Kupchik 9 each. At the Stockholm Olympics, overqualified for 2nd place in comparison to the opponents from other countries, Fine pulled 76.7 percent of possible points, the second highest percentage after Flohr, who scored 78.7 percent at board one for Czechoslovakia.

The events of 1937, and the years after, are of importance in Fine's steady struggle with Keres: at Margate 1937; at Baden-Semmering 1937 (1st, Keres 9, 2nd, Fine 8, with Capablanca, Reshevsky, and Flohr trailing); and at Hastings 1937–38, where

Fine suffered a setback when he and Flohr took 4th and 5th prize only, behind Reshevsky (7 points) and Alexander and Keres (6½ points each). At New York 1938, Fine's 12½ points and 2nd prize were superseded by Reshevsky's 13 points, but the eternal rivals Simonson, Horowitz, Kashdan, Dake, Kupchik, and Treysman were left far behind. While conspicuously excelling at all tournaments, Fine never won the U.S. Championship! This failure critically influenced his possible claim to World Championship candidacy in 1946.

TO EUROPE AND BACK

Fine's greatest achievement was Amsterdam 1938—the AVRO Tournament, organized exclusively for the purpose of picking a challenger to World Champion A. Alekhine. Fine and Keres both scored 8½ points each, sharing 1st and 2nd place, ahead of Botvinnik 7½; Alekhine, Euwe, and Reshevsky 7 each; Capablanca 6; and Flohr 4½. But instead of arranging an immediate tie-breaking match between the two joint tournament winners, Fine and Keres, the tournament officials chose one of the contrived statistical systems for tie-breaking, in this case, the "Berger-Sonneborn," on account of which Keres became the official candidate on the sole strength of his individual 1½:½ score against Fine.[9]

Hence, while Keres had the right of first claim, Fine gained the right to challenge Keres to a match before or after the conclusion of any other championship contest; and Fine's more deliberate style and pragmatic attitude might have helped him to prevail. However, no such match was on the immediate horizon, and the gathering clouds of World War II prevented any such plans for another decade.

At Amsterdam 1938, both Botvinnik and Fine were at the height of their power. Fine's victory over Botvinnik is imposing.

[9] Many challengers—Steinitz–Zukertort after London 1883; Alkehine–Capablanca after New York 1927; Euwe–Alekhine before 1935; and Fischer–Spassky —had a minus score to start with. Therefore the singlehanded decision by tie-break was inconclusive in such an important case.

## AVRO TOURNAMENT

Amsterdam 1938
*French Defense*

R. FINE              M. BOTVINNIK

| 1 | P–K4 | P–K3 |
|---|------|------|
| 2 | P–Q4 | P–Q4 |
| 3 | N–QB3 | B–N5 |
| 4 | P–K5 | P–QB4 |
| 5 | PxP | |

The less usual line of many in this, the Winawer Variation of the French. It was extensively systematized by Nimzowitsch.

Both Botvinnik and Fine were at home with the popular openings of the prewar period. Fine had been collecting all contemporary material on the openings for the 6th edition of *MCO* and was familiar with the theory of the French. Botvinnik was known as a connoisseur of the Caro-Kann and of the French Defense. He was the USSR's most persevering, ascetic, controlled (in every sense), and ambitious aspirant to chess fame—and, undoubtedly, the most gifted. Separating himself from the objective chronicler of established analysis, practicing grandmaster Fine had to choose a little-explored avenue to create some surprise for the Moscovite.

In the 1930s, one of the most popular continuations was 5 P–QR3 BxNch 6 PxB N–K2 7 Q–N4 N–B4 8 B–Q3 P–KR4 9 Q–B4 PxP 10 PxP Q–R5! 11 N–B3 QxQ 12 BxQ N–B3 13 P–B3 B–Q2= (Bogolyubov–Flohr, Nottingham 1936). Here,

less favorable is 6 . . . Q–B2; e.g., 7 N–B3 N–K2 8 P–KR4! P–QN3 9 P–R5 P–KR3 10 P–R4! B–R3 11 B–N5ch BxB 12 PxB (as in L. Steiner–Foltys, Lodž 1938). 5 P–QR3, forcing the exchange, leaves White with the pair of bishops, but Black's pieces have greater mobility.

However, White need not compel Black's bishop to declare himself at once. He has other options; e.g., 5 B–Q2, when 5 . . . PxP? 6 N–N5 BxBch 7 QxB N–QB3 8 N–KB3 P–B3 9 Q–B4 N–R3 10 N–Q6ch K–B1 is good for White (as in Fine–Capablanca, AVRO 1938). Better is 5 . . . N–K2 6 P–QR3 BxN 7 PxB QN–B3 8 N–B3 Q–B2; or 6 N–N5 BxBch 7 QxB O–O 8 P–QB3 Q–N3, as recommended by Fine in *MCO*, 6th ed. 6 N–B3 QN–B3 7 PxP reverts to the main line of this game.

Later on 5 Q–N4 came to the fore; e.g., 5 . . . N–K2 6 PxP (6 QxNP R–N1 7 Q–R6 PxP 8 P–QR3 B–R4 9 P–QN4 Q–B2 10 N–N5 QxPch 11 N–K2 B–N3 12 B–B4 Q–N2=) QN–B3 (also 6 . . . BxNch 7 PxB N–N3 8 N–B3 N–Q2 9 B–K3 Q–R4=) 7 B–Q2 N–B4 8 N–B3 BxP 9 B–Q3 P–KR4 10 Q–KB4 QN–K2 11 R–KR3 P–QR3 12 O–O–O N–N3= (*MCO*, 11th ed., 1972). But this sharp attack has lost most of its impetus. The text, 5 PxP, was tried by Bogolyubov against Alekhine at Bad Nauheim 1937, and after 5 . . . N–QB3 6 N–B3 P–B3? 7 B–QN5 BxP 8 O–O B–Q2 9 R–K1 PxP? 10 NxKP, White had the superior game.

The tempting 5 . . . BxNch 6 PxB Q–R4 triples White's pawn, but Black's "attack" soon peters out; e.g., 7 B–Q2 N–QB3 8 Q–N4! KN–K2 9 N–B3 QxBP 10 B–Q3, and White holds all the aces! Hence:

| 5 . . . | N–K2 |
| 6 N–B3 | QN–B3? |

Preferable is 6 . . . Q–B2 7 B–N5ch (7 B–KB4 N–N3 8 B–N3 QxBP) B–Q2 8 BxBch NxB!

| 7 B–Q3 | P–Q5?! |

This is sharper than 7 . . . N–N3 8 BxN RPxB 9 B–K3; or 8 Q–K2 P–Q5 9 P–QR3 Q–R4 10 R–QN1 PxN 11 B–K3—and riskier!

| 8 P–QR3 | B–R4 |
| 9 P–QN4 |  |

A complex setup, requiring an accurate forecast arrived at during prepared analysis or in over-the-board play. For the most part, the fragmented details of diverse lines fall into an apparently uniform pattern only *a posteriori*. In practice, the seemingly compact course of a grandiose game is a synthesis of many factors. Fine could not foresee what defense Botvinnik would adopt. He kept a memory bank of responses, suitable against individual styles, but one cannot mentally computerize all and sundry permutations. The final analysis is left to the occasion. Else, why ponder, with the clock ticking? The following vacillations prove the point.

| 9 . . . | NxNP |

Winning two pawns and maintaining the pin, it almost works. Anyhow, after 9 . . . PxN 10 PxB QxP 11 Q–K2 QxBP 12 O–O O–O 13 B–KN5 QxP/R5 14 Q–K4 N–N3 15 R–K1. White has a crushing advantage in space.

| 10 PxN | BxP |
| 11 B–N5ch? | N–B3 |

The first piece of evidence that 5 PxP had taken Botvinnik by surprise, otherwise Black would have replied: 11 . . . B–Q2 12 QxP BxNch 13 QxB BxB, as worked out in later research. For the same reason, Fine might therefore have preferred 11 O–O! BxN 12 R–N1! with a mobile knight and a good pair of bishops; e.g., 12 . . . Q–B2 (12 . . . O–O 13 N–N5 P–KR3 14 Q–R5 QxKP 15 P–B4+) 13 B–R3 N–B 14 Q–K2. Both point and counterpoint underscore that the opponents were already out of their own book and improvising. From now on, Fine's intuition and ironclad technique ensure him of victory in a short time. He assumes command of the ranks and files!

| 12 BxNch | PxB |
|---|---|
| 13 R–R4 | BxNch |
| 14 B–Q2 | P–B3 |

Trying to instill a little dynamic fluidity by opening some lines for Black's queen and rook. But Fine doesn't fall for it.

| 15 O–O | O–O |
|---|---|
| 16 Q–K1 | P–QR4 |
| 17 BxB | QxP |
| 18 Q–K1 | P–QR4 |
| 19 QxP | B–R3 |
| 20 KR–R1 | B–N4 |
| 21 R–Q4 | |

Ordinarily, one would take what's up for grabs by 20 RxP. But Fine's positional instinct tells him that to occupy square Q6 with a tempo, and to dominate the center, is better strategy, as the QRP can be blocked at will if necessary. There is a drop of poison in the future World Champion's bait of 21 RxP RxR because 22 QxR QxQ 23 RxQ reduces the position to a possible draw, whereas 22 RxR Q–Q8ch 23 N–K1 Q–K7 spells disaster for White.

| 21 . . . | Q–K2 |
|---|---|
| 22 R–Q6 | P–R5 |

Black must call White's bluff, if a bluff it was, and ask him to show how to block the advance. If 22 . . . KR–Q1 23 R/1–Q1 RxR 24 BPxR Q–KB2 25 P–Q7 R–Q1 26 QxRP RxP 27 Q–R8ch wins!

| 23 Q–K3 | R–R2 |
|---|---|
| 24 N–Q2!! | |

Threatening 25 P–QB4, and Black has no more moves (besides, it prepares the consolidating P–KB4). What comes next is mere motion.

| 24 . . . | P–R6 |
|---|---|
| 25 P–QB4 | B–R5 |
| 26 PxP | QxP |
| 27 RxP | R–K1 |
| 28 P–R4 | R/2–R1 |
| 29 N–B3 | Q–N7 |
| 30 N–K5 | Q–N8ch |
| 31 K–R2 | Q–B4 |
| 32 Q–KN3 | |

Black resigns, as behooves a player of high caliber in an ending such as this. Botvinnik admits that he too foresees the inexorable end through Fine's R–KB3–B7 and R/6–Q7. Hopeful souls might try 32 . . . Q–N8 33 R–Q7 P–N3 34 P–R5 B–B7 35 RxR RxR 36 Q–K5 Q–R8! But White has 35 NxNP PxN 36 Q–K5!+; or if 32 . . . R–R2 33 NxP+.

Reuben Fine's sojourn in Europe bore other fruits; notably, his first marriage, to Miss Keesing, who was connected with the prominent Dutch publishing house. He later cooperated, with Hans Kmoch as editor, in setting up Keesings *Chess Archives*, which was kept up to date in Holland through 1944. The *Archives* were a loose-leaf collection of current matches and tournaments (starting with AVRO 1938), giving all games, problems, endings, and studies; combinations and brilliancies; opening lines, strategic themes, and tactical turns—all supported by an ingenious chart of symbols that might have served as a Western precedent to the later and even more condensed Yugoslav *Chess Informant*.[10]

While the clouds of war were gathering, Fine came home for good, and during the following years he may have slowly forsaken his ambitions for the championship, national or otherwise.

Probably one of the best summaries of Fine's career, based on instructive games, is his *A Passion for Chess* (New York: McKay, 1958; previously titled *Lessons from My Games*). While relaxing after his last trip to Europe, Fine wrote his piece of lasting value, the unique compendium of 580 packed pages, *Basic Chess Endings* (New York: McKay, 1941). Among further titles of lasting value from his pen is an anthology of selected games played on the domestic scene during the war, in isolation, but by no means below any international standards. Reuben Fine's *Fifty Chess Masterpieces 1941–1944* (New York: Dover, 1977) conveys an impressive picture of America's chess production during that period, and contains individual essays on general facets of chess.[11]

As previously pointed out, Fine had also been responsible for the sixth edition of *MCO* (1938), and under his own steam followed up with his manual on the openings, *Practical Chess Openings* (Philadelphia: McKay, 1948).

He never lost touch with the fine points of his avocation. He also was the unchallenged leader in speed chess, pulverizing the strongest—Denker, Helms, Horowitz, Kashdan, Kevitz, Pavey, and others. It was a legacy, both of talent and innumerable hours spent at strong "skittles"—the sure way to build the memory grooves that are more important for success than dry instruction and study.

This fact, along with his ability to visualize without view of a chessboard, enabled Fine to produce another singular first in 1945. He won four simultaneous games which he played blindfold at ten seconds per move. One game was against rapid-transit veteran Herman Helms, another one against Walter Shipman, several times Manhattan Chess Club and New York State champion. The shortest of the games, shown here, pitted Fine against future World Champion candidate R. Byrne, then only fifteen years old.

---

[10] The original *Archives* are still being continued in Germany as "Schach—Archiv," in loose leaf format, monthly.

[11] It was originally published in 1945 by *Chess Review* under the title *Chess Marches On*.

## BLINDFOLD SPEED SEANCE

New York 1945
*Queen's Pawn Game*

R. FINE        R. BYRNE

| | |
|---|---|
| 1 P–Q4 | P–Q4 |
| 2 P–K3 | N–KB3 |
| 3 N–KB3 | P–KN3!? |
| 4 B–Q3 | B–N2 |
| 5 O–O | QN–Q2 |
| 6 P–QN3 | O–O |

Black had employed an unusual defense to throw White off the beaten path and to get the better out of early complications. Actually, this method helps the blindfold player to keep the positions more distinctly apart, and early digressions from the book assist the more experienced master.

| | |
|---|---|
| 7 B–N2 | P–B4 |
| 8 QN–Q2 | P–QR3 |
| 9 Q–K2 | P–QN4 |
| 10 P–B4! | BPxP |
| 11 KPxP | NPxP |
| 12 PxP | N–N3 |
| 13 QR–N1 | N–R5? |
| 14 B–R1 | PxP |

| | |
|---|---|
| 15 NxP | B–K3 |
| 16 N/B4–K5 | P–QR4 |

White threatens to win the rook's pawn.

| | |
|---|---|
| 17 B–N5 | N–N3 |
| 18 N–B6 | Q–Q3 |
| 19 N–N5!! | B–N5? |
| 20 QxP | N–B1 |
| 21 Q–N7 | |

Black's game deteriorates suddenly, as often happens to the weaker in speed chess. 19 . . . KR–B1 would have been better, hoping for a slip on White's part. 20 QxP and 21 Q–N7 are the death blows.

| | |
|---|---|
| 21 . . . | P–R3 |
| 22 QxR | PxN |
| 23 N–K5 | B–B4 |
| 24 QR–B1 | N–K2 |
| 25 QxP | N3/B3–Q4 |
| 26 B–B4 | N–B5 |
| 27 Q–B5 | Q–Q1 |
| 28 KR–K1 | Q–R1 |
| 29 B–B1 | N/K2–Q4 |
| 30 P–B3 | R–B1 |
| 31 P–QR4 | |

And Black loses after some more wood-shifting.

A SECOND CAREER

In a way, Fine's failure to achieve a better record against Keres in the 1938 AVRO Tournament, punctuated by a slip in a superior position, may have helped his pursuit of a "respectable" (that means "more stable") livelihood. From then on, he turned his energies to a professional career, acquiring his PhD in psychology and choosing psychoanalysis as his special discipline. He subsequently branched out into running the Center for Creative Living in New York. His particular choice of occupation might be significant; to quote two passages about the nature of chess:[12]

[12] From Walter Korn, "Chess," *Encyclopaedia Britannica*, Rev. ed. 1974, Macropedia Vol. 4, pp. 195 and 204.

Chess has been likened to the logistics and conduct of war (*e.g.*, F. K. Young: *Chess Generalship*, Boston, 1910) in a somewhat inconclusive interpretation of the Chess features of attack and defense, aiming at the surrender of the opponent's King. Nevertheless, the game is only a rather limited simulation of war or, in Freudian terms, a sublimation of that aggressive impulse. More likely, the game contains elements of [Sino-] Indian symbolism and other allegories. . . .

After the turn of the 19th century, there appeared some German works on Chess written in the vein of speculative philosophy. They were followed by pamphlets of psychoanalytical precept (*e.g.*, by Reuben Fine, Ernest Jones, *et al.*), dealing also with aspects of psychosis. But the ambiguity of these concepts and their absence of true clinical diagnoses precluded reliable conclusions.

Let us reverse for a moment the role of the psychoanalyst looking at the player. In curious counteraction, the sublimation of chess could as well have become chess player Fine's sublimation of the game itself into a profession based on analysis of human motivation and behavior.

Fine's departure into psychology—just as Em. Lasker's greater preoccupation with philosophy rather than mathematics—might have provided a satisfying compromise between the commitment to a "sensible" career and a "reasonable" measure of fulfillment through chess. As Fine himself lucidly explained in his *The Psychology of the Chess Player* the chess player who has broad education and interests outside of chess, may make for a fuller personality than the one totally immersed in the game and nothing but the game.[13] The acceptance of the axiom that the highly advanced specialist of chess requires exclusive full-time dedication might spell danger; it also helps spread an illusion about its importance, being considered superior merely because it commands, or allows, such absorption.

It is difficult to see how the complexities of Oedipal and other Freudian theorems can be universally valid for the players of a game that may have sprung, three millennia ago, from the "cosmic allegories" of Sino-Indian symbolism;[14] or may abide by other elements of functional analyses.

Some of R. Fine's own preoccupation with ambivalent disclaimers of full sanity of some of the world chess champions resembled a possible alibi for his own forfeiture of the crown; but Fine could afford the critique. His disappointment might have

---

[13] A view shared by Adriaan D. De Groot and others.
[14] Professor Pavle Bidev in *FIDE Magazine*, 1964, Nos. 2 and 4; and 1965, No. 2.

stemmed from such unrealized hopes for the chess championship, and we will have a look at their roots in the next section.

## CHAMPIONSHIP: A DREAM UNFULFILLED

At the end of the war, a tendency became manifest which had been developing in the USSR since 1920: of chess as another effective ideological tool. At the conclusion of the All-Russian Chess "Olympiad," Moscow 1920 (won by Alekhine, prior to his emigration), Ilyin-Zhenevsky declared that "in this country [the USSR] where the workers have gained victory, chess cannot be apolitical as in capitalist countries."[15] He, and other political friends and chess amateurs, were also aware of the aura of intelligence which surrounded the game of chess, and thus helped universally and globally to glorify the intellectual superiority of a group that excelled in chess.

With World War II coming to an end during 1945, the succession to the world chess championship again became acute. The AVRO Tournament 1938 had established Keres' right to challenge Alekhine, and Fine's corresponding right to a contest with Keres or Alekhine, whatever was offered first. The intervening war years and their aftermath brought about some shifts in emphasis that needed a determination. Keres had been playing in some European tournaments in 1942 and 1943, but *pro tem* disappeared back into his native Estonia, soon thereafter annexed by the Soviet Union, which was sponsoring its own crop of candidates. P. Keres had narrowly lost to Botvinnik in the four-round USSR "Absolute" Championship, Moscow-Leningrad 1941 (1 loss, 3 draws), but he still was the FIDE candidate. R. Fine had been unlucky on the U.S. domestic scene. In New York in 1940 and in Hollywood in 1945, he placed 2nd, with S. Reshevsky in 1st place; and the U.S. Championship 1944 had been won by A. Denker, with Fine the runner-up. Thus A. Denker and S. Reshevsky had also become potential challengers, although proven international success and the FIDE nomination, not the vicissitudes of domestic results only, weighed heavily in Fine's favor. The other candidate entering the picture was the Soviet Union's M. Botvinnik, against whom Reuben Fine had scored 1½:½ during their last encounter at Amsterdam 1938.

At this point, challenges and match and tournament plans became shrouded in politics. Feelings were running high about Alekhine's suspected collaboration with the Germans; and American and world reaction to the evidence of death camps, as reports filtered back from the Allied armies, was one of revulsion. The

[15] D. J. Richards, *Soviet Chess* (Oxford: University Press, 1965), p. 13.

story of those days and their bearing on chess was factually, and in fresh memory, recorded and later reproduced by I. A. Horowitz and P. L. Rothenberg in *The Personality of Chess*. Another penetrating record of the political wrangle over the world championship in the years 1946–1948, and the Soviet Union's maneuvering to nail it down, may be found in R. Fine, *The World's Great Chess Games* (New York: McKay, rev. ed., 1976), pp. 223–24.

Meanwhile, the USSR, exploiting Alekhine's formal legitimacy as holder of the title, and impervious to genuine moral questions, proposed a title match Alekhine–Botvinnik to be held in Moscow. The Soviet Union was not yet a signatory to FIDE and bypassing that body, issued its invitation through the British Chess Federation in the summer of 1945. It caused a justified storm of protest by American and many European chess federations, prompting the British Chess Federation to give their precipitate mediation a second thought.

With common sense and in line with protocol, Reuben Fine suggested to hold another elimination match of six players in order to determine, or at least reaffirm, a new pretender to the crown, pending an objective clarification by FIDE of Alekhine's role and status. Fine, then still at the height of his ability, and still a great danger to other groups' aspirations, saw his and the U.S. Chess Federation's advice turned down. Shortly after, Alekhine died, and three years elapsed before the vacuum was filled in an orderly manner, in 1948. But Fine, who could not afford the considerable loss in his professional income (his appeal to the USCF to contribute was turned down), did not participate . . . "and [Fine] again lost another tangible and justified chance." (J. Silbermann and W. Unzicker, *Geschichte des Schachs* Munich: Bertelsmann, 1975, p. 208.)

These facts are worth recalling in the light of an aggressive rewrite of history attempted by A. Kotov in *Alexander Alekhine* (London: Batsford, 1975; New York: RHM, 1975). Kotov's book is an abbreviated translation of the 1955–58 Russian and German edition, but the later version specifically contains an added chapter "The War and Chess." This chapter unabashedly spreads Kotov's attack that "certain over-active members [of the USCF]—R. Fine, A. Denker and others . . .[16] tried to starve Alekhine to death, and for various suspicious reasons"; and that "the complaisant organizers . . . in England . . . decided not to spoil relations with the all-powerful 'Yankees' and it was the poor champion who had to

[16] In his memoirs, Kotov pokes unmitigated fun on Reshevsky's Jewish orthodoxy. Kotov has an individual minus score against Reshevsky, and lost 1½:½ against I. Kashdan on board five in the U.S.–USSR match in 1946.

lose. . . ." While Kotov ignores Alekhine's disparaging comments about the Soviets and that Alekhine played chess in Central Europe while France, and large parts of Russia, were under German occupation, he also deplores that the transfer of Alekhine's body to Moscow was blocked by his American widow Grace Wishaar. Thanks to her intercession, Alekhine's grave has since remained in Paris, accessible to all.

## THE ECLECTIC SCHOOL

Fine, Kashdan, and their contemporaries were called Pragmatists, who tenaciously extended any small advantage once achieved; and then drily wound up the game by mere technique learned from Capablanca. These simplifications give no credit to the considerable merits of their own style. Their generation did away with the false luster of preconceived theories searching for ultimate truths. They had absorbed the brilliance of the speculative and romantic schools and surely employed it against the rare slips of their equally sophisticated opponents. They had digested the novel strategies of the Hypermoderns and moulded their findings, Capa's technique, Tarrasch's and Steinitz's methodologies, and Lasker's subjectivity into a frame of fearsome efficiency. They were awesomely practical and versed in all facets of Caïssa's gift.[17] But even the strongest met with some stumbling blocks; e.g., with Arnold Denker.

ARNOLD DENKER (b. 1914) rose to the top of the domestic arena when he secured 1st prize and the U.S. Championship at New York 1944. He beat Reuben Fine in their individual and decisive encounter. Denker—which in German means "the thinker"—was a master of the whirlwind attack and the rapid mop-up. As a man, he was direct, impetuous, and outspoken.

He was fifteen when he won a brilliancy prize for a Manhattan Chess Club tournament game in 1929, against S. Feit. Denker butchered his opponent in twenty-three moves in a game which was included in all the bedside books on brilliancies by Chernev, Reinfeld, K. Richter (Germany), and many others.[18]

Denker was fearsome because of his uninhibited treatment, whoever his adversary, and because of his lightning strokes that punished a careless opponent. He did not have the patience to make it into the top class, but the following game was a crucial "spoiler,"

[17] Caïssa, the Muse, or Dryad, or Deity of Chess, as invented by the British orientalist Sir William Jones in a poem on chess (1763).
[18] Irving Chernev's collection is *1000 Best Short Games of Chess* (New York: Simon & Schuster, 1955).

with an agonizing effect on his victim. Fine expected to usurp this championship, with Reshevsky absent and eighteen participants of less caliber participating (or at least they were not of the caliber to deny him a steady momentum). When this game was played in the 7th round, Fine was 2nd in the lead, ½ point behind Denker, who also appeared to be in the best of form. Hence, Fine played for a win—sharp, taking risks, but allowing Denker just the kind of position he excelled in, and Denker had the "Indian Sign" on Fine.

## U.S. CHAMPIONSHIP

### New York 1944
*Nimzo-Indian Defense*

A. DENKER                           R. FINE

| 1 | P–Q4 | N–KB3 |
|---|------|-------|
| 2 | P–QB4 | P–K3 |
| 3 | N–QB3 | B–N5 |
| 4 | P–K3 | P–QN3 |
| 5 | B–Q3 | B–N2 |

Forceful is also 5 . . . P–B4 6 N–B3 O–O 7 P–Q5! P–QN4!

| 6 | N–B3 | N–K5 |
|---|------|------|
| 7 | O–O |  |

Offering a pawn for a strong attack which is difficult to meet; e.g., 7 . . . BxN 8 PxB NxQBP 9 Q–B2 BxN 10 PxB Q–N4ch 11 K–R1 Q–KR4 12 R–KN1 QxBPch 13 R–N2 P–KB4 14 B–N2 N–K5 15 R–KB1 N–QB3 16 B–K2 Q–R6 17 P–Q5 N–K2 18 RxP R–KN1, and the game will level out. But Fine wants to force a win, otherwise he should have played 7 . . . P–KB4. In terms of theory, this game was a first.

| 7 | . . . | NxN |
|---|-------|-----|
| 8 | PxN | BxP |
| 9 | R–N1 | B–R4 |
| 10 | B–R3 | P–Q3 |

| 11 | P–B5!! | O–O |
|----|--------|-----|
| 12 | PxQP | PxP |
| 13 | P–K4 | R–K1 |
| 14 | P–K5 | PxP |
| 15 | NxP |  |

If now 15 . . . N–B3 16 BxPch! KxB 17 Q–R5ch K–N1 18 QxPch, followed by 19 R–N3 winning; and if 15 . . . P–KR3 16 Q–R5 Q–B3 17 NxP.

| 15 . . . | Q–N4 |
|----------|------|

Generally accepted as the losing move, but a consortium of commentators has come to the conclusion that also Fine's suggested 15 . . . P–N3 does not save the game after 16 B–N5 Q–Q4, although it might retard the loss. The remainder of the game is given without notes:

| 16 | P–N3 | P–N3 |
|----|------|------|
| 17 | Q–R4! | Q–Q1 |
| 18 | K2–QB1 | P–QN4 |
| 19 | BxQNP | Q–Q4 |
| 20 | P–B3 | B–N3 |
| 21 | R–B5 | BxR |
| 22 | BxB | R–KB1 |
| 23 | B–B4 | B–B3 |
| 24 | BxQ | BxQ |
| 25 | BxQR | Resigns |

Painful.

In the 1948 New York International, Fine made it to 1st place (8 points) against such elite as Najdorf 6½, Euwe 5, Pilnick 5, Horowitz 4½, Kramer 4½, Bisguier 4, and Kashdan 4. Denker was in 9th place (2) and H. Steiner last (1½). That was Fine's last but one "official" U.S. performance. The same event in 1951 pushed him back to 4th place. After that, he no longer actively and earnestly participated in public or competed in professional contests.

The puzzle remains, whether Reuben Fine had been discouragingly deprived of a legitimate, supreme, role for America in World Chess.

# 9.

# The War Years and After

## THE SUPERPOWERS NAME THE GAME

The FIDE motto *gens una sumus*—meaning that players are united by the common bond of chess—often has meant "no holds barred," with many an occasion for an inter- and intranational *casus belli*. Out of once simple beginnings have mushroomed elaborate Laws of Chess, Tournament Rules and Regulations, and a separate enforcing body of functionaries who are often steeped less in chess than in legal maneuvering.

The U.S.–USSR team matches, by radio in 1945 and face to face in 1946, 1954, and 1955, provided evidence of the USSR's successful use of chess as a massively expanding weapon; while the encounters were individual, the game proved to be merely another instrument in the Soviet cultural-political struggle.

Although the Yugoslavs have been in part dissidents as far as interpretation of a political ideology is involved, they adopted the same attitude toward chess as did Moscow. They used their more strategic location in Central Europe to mold chess into a strong and profitable tool for literary penetration into both the East and the West. Their effort was helped by their adoption of both Cyrillic and Latin lettering in their orthography. It aided their publishing industry and, under cover of chess, the free movement of East European reporters, ideologists, and players throughout the West and the United States. Along with increasing prestige and promotion, it created a disadvantage to American chess authors' competitive position vis-à-vis their own publishers. This situation was aggravated when mass-produced, inexpensively translated chess texts poured into the United States via foreign countries, undermining the American producers' cost-estimates for worthwhile chess books, and harming the prospects for, and authors of, original American texts.

Other complications arose, in technical respects: under the banner of unification, a drive was launched by the World Chess Federation to adopt Europe's algebraic notation as the universal official chess language, thus devaluating the picturesque tradition of the English and Spanish descriptive notation with its own functional merits; the intensification of European contests, subject to increased regulatory demands within Europe's mutually more accessible spheres, created obstacles to fruitful American participation in foreign events and to American competition for International titles.

However, these developments did not deter strong new cadres of players from arising in the United States and letting the future assess their national and international impact. For the moment, it was the hobby that took charge, over and above any regulations.

## THE NEW GENERATION

After World War II, the two leading proponents in the United States were Arthur Bisguier and Larry Evans. Both became chess professionals. They were soon after joined by Robert Byrne and William Lombardy. All four of them became grandmasters.

Bisguier's and Evans' tournament performance was somewhat uneven. Always landing near the very top (except when affected by indispositions, which are a legitimate factor with humans), they somehow lacked the combination of consistent punch and weight that opens the road to the chess world's top. Nevertheless, they were an ever-present danger to opponents of any strength, and reliable pillars in all important national and foreign events.

### ARTHUR BISGUIER

Arthur Bisguier (b. 1929), a rotund and affable man, finished in 1st place, just a notch ahead of Evans, in the U.S. Championship 1954, and in the strong Rosenwald Tourney, New York 1955. But he was more at home with the gyrations of U.S. Open Tournaments, which he topped in 1950, 1956, and 1959. While he dubbed himself a classicist (in these days an innovation), he was not adverse to trying the novel and unusual—and he sometimes suffered the consequences. He became active in the domestic organization of chess, and authored a few books; e.g. (with A. Soltis), *American Chess Masters* (New York: Macmillan 1974).

The following crystal-clear brevity was inflicted in classical style upon Bent Larsen, a formidable member of the upper chess fraternity for many years. Larsen committed one innocent slip—an unfavorable transposition of moves in an otherwise equalizing sequence —which was promptly exposed as such by White. One inaccurate move (12th), and Black is crushed even before the 20th move.

### Zagreb, Yugoslavia 1965
*(Pirć-) Robatsch Defense*

A. BISGUIER      B. LARSEN

| | |
|---|---|
| 1 P–Q4 | P–KN3 |

A dexterous defense which can be sprung against almost any White opening move. It was widely popularized by the Austrian master Karl Robatsch, with the idea of giving Black's KN the alternative of moving to . . . K2 or even to . . . R3; as different from *1* P–Q4 P–Q3 2 P–K4 N–KB3 (the Pirć Defense proper) 3 N–QB3 P–KN3.

The Pirć Defense, on the other hand, forces White to move out his QN before he has been able to play P–QB4, whereas the Robatsch leaves White the choice of a three-pawn or four-pawn attack first (P–QB4 and/or P–KB4), with the knights to be posted behind instead of in front of the respective pawns—just to give a few pointers in an otherwise very flexible treatment.

Larsen had a predilection for early fianchettoes and often answered . . . P–QN3, or, when White, played *1* P–QN3.

| | |
|---|---|
| 2 P–K4 | B–N2 |
| 3 P–KB4 | |

Two different knight moves can be played here, both disregarding a BP or KP push; i.e., (a) *3* N–KB3 N–KB3 4 N–B3 P–Q3 5 B–K2 O–O 6 O–O P–B3! 7 P–KR3 P–QN4 8 P–K5 N–K1 9 B–KB4 B–N2 *10* Q–Q2!! N–Q2 *11* KR–Q1 N–N3= (Diesen–Rohde, U.S. Jr. Championship 1976); or (b) *3* N–QB3 P–QB3 4 B–QB4 P–Q3 5 Q–K2 P–QN4 6 NxP P–Q4 7 B–B4 N–QR3 8 PxP PxN 9 BxPch K–B1, with promising ideas on both sides (Regan–Soltis, 7th USCF International Tournament, New York 1977).

| | |
|---|---|
| 3 . . . | P–Q3 |
| 4 N–KB3 | N–KB3 |
| 5 B–Q3! | O–O |
| 6 O–O | |

For 6 N–B3 see notes to Byrne–Korchnoi, p. 189.

| | |
|---|---|
| 6 . . . | QN–Q2? |

Too passive. Black should have generated some initiative here, perhaps with 6 . . . N–B3! White may reply with another strategic device available to him as long as N–QB3 is not on the board; namely, the underpinning with 7 P–B3. The game might then continue something like 7 . . . B–N5 8 QN–Q2 P–K4!

## 7 P–K5!

This prevents for good the thematic counterthrust 7 ... P–K4, and White consequently storms Black's hedgehog defense.

| 7 ... | N–K1 |
|---|---|
| 8 Q–K1 | P–QB4 |
| 9 P–B5! | |

White already has a variety of choices and picks a sacrificial but apparently incisive one. 9 P–B4 P–K3 would uphold Black's strategy. Better is 9 P–K6 PxP 10 N–N5 N–B2 11 Q–R4 N–B3 12 PxP PxP, and White commands more space.

| 9 ... | PxKP |
|---|---|
| 10 PxNP! | RPxP |
| 11 Q–R4 | KPxP |

Wins a pawn, but allows all White pieces to enter the fray rapidly. White's next move removes Black's strong bishop.

## 12 B–KR6

Black is two pawns up but very restricted in his maneuvers. Will White be able to capitalize?

| 12 ... | N/1–B3? |
|---|---|

He already does. Black wants to keep the option ... N–K4, but he had better defensive chances after 12 ... N/2–B3. Of course, 13 N–N5 Q–B2 14 N–Q2 B–B4 15 BxB gives White a strong attack. Nevertheless, the text does not help. If 12 ... BxB 13 QxB N/2–B3 14 N–Q2 B–B4 15 R–KB1!

## 13 N–N5          N–K4

Played to remove White's bishop. If 13 ... N–R4 14 BxB KxB 15 RxPch!! RxR 16 N–K6ch, winning the queen. Another reason why 12 ... N/2–B3 was mandatory.

## 14 RxN!          B–R1

A desperate though subtle defense. If 14 ... BxR 15 B–N7 wins and if 14 ... PxR 15 BxB wins. If 14 ... N–N5 15 BxB KxB 16 RxBPch! RxR 17 Q–R7ch K–B3 18 NxR, with mate or capture of Black's queen. After Black's last move, 15 B–N7 is answered 15 ... KxB 16 Q–R7ch KxR and Black escapes.

| 15 R–B1! | R–K1 |
|---|---|
| 16 B–B8! | |

An aesthetic delight. It clears the line for White's renewed threat of mate, and if Black captures the bishop, he blocks his own escape square.

| 16 ... | B–B3 |
|---|---|
| 17 RxB! | PxR |
| 18 Q–R6! | |

The self-block remains in place and if 18 ... PxN 19 Q–N7 mate. Black resigned. This simple miniature illustrates the swift punishment grandmasters can mete out even against each other for the slightest slip.

LARRY M. EVANS

Larry M. Evans (b. 1932), three years younger than Bisguier, showed solid staying power over a prolonged period.[1] His style differed greatly from Bisguier's. Evans was a tenacious and tricky defender who struck out when cornered, and often turned the tables in his favor when least expected. To retain spirit in adversity is a requisite of grandmastership. Hence, Evans was difficult to beat even when Black, although he felt uncomfortable in transparent positions.

At the age of nineteen, in 1951, Evans won the U.S. Open Championship at Fort Worth, Texas, and several times thereafter. In the same year he defeated Reshevsky in the formal U.S. Championship, the man with whom he and Bisguier kept a running battle. The victory was all the more important since Reshevsky usually bested both. In 1954, Evans beat Taimanov 2½:1½ in the U.S.–USSR match in New York; and during the 1950, 1952, and 1958 Olympics, he attained a high percentage on his respective board (Bisguier also participated). In 1956, Evans went on a goodwill chess tour to Europe, sponsored—as an exception—by the U.S. Department of State. In the 1961–62 U.S. Championship, Evans again came 1st, ahead of R. Byrne, but Bisguier, Fischer, and Reshevsky did not compete. In 1963–64 and in 1966–67, he was runner-up to Fischer, who placed 1st. As late as 1968 Evans again secured the U.S. Championship, with 8½ points, ahead of R. Byrne 8, Reshevsky 7, Benko 6½, Lombardy 6, Bisguier 6, Rossolimo 5½, Saidy 5½, Zuckerman 5½, and Horowitz 4—aside from Fischer, the best gathering of American chess players. As late as 1975, Evans came 2nd in the 5th Annual Louis D. Statham Masters-Plus Tournament at Lone Pine, California, which was attended by twenty-two international masters and grandmasters. At the end of the same year he secured 1st prize in Portimao, Portugal.

Evans devoted himself to full-time journalism, directing a syndicated chess column and authoring a number of books. He also may claim credit for his consultancy on Fischer's *My 60 Best Games of Chess* and for the revision of the 10th edition of *MCO*. Evans is a fast, clear writer with an adaptable prose, and chess has served as a good vehicle for his literary aspirations. Another one of his talents is writing scripts for stage or screen, including some with devious plots! For a while he concentrated on trying to beat the odds and the bankers at the casinos of Nevada, where he was domiciled.

---

[1] Evans is not to be confused with Captain W. D. Evans (b. 1790), whose lasting but only legacy was the Evans Gambit. There also emerged in the 1970s a young American master named Larry D. Evans.

In the game shown here, Evans' opponent, B. Zuckerman, a strong international master, takes chances—and pays for them.

## U.S. CHAMPIONSHIP

**New York 1966–67**
*Sicilian Defense*

| L. EVANS | B. ZUCKERMAN |
|---|---|
| 1 P–K4 | P–QB4 |
| 2 N–KB3 | P–Q3 |
| 3 P–Q4 | PxP |
| 4 NxP | N–KB3 |
| 5 N–QB3 | P–KN3 |
| 6 B–K3 | |

The preferred continuation as against 6 P–B4 N–B3! or 6 B–K2 N–B3! The text has independent value as an introduction to the Yugoslav Attack, 7 P–B3, etc., as shown in the further course of the game.

| 6 . . . | N–B3 |
|---|---|
| 7 P–B3 | B–N2 |
| 8 Q–Q2 | O–O |
| 9 O–O–O | |

Modern routine is 9 B–QB4 B–Q2 10 P–KR4 R–B1 11 B–N3 N–K4 12 O–O–O N–B5 13 BxN RxB 14 P–R5 NxRP 15 P–KN4 N–B3 16 N/4–K2 Q–R4 17 B–R6 BxB 18 QxB KR–B1 19 R–Q3! (Karpov–Korchnoi 1974). 9 B–QB4 posts the bishop on the most useful square and prevents . . . P–Q4; it also adds a piece to White's queen-side defense and creates the smooth unfolding of White's attack on the king-side.

For further elaborations and sidelines, compare with the game Grefe–Tarjan, El Paso 1973, p. 259.

| 9 . . . | NxN |
|---|---|
| 10 BxN | B–K3 |
| 11 K–N1 | Q–B2 |

Bad is at once 11 . . . Q–R4 12 N–Q5, but useful is 11 . . . P–QR3 12 P–KR4 P–QN4 13 P–R5 P–N5 14 N–Q5 BxN 15 PxB Q–R4 16 B–B4 KR–B1 17 B–N3 Q–N4 18 P–N4 P–R4, and White's attack is at a standstill.

| 12 P–KR4 | KR–B1 |
|---|---|
| 13 P–R5 | NxP? |

In this particular case, the capture is risky and unnecessary. Right was 13 . . . Q–R4 14 PxP (14 N–Q5 QxQ 15 NxPch? K–B1) RPxP 15 P–R3 QR–N1 16 Q–B4 Q–B2 17 P–K5 N–Q4! In a later game between the same opponents, during the U.S. Championship 1969, White chose 16 P–KN4 P–QN4 17 N–Q5 QxQ 18 RxQ NxN 19 PxN BxQP 20 BxB BxP=. Lastly, if 16 BxN BxB 17 N–Q5 QxQ 18 NxBch K–N2!=.

| 14 BxB | KxB |
|---|---|
| 15 P–KN4 | N–B3 |
| 16 Q–R6ch | K–N1 |
| 17 P–K5 | |

The decisive line clearance for White's bishop.

| 17 . . . | PxP |
| 18 P–N5 | N–R4 |
| 19 B–Q3 | P–K5 |

White's threat was 20 RxN. Black's reply clears the square for . . . Q–K4 and . . . Q–N2. If 19 . . . P–B4 20 RxN PxR 21 QxBch K–R1 22 QxBP!

| 20 RxN! | PxR |
| 21 NxP | |

Black has no defense after 21 BxP Q–K4 22 BxPch K–R1 23 B–K4ch K–N1 24 BxP KR–N1 25 BxR QxN 26 R–Q8ch

either, but the text is intuitively more elegant, mobilizing the knight for sacrifice.

| 21 . . . | Q–KB4 |

If 21 . . . Q–K4 22 N–B6ch PxN 23 PxP Q–N6 24 BxPch K–R1 25 B–N6ch! This finale echoes the one in the game.

| 22 N–B6ch | PxN |
| 23 BxPch | K–R1 |
| 24 B–B5ch | K–N1 |
| 25 Q–R7ch | K–B1 |
| 26 Q–R8ch | K–K2 |
| 27 PxP mate | |

ROBERT BYRNE

Robert Byrne became an international master in 1952, but matured into grandmastership at a much later date, 1964, after he decided to leave the academic field and devote full time to chess. "Retiring" from a tenured career full of academic politics, he retained the prestige of his former career and maintained the aura of scholastic righteousness, with its tensions, idiosyncrasies, and also its methodical precision. In Fall 1972, Byrne succeeded Horowitz as the chess columnist of the *New York Times* and has since then conducted the column in a crisp, orderly, and very aloof fashion. His writing and playing style were very deliberate, although this disposition can carry the danger of rigidly following a preconceived principle, perhaps missing a strategic or technical change at crucial moments. (This rigidity, incidentally, was one of the weaknesses of Nimzowitsch, the author of *My System* and *The Blockade,* and one of Byrne's patron saints.) Apparently the three-times-a-week regularity of meeting a columnist's deadline fitted Byrne's measured composure. The substance was almost exclusively dedicated to masterplay and analysis, but any dryness was happily broken by the columnist's knack for both humorous and sophisticated headlines. This has provided some variety amid the monotony: Chess is not just grandmaster play and high-grade analysis of only a few sectors chosen from a whole framework of theory; it has many aspects of humanity, as had been perceived in predecessor Horowitz's selections. But Byrne's column is solid, competent and a frequent "eyewitness report."

Byrne's slow tempo of maturing and his careful dosage seem to have contributed to a steady growth of, and stability in, his playing strength. In 1964 he made it to grandmastership. Withstanding the rigors of the Leningrad Interzonal 1973, he attained 3rd place and thus qualified for a subsequent World Championship candidates' elimination match against former World Champion Spassky.

Our first specimen of Byrne's games is from the 17th U.S. Championship 1965–66, which resulted in: Fischer 8½, R. Byrne and Reshevsky 7½ each, Addison and Zuckerman 6½ each, Rossolimo 6, Benko, Evans, and Saidy 5 each. It was rated as a Zonal tournament and enabled Byrne, together with Fischer, to join the chess elite at Sousse 1967.

### U.S. CHAMPIONSHIP

#### New York 1965–66
*Sicilian Defense*

R. BYRNE          L. EVANS

| 1 | P–K4 | P–QB4 |
|---|------|-------|
| 2 | N–KB3 | P–Q3 |
| 3 | P–Q4 | PxP |
| 4 | NxP | N–KB3 |
| 5 | N–QB3 | P–QR3 |

The aforementioned game Evans–Zuckerman used the Dragon, whereas Black's choice here invites the Najdorf Variation.

#### 6 B–KN5     P–K3

Obviously, 6 . . . P–KN3 is out, but 6 . . . QN–Q2 retains the possibility of a later . . . P–KN3, and also the option . . . P–K4; but it is under a cloud because of 7 B–QB4 Q–R4 8 Q–Q2 P–K3 9 O–O–O P–N4 10 B–N3! B–N2 11 KR–K1± (*MCO*, 11th ed.).

#### 7 P–B4     Q–N3

Sharp is 7 . . . B–K2 8 Q–B3 Q–B2 as in Timman–Kavalek,

shown on p. 250; or 8 . . . P–R3 9 B–R4 P–KN4 10 PxP KN–Q2 11 NxP! PxN 12 Q–R5ch K–B1! 13 B–QN5 R–R2!! But the definitive game with this line, Gligoric–Fischer, Portorož 1958, ended in a draw.

After 7 . . . Q–N3 8 N–N3, White's game maintains a healthy complexion, but one of the later preferences was 7 . . . P–N4 8 P–K5 PxP 9 PxP Q–B2! 10 Q–Q2 QN–Q2 or 10 PxN Q–K4ch=. The forthcoming "poisoned pawn" sacrifice offers a conduit for the queen's rook to exert pressure on the vertical, after attacking Black's queen by R–QN1.

#### 8 Q–Q2     QxN
#### 9 R–QN1

All this move does now is force Black's queen back on a good defensive square from which it can quickly return into Black's center. More sustaining is 9 N–N3! N–B3 10 BxN PxB 11 N–R4 Q–R6 12 N–N6 R–QN1 13 N–B4 Q–R5 14 K–B2 P–

B4 (as in Timman–H. Olafsson, Reykjavik 1976); or 9 . . . QN–Q2 10 BxN PxB 11 B–K2 N–B4 12 O–O B–Q2=; or 9 . . . Q–R6 10 BxN PxB 11 B–K2 N–B3 12 O–O B–Q2 13 P–B5 N–K4 14 PxP PxP 15 B–R5ch K–Q1= (Tal–Portisch, Varese 1976).

| 9 . . . | Q–R6 |
| 10 P–K5 | PxP |

Not 10 . . . KN–Q2 11 P–B5 NxP 12 PxP PxP 13 B–K2 N–B3 14 NxN PxN 15 N–K4! P–Q4 16 O–O Q–R4 17 B–R5ch K–Q2 18 RxB resigns (Keres–Fuderer, Goeteborg 1955).

| 11 PxP | KN–Q2 |
| 12 B–QB4 | B–N5 |

When this game occurred, 12 . . . B–K2 had been discarded as a dead end; e.g., 13 BxP O–O 14 O–O BxB 15 QxB P–R3! 16 Q–R5 PxB (16 . . . QxN 17 RxP!±) 17 NxP RxRch 18 RxR Q–K2 19 Q–B5 N–N3 20 Q–B8ch±.

| 13 R–N3 | Q–R4 |
| 14 O–O | O–O |

Quite a position. 14 P–QR3 QxPch (or deflecting Black's bishop and queen with 14 . . . BxP 15 RxB QxR 16 O–O NxP 17 Q–B4 QN–Q2) 15 K–Q1 BxN 16 RxB P–R3 may stand further experimentation.

In the game's position, Black was believed to have the edge after White finally carried out the tactical plan inherent in his

whole formation: 15 NxP!? PxN 16 BxPch K–R1 17 RxRch BxR 18 Q–B4 N–QB3 19 Q–B7 N–B3 20 BxB NxP 21 Q–K6 N–N5! and White resigned (Tringov–Fischer, Havana 1965). But ardent analyst Robert Byrne burned some midnight oil and came up with a different idea. It had the element of surprise, and if there was a hole in the idea, he must have not seen it, else he would rather have refrained than risked.

### 15 B–B6!!?

A bombshell which rapidly mobilizes all of White's men for attack, including the queen's rook after N–K4.

| 15 . . . | PxB |

After 15 . . . NxP, White again would have deflected Black's forces by 16 RxB QxR 17 BxN QxB 18 BxP KxB 19 Q–N5ch K–R1 20 Q–B6ch K–N1 21 R–B4 P–K4 22 N–B5 BxN 23 RxQ B–K3 24 N–K5 and wins. However, under the shock of

White's 15th move, Evans' resistance gave way, and he missed what was probably his first and last chance to retaliate, at least somehow. He may have been overconfident because he did not reckon with Byrne's powerful follow-up on move 16.

A dialogue of comments in *Chess Life*, 1966, by Evans in the January and Byrne in the March issue, deals with Black's improvement 15 . . . NxB! 16 PxN R–Q1; Byrne concedes that after 17 RxB (best!) QxR 18 Q–N5 P–KN3 19 N–K4 or 19 R–B4, "White has a dangerous attack," but that "Black is not without further defensive resources." The statement sounds contradictory, as 19 N–K4 RxN is hardly good for White, whereas 19 R–B4 P–N4 20 B any RxN; or 20 KNxNP PxN 21 BxNP QxN 22 Q–R6 Q–B5ch; or 19 . . . RxN 20 Q–R6 Q–B1 21 QxQch KxQ 22 RxR N–B3 might work out in Black's favor.

As it happened, Byrne stuck to his guns against Zuckerman, New York 1967, playing 19 R–B4; and after 19 . . . RxN 20 Q–R6 Q–B1 21 QxQch KxQ 22 RxR N–B3, instead of playing 23 R–Q6, he might have proven his point with 23 R–R4 K–N1 24 N–K4 with pressure.

**16 Q–R6!!**

This is the blow unforeseen by Black. He had expected 16 PxP K–R1 17 Q–R6 R–N1 and White has a harder task making

up for his material deficit. As shown later by A. O'Kelly, White also wins by 18 B–Q3 N–B1 19 N–B3 BxN 20 RxB QxR 21 P–KR4!

With the text, White intends 17 N–Q5 and 18 R–N3. Right after the game began circulating, Hans Johner proposed 16 . . . BxN 17 R–B4 BxNch 18 RxB Q–K1ch, or 17 PxP NxP 18 QxN N–Q2—but it was all academic! Byrne's own brilliant plan was to answer 16 . . . BxN with 17 B–Q3! BxNch 18 K–R1 P–B4 19 BxP PxB 20 R–N3ch K–R1 21 Q–N7 mate.

**16 . . .          QxKP**

If 16 . . . NxP 17 N–K4! Evans noted that after 16 . . . Q–B4 17 B–Q3 QxNch 18 K–R1 P–B4 19 RxP QxB, "Black may be able to survive"; but 20 R–N5ch Q–N3 21 N–K4 K–R1 22 RxQ PxR 23 R–KB3, or possibly 17 R–B4, puts an end to analytical shadowboxing. Nevertheless, Black tenaciously fights back against all odds for another twenty moves.

**17 N–B5!**

Blocking . . . P–B4 with access for Black's queen to . . . B3.

**17 . . .          PxN**
**18 N–K4!!**

Hammerblows follow one another. As has been inherent in the whole opening strategy, this move clears the rank for R–KR3 (or R–N3).

If *18* . . . QxN *19* R–N3ch Q–N5 *20* RxQch PxR *21* B–Q3 P–B4 *22* BxBP N–KB3 *23* Q–N5ch K–R1 *24* QxNch K–N1 *25* BxPch! KxB *26* Q–R4ch K–N1 *27* Q–N5ch K–R1 *28* R–B6++. If *18* . . . R–K1 *19* R–KR3 R–K3 (Evans quoted *19* . . . N–B1 *20* NxPch QxN *21* QxQ B–K3 *22* BxB PxB *23* R–N3ch with equality, but *23* RxB leaves Black with only two knights versus queen) *20* BxR PxB *21* QxPch K–B1 *22* Q–R8ch K–K2 *23* R–R7 mate. If *18* . . . P–B5 *19* RxP P–B4 *20* R–N3ch K–R1 *21* QxPch KxQ *22* R–R4 mate. No better would be *18* . . . R–K1 *19* R–KR3 N–B1 *20* NxPch QxN *21* QxQ B–K3 *22* BxB±.

Thus, Evans picks the only available detour.

| 18 . . . | B–Q7?! |
|---|---|
| 19 NxB | Q–Q5ch |
| 20 K–R1 | N–K4 |
| 21 R–N3ch | N–N5 |

Black has been able to regroup, thus gaining some respite. No game has ever been won or drawn by precipitate resigna-tion. If *21* . . . N–N3 *22* R–KR3 wins.

| 22 P–KR3 | Q–K4 |
|---|---|
| 23 R–B4 | Q–K8ch |
| 24 N–B1 | QxR |
| 25 RxNch | QxR |

If *25* . . . PxR *26* NxQ and *27* N–R5 wins. Black has reduced the forces by useful exchanges and has two rooks for the queen; but the threat N–N3–R5 still prevails.

| 26 PxQ | N–Q2 |
|---|---|
| 27 N–N3 | K–R1 |
| 28 B–Q3 | R–KN1 |

Quicker is *28* NxP R–KN1 *29* BxP RxP *30* B–K8.

| 29 BxBP | R–N3 |
|---|---|
| 30 BxR | PxB |
| 31 N–K4 | P–QN4 |
| 32 P–N5 | B–N2 |
| 33 NxP | N–B1 |

Byrne castigates himself for omitting *33* PxP R–KN1 *34* N–N5 NxP *35* N–B7 mate, but whatever he plays, he must win.

| 34 Q–R2! | B–B1 |
|---|---|
| 35 Q–K5 | N–K3 |
| 36 N–Q7ch | Resigns |

In their chess annotations, Byrne's and Evans' comments gen-erally stood out for their critical objectivity. One is therefore struck by the conflicting claims, counterclaims and rebuttals as offered by such masters as Byrne and Evans themselves, and by Johner, O'Kelly, and others not mentioned here. It goes to show that even with the intense concentration that masters devote in good faith to analysis over the board or thereafter, an infinite number of variants and permutations can get the better of them. One easily sees and comments on what one wants to, and not necessarily on what there is. An element of transcendental existentialism is inherent in these battles and, via brilliancy and blunder, with the forces initially even, it is the psychological shock effect that counts.

Hence, Byrne showed independent shrewdness by unsettling his enemy with an opening line that was under a cloud because of Fischer's (as Black) earlier victory over Tringov.

Possibly, Byrne's success at the Leningrad Interzonal in 1973, combined with his role at the *New York Times* and its subsidiaries, secured him one of the rare invitations extended to Western masters—in this case, to the Alekhine Memorial Tourney, Moscow 1975. He placed only 11th (with 6 points), but in a very strong field of sixteen contestants, scoring victories over some of the strongest, among them Victor Korchnoi, who the year before had suffered his cruel and disheartening loss to Karpov.

Byrne summoned boldness in cutting endless entangled opening analyses to the bone.

### ALEKHINE MEMORIAL TOURNAMENT

#### Moscow 1975
*Pirc Defense*

| R. BYRNE | V. KORCHNOI |
|---|---|
| 1 P–K4 | P–Q3 |
| 2 P–Q4 | N–KB3 |
| 3 N–QB3 | P–KN3 |
| 4 P–B4 | B–N2 |
| 5 N–B3 | O–O |
| 6 B–Q3 | B–N5 |

Hardly the best move (although Korchnoi may have had some novelty in store)—had the game taken its normal theoretical course according to book. But if so, then White's 10th move foiled it.

Altogether, the Pirc Defense is difficult even after the alternative 6 . . . N–B3 7 P–K5 PxP 8 QPxP N–Q4 9 B–Q2! N/4–N5 10 B–K4 B–B4. But there is no end to new discoveries, for instance, Tal's "new" (1974) move 6 . . . N–R3! Ultimately, this is best followed by 7 P–K5 (7 O–O P–B4 8 PxP NxP) N–Q2 8 N–K4 P–QB4, dissolving all tension, as pushing with 9 P–K6 PxKP 10 N/4–N5 N–B3 11 N–R4 N–QN5 or even 10 . . . R–B3 holds everything.

| 7 P–KR3 | BxN |
|---|---|
| 8 QxB | N–B3 |
| 9 B–K3 | N–Q2 |

No particular advantage accrues from 9 . . . P–K4 10 QPxP PxP 11 P–B5 N–Q5! 12 Q–B2 PxP 13 PxP P–N4 14 O–O P–B4 15 N–K4! After 9 . . . N–Q2, the established routine was 10 Q–B2, followed by either 10 . . . N–N5 or 10 . . . P–K4!—the standard liberating move in this system. But Byrne very simply and logically nips that pawn push in the bud.

**10 P–K4!    N–N5**

If *10 . . .* PxP *11* QPxP N–N5
*12* O–O–O P–QB3 *13* B–B4.

**11 O–O–O!**

Elementary. *11* QxP NxBch *12*
PxN R–N1 *13* QxRP RxP
favors Black.

**11 . . .          P–QB4**

*11 . . .* NxBch *12* RxN P–QB3
*13* P–KR4 would unleash a decisive king-side attack.

**12 PxBP          Q–R4**

*12 . . .* PxKP *13* B–N5 N–QB3
*14* BxN PxB *15* QxP±.

**13 BPxP          PxP**
**14 P–QR3          PxP**

Either *14 . . .* NxBP *15* RxN
N–N3 *16* BxN QxB *17* RxP, or
*14 . . .* N–QB3 *15* B–K4 loses
Black a pawn (R. Byrne).

| 15 | PxN | Q–R8ch |
| 16 | K–Q2 | QxP |
| 17 | N–Q5! | PxP |
| 18 | QxP | QR–Q1 |
| 19 | R–QN1 | Q–K4 |

If *19 . . .* Q–R7 *20* B–B4 Q–R6
*21* R–N3 Q–R5 *22* B–Q4 N–
N3 *23* NxN PxB *24* R–Q3±.

| 20 | QxQ | NxQ |
| 21 | N–B4 | KR–K1 |
| 22 | B–B2 | P–QR3 |
| 23 | KR–KB1 | |

White, a piece up, wins in another sixteen moves.

Byrne continued as one of the United States' consistently stable
chess delegates. After a slow start, he worked his way up to sharing
3rd–4th prize with grandmaster Huebner at Las Palmas 1976 (Geller
and Larsen 10 points each; Byrne and Huebner 9½ each; Portisch,
Gheorghiu, and Tseshkovsky 9 each; Sigurjonsson 8½; Rogoff of
the United States 8; with eight more strong players to follow—altogether sixteen entrants). In January 1976, Byrne had placed first
at Torremolinos, Spain, with Larry Christiansen of California coming 2nd with 9 points and gaining the first foothold toward the
grandmaster title.

In July 1976 Byrne narrowly missed securing participation in the
1977 candidates matches, as he occupied 5th–7th place only in the
Biel (Bienne) Interzonal. He was overtaken by Bent Larsen (1st),
whom he had thrashed in their individual game; by Petrosian and
Portisch, with whom he had drawn; and he defeated Smyslov. Byrne
failed by just ½ point, drawing one game too many!

### WILLIAM LOMBARDY

William Lombardy (b. 1937) first drew attention by winning all
eleven games at the 4th World Junior Championship at Toronto
1957. This particular FIDE-sponsored event was not yet one of the
strongest; but Lombardy's unflinching climb must be rated on its

own merits of obstinate determination, something that Bill applied also to his personal conduct. Previously a big hulk of a man, Lombardy looked tall and trim at Lone Pine in 1977, telling all that he had lost around forty pounds in the year past by a strict and consistent dietary regimen, and that he felt much better in every way.

Lombardy achieved his grandmastership in 1960 and remained always at or near the top in leading events, including his impressive results in the U.S. Olympic teams. He studied psychology at the tough City College of New York, then switched over to theology and teaching, but devoted increasingly more time also to the other gospel, chess. An author of several books (partly in cooperation with Daniels)[2] and chess magazine serials, Lombardy has also functioned as chess consultant to publishing houses.

The following game is one of those which started Lombardy on his international career. It shows the rapid fall of a faulty conception—and the punishment for it.

### Toronto 1957
### Nimzo-Indian Defense

M. GERUSEL            W. LOMBARDY
(W. GERMANY)              (U.S.)

| 1 | P–Q4 | N–KB3 |
|---|------|-------|
| 2 | P–QB4 | P–K3 |
| 3 | N–QB3 | B–N5 |
| 4 | Q–B2 | N–QB3 |

Other favored lines, but quite defensible for Black, are 4 P–K3 or 4 P–QR3 BxNch 5 PxB P–QN3. 4 Q–B2 is considered too stodgy; Black's answer makes it a Milner–Barry Variation.

| 5 | N–B3 | P–Q4 |
|---|------|------|
| 6 | P–QR3 | BxNch |
| 7 | QxB | N–K5 |
| 8 | Q–B2 | P–K4 |
| 9 | PxKP | B–B4 |
| 10 | Q–R4 | O–O |
| 11 | B–K3 | P–Q5 |

Coupled with White's next move, this maneuver is not compatible with the position. It aggressively occupies a slope for the bishop, with the QR to occupy Q1—and to develop the king-side with P–KN3, B–N2, and O–O. But White underrates the force of Black's immediate counter. Therefore it might have been better to examine 11 P–K3 (11 PxP? QxP 12 B–B4 QR–Q1 13 P–K3 N–Q7!? 14 B–K2 NxNch 15 BxN Q–Q7ch) N–B4 12 Q–Q1 PxP 13 QxQ QRxQ 14 BxP N–Q6ch 15 BxN BxB 16 B–Q2 KR–K1 17 B–B3 B–K5 18 R–QB1.

### 12 R–Q1!?

Gerusel still wasn't aware of Black's follow-up, else he might

[2] W. Lombardy and D. Daniels, U.S. Championship Chess (New York: McKay, 1975), covering the period till 1973.

as well have castled, avoiding
an immediate loss, with tempo,
of the KB pawn. He might have
overlooked Black's 15th move,
otherwise his taking risks is no
longer sound. Yet, the same key
move decides after *12 O–O–O
PxB 13 RxQ KRxQ 14 N–R4!
B–K3! (14 . . . NxBP 15 NxB
NxR 16 NxKP) 15 P–B4 P–
QR3! 16 P–KB5 N–B4 17 Q–
B2 R–Q7+.*

| 12 . . . | PxB! |
| 13 RxQ | PxPch! |

| 14 K–Q1 | KRxQch |
| 15 K–B1 | P–QR3! |

Threatening to win the queen
by . . . N–B4.

| 16 Q–N3 | N–B4 |
| 17 Q–B3 | |

Or *17 Q–K3 N–R4 18 P–QN4
N/B–N6ch 19 K–N2 NxPch*
wins.

| 17 . . . | N–R4 |
| 18 P–K4 | N/R–N6ch |
| 19 Resigns | |

That Lombardy's victory was not just a freak of chance was convincingly underscored when he led the American Students' team to
victory ahead of the USSR, Yugoslavia, and Czechoslovakia in the
7th Student Olympiad, Leningrad 1960—during the heyday of
Soviet chess. Lombardy, at top board, led with 92 percent (!),
beating Spassky (83 percent) in their individual tussle. Best on
board two was Kalme (88 percent) and Raymond Weinstein (75
percent) on board three. Other members of the U.S. team were
Anthony Saidy, Edgar Mednis, and Eliot Hearst.[3]

## CHESS BY MAIL: BERLINER

Whenever an American—be it Morphy, Pillsbury, Capablanca; or
the Olympians; or Lombardy and the U.S. Students' Team—went
abroad and conquered, it jolted the well-knit fabric of structured
organization. Somehow, these men were considered freaks.

A similar shock was injected into the 5th World Correspondence
Chess Championship (1965–68), which ended with the emergence

[3] At the same event, Milan Vukcević shared 88 percent on second board, for
the Yugoslav team. He later moved to the United States, placing exceedingly
well in its national tournaments. He came third (after Brown and Rogoff) in
the U.S. Championship 1975, leaving behind R. Byrne, Reshevsky, Lombardy,
Bisguier, and seven more grand- and international masters. Now spelled "Vukcevich," he became professor of metallurgy in Ohio, and was to be heard of
again in chess activity of later years.

of a new World Champion: Hans Berliner of the United States (b. 1929—in Berlin!). As described by *Correspondence Chess*, May 1968 (the quarterly journal of the British Correspondence Chess Association), "his victory was a resounding one, for his winning margin was the greatest on record and in a field of his class it is spectacular!!"

Correspondence chess is confined to either a particular group of devotees, or to players geographically or by occupation or disposition so remote from centers of activity that postal chess is their substitute for club-tournament chess. It may serve as the shooting range for novelties, or a sparring ring for practice: Paul Keres, for example, was a prolific mail-chesser. The one ingredient which is missing, though, is the climate of physical presence, personal magnetism, and audience participation, with its synergetic excitements. Chess by mail is like watching football or a concert on television rather than being at the event in person. It might provide a penpal. It is a useful substitute for individuals who are wary of travel, of crowds, or of "kibitzers"—or who prefer to play under pseudonyms.[4]

Postal chess also drops the requirement of instant decision-making over the board (and its extraneous influences) and replaces it with the possibility of a studious, detached, prolonged, and perfectionist analysis. The element of "Chess House" skittles that provide some training in varied opening lines is replaced by the greater depth and intensity when searching the "book" for answers. The tedium of dry study is relieved by the active, though distant, presence of the postal antagonist. The psychotechnical probing is perhaps more elusive, yet far more potent. I will try to catch some of the finer points in my commentary to the next game.

Since Berliner had once lost an important game with White in the Two Knights' Defense with 4 N–N5, he regarded the move as inferior. This is not conclusive proof in favor of his opinion about this opening, but it suffices for his present conclusions. In this tourney he was Black against International Correspondence Chess grandmaster Estrin, a specialist in this opening, who had published several monographs on it in Russian, German, and English. Therefore, Berliner spent considerable time researching this variation (which he expected Estrin to employ). This is psychological ploy number one—to rattle the opponent by playing to his strength, and making him think, What does my opponent have up *his* sleeve?

[4] Some postal chess rules forbid entry under a code name, although there is really no legality to such a prohibition. It is the true disclosure and verification of playing strength, and the results, that count in the end.

## CORRESPONDENCE CHESS CHAMPIONSHIP

1965–68
*Two Knights' Defense*

YA. ESTRIN          H. BERLINER
(USSR)                    (U.S.)

| 1 | P–K4 | P–K4 |
|---|------|------|
| 2 | N–KB3 | N–QB3 |
| 3 | B–B4 | N–B3 |
| 4 | N–N5? | |

"It is a truism that no piece should be moved a second time this early," said H. Berliner, emphasizing a Tarrasch precept.

Black's self-assured posture is not true either, because the knight's sally here is of such nature that it radically changes strategy by virtue of an almost forced loss of one of Black's pawns. It gives the opening a distinct flavor as it avoids transposition into other king's pawn openings or into an obligatory Max Lange Attack. Therefore, 4 N–N5 may be one of the instances where truisms call for a probe, regardless of the outcome of this particular game. But apart from conviction, which often helps, Berliner's choice was subjectively right, as will be seen.

| 4 . . . | P–Q4 |
|---------|------|
| 5 PxP | P–N4! |

The ingenious invention of American master Olaf Ulvestad, first analyzed in detail in his *Chess Charts* (New York: 1941). It anticipates a maneuver that occurs in the Fritz Variation of an earlier date, after 5 . . . N–Q5 6 P–QB3 P–N4! 7 B–B1, but maintained its own standing because of the involved alternatives 6 PxN PxB 7 N–QB3 or 6 BxP QxP 7 N–QB3 QxP 8 Q–B3 QxQ 9 NxQ B–Q2 10 O–O B–Q3 11 BxN BxB 12 N–K5 BxN 13 R–K1, with more space.

### 6 B–B1?!

At the time, this move was considered White's best, but it is still only the valve to a stream of complications that explain the soundness of Berliner's decision to use this overture. Estrin also toyed with 6 PxN PxB 7 N–QB3 P–KR3 8 KN–K4 NxN 9 NxN Q–Q4 10 Q–B3.[5]

---

[5] A correspondence player is hard put to conduct a game whose opening has been analyzed at length. He cannot hope that his well-read opponent will choose an inferior variation. Thus, the sooner he gets into a balanced position that contains still uncharted passages, the more opportunity he has to display his own initiative and talent.

Even a postal position cannot be analyzed endlessly, because the correspondence chess player also has a time limit to adhere to. The postal player has a given number of days in which to reply, and *Sitzfleisch* must be matched by the right selection before his time runs out. The quarrels between player and time-controlling umpire that may be used to unnerve the opponent in tournament chess are equally accessible to correspondence chess players!

**6 . . .  N–Q5**

An alternative, useful in mail chess, was 6 . . . P–KR3 7 N–KB3 QxP 8 N–B3 Q–K3 9 BxP B–N2 10 Q–K2 O–O–O 11 P–Q3 B–B4, with an undefined position.

**7 P–QB3  NxP**

This is where Ulvestad merges with A. Fritz in *Deutsche Schachzeitung*, 1904.

**8 N–K4**

8 NxBP or 8 PxN are variants still unresolved as to their final effect. The text is more popular.

**8 . . .  Q–R5**

8 . . . N–K3 was "book," with a slight tilt in Black's favor. Again, Berliner probes the unknown.

**9 N–N3  B–KN5**
**10 P–B3  P–K5!**

This was the Berliner innovation that upset the applecart 10 . . . N–B5 11 BxPch K–Q1 12 O–O B–B4ch 13 P–Q4 PxP 14 N–K4! N/Q4–K6 15 Q–N3! (not 11 Q–K2 B–Q3 12 Q–B2 NxN 13 BxPch B–Q2 14 BxBch KxB 15 QxN N–B5 16 QxQ NxPch 17 K–K2 NxQ=). The novelty showed great foresight.

**11 PxN  B–Q3!**
**12 BxPch  K–Q1**

12 . . . B–Q2? 13 BxBch KxB 14 K–B2 secures the additional material.

**13 O–O!**

If 13 PxB BxNch 14 PxB QxRch 15 B–B1 N–N5 16 N–B3 R–K1, with an ongoing attack. If 13 K–B3 P–KB4! overwhelms. So far, so good.

**13 . . .  PxP**
**14 RxP!?**

Estrin believes he arrested Black's momentum. This juncture between the old, the new, and the newest, caused Estrin in a later game to develop 14 Q–N3!? After the text Black pulls another ace and at last upsets White's equilibrium. (Subsequently Berliner, distrusting 14 Q–N3, advocated 14 O–O, but gave no supporting analysis to either move.)

**14 . . .  R–QN1**
**15 B–K2?**

It is extremely difficult to walk unerringly in a strange land—that is what Berliner's effort led specialist Estrin into. It is a question if Berliner's suggested 15 B–B1 really can save White; e.g., 15 . . . R–K1 16 N–B3 N–B3 (not 16 . . . P–QB3? 17 N–K2! BxR 18 PxB) 17 B–N5 R–K2 18 Q–B1 BxR 19 QxB QxQPch. A correspondence game Jovčić–Koshnitsky 1969 continued 15 P–R4, which allows the bishop to keep square K8 under observation; but in view of Black's labyrinthian choice of 15 . . . P–QR3 16

BxP N–N5 *17* B–K2 BxR; or
*15* . . . P–KB4; or *15* . . . P–QR4
*16* N–B3 N–N5 *17* Q–B1 BxR
*18* QxB QxQPch *19* K–B1 BxN
*20* PxB R–N3, the addition of
the evaluation symbol ± in
books on the openings (e.g., in
the *Encyclopaedia of Chess
Openings*, abbreviated as *ECO*)
is not conclusive without
further practical elaboration.

| | |
|---|---|
| *15* . . . | BxR |
| *16* BxB | QxQPch |
| *17* K–R1 | BxN |
| *18* PxB | R–N3 |
| *19* P–Q3 | N–K6 |
| *20* BxN | QxB |
| *21* B–N4 | |

The only move to prevent mate.
But as the KR file has thus been
defused (*21* . . . R–R3ch *22* B–
R3), Black uses his king-side
pawns to demolish White and
get his king's rook into play.

| | |
|---|---|
| *21* . . . | P–KR4 |
| *22* B–R3 | P–N4 |
| *23* N–Q2 | P–N5 |
| *24* N–B4 | QxNP |
| *25* NxR | PxB |
| *26* Q–B3 | PxPch |
| *27* QxP | QxQch |
| *28* KxQ | BPxN! |

These positions are the test case
for mastery. Daring, and opponents' oversights, might help
middlegame positions end in
some brilliant finish; but where
experts battle with their last
ounce of tactical know-how and
positional instinct, the nuances
of endgame skill decide. A master simplifies into an endgame

when he believes that technique
will secure him victory.

In this position, Black has an
extra pawn which may or may
not be enough to win, but it
helps him dictate the wing he
operates on. White is tied to
watching Black's passed pawns,
and Black can thus choose the
right moment to move his
pawns forward. But for this to
happen, all of them must remain intact, so that Black can
win one or both and promote. If
*28* . . . RPxN *29* P–R4 and *30*
P–R5, and White neutralizes
the queen's wing.

| | |
|---|---|
| *29* R–KB1 | K–K2 |
| *30* R–K1ch | K–Q3 |
| *31* R–KB1 | R–QB1! |
| *32* RxP | R–B2 |

Very well played. Black pre-
serves both connected pawns,
and although the material is
even, PR4 is a compelling
passed pawn, which White's
king must guard. Black will
gobble up the queen-side pawns
and the queen's pawn is feeble.

| | |
|---|---|
| *33* R–B2 | K–K4 |
| *34* P–R4 | |

A flabby response which weakens the pawn chain and impairs
White's rook's ability to defend
them. A temporizing *34* K–N3
seems better but also loses; e.g.,
*34* K–N3 K–Q5 *35* K–R4 KxP
*36* KxP R–B7 *37* R–B3ch K–Q7
*38* P–N3 K–B8 *39* P–R4 R–
QN7 *40* P–R5 P–N4 *41* P–R6
P–N5 *42* K–N4 K–B2 *43* R–B7
RxP *44* RxP R–QR6+.

| 34 . . . | K–Q5 | 40 R–QN7 | R–N5ch |
|----------|------|----------|--------|
| 35 P–R5  | KxP  | 41 K–B3  | P–N5   |
| 36 R–B3ch| K–B7 | 42 RxRP  | P–N6   |
| 37 P–N4  | P–N4 | 43 Resigns | |
| 38 P–R6  | R–B5 | | |
| 39 R–B7  | RxP  | | |

If 43 R–B7ch K–N8 44 R–B5 R–QR5, curtain!

Berliner's success was remarkable. That success may have been complemented by his professional work with computers. Or, vice versa, mail chess may have contributed to his choice of a precise discipline as his field of work.

Correspondence chess, as I have noted, allows a greater scope for exact planning than does over-the-board play. Surprises can often be eliminated by preparation and calculation; for one has access to source materials during play, and a great deal of time in which to use them. A library is often used in place of one's own memory, and thus one's human fallibility is somewhat lessened.

There's a danger here, though. Total truth is unattainable; yet the quest is tempting. The desire for, and illusion of, chess perfection may lead to the conclusion that chess charts and calculations can be precisely computerized—that the use of artificial or machine intelligence can supersede and even overtake the brain's function in the game of chess, with all its sequences, middlegame tactics and strategies, and endgame art and precision. Not quite so as yet. The computer may replace part of some of the routine load but, in Berliner's own words, "the average human being vastly underrates the computing machine that was put into his head by nature. . . ." (*Chess Life & Review*, October 1975).

By merit of domestic success, Hans Berliner took part in the 1952 Olympics in Helsinki. He played reserve board two and scored 50 percent of possible points. He participated in some U.S. Championships (1954, 1957, 1960, 1962), placing himself very laudably, but never near the top. His forte was chess *par distance research*.

At the 1965–68 World Correspondence Chess Preliminaries and Championship, his final commanding lead was 14 points without a single loss, ahead of many illustrious names in mail chess. He finally nailed down—for himself, and thus also for the United States—the coveted title of International Correspondence Chess Grandmaster.

While Berliner has shunned significant tournament chess since, his achievement ex cathedra coincided with a deep preoccupation with computer programming, and prominently so with computer chess. (This and similar subjects in the province of chess cybernetics are further looked at in Chapter 14.)

# 10.

# The Artistic Pathfinders

## ENDGAME STUDY AND PRACTICAL PLAY

In playing through the games given on these pages, we witnessed the importance of the theory and practice of the endgame. Knowledge of minute finesses in handling the reduced material may turn a possible defeat into a draw. The power of accumulating subtle positional advantages in the concluding stage is the essential turning point toward victory. The ending is a more definite, less changeable, and better-founded portion of the game than the opening. In somewhat primitive but true comparison, the virtuosity of endgame play reminds one of the "squeeze" in contract bridge, where a skillfully forced discard might make or break the contract.

Capablanca never "studied" the game, still less the opening, which he treated heuristically. But he ingested books on the endings as part of building a decisive precision machinery. Capablanca is reputed to have sensed the theme and the solution to an endgame about to be shown to him, even before it was fully set up on the board! Also Emanuel Lasker was a remarkably fast solver.

What good is it to learn the routine of how to win in the opening, to slither into a meaningless middlegame, just hoping for the opponent's blunder—only to end up with a bishop and knight, or king and two knights versus king and one pawn, and lack all preparation or talent to win that position within the permitted maximum of moves?

Fischer, for instance, was considered the walking symbol of chess at its sportive height; but he also was one of the most erudite dictionaries of endgame technique. He certainly had devoured Fine's *Basic Chess Endings* and all of Averbakh's, Berger's, Bilguer's, Chéron's, Rabinovich's, and others' books on the final phase of the game. The following pièce de résistance is clearer in its conception, simpler in straightforward execution, and better suited to demonstrate aesthetic beauty than the routine completion of a game by following the general principles of theory as "a matter of technique."

The diagram shows a blocked, drawish position where Black's king cannot penetrate and utilize his pawn plus. But there is a difference between this and a similar position in a Fischer–Spassky game which we will analyze later (there the position was part of match strategy— the draw was assured, and Fischer's sadomasochistic taunting only jeopardized the easy draw without the tempting compensation of a potential win). This, and the next two diagrams, with my own notes, are taken from W. Korn, *American Chess Art—250 Portraits of Endgame Study* (New York: Pitman, 1974). In the sphere of endgame studies, the collection is an American first, covering compositions from the year 1850 up to the present, including contemporary artists; for example, H. Branton, R. Brieger, J. E. Peckover, O. Weinberger, and many others. The history and technique of these facets of "chess art" are explained in an understandable fashion.

In the following endgame, arrived at in Bisguier–Fischer, Black unlocks the floodgates.

### U.S. CHAMPIONSHIP
#### 1967

#### New York 1967
#### Round 11

A. B. BISGUIER          R. J. FISCHER

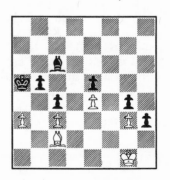

1 ...          BxP!!

Black gives up a bishop for two pawns.

2 BxB          K–R5
3 B–B5          K–N6!!

If 3 . . . KxP 4 BxP P–N5 5 PxP P–B6 6 B–Q1+.

4 BxP          P–K5
5 BxP

Releasing the king from watching Black's RP. But it is too late.

5 . . .          KxBP
6 P–N4          K–Q7!!

A last finesse, gaining all-important time for the right pawn to queen.

If 6 . . . P–K6 7 B–B1!—preventing Black's BP from queening with a tempo-saving check in subvariations 7 . . . K–Q7 8

P–N5; and now (a) 8 . . . P–B6 9 P–N6 P–B7 10 P–N7 P–B8(Q) 11 B–N8(Q) P–K7 12 Q–R2ch=; or (b) 8 . . . P–K7 9 BxP KxB 10 P–N6 P–B6 11 P–N7 P–B7 12 P–N8(Q) P–B8(Q)ch 13 K–N2 QxP 14 Q–K8ch and 15 QxP=.

| 7 B–N2 | P–K6 |
| 8 B–B3 | P–B6 |

And Black wins.

The next diagram is another blend of practical perfection needed to win the position that by all other signs looks like a draw, and of the artistic attraction of the setting and solution.

### INTERNATIONAL TOURNAMENT

#### Palma de Mallorca 1970

S. RESHEVSKY      B. IVKOV

This was the position after Black's 82nd move:

A compact miniature of *telescopic proportions*. An ordinary mortal would agree to a draw. The pawn cannot advance without being captured, securing the draw for Black. The knight, on the other hand, must not be taken, as the pawn would fall. Black's king can shuttle to and from the squares B4, N4, R4, and even the square R3 is available if the bishop moves away.

| 1 B–R3!! | K–B4 |
| 2 B–Q7!! | |

Black has become helpless against either the loss of his knight or the pawn's marching. If 1 . . . K–R3 2 B–B1ch K–R4 3 B–B4!—cutting off both the knight's checking square and Black's king's square N4. If 1 . . . K–R4 2 B–N4 K–N4 3 B–K2ch K–B4 4 B–B4!! N–B3 5 P–N7, and Black must again relinquish all guards. A tightly knit ending with three variations, conceived by a venerable grandmaster.

The following example is a true "composed" ending, the idea for which germinated from a practical ending in a club game, where Black's rook was "misplaced"; but the position created a "motif," capable of being reduced to sharp, crystal-clear form.

### 1ST PRIZE, "BOHEMIA" STUDY TOURNEY, 1933

*White to move and win*

WALTER KORN

| 1 P–R6 | P–R6! |
| 2 PxP | R–QR5 |
| 3 P–R7 | RxP/6 |

The low-key overture has served to deflect Black's rook from the fifth to the sixth rank. The importance of that detour becomes plain as play proceeds. At this moment, both white pawns are threatened with capture, voiding a win. Therefore, White first protects the other pawn as well.

| 4 N–Q8! | R–N6ch |
| 5 N–N7 | R–QR6 |
| 6 N–Q6! | R–N6ch |
| 7 K–B7 | R–QR6 |
| 8 K–N7 | R–N6ch |
| 9 N–N5!! | |

Now it transpires why Black's rook was initially forced on to the sixth rank. In consequence of White's oblique zigzag N–Q8–N7–Q6–N5, the rook can no longer go back to QR6 to deter the rook's pawn from queening, as the knight controls the square; but the knit is *en prise*!

| 9 . . . | RxNch |
| 10 K–R6! | R–N8 |
| 11 P–B8(Q)ch | KxQ |
| 12 P–R8(Q)ch | |

and White wins.

A brief explanation of the terms, the economics, and what subsequently derives as the "aesthetics" of chess art, might be in order. In its entirely gamelike appearance and with a natural flow of moves, this type of endgame study is called "positional." Because the composition contains no more than seven pieces, it is called a "miniature." Each piece, having had its say, disappears in the wings, until the sole winning force of queen against rook remains for the last bow. This requirement determines a study's "economy," fully observed here.

Apart from the introduction (moves 1–3), the main play (4–9), and the windup (10–12), the solution also contains a substantially important false lead which is not supposed to work, but gently adds to the difficulty of finding the right road to the win; it is called a "try," and here consists of another attempted, but not as effective, defense (*1* P–R6) RxP 2 P–R7 K–B3 3 N–Q8!! RxP 4 KxR K–K4 5 K–R6 K–K5 6 K–R5 K–Q6 7 KxP, securing the pawn and win; whereas 3 P–R8(Q) R–B1ch 4 K–N7 RxQ 5 KxR K–K3 6 N–Q4ch K–Q4 7 N–B2 K–B5 8 N–R1 K–Q6 9 K–R7 K–Q7 *10* K–R6 K–B8 does not win here. A "try" may be either an alternative defense of Black's which does not work out, or another opening move of White's which might look promising but, likewise, is supposed to fail.

It is precisely this kind of monolithic structure that allows for just one, and only one, opening move—otherwise the setting is called "cooked"—which marks the difference between a mere ending and an endgame study. This latter, together with problems (another branch of chess), is called "chess composition."

It should be noted that the distinction between a problem (including fairy chess) and an endgame study (or composed ending) is not difficult—it is very explicit. The orthodox chess problem requires a mate to be achieved within a definite number of moves; its construction and material need bear no relation to the actual game, and the "tasks" and "themes" dominate. The endgame study stipulates a given outcome (to win or to draw), without a stated limit to the number of moves. The composed ending is less construed and formalistic than the problem, and often demands a profound knowledge not only of basic but also of complex endgame theory, thus providing a close link with practical chess play. An endgame study may cause problems, but by definition is not a problem, although questionable authorities often mix up these terms. In terms of chess "property" rights, chess composition is a distinct invention and the product by an identifiable composer. Especially if the composition is a prize winner, it is traceable to an individual author. Yet, studies and problems are often quoted as examples without any mention of their original source and composer, inadvertently giving the impression that they were the columnist's creation.

## THE HEYDAYS OF AMERICAN CHESS COMPOSITION

While problem-making often leads to abstractions that are strange to any mind not steeped in formal exercise, American compositions did attain heights of international recognition. The general awakening began in the 1850s, not only with Hazeltine, Perrin, Cook, and the Loyd brothers, but also when chess columns sprang up in the *Albion*, the *Saturday Courier*, the *Chess Monthly*, the *New York Clipper*, and scores of others to follow.

The name of (William) Meredith (1835–1903) came to be known worldwide as the label for his specialty: highly artistic two-movers, containing between eight to twelve men, including kings.

## THOMPSON'S GENIUS

The majority of problem compositions of the earlier period appeared in John J. Brownson's *Dubuque Chess Journal* (actually edited by Orestes A. Brown, Jr., a contemporary composer and co-owner). Interesting is the high-quality output of problemist T. A. Thompson, a freed black slave. His talent was recognized and greatly furthered by John K. Hanshew, when Thompson came to Philadelphia to show him his art work. Hanshew's description in the *Maryland Chess Review* refers to Mr. Thompson's ("a black gentleman's") visit, and to the subsequent publication by the *Dubuque Chess Journal* of Thompson's collection of problems.

The editor's preface to *Chess Problems* by Theophilus A. Thompson (Dubuque, Iowa: 1873) conveys a topical human interest story:

T. A. Thompson (colored) was born in Frederick City, Maryland, on the 21st day of April 1855. At 13th years of age he left his native city and went to live with a family in Carroll County in the capacity of house servant. In 1870, he returned to Frederick, where he has lived ever since.

He saw a chess board and men used for the first time in April 1872, when he witnessed a contest between Mr. S. of Ohio and Mr. H. of Frederick City. Although he could not understand the game and dared not ask questions for fear of annoying the players, he watched every move with the closest attention. The party finished, he went home, fully determined to learn the game.

Mr. H. having heard of his ardent desire loaned him a chess board and a set of chess men, gave him some instructions, and left him a few two-move problems to solve. Thus, thanks to the kind assistance of John K. Hanshew, our hero became possessed of the open sesame to Caïssa's gardens of ever increasing intellectual delights.

Hearing last summer of the Dubuque Chess Journal, he soon became a subscriber, a student, and a contributor. Hereto, accumulating the following rich store of chess compositions that are offered for perusal to the general chess reader with great pleasure and much confidence by the proprietors of the Dubuque Chess Journal—Dubuque, June 1st, 1873.

The frontispiece of the Thompson volume shows an ingenious triple-faced four-mover wherein either "White to play mates in four," or "Black to play mates in four," or either "White or Black on the move compels self-mate in four moves." Literally, a chameleon.

"Either to play and mate, or compel self-mate in four moves."
  I. *White (W) or Black (B) to mate:*
     (W) 1 NxQ B–N5ch 2 K–K2 RxN 3 R–B7 and mate next move cannot be prevented. If 2 . . . R–B7ch 3 NxR and 4 Q–N8 mate. If 1 . . . R–B8ch 2 KxR P–K7ch 3 KxP any 4 Q–N8 mate. (b) 1 R–B8ch KxR 2 Q–B6ch K–K1 3 Q–B7ch and 4 Q–Q7 mate.
  II. *White (Q) or Black (B) to compel self-mate:*
     (W) 1 Q–N8ch QxQ 2 O–O–Och R–Q5 3 R–B8ch RxRch 4 N–B6ch RxN mate. (b) 1 B–N5ch R–B3 (if 1 . . . RxB 2 R–B8ch KxR 3 Q–Q8ch RxQ mate) 2 BxRch PxB 3 R–B8ch KxR 4 Q–Q8ch RxQ mate.

An admirable construction of reciprocal compulsion. In each variant, the defending moves of either White or Black are forced. It is an exquisite specimen of abstract thinking and formal exercise and a very advanced "heterodox" conception (only after 1960 has the self-mate been classed as orthodox).

Thompson's determination, and speedy acquisition of chess mastery, is astounding. He had had no formal education, learned chess from mere observation in April 1872, and had a complete collection of first-class problems published just one year later by the leading chess publisher of the period.

Equally impressive is the literary taste expressed in Thompson's consistent use of the term "self-mate." It took the famous originator of fairy chess, T. R. Dawson of *The Chess Amateur,* till 1922 to achieve legitimacy for the obviously more natural term "self-mate" in place of the then fashionable expression "sui-mate." Thompson was also free of the snobism often found in the composers' community.

## A RECORD ACHIEVEMENT

Walking the bridge from a previous speculative era, across and over the age of rationality, right into the transpersonal, transcendental, and extrasensory realms of latter days, we conclude this discussion with a fascinating product of "fifth-dimensional" relationships. It is a two-mover, the identical setting of which was perceived by two different composers located in vastly different and partly isolated regions, and submitted by each of them separately to American Alain C. White's highly respected and authoritative *Good Companions* tourney of July 1920—winning a joint first prize. To quote the British problemist Brian Harley, previous chess editor of the London *Observer* and the author, among other books, of *Mate in Two Moves* (England: 1931, p. 61):

> The following position is without doubt the finest known exposition of the [self-block] theme. The two composers, living as far apart as San Francisco [A. J. Fink (1890–1956), a strong West Coast player as well] and Tahiti [Frank J. Stimson (1883–1958), American diplomat, philosopher, architect, and writer of mysteries, who retired to the Island of Moorea, adopting the native name of Ua Tane], had a curious simultaneous experience, one dreaming the position and the other the Key; Ua Tane . . . believes there was thought-transference at work, due to the operations of a friend, an amateur medium, who was shown the idea of the problem.

According to Harley, whom I met after the War somewhere near Portsmouth, England, he apparently had written to Ua Tane for confirmation regarding the role of the medium.

As to the structure of the problem, it is a record achievement (or Task Record) of eight self-blocks, with distinctly different White mates. Its construction was even more highly praised in M. Lipton, R. C. O. Matthews and J. M. Rice, *Chess Problems: Introduction to an Art* (New York: Citadel Press, 1965), and in Rice's opinion is as yet unsurpassed (the authors are British). Here is the diagram of this American record, the solution of which will, in its harmony, impress also the total layman of the craft.

## A. J. FINK AND
## J. F. STIMSON (UA TANE)

First Prize, *Good Companions,*
1920

*White to play, mates in two*

*1 R–B8*

A tempo move creating a *zug-zwang* in a virtually unchanged position. Whichever defense Black now chooses, his move blocks one of the previously available escape squares, each time allowing White to administer a different mate:

| 1 ... PxBP | 2 R–Q8 mate |
| 1 ... NxP | 2 N–B7 mate |
| 1 ... N–Q5 | 2 N–B4 mate |
| 1 ... R–Q5 | 2 N–B3 mate |
| 1 ... N–B4 | 2 NxN4 mate |
| 1 ... P–Q3 | 2 P–K6 mate |
| 1 ... P–K3 | 2 Q–K4 mate |
| 1 ... PxKP | 2 QxQP mate |

Composition is less subject to age or geriatric influences than tournament play is. Many extraneous factors remain within the artist's discretion. Composition, and its appreciation, can be applied at any time up to one's ripe old age. Solving and composing competitions to take part in, have also been around, although they pedagogically have been somewhat neglected by the powers that be.

A DISTINGUISHED HISTORY

The United States may look back to a distinguished history also in the egghead sphere of chess composition. It has retained its popularity, and its specimens have not disappeared from the columns and the magazine pages.

An early anthology was Cook's (et al.) *American Chess-Nuts* (New York: A. W. King, 1868).[1] Then came Wurzburg, White, Hume's *The Golden Argosy* (Straud: 1929), a collection of Shinkman's output. But the greatest assistance in this sector of

---

[1] The hilariously double-edged expression "Chess-Nuts" was first employed as the pseudonym of an anonymous "letter-to-the-editor" correspondent of the chess column in the *Illustrated London News* in the mid-nineteenth century. The column, along with the signature, was later taken over by Howard Staunton. The fitting appellation was most likely coined by Charles Dickens, who was a student of chess. At the time just before the term first appeared in the column, Dickens described some of his analytical and solving efforts as little "Chess-Nuts"—as is corroborated by his letters and by biographies about him.

chess was rendered not only to domestic but also to the chess world's problem composition in general, by the munificent patronage of Alain Campbell White (1880–1951), who as a Harvard College freshman already conceived the idea of collecting and furthering problem composition.[2] A talented composer himself, he coedited (with George Hume), financed, published, and freely distributed monographs and about thirty books of collected problems by individual authors, widely known as the *Christmas Series*. He was the author of the complete, monumental anthology of Samuel Loyd's compositions. White was the first to initiate an exact classification by themes and to compile a collection of about 200,000 problems (later on divided up among British trustees), a task of classification that has not yet been duplicated in the province of endgame study composition.

Gustavus Charles Reichhelm (1839–1905) of Philadelphia, one of the architects of the "Theory of Corresponding [or "related"] Squares"—a basic tenet in king and pawn "opposition" and tempo play—was a famed composer of endgame studies.[3] Reichhelm also was one of the strongest amateurs in the second part of the nineteenth century; we already noted his successes elsewhere. His, and other important games of the period, have been transmitted to us in his exemplary chronicle *Chess in Philadelphia* (1898). It was coedited by Walter Penn Shipley and meticulously narrates American chess life then.

The American chess problemists maintained a narrow but significant foothold, up to the present day—as composers, authors, and otherwise; to name a few, V. L. Eaton, K. S. Howard, F. Gamage, J. Buchwald, E. Hassberg, N. Guttman, E. Holladay, and V. Wilson. Buchwald and Hassberg's extensive collections of problems are now housed at the Cleveland Public Library. Vaux Wilson originated an internationally recognized system of evaluating problems—a set of important criteria used by judges in problem competitions. Vincent L. Eaton coined the parallel term "problematist," a term preferred by some to "problemists."

Toward the turn of the century, orthodox problems and endgame study composition have lost ground to heterodox, or "fairy chess," problems.[4] This form moved away most considerably from the realities of practical chess, into its own sphere of construction,

---

[2] White was no relation to his namesake John J. White of Cleveland who built a chess treasure of different sort.

[3] Although his name was often misspelled "Reichelm," he never deserted his parents' original spelling.

[4] An erudite exposition of fairy chess may be found in Anthony Dickins, *A Guide to Fairy Chess* (New York: Dover, 1971). Dickins is British.

outside the old rules of orthodoxy, with different kind of material (chessmen added) and on new and often eccentric ground. But it is not an exclusive involvement. Many masters, for example, Milan Vukcevich and Pal Benko, practiced both strong actual play and exquisite composition of fairy chess problems (and of regular endgame studies).[5]

A good part of contemporary composition after mid-twentieth century has carried a multinational label. Apart from Vukcevich, the banner was carried also by Pal Benko, born in France in 1928 of Hungarian parents. He was several times Hungarian national champion or runner-up. Pal and his parents left Hungary for the United States in 1956. He acquired U.S. citizenship in 1962 and occupied board two for the United States at the Varna Olympics 1962, scoring 66 points out of 73 games played. He was awarded the grandmaster title in 1958 and has shown widely varying tournament results, mostly because he strives for beauty rather than success, with his love concentrated on the chess arts. For years, he conducted a column on chess composition in *Chess Life & Review* and holds the world record—likely to stand for a long time—of a so-called "serial" of forty mate-in-three-moves problems (see *CL&R*, 1974, No. 2, p. 118). He also specializes in series of self-mates and help-mates and in a charming old pastime called "letter (or picture) problems." His endgame studies have won him a number of first prizes. He also wrote a monograph on the Benko Gambit, an in-depth analysis of a line formerly, and haphazardly, named the Volga Gambit.

Another international and a strict adherent of chess for chess art's sake—or of beauty first and never mind the score or the kudos—was Nicolas ("Nick") Rossolimo (1910–1975), whose tournament results as a grandmaster were equally uneven because of this "weakness." His compositions occupy a high place.

Two homegrown grandmasters, who combine their competitive talents with a thorough knowledge of endgame strategy, have been mentioned before, but we recall their achievements because they should not be omitted from this particular context: Isaac Kashdan (some of his pieces were composed in partnership with Al Horowitz) and, on top of the tower, Reuben Fine. His *Basic Chess Endings* has been translated into many languages and reprinted by the original publishers over and over again. Any new reprint could well benefit by the addition of an appendix.

---

[5] A good selection, with biographical sketches and explanations of the problems, is given in Kenneth S. Howard, *Spectacular Chess Problems* (New York: Dover, 1965), and in a few other of his titles, also published by Dover.

While Fine's work may not be as profound as for instance André Chéron's *La Fin de Partie* (also translated into German, 1960–65), Fine keeps his nose to the grindstone of practicality, not becoming excessively purist.

All these ingredients: competitive tournament chess and the preparation for it; recreational and leisurely games, coupled with helpful instruction; practical endgame training; devotion to the chess arts, be they problems or studies; and journalistic and editorial enlightenment about the universe of chess—all are an integral part of the game and have rarely been given the necessary time, the deserved space, or the knowledgeable manpower so desirable for an optimum enjoyment of the pastime.

# 11.

# Fischer: Nothing but Chess

## THE ENIGMA OF A RECLUSE

Volumes have been written about Bobby Fischer (b. March 9, 1943). I will try to coordinate numerous fragments of the prodigy's seeming inconsistencies. I will also look at his games, to define any pioneering role he might have played, but I will do it with an irreverent, freethinker's sentiment.

Obviously, we no longer talk about early American pioneering, but rather its parallels—the later breakthroughs in accustomed credos, and their wide repercussions. Under scrutiny are both the pioneer as an individual, and the tenets of a given period.

The person Bobby Fischer was not the product of a cohesive home in the traditional sense; we know that his father was moved out of the family when the boy was two. It is indeed a matter of conjecture whether the break was inobtrusive or eruptive. If the latter were the case, it may have left an unstabilizing impression on the child at this early, impressionable age. His mother at once assumed both the maternal and paternal roles, becoming the object of both the boy's affection and distrust. This conflict of polar extremes could not be resolved within the confines of one home, and a very mobile home at that. Without doubt, mother's love was overpowering.[1] Such dominance can create docility (with the bachelor son forever sticking to mother), or hostility (toward either sex), or a fervent wish to build one's own world (or dream world). It often ends in rejection of the parents. Much of Fischer's drive, stubbornness, and I.Q. seems to have been inherited from his mother.

---

[1] To quote James A. Michener's "The Jungle World of Juvenile Sports" (*Reader's Digest*, December 1975): "Mothers especially wanted their gifted sons to play the whole game and score the maximum of points: . . . there is an ego factor here . . . and the son inherits the mother's own ego factor!"

Had Fischer been a musical marvel, his mother might have sacrificed all for getting the best teacher—and still not necessarily reaped the reward of her son's utmost love and gratitude for spurring him on during leisurely and playful adolescence. But music is somewhat more tangible and secure than chess, which was Fischer's dreamland. When his mother realized his talent, she drove him on and implored others to recognize him; but she also drove herself out of his world, which was being invaded. With the exception of Bobby's own drive and ambition, the prerequisites for an even development and a balanced progress in life were aborted. Being unreligious, but probably a maverick, he might have been called names. Resenting any label, yet feeling a void, he later found a creed, significant in its fundamentally strict observance of the Sabbath. It is paradoxical that Fischer joined the Christian denomination of the Church of God, for it both dissociated him from a purported Judaic origin, yet carried over some Mosaic precepts.

It is not too far-fetched to see a connection here with Reshevsky. Reshevsky, who perhaps became Fischer's father-figure, adheres to strict religious tenets; Fischer takes up religion, but does him one better by entering fundamentalism. He discards Judaism, but accepts the beaten victim's belief in God and order. After all, some ancestors "ate their dead with honor—hoping to retain some vestige of strength and virtue that had died" (H. G. Wells, *The Outline of History* [New York: Garden City, 1961], p. 137).

Uneven early impressions may lend impetus to strong impulses, often difficult to resist. More relevant than other players' incidental origin or religion may have been Fischer's compelling quest for some suitable semiethical code. It would keep him on the right path; contain some elements fitting his ambivalence about strictness or need for dissent; and imbue him with some sense of direction, however imaginary.

By mere speculative inference: His mother, Dr. Regina Fischer-Pustan, a nurse, and later a medical doctor, was often in the front line of protesters. Fischer might have absorbed a strain of rebelliousness from her, and campaign for his own causes, yet remain torn by an inner conflict because of his urge for rightful recognition.

Otherwise, Fischer was reasonably "normal." He developed a good physique and adhered to regular workouts, including a good game of tennis. He acquired a taste for good appearance and strove for dignity, complaining that certain segments of players "had no class." Yet, he visibly felt uncomfortable in public.

Arrangements by him or in his behalf sometimes ended in turmoil. He frequently sought legal shelter when only simple decisions were needed. There were vacillations about terms (for matches, TV rights, and the like) and disavowals of attorneys called in and then discarded.

Finding such difficulties in decision-making in life, Fischer turned away from its conflicts and found solace instead in the consequential but artificial structure of chess. Chess provided an empire, and it also pretended perfection and dominance.

Fischer's rise was assisted (if not caused) by tremendous bursts of ambition and will power. It was a costly rise if, for a while, he may have believed that what suited himself, suited the world; that the subjective conditions most conducive to his best efforts, were also the objective conditions best for chess. The chess world, therefore, had to abide by them, and by him.

The element that Fischer added to chess history was: he had become the quintessence of chess sine qua non; to a degree of obsession without parallel. It is necessary to characterize this potent ingredient, because such volcanic eruptions of genius seem so endemic to this subcontinent.

Fischer is one of the first instances of a prodigy who was not held back by any attempts to make his life a "normal" one. Morphy was hampered by the orderly conventions of home and education. Capablanca's natural talent was easily strong enough to propel him through a life span that was filled with the ambition, but not the fever, of chess; he remained above the scene. They were the children of a chess ideology based on preconceived planning; whereas the chess concepts of the latter half of Fischer's century are based on creating and maintaining complexities and fluidities, distrusting accepted stratagems, and remaining elastic enough to alternate tactically from active defense to dynamic aggression.

Fischer started chess at the age of six and chose to give it his exclusive attention. It is not just that chess obliterated his other interests; Fischer must have had an innate ability and desire for the game. After all, a kid hanging around boy's clubs and playgrounds has many distractions and temptations to fall for. The mental associations in chess must have struck a responsive cord in Bobby. At nine, although the future effects of chess were not yet apparent, he was a disinterested pupil in school—as far as permitted by the laxities in the educational system. But later he struck back at the system with determination, refusing to acquire general knowledge by rote, of a tradition which he thought to be of no future use.

I first met Fischer when visiting John and Ethel Collins at their Brooklyn home—called the Hawthorne Chess Club—in Fall 1955 or so. Frank Brady, in his *Profile of a Prodigy* (New York: McKay, rev. ed., 1973) sympathetically relates as "fortunate and revealing that Bobby chose the Collins's [sic] as his alter familia, indicating a facet

of his personality that he rarely shows to the public; that of a genial
and soft spoken member of the household with a need for lasting
and meaningful relationship." There are other testimonials, by
former schoolmates (like James Buff, now on the West Coast), who
disclose instances of Fischer's upright observance of pledges and
repairing of wrongs. As is movingly described in J. Collins, *My Seven
Chess Prodigies* (New York: Simon & Schuster, 1975), the Collinses'
devotion to younger players was proverbial and unlimited. While
for reasons unknown, Fischer did not come through with an
assumed promise to provide Jack's book with a Foreword, the
Collinses did not let this affect their relationship. They placed chess
first, with Fischer as its proponent—and with personal polarizations
to be taken in stride and Fischer to be taken as he was. He simply
seemed unable to discern when he could advance himself without
needlessly hurting others.[2]


## ASCENT INTO STARDOM

Fischer's ascent from 1956 onwards was accentuated not only by
his superiority, but also by his nonconformist dissent from standards, intuitively making changes that benefited the professional
chess community everywhere. In this respect he is to be given credit
for striving to stand fully on his own. The emergence of a formidable non-Soviet challenger confronting a well-supported Eastern
chess apparatus lifted the aspirations and the self-confidence of
other competitors throughout the world. It also improved the global
status of chess.

Let us begin with Fischer's own beginnings. International master,
FIDE judge, and author of several books, Hans Kmoch (1894–
1973), for three decades the game's annotator for *Chess Review*,
called the next game "the game of the century" and the well-
deserved epithet stuck. This game established thirteen-year-old
Fischer's transition from a promising prodigy to a heavyweight, al-
though at the tournament he placed only 8th–9th, together with
Seidman; ahead of him were Reshevsky 9; Bisguier 7; Feuerstein and
Mednis 6½ each; and S. Bernstein, D. Byrne, and Turner 5½ each.
But next year, at the 1957 U.S. Championship, Fischer shot up into
1st place (10½ points), and did not lose a single game. He was
followed by Reshevsky 9½; Sherwin 9; Lombardy 7½; Berliner 7;
Denker, Feuerstein, and Mednis 6½ each; Seidman 6; and S.
Bernstein and Bisguier 5 each. He likewise played in and won the

2 Collins also compiled *Maxims of Chess* (New York: McKay, 1978).

1958–59, 1959–60, 1960–61, 1962–63, 1963–64, 1965–66, and 1966–67 U.S. Championships with a total of seventy-seven games, out of which he lost only three (one each against R. Byrne, E. Mednis, and S. Reshevsky). The 1963–64 Championship was a total blackout: Fischer won all eleven games!

Now back to Fischer's First Brilliancy prize for this win against Robert Byrne's younger brother Donald, who became an international master in 1962.[3]

## ROSENWALD TOURNAMENT

### New York 1956
*Gruenfeld Defense*

| D. BYRNE | R. J. FISCHER |
|----------|---------------|
| 1 N–KB3 | N–KB3 |
| 2 P–B4 | P–KN3 |
| 3 N–B3 | B–N2 |
| 4 P–Q4 | O–O |
| 5 B–B4 | P–Q4 |

White started with a Réti opening, then varied with an English opening; now Fischer creates a Gruenfeld Indian Defense and a surprise; it was his first venture with this defense in serious tournament play. It also transforms Réti's diagonal influence into a fight in and for the center.

Actually, White's 5 B–B4, meant to maintain a careful equilibrium, contains a grain of timidity. It's proven so by White's change of heart on his 11th move. Probably Byrne, having studied Fischer's opening repertoire (or perhaps not yet taking him too seriously), may have been sure that Black would play 5 . . . P–Q3 when, after 6 P–K3 P–B3 7 B–K2 Q–R4 8 O–O N–R4 9 B–N5, a position with some latent venom would arise, suited to Donald Byrne's style. Otherwise, White could have more aggressively played 5 P–K4! with a regular King's Indian Defense. After 5 B–B4, Fischer's 5 . . . P–Q4 channels the game into a variation where 5 B–B4, coupled with the stereotype 6 Q–N3, is counterproductive.

### 6 Q–N3?

A key move, but one tempo too late. For comparison, the main line with this move arises after 1 P–Q4 N–KB3 2 P–QB4 P–KN3 3 N–QB3 P–Q4 4 N–B3 B–N2 5 Q–N3 at once, when 5 . . . PxP 6 QxBP O–O 7 P–K4 is accepted as the proper strategy, with White's queen's

---

[3] Donald Byrne (1930–1976) could not keep pace with his brother Robert's steadier progress in chess because he suffered from a progressive skin disease which finally took its toll. He was a college teacher, was awarded the international master title in 1962, and served as the U.S. Olympic team captain in 1966, 1968, and 1972, sometimes filling in most successfully as a player.

bishop aiming for N5, whereas B–B4 would be generally meek. The threat to Black's QBP is futile here, and in similar lines with B–B4; e.g., 6 PxP NxP 7 NxN QxN 8 BxP N–B3 9 P–K3 B–N5; or also 8 . . . N–R3 9 B–N3 B–B4 10 P–QR3 QR–B1, and Black has strong initiatives.

Thus, the correct positional treatment in the line with B–B4 is either 1 P–Q4 N–KB3 2 P–QB4 P–KN3 3 N–QB3 P–Q4 4 B–B4 B–N2 5 P–K3 O–O; and now (a) 6 N–B3 P–B4=, or (b) 6 Q–N3 P–B3 7 N–B3 Q–R4, or (c) 6 R–B1 P–B4 7 PxBP B–K3! 8 N–B3 N–B3 (Botvinnik).

Returning to the position on the board after 5 . . . P–Q4, White can naturally exert pressure on the QB file by 6 R–B1, maintaining the option of P–K3 or P–K4. The text 6 Q–N3 looks like the confusing of thematic strategies and like a point scored by Fischer. Instead of 6 . . . P–B3, Black now "surrenders" the center because he gains chances to attack White's queen instead.

| 6 . . . | PxP |
| 7 QxBP | P–B3 |
| 8 P–K4 | QN–Q2 |

Theory recommended 8 . . . P–QN4 9 Q–N3 Q–R4 or 8 . . . KN–Q2, but Fischer's move neutralizes White's center more effectively and at the same time develops another piece without compromising his pawn posi-

tion. White's 8 P–K4 relinquishes the chance of defending the QP by 8 P–K3. The injection of an original idea in an effortless manner already shows the grandmaster touch. After 9 P–K5, Black has either 9 . . . N–N3 and 10 . . . KN–Q4 or 9 . . . N–Q4 10 NxN PxN 11 QxP NxP! (Fischer).

| 9 R–Q1 | N–N3 |
| 10 Q–B5? | |

Once more 10 Q–N3 was called for.

| 10 . . . | B–N5! |

Actively played, and planning 11 . . . KN–Q2 12 Q–R3 P–K4 13 PxP Q–K1. In reply, 11 B–K2 would have been a sound developing move, as the aforementioned freeing maneuver cannot be prevented. But White believes that he can contain Black, that his next move inhibits . . . P–K4, and that he has time to complete his development with either B–K2 or perhaps B–Q3, followed by O–O.

| 11 B–KN5!? | N–R5!! |

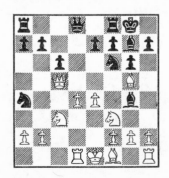

A diabolical offering, ingenious to conceive and presaging more to come. While Black's queen's knight is for the taking, it is invulnerable because of 12 NxN NxP; and now (a) 13 QxKP with either 13 . . . QxQ 14 BxQ KR–K1 15 B–K2 RxB 16 O–O P–QN4! or 13 . . . Q–R4ch! 14 P–N4 (14 N–B3 NxN and 15 . . . R–K1+) QxN 15 QxN KR–K1 16 B–K7 (16 N–K5 QxR mate) BxN 17 QxB (PxB B–B3+) RxBch 18 B–K2 QR–K1 19 R–Q2 QxNP+. (b) 13 BxP NxQ 14 BxQ NxN 15 B–KN5 BxN 16 PxB NxP, with a won ending. (c) 13 Q–N4 NxB 14 NxN BxR 15 KxB BxP 16 Q–Q2 BxP, likewise with a won endgame. (d) 13 Q–B1 Q–R4ch 14 N–B3 BxN 15 PxB QxB∓, or 13 . . . BxN 14 PxB Q–R4ch 15 B–Q2 NxB 16 QxN QxN∓. Thus White's restrained reply is mandatory. But the value of the game is enhanced when Black generates his best resources.

12 Q–R3          NxN
13 PxN           NxP!!
14 BxP           Q–N3!!

Black keeps making the very moves that White believes to have saved himself from; e.g., (a) 15 BxR BxB 16 Q–N3 NxQBP! 17 QxQ (17 QxN? B–N5!) PxQ 18 R–R1 R–K1ch 19 K–Q2 N–K5ch 20 K–B2 NxP 21 KR–N1 B–B4ch wins. Or (b) 15 B–K2 KR–K1, with the threat . . . BxN. Byrne had

reckoned with 14 . . . Q–K1? 15 R–Q3!

## 15 B–B4

White must refuse the offer of the exchange (initiated by 13 . . . NxP) because of 15 BxR BxB 16 Q–N3 NxQBP 17 QxQ (not 17 QxN B–N5 capturing the queen) PxQ 18 R–R1 R–K1ch 19 K–Q2 N–K5ch 20 K–B2 NxP 21 R–KN1 B–B4ch, with an irresistible attack.

15 . . .          NxQBP

15 . . . KR–K1 16 O–O NxQBP 17 B–B5 N–N4 18 BxN/5 QxB 19 R–QN1 Q–B5 20 RxP would allow White very promising counterplay. But Black's text continues the mocking sparkle, in anticipation of his 17th move —else the concept would be faulty.

## 16 B–B5?!

A sharp counterstroke, showing confidence in the solidity of White's setup.

If 16 BxR BxB 17 Q–N3 R–K1ch 18 K–B1 QxQ 19 BxQ NxR 20 BxN and Black is a pawn to the good. If 16 QxN KR–K1 17 Q–R3 R–KB1, regaining the piece and keeping the pawn with a commanding positional lead. The attack on Black's queen, however, seems to tilt the balance and gain material for White.

16 . . .          KR–K1ch
17 K–B1           B–K3!!

The acme of imagination, confronting White with a devilish choice. Although he picks the greater evil, there actually is not much of a lesser one to choose from. If 18 BxB Q–N4ch 19 K–N1 N–K7ch 20 K–B1 N–N6 dbl. ch. 21 K–N1 Q–B8ch 22 RxQ N–K7 mate. If 18 QxN QxB 19 PxQ BxQ, with a winning pawn ahead. If 18 B–Q3 N–N4 19 Q–N4 Q–B2 20 P–QR4 P–QR4!

The precision of Black's combination, started with 11 . . . N–R5, becomes even more evident if it is realized that 17 . . . B–K3! is also the only move that saves Black from defeat, while also keeping the draw in hand by perpetual check after 21 K–N1—unless there is more in it for Black, and there is! If 17 . . . N–N4 18 BxPch KxB 19 Q–N3ch B–K3 20 N–N5ch K–N1 21 NxB NxP 22 NxNch QxQ 23 NxQ+.

| 18 BxQ | BxBch |
| 19 K–N1 | N–K7ch |
| 20 K–B1 | NxPch |
| 21 K–N1 | |

Amusing is 21 R–Q3? PxB 22 Q–B3 NxN 23 QxB R–K8 mate. The interpolation of 20 . . . NxPch later provides protection for the knight on QB6.

| 21 . . . | N–K7ch |
| 22 K–B1 | N–B6ch |
| 23 K–N1 | PxB |
| 24 Q–N4 | R–R5! |

Not 24 . . . NxR? 25 QxB. If 24 Q–B1 N–K7ch+ and if 24 Q–Q6 QR–Q1! 25 QxR N–K7ch 26 K–B1 N–Q4ch! and 27 . . . RxQ!

**25 QxP**

Still not 25 Q–Q6 NxR 26 QxN RxP and 27 . . . R–R8. Black's next capture leaves him with two bishops and a rook, a passed pawn, and greater mobility—enough for a sure win.

| 25 . . . | NxR |
| 26 P–KR3 | RxP |
| 27 K–R2 | NxP |
| 28 R–K1 | RxR |
| 29 Q–Q8ch | B–B1 |
| 30 NxR | B–Q4 |
| 31 N–B3 | N–K5 |
| 32 Q–N8 | P–QN4 |
| 33 P–R4 | P–R4 |
| 34 N–K5 | K–N2 |
| 35 K–N1 | B–B4ch |
| 36 K–B1 | N–N6ch |

36 K–R2 B–Q3 37 Q–K8ch N–B3 is another killer.

| 37 K–K1 | B–N5ch |
| 38 K–Q1 | B–N6ch |
| 39 K–B1 | N–K7ch |
| 40 K–N1 | N–B6ch |
| 41 K–B1 | R–QB7 mate |

The older Byrne brother, Robert, was also unlucky against Fischer, in a thrilling game which was awarded First Brilliancy prize. *The South African Chess Quarterly* described the encounter as fabulous and unparalleled, with Black turning White's safe and solid position at the 11th move into a loss within eleven more moves.

The game is given in Robert J. Fischer's *My 60 Memorable Games* (New York: Simon & Schuster, 1969) with his own elaborate notes; I therefore report its impressive course with only short comments. The highlights tell their own story with penetrating clarity.

## U.S. CHAMPIONSHIP

### New York 1963–64
*Gruenfeld Defense*

| R. BYRNE | R. J. FISCHER |
|----------|---------------|
| 1 P–Q4 | N–KB3 |
| 2 P–QB4 | P–KN3 |
| 3 P–KN3 | P–B3 |
| 4 B–N2 | P–Q4 |
| 5 PxP | PxP |
| 6 N–QB3 | B–N2 |
| 7 P–K3 | O–O |
| 8 KN–K2 | N–B3 |
| 9 O–O | P–N3 |
| 10 P–N3 | B–QR3 |

When this tournament was played, Fischer was a steamroller flattening all before him. This explains his opponent's impulse to simplify whenever possible, to blunt Fischer's progress, and score at least a draw. Therefore, Byrne as White chose the simpler 5th, 7th, and 10th moves in favor of the more complicated 7 N–R3 or 7 N–B3 or 10 N–B4.

| 11 B–QR3 | R–K1 |
|----------|------|
| 12 Q–Q2 | P–K4! |

Apparently Fischer considered 12 . . . P–K3 as solid but drawish and preferred to unbalance

the position—and Byrne! Byrne did not expect Black to settle himself with an isolated QP.

| 13 PxP | NxP |
|--------|-----|
| 14 KR–Q1? | |

The question mark is paradoxical, yet true. Black has a hold on the diagonal QR3–KB8 and pins White's knight. It is natural that White move the KR out of the pin and onto the Q-file, exerting still more pressure upon Black's "isolani." Just as sensibly, the QR is presumed to occupy the open QB file. Besides, as has been generally pointed out, *14 QR–Q1* might have been answered by . . . Q–B1 *15 B–N2 Q–KB4*, or *15 NxP NxN 16 BxN R–Q1 17 P–B4 RxB!* with a new ball game. But Fischer comments that he saw . . . Q–B1 in after-game analysis long after! Would he have seen it during the game?

| 14 . . . | N–Q6! |
|----------|-------|
| 15 Q–B2! | NxP!? |

Byrne himself said that he could not figure out why Black chose a line which seemed to lose in the long run, until he was confronted with the dazzling shocker 18 . . . NxB; it provided a cue, although the final blow occurred three moves later. Black's positional feel and instinct, combined into foresight, at work.

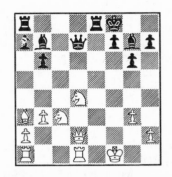

| 16 | KxN | N–N5ch |
| 17 | K–N1 | NxKP |
| 18 | Q–Q2! | NxB! |
| 19 | KxN | P–Q5! |
| 20 | NxP | B–N2ch |
| 21 | K–B1 | |

If 21 K–N1 BxNch 22 QxB R–K6ch 23 K–B2 QxQch 24 RxQ RxR wins. If 21 K–B2 QxQ 22 B–N2 Q–R6 23 N–B3 B–KR3 24 Q–Q3 B–K6ch 25 QxB RxQ 26 KxR R–K1ch 27 K–B2 Q–B4 wins.

| 21 . . . | | Q–Q2! |

White resigned. If 22 Q–KB2 Q–R6ch 23 K–N1 R–K8ch 24 RxR BxN; or 22 N/4–N5 Q–R6ch 23 K–N1 B–KR3, all winning rapidly.

Observed with hindsight, the removal of White's KR from its wing at move 14 KR–Q1 actually invited Black's devastating king-side attack!

Notice of the game went around the world.

## DEFENDER OF PRINCIPLES

As he matured as a chess player, Fischer passed through periods of distinct crises, each one based on stubbornly held principles. He often gained his point partly because he was Fischer, the chess hero, partly because the climate was right for a change.

In 1962 Fischer started his campaign against the system whereby one candidateless tourney decided who shall challenge the sitting champion. Fischer argued that the Soviet Union's numerical preponderance heavily favored one of their players to succeed with the assistance of team tactics. In 1965 Fischer's view was upheld, and FIDE changed the procedure to a series of matches to determine the ultimate challenger. Also in 1965, Fischer decided to take part in the Capablanca Memorial Tournament, held in Havana, Cuba, in August–September. This decision was in spite of the U.S. Department of State's decree forbidding travel to Cuba, except for "news-gathering journalists." Enthusiastically endorsed by Cuba, which was interested in his participation, Fischer, unable to attend personally, devised the stratagem of teletype (and supporting telephone) communications from New York to Havana, thus bypassing the U.S. government's embargo.

The next imbroglio happened at the Sousse Interzonal Tournament 1967, which seemed obligatory for Fischer to attend in order to qualify for the World Championship. After the 9th game—with 7½ points to his credit and clearly headed for first place—Fischer asked for a simple and well-reasoned adjustment of his overcrowded schedule. A partly prejudiced and partly inept group of arbiters turned him down and forfeited his 10th game against Gipslis when he did not turn up, pending a disposition of his protest. Fischer had been requested to play regardless, and to await a decision later—one of the persistent bureaucratic demands which disregard the realistic fact of life that a fighter won't continue with a Damoclean sword over his head, hoping for relief after the resolution of some intangible regulation.

After some persuasion, Fischer did arrive, fifty-three minutes late, for his next game against Reshevsky, and beat Sammy within eighteen moves! But he was finally denied a replay against Gipslis— and against Hort and Larsen, whose games he forfeited under similar circumstances. Since he could not cope single-handedly with officialdom and grandmaster jealousies at Sousse, Fischer quit. His unconventional behavior caused a European outcry over his "rudeness," adding insult to his own injury. A venerable Swiss chess journalist suggested in his column that the undisciplined juvenile ("der Halbwuechsige") be subjected to a thorough spanking ("eine Tracht Pruegel")—this, in an era when young men of twenty-four rise to become staff officers and die in war, or unabashedly become millionnaires.

The sociological background of this affair was delineated by me, in *Chess Review* of April 1968, as "The Purgatory of Robert J. Fischer" (a heading superficially diagnosed by one Fischer biographer as "ominous sounding"):

. . . many regions, near and far, are now affected by peculiar rumblings of revolt calling for reform. Bearded artists, skeptical students, unionized writers, poets and the like, rebel against staled ideologies which have always been anathema to the iconoclast.

The iconoclast, indeed, is hard to defend. He is so often unpredictable in his reaction and erratic behavior. He is a square peg in a round hole even while he denies he is a square! So he stands a seemingly justified target for authoritative rebuke. When he does not conform to the "club," it is turned as a bludgeon against him. Such happened to Bobby Fischer in Sousse.

A serious competition must undoubtedly be governed by generally applicable rules, which will be respected if impeccably and rationally administered by persons of proven stature and experience. That last clause comes into question as applied to the events at Sousse.

Another issue also arises. In countries where even leisure is officially organized and subsidized and so professionalized, the chessplayer is not an individual, but a protected member of a particular social pyramid, which expects him to cooperate in upholding his country's prestige in return for secure financial shelter. But the success of an American master is based entirely on his own inventive effort. He has to be a "prima donna" with just the right doses of temperament and cunning to propel him to success. He lays his own money and his existence on the line of competition. Right or wrong, this is the fact of life. And the American master has done remarkably well in his environment for overwhelmingly harassed amateurs.

It is too much to demand, however, that he must abide too obediently by all the dictates of an aging collective group and discard all his artistic temperament and idiosyncrasies.

Because of some mistakes—which were matched by errors in judgment on the part of the organizers—Robert J. Fischer was excluded from an all-important event by legalistic means, partly arising out of fear. Unless a remedy is found, Fischer will become the shadow prime minister: no one will be able to call himself the undisputed champion of the world. Some remedy must be found, with the arguments to be decided over the chessboard.

Despite the fact that their own interest was at stake, the Yugoslav team seems to have been the only one to keep aloof. The affair at Sousse set the lone fighter back by four years and, undoubtedly, must have left him with a deep sore. At last, the final decision came over the chess board: the 1970 Olympics in Giessen; the 3:1 victory over Petrosian at Belgrade 1970; and Fischer's commanding margin in Zagreb 1970.

In 1970, the FIDE presidency passed from Folke Rogard to the knowledgeable former World Chess Champion Max Euwe. Perhaps helped by his better insight as well, the World Chess Federation felt constrained to admit Fischer to the Palma de Mallorca Interzonal, provided that any one of the three American qualifiers would step aside in Fischer's favor. West Coast international master William Addison exercised his right to participate—ignoring the exhortations of the USCF executive—in the hope to make the grandmaster norm, but finished 18th out of twenty-four contestants; Reshevsky was not the man to yield to Fischer, and finished 17th; but Pal Benko obliged. When Bill Lombardy, next in line as a substitute, also bowed out in Fischer's favor, the road was open for Bobby to proceed to the top of the ladder in the Interzonal, cap his success with an enormous plus score at Buenos Aires 1970, and finally crush Larsen, Taimanov, and Spassky—in unprecedented fashion.

The overtures, the ploys, and the pandemonium preceding the final takeoff, were indeed unique in the annals of chess championships. Among the imponderables were the on, off, and on again travel plans to the Reykjavik location; the hide and seek with the press and other media; the bull sessions with Fischer's exasperated, and exasperating, entourage; the confrontations with the Icelandic organizers; and the seesaw of terms approved, rejected, and again accepted, when the British "angel" James D. Slater upped the Fischer–Spassky stake and coupled it with the derisive question whether Fischer was chicken; he indeed got Fischer to respond.[4] Some of the chess reactions in this intricate web of the 1972 World Championship are next on the agenda.

## THE BIZARRE INCIDENT AT REYKJAVIK

Fischer gave up two games at Reykjavik. Was it the first nail in Spassky's coffin? A paradoxical statement—but had there been anything predictable since Fischer went amok?

Inexplicable by all rational standards, and in a manner which even an average player would not try, a champion throws away an obvious and inevitable draw in the 1st match game, playing 29 . . . BxKRP!? Some of the innumerable reports have it that Fischer blundered, playing hastily and nervously. No wonder, we say: the greater the artist, the greater the butterflies to overcome at the start. But what kind of butterflies would induce *such* a simply incredible move? Before we continue dissecting, let us diagram the position we are talking about, after White's 29 P–N5, in the 1st game of the World Championship Match, Reykjavik, July 11, 1972:

---

[4] The nagging thought: Was it the British, in the person of Slater, who presented the United States with a new champion?

B. V. SPASSKY                                                    R. J. FISCHER

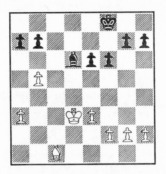

In this position, Black played the notorious 29 . . . BxKRP!? and we gave the move a contradictory exclamation mark, both because of psychology and because of the facts involved. Another view holds that Fischer's deed disdainfully indicated: "Well, obviously 29 . . . K–K2 draws now, but a draw? So easily? Let's see how far you can be pushed and show me?" (but the reader is advised not to emulate any such hypothetical tactics). If one witnesses that Fischer, losing this one bet, proceeded to forfeit another point and thereafter win the match (suffering just one more, this time genuine, loss), must not one admit that Fischer's stance succeeded? Did Fischer have his "evil eye" indeed not on Spassky but on the next World Championship contender?

For Robert Fischer even this so-called incredible blunder was not the ultimate loser, but simply imprudent. Yet, the "simple ending" created a wealth of postmortems, with grandmasters from all over the world sharply differing in their analyses for years thereafter— with only a few correctly pinpointing where and how Fischer subsequently still missed to draw.

Spassky played accurately in reply to Fischer's thumbing his nose at him with yet undiscernible effect. Fischer also mocked the galaxy of experts who kept racking their brains to find the definitive solution in a "plain" ending which everyone had been sure led to an immediate loss. Ironically, during the active phase, Fischer himself failed to concentrate successfully on the contingencies that might have saved the draw.

Fischer was indeed a master of endgame tactics, but it appears that the motives underlying this particular game were somewhat special and outside proficiency. In the role of Dr. Jekyll and Mr. Hyde, Fischer shed the pose of the good endgame doctor, and with Spassky played the Mr. Hyde. As attorney for the defense, we must not dismiss the somber thought that the nonchalent yet erratic 29th move might have given Fischer cause to ponder later on: "Did I blow a piece—or my nerves?" While Fischer did recoup his full powers, were there sinister traces of nervous difficulties that the incessant pressure of chess might sometimes produce?

As to the endless analyses of this ending, which for years stayed on with the world's chosen best, I am not attempting to belittle proven credentials; I merely use their exasperated probing as an example of the bottomless snake pit of championship chess interpretations.

In a nutshell: Fischer lost game 1, creating a lot of psychological undertones; and he lost game 2 by outright forfeit. Yugoslavia's A. Pasternjak, in *Bobby Fischer* (Munich: Copress, 1974), speculates that gentlemanly Boris Spassky lost the psychological war when—perhaps under governmental instruction—he cooperated in the acceptance of the forfeit as an established fact, a forfeit which had resulted from Fischer's insistence on no television cameras and which had no direct bearing on chess, on Spassky's income, or other interests in the televised match controversy. It was a triangular dispute between Fischer (the financial winner or loser), and the Icelanders and the producer Chester Fox, and was resolved in Fischer's favor somewhat belatedly—after his clock had been running for forty-five minutes; and Fischer did not feel that he could absorb such a handicap at that point. Spassky, purportedly eager to fight, won the second game by default on extraneous grounds, and the score stood at 2:0. Ready to withdraw (as usual!), Fischer was persuaded—perhaps by Dr. Henry Kissinger; perhaps by his sister Joan Targ, who still was his alter familia rather than the Collinses; perhaps by his attorneys, seconds, and friends; or last but not least by the purse—to continue the match in spite of two points down. By that time, Fischer also was the embodiment of cold fury and determination, all of which might have helped to overcome the stage fright before facing the last hurdle: World Champion Spassky, against whom he had never before won a game out of five played. Three he had lost and two were drawn, and now he was another 2 points down. (We have here an interesting parallel to Capablanca–Alekhine, with the latter having a minus score of 5:0 before the start of their 1927 championship match.)

The miracle happened: Fischer won game 3, breaking the spell and restoring his self-confidence by gaining on the match score: 2:1. Game 4 was a draw, with a score of 2½:1½; game 5, a win for Fischer, levelling the score to 2½:2½. In the preceding match Fischer–Petrosian, Buenos Aires 1971, Fischer had crushed his adversary's stamina in the 6th game. With a more dramatic prologue, history was repeated with the 6th match game Fischer–Spassky. The foreplay already presaged a crisis for Black. Only two times in his past had Fischer adopted the English Opening, and that possibly was mere probing. The Russian analysts suspected Fischer to be weak in the sector of openings and always worked feverishly to unnerve him with theoretical innovations. But Fischer, like Capablanca, had a wide grasp of the game's methodology, had a systematic, conceptual feel of total strategy, and of his opponents' soft spots; he was superb in the middlegame and in the endgame.

Copying the style of chess enthusiast and music critic Harold C. Schonberg, who authored *Grandmasters of Chess* (Philadelphia: Lippincott, 1973), a book written in admirable prose, grandmaster M. Najdorf called the next duet a "game like a symphony by Mozart." (If one likes just Mozart.)

Match Game 6
**Reykjavik 1972**
*Queen's Gambit Declined*
*(by transposition)*

R. J. FISCHER              B. SPASSKY

| 1 P–QB4 | P–K3 |
| 2 N–KB3 | P–Q4 |
| 3 P–Q4?! | N–KB3 |

*Item:* For the first time, Fischer adopts the Queen's Gambit in serious play, and catches Black unprepared for that.

*Item:* White knows that Spassky persistently played the Tartakover Variation, considered it the most flexible defense, and had never yet lost a game with it; and that, to be safe, Black will now follow in these footsteps.

*Item:* Spassky occupies a hot seat, wondering what new turn Fischer may have discovered among the preferences chosen by Black in the past; but he must wait and see.

The game is now steered, through known channels of theory, straight into a middlegame which is Fischer's true fishpond. He bypasses the endless and sickening routines of "opening research."

| 4 N–B3 | B–K2 |
| 5 B–N5 | O–O |
| 6 P–K3 | P–KR3 |
| 7 B–R4 | P–QN3 |

Aggressive is 7 . . . N–K5, the Lasker Defense, but with years of analysis behind it, it dissipates tension too early, leaving Black with a slight positional disadvantage to face in the endgame. The text maintains greater "dis-balance"; despite Black's loss here, the Tartakover Variation is not as bad as the coming defeat may make it look.

When Fischer resorted to the same defense (when Black) against Petrosian at Belgrade 1959, and at Curacao 1962, both games were drawn. He won as Black against Bertok at Stockholm 1962. Fischer was thus able to put himself into Spassky's shoes.

Briefly glancing at other stratagems against 7 . . . P–QN3: in a game played just before this match; i.e.; Portisch–Ivkov, Wijk aan Zee 1972, White postponed 4 N–B3 in favor of 4 B–N5 B–K2 5 P–K3 P–KR3 6 B–R4 O–O 7 R–B1 P–QN3 8 PxP NxP 9 NxN PxN 10 BxB QxB 11 B–K2! P–QR4! 12 B–B3! Q–N5ch 13 Q–Q2 P–QB3 14 R–B3! Q–Q3 15 N–K2±, but 12 . . . Q–Q3 at once would have been more stable. The sequence shows some of the ideas in the Tartakover Variation and the stratagems apparent in this game, which continues in the conventional fashion. (Actually, the 11 B–K2 to B3 maneuver was invented by Flohr–Bondarevsky, Moscow 1947; anything new is something old.)

| 8 PxP | NxP |
| 9 BxB | QxB |
| 10 NxN | PxN |
| 11 R–B1 | B–K3 |

The bishop's best square! The fianchetto 7 . . . P–QN3 does not prepare . . . B–N2, but . . . P–QB4. It remains to be seen if Black's combined but "hang-

ing" pawns on QB4 and Q4 are an asset or a liability.

| 12 Q–R4 | P–QB4 |
| 13 Q–R3 | R–B1 |
| 14 B–N5! | P–QR3 |

14 B–K2 N–Q2 was usual before Furman, against Geller, Moscow 1970, played 14 B–N5 to provoke the weakening 14 . . . P–QR3, even though it was followed up by . . . Q–N2. Furman–Zaitsev, Tallin 1971, tried to ignore White's maneuver with 14 . . . P–QR4!? (as a prelude to 15 . . . Q–N5ch) 15 R–B3! P–QB4; 16 B–Q3 Q–R2! 17 B–N5 N–R3 18 O–O N–B2 19 B–B6 P–B5! but the line is not too inspiring.

Nevertheless, Spassky might have tried for other ways; e.g., (a) 14 . . . K–B1?! 15 PxP RxP 16 RxR QxR! 17 K–Q2 QxQ 18 QxQ N–Q2 19 BxN BxB 20 N–K5 B–K1 21 R–QB1 K–K2 22 K–Q3 P–B3 23 N–B3 K–Q3 24 K–Q4 B–Q2 25 N–Q2 R–K1= (J. Zelinskis–V. Sichov, correspondence, USSR 1971); or (b) 14 . . . Q–N2! 15 PxP PxP 16 RxP (16 B–R4 N–R3!) RxR 17 QxR P–R3 18 B–Q3 QxNP 19 O–O N–Q2 20 Q–B6 R–N1 21 N–Q4 Q–N3= (*Das Schach-Archiv,* 1973).

Obviously, Spassky and his trainers Geller and others had spent the time before the match intensively preparing for replies to Fischer's sacrosanct 1 P–K4, and thus Spassky himself neglected to familiarize himself with the innovations found after the Furman–Geller game. They had not counted on Fischer's sudden switch, which accounts for Spassky's sticking with what he knew so far. And he fumbled.

| 15 PxP | PxP |
| 16 O–O | R–R2 |

In this position, Spassky should have followed with Geller's own improvement over the doubtful text move, and played 16 . . . Q–N2 17 B–K2 (17 B–R4 B–Q2!) N–Q2, although White still maintains pressure with 18 R–B3 and 19 KR–B1.

| 17 B–K2 | N–Q2?? |

Here we have that fumble. Spassky remembered that something had been wrong with Geller's continuation against Furman; i.e., 17 . . . P–QR4 18 R–B3 N–Q2 19 KR–B1 R–K1 20 B–N5! B–N5 21 N–Q2! and he therefore chooses the more natural 17 . . . N–Q2—but it was no longer natural.

Petrosian put forth 17 . . . P–B5 18 QxQ RxQ 19 N–Q4 N–B3, but 20 NxB PxN 21 P–QN3 N–R4 22 PxP NxP 23 P–K4 R/K2–QB2 24 B–N4 is good for White. Tal thought of 17 . . . Q–B1 now instead of later, but these afterthoughts are moot. Whatever Black's strategy, Fischer is already on the march.

| 18 N–Q4! | Q–B1? |

Purely for the sake of analysis: if 18 . . . N–B3 19 N–N3! N–K5 20 P–B3±; or 19 . . . R/2–B2 20 BxP R–R1 21 RxP±; or 19 . . . N–Q2 20 R–B3 K–B1 21 KR–B1±; or 19 . . . P–B5 20 QxQ RxQ 21 N–Q4±.

There is of course 18 . . . K–B1, or 18 . . . N–B1; 19 NxB PxN; or 18 . . . N–N3 19 Q–R5 N–B5, but after Spassky's choice, Fischer's grip tightens even faster. Spassky might have expected 19 N–N3, but not Fischer's next two moves, which look like good prior homework.

| 19 NxB! | PxN |
| 20 P–K4!! | P–Q5?! |

This move has been questioned in many quarters, as it immobilizes Black's center, but there might be no better substitute. If 20 . . . N–B3 21 P–K5 N–Q2 22 B–N4 Q–K2 23 P–B4±; if 20 . . . P–B5 21 Q–R3! Q–B2 22 B–N4 R–K1 23 B–R5! (23 PxP PxP 24 KR–K1 RxRch 25 RxR N–B1= —Tal) P–N3 24 B–K2± (S. Flohr and I. Nei).

| 21 P–B4 | Q–K2 |
| 22 P–K5 | R–N1? |

22 . . . N–N3 at once would have been a last tactical hope.

| 23 B–B4 | K–R1 |

Now 23 . . . N–N3 comes too late because of 24 Q–QN3 K–B2 25 P–B5!+. Black is helpless against Fischer's generating king-side attack. White carefully prevents any countermeasures and finally smashes through with a mating attack.

| | |
|---|---|
| 24 Q–R3 | N–B1 |
| 25 P–QN3 | P–QR4 |
| 26 P–B5! | PxP |
| 27 KRxP | N–R2! |
| 28 QR–B1! | Q–Q1 |
| 29 Q–N3 | R–K2 |
| 30 P–KR4 | R/1–N2 |
| 31 P–K6! | R/N2–B2 |
| 32 Q–K5 | Q–K1 |
| 33 P–R4 | Q–Q1 |
| 34 R/1–B2 | Q–K1 |
| 35 R/2–B3 | Q–Q1 |
| 36 B–Q3 | Q–K1 |
| 37 Q–K4! | N–B3 |

Black's hopeless queen shuttle is at a merciful end. The threat was 38 R–B8ch NxR 39 RxNch with mate next.

If 37 . . . P–N3 38 Q–K5ch R–N2 39 R–B7 RxR 40 RxR Q–KN1 41 BxNP and 42 P–K7+. 37 R–B7 RxR 38 PxR QxQ 39 P–B8(Q)ch also ends the agony.

| | |
|---|---|
| 38 RxN | PxR |
| 39 RxP | K–N1 |
| 40 B–B4 | K–R1 |

41 R–B7 was threatened. If 40 . . . Q–Q1 41 Q–N6ch+; or 40 . . . Q–R4 41 R–N6ch K–R1 42 Q–R8ch and mate next.

| | |
|---|---|
| 41 Q–B4 | Resigns |

Threat: 42 R–B8ch. If 41 . . . R–B1 42 RxPch R–R2 43 Q–B6ch K–N1 44 P–K7ch R–B2 45 R–R8 mate.

With this game, Spassky's spirit broke. He did not recover it during this match. With the termination of the 21st game, with 7 wins, 3 losses, 11 draws, and a total score of 12½:8½, the match of the century ended in Fischer's favor.

From here on, during a vacuum of three years to come, the chess world's attention was riveted on the firm expectation that Fischer was not to let go, not let go soon, nay, never let go, of that hold to the highest chess honors. It did not work out this way. Fischer developed a trend that had been emerging but became manifest after 1972: to become an utter recluse. While Morphy refused appointments, he never concealed his abode; he could be found even if he did not respond. Fischer denied even the chance to be contacted and became a hermit.

## FISCHER BOWS OUT

As a sequel, when the championship turned full cycle again in 1975, it created a twilight of the gods when Fischer renounced his title rather than play under any but his own terms; *terms* that have been proven right, but were intransigently posed at the wrong time, either too late in the season or maybe prematurely. After a decisive re-affirmation of his title in a match with Karpov, had it come to it, Fischer's terms might have been accepted and his powers remained undisputed even if he had consequently retired. Robert Byrne, in the *New York Times*, voiced the opinion that Fischer's refusal to play Karpov was due to unsurmountable fear. Fear is a part of the artist's syndrome but to make it the sole, cowardly cause may be too simple. If Byrne's *reveille* tried to reawaken Slater's earlier challenge, it was sounded too late. Actually, Fischer might have suffered from his own reflections, looking back at the match games with Spassky. Fischer had scored no win ever against Spassky before the 3rd match game. Game 3 provided a break by virtue of Fischer's controversial, though upsetting, move 11 . . . N–R4. With his in-cisive power of analysis, Fischer might have pondered how often and how far luck, determination, and health may keep a man at the top—what did the magic crystal tell him?

Apart from these speculations, what were the unmet terms? Up to the "match of the century," the rules provided that whoever had the better score out of 24 games, became champion. (Incidentally, had this rule been effective for the Alekhin–Capablanca match of 1927, the contest would have ended at 13:11 for Alekhin; or 4 wins, 2 losses, 18 draws, at a saving of another ten games. The remaining drama, climaxing in Alekhin's victory in the 32nd and 34th and final game would have not been enacted and Alekhin's success would have been less convincing.)

Shortly after the 1972 match, Fischer concluded that a 12½ (to 8½) margin and the concomitant limitation to an arbitrary number of 24 games were both inconclusive and risky. In October 1972, FIDE changed the ruling to 6 wins out of a maximum of 30 games, draws not counting; and, if after 30 games no player has scored the required 6 wins, the winner of the match was the player who had a lead of at least 2 points. Fischer considered these limitations too narrow and insisted on 10 wins, draws not counting, and no limita-tions to the number of games played. Fischer also proposed that at a score of 9:9 a World Championship match be terminated with the incumbent champion retaining the title. In practical terms, this stipulation meant that the champion considered a challenger's winning margin of 1 point (e.g., 10:9) as too unconvincing to make the incumbent champion lose his title.

Fischer had a precedent to lean on in the Lasker–Schlechter challenge of 1909–10, which anticipated a title match of 30 games, with Schlechter having to win at least 2 more games than his op-ponent to be able to claim both match *and* title (i.e., 16:14 points).

Thus at 14½:14½, the challenger would not have won the title even if he had won the last, remaining, game and the match. The longer match did not materialize because of lack of backing for Schlechter, and it was reduced to 10 games; with Lasker, naturally, retaining the title when the match ended in a 5:5 tie. When Fischer's suggestions were voted down by FIDE in July 1974, and again in March 1975, Fischer resigned the crown. As the result, Anatoly (Tolya) Evgenyevich Karpov formally received the World Chess Federation's blessing as the World Chess Champion. He successfully went out to prove his worth by continuously winning a large number of strong international tournaments.

## FISCHER PARTIALLY VINDICATED?

The elimination match Karpov–Korchnoi (1974) ended with a score 3:2, with 19 draws—not a convincing decision within a total of twenty-four games. Korchnoi had to battle official favoritism with its depressing effects, and also the limited number of available rounds, which came to an end just when the odds were changing.

The match Karpov–Korchnoi in 1974 underlined Fischer's objections to putting a limit on the number of games before a differential of a score was attained, sufficiently high to topple the title holder.

Indeed, Fischer's arguments were partially met in 1977, when FIDE decided to remove the limit on the number of games to be played to win the World Championship. The match was to go on until one of the two parties had scored the first 6 wins. While well-fought-out draws often are a worthy outcome of a powerful struggle between near-equals, the revival of the provision of draws not counting also seemed to support the fighting spirit expected by the audience. The limitation to six wins also reduced the financial risks and other involvements.

With more detachment provided with the passing of time since the raging fires of the aborted Fischer–Karpov match, a few well-founded surveys were published, in favor of Fischer's arguments; namely (1) *The Meaning of Bobby Fischer's Decision*, by Barrie Richmond, M.D. (*CL&R*, 1975, No. 7), a psychological dissection of attitudes; (2) *Bobby Fischer: An Era Denied*, by Charles Kalme (*CL&R*, 1975, No. 11), mostly dealing with the statistical probabilities of Fischer's demand; and, actually preceding both of the above opinions: (3) "The Crucial Game—The 15th Match Game Korchnoi–Karpov," by Walter Korn (*Atlantic Chess News*, 1975, No. 5), trying to prove in its conclusions the correctness of Fischer's terms for a championship match.

Apart from any vindication of Fischer's standpoint, he created one disconcerting thought that was to haunt any current chess power for a long time to come; namely, that no dominance lasted forever—that someone could always come back or arise.

During the latter part of the 1970s, the tensions in the chess world had grown very acute. In addition to the emigration of grandmasters Lein and Shamkovich to the U.S.; of Liberzon, Dzhindzhikhashvili, Kushnir, Pachman, etc.; Spassky effected a "sabbatical" in the West, and Sosonko and Korchnoi defected. Korchnoi in particular decried the politicization of Soviet chess and its frequent violations of FIDE's tenets to suit the USSR's ends. In some instances, the Soviet Union was indeed obliged to drop some of its injunctions against participation of its chess dissidents in international matches anywhere.

In regard to Fischer and as time went on, the American onlooker reluctantly had to realize that the United States and the chess world may have to live on without such specific product; or, rather, find idols who represented a complete personality, beyond enormously skillful technique and drive.

## PRIVACY OR EXPOSURE

Chess is a sensitive absorption which may be privately recreational, yet contains the ambition to be overtly recognized. The conflict between privacy or promotion, American way, can be crucial. Concrete questions arise: Was Fischer intoxicated with success, and thus unable to cope with relapses? Did he abhor any regulations to an extent which became incompatible with reality? Was he messianic or just too principled? Was he after money only as a status symbol? But that cult was accorded "Bobby" only, not Chess!

Let us now look at some of the deceptive confusions that occurred during the Fischer–Spassky match: Fischer's clash with Fox over the televising of play and his defamation suit against Darrach. Tactics or views aside, there is a core of substance.

Fischer's managers arranged for the match to be televised, by "hidden, noiseless" camera, for viewing over closed circuit T.V., with a fee paid to the financial organizers of the match. This followed the pattern set mainly for mass sports events, but Fischer repudiated the agreement. He insisted that it interfered with his play. Perhaps he resented personal exposure to the medium, or was, indeed, hypersensitive to any suspected source of noise. This behavior—or even bacterio- or mysophobia—is not strange to prodigies and only they can judge; and they cannot be called paranoid.

Needless to say, any rights to, or use of, television as such, will be individually solved in future contests and might indeed become an important instrument of projection and propagation.

A further, related, incident arose with the demand to play part of the match in complete solitude, with only a referee present. Such request may be rooted in psychological need; or may be practical, with an eye on copyright. American chess history provides a precedent. The Capablanca–Lasker match in 1929 stipulated secrecy for the games that were attended by an umpire and one witness each. In one of them, Hartwig Cassel of the *American Chess Bulletin* and a reporter for New York's *Sun* and for the *Staatszeitung*, invoked the right to disclosure and passed the scores on to the press, without requesting a reward. It spoiled some expectations of income for the organizers, but they put up no fuss. It is uncertain, indeed, that closed proceedings would be commendable. Players' comments can be subjective, with improvements withheld for future use. Except by specific legislation, games (especially when played in a competition) cannot be copyrighted, an opinion held by several authorities; and misuse by confidential arrangement could become a danger. Only Chess Composition (e.g., problems and endgame studies) is copyrightable material, in the province of chess art. Yet, it is most flagrantly plagiarized and reproduced without "royalties" or the mention of source. A different approach might, of course, evolve with the advent of audio-visual techniques.

Ironically, during the Korchnoi–Spassky match, Belgrade 1978, and the Karpov–Korchnoi World Chess Championship, Bagoino 1978, similar issues surfaced of players' isolation from the public, or the opponent's right to choose solitude even away from the board. Thus one wonders whether Fischer evolved something overdue.

A tragicomic touch entered later, when Fischer sued Brad Darrach, a photo-reporter covering the Reykjavik match for *Life* magazine. Purportedly, Darrach had been pledged to cover the event and not utilize his role otherwise, but he subsequently published a book which, partly in the shape of a fiction, was somewhat critical of the Reykjavik scene. While Darrach claimed the privilege of describing a "public person," Fischer resented the intrusion of his privacy. Legal outcomes aside, Fischer made the chess world aware of the ins and outs of privacy and publicity for the player and his output. He was eternally on the escape from publicity and involved in a struggle to be left out of the public's obnoxious glare and to have the right to his own life.

Fischer left a number of legacies: first, that in chess as well as in other competitions, the impressive performers were entitled not to a few crumbs off the table, but to a proportionate reward; secondly,

for better or worse, a change in chess style. Fischer developed
extreme sensitivity to any external and environmental influences to
such a degree that it became difficult to draw the line, and limits,
between "psychological chess warfare" or sheer personal upset on
one hand, and the good old focusing-on-the-game on the other.
Chess is, after all, a game not of one but of two participants, each
with his own idiosyncracies, and a modicum is therefore imperative.
Thirdly, he left a legacy of doubt if he indeed "shall return." Fischer
is known to have met with Karpov in 1976, and with Korchnoi in
1977 to discuss an individual match—on his own terms. In 1977, he
also, experimentally, played against a high-caliber Greenblatt Computer Chess program in Los Angeles, winning all three games in
superb style.

# 12.

# Chess Lore and Chess Symbology

## CHESS CHRONICLES AND CHRONICLERS

Allowing a tolerance of three years, the American Bicentennial of 1976 may also include the Chess Bicentennial, when one considers that the original English publication of Ben Franklin's *The Morals of Chess* was in 1779. Preceded by centuries of ancient chess symbolism, Franklin's essay was a down-to-earth utilitarian manifesto about the new continent's acquisition of a valuable hobby to spread among the people.

America's contribution to chess, domestically and internationally, rests not only on the visible results of tournament games and its players, but also on the inducement of, and support by a rich, home-grown treasure trove. It embraces chess literature (factual and fiction); fine arts; the labor and the money devoted to the enrichment of chess; and other spheres of American chess tradition.

According to their time and place, some of the annals of American chess have already been given credit in foregoing chapters. We briefly repeat the chronology.

TABULATION OF EVENTS

| 1857 | First American Chess Congress | New York | 1st: P. Morphy |
|------|-------------------------------|----------|----------------|
| 1871 | Second American Chess Congress | Cleveland | 1st: G. H. Mackenzie |
| 1874 | Third American Chess Congress | Chicago | 1st: G. H. Mackenzie |
| 1876 | Fourth American Chess Congress | Philadelphia | 1st: J. Mason |
| 1880 | Fifth American Chess Congress | New York | 1st: G. H. Mackenzie |

234

1889   Sixth American         New York      1st, tie, M. Weiss
          Chess Congress                  and M. Chigorin
                                          6th: S. Lipschuetz
(Lipschuetz placed 6th, but 1st among American participants, thus earning the U.S. Championship title)
For subsequent title-holders we refer to the foregoing chapters.

REPOSITORIES OF INFORMATION

Jeremy Gaige, *Chess Tournament Crosstables*, Vol. I–IV (Philadelphia: 1974), a comprehensive, global coverage of tournaments, with the results shown round by round, and covering the period till 1930 (except matches).

Kenneth Harkness, *Official Chess Handbook;* "approved by the United States Chess Federation" (New York: McKay, 1967), covering events and top prize-winners during the period ending 1966.

Gene McCormick, "A Brief, Contentious History of U.S. Chess Championships" (*Chess Life & Review*, December 1977)

"Yearbook"—*Chess Life & Review's* annual summaries of American competitions; of masters' participation in tournaments abroad; etc.

USCF "Directory of Affiliates" (1978–   ); mostly chess clubs.

"Official USCF Guide"—annual, loose leaf (1979–   )

Douglas A. Betts, *Chess—An Annotated Bibliography of Works Published in the English Language, 1850–1968* (Boston: Hall, 1964).

The John G. White chess collection at the Cleveland Public Library is America's—and probably the world's—most comprehensive public storage of chess bibliography. Its donor, John Griswold White (1845–1925) of Cleveland, a wealthy attorney, also provided a trust fund of $275,000 for continued maintenance of his collection, which contains many ancient and priceless first editions, manuscripts, books, periodicals and chess sets. An extensive card-index of the John G. White Department's holdings was published in 1964 by Hall & Co. of Boston, but new publications have been added continuously by the curator, Alice N. Loranth.

Being different from "national" libraries (e.g., the Royal Dutch or the Yugoslav National), American public libraries must purchase out of their own municipal budgets and are gravely affected when the eroding financial support is further diminished by the flow of patrons' funds into more glamorous undertakings of less lasting value.

The New York Public Library possesses Frank J. Marshall's collection, later donated by Gustavus A. Pfeiffer. James E. Gates of Columbus, Georgia, was reputed to own the largest private assemblage of rare and valuable chess books in the United States, with

R. G. Hennessey of Los Angeles following closely; but no catalogs describing the content have yet been available. Albrecht Buschke of New York disposed of his valuable chess books after migrating to this country, but his expertise in matters of chess was put to frequent use. Kenneth Smith, American master, founder and co-editor of *Chess Digest Magazine*, has ranked among the largest distributors (and as an occasional publisher) of chess books and periodicals of English and foreign parentage. Fred Wilson of New York and D. Brandreth of Delaware also have some chess titles to their credit.

Within the various chapters of this book, we have mentioned some of the highlights of U.S. chess publication; e.g., the works of E. C. Cook, Fiske, Hagedorn, Hazeltine, Keidanz, Reichhelm, Shinkman. One may also include a number of leading contributions in the popular field of opening theory:

J. W. Miller, *The American Supplement to* [W. Cook's] *"Synopsis", Containing American Inventions in the Chess Openings* (Cincinnati, 1884).

Mordechai Morgan, *The Chess Digest*, 4 vols. (Philadelphia, 1901–5), a "most comprehensive encyclopedia of the openings in tabular form, with notes on over nineteen-thousand games." "Miller's *Supplement* owed most of its American analyses to Judd, Maurian, and Sellmann.[1]

## THE DIALECTICS OF CHESS

Apart from functional chess writing, America has produced a cornucopia of exquisite and imaginative chess fiction, which intermixes reality and well-invented legends. Morphy found a loving biographer in Francis Parkinson Keynes' *The Chess Players* (New York: Farrar, Straus & Giroux, and Fawcett, 1960). The story revolves around a few definite facts, but displays deep insight. I quote a passage: "We also know that, before leaving Paris in 1865, Paul Morphy suffered some sort of severe shock which resulted in a nervous breakdown. We have no idea what it was: again, imagination must enter the picture, but *imagination properly controlled*" (italics mine—W.K.). An extensive documentary about Morphy as man and chess player was compiled by Brooklyn's ardent collector

---

[1] The *Supplement* also listed all United States and Canadian chess clubs by name and address. The Methuselah among the clubs has been the Manhattan Chess Club of New York, which was organized on December 18, 1977. The oldest meeting place de facto but not de jure has been the chess room of the Mechanics' Institute (formerly the Mercantile Library) in Downtown San Francisco, dating back to 1850; but it was not incorporated as a chess club in its own right.

of Morphy memorabilia, David Lawson, in his book *Paul Morphy: The Pride and Sorrow of Chess* (New York: McKay, 1976). Both Keynes and Lawson convey total environmental and biographical detail just as Brady's book about Fischer does—two ingredients not often found together.

Inspired by the Fischer spell, another fictional, but rational, account was related in J. W. Ellison's *Master Prim*. It contains some revealing dialogue between a news-conscious editor and a chess-conscious reporter, who warns that chess players are very negative and alienated people who don't make good copy.

Two novels, one by an American passer-by, the other by a late-comer, but both widely read here, were written by Zweig, and by Nabokov. Stefan Zweig's *The Royal Game*, translated by Ben W. Huebsch, was published in the *Woman's Home Companion*, New York, March 1944. The book, which poetically penetrates a chess player's mind, was reprinted in *Chess Review*, November 1944. Dr. Henry Davidson, author of A *Short History of Chess* (New York: McKay, 1949), appended a comment to the effect that Zweig's narrative is not entirely flattering as it leaves unanswered the question whether an otherwise deficient mind (an *idiot savant*), who is the book's hero, could still be an outstanding success in a special faculty like chess.

Similar to Zweig but more expansive is Vladimir Nabokov's *The Defense* (in the Russian original, *The Luzhin Defense*) which appeared in *The New Yorker* and later as a book by Putnam (New York: 1964). Nabokov (1899–1977) arrived in the United States in 1939, became a citizen in 1945, and taught at American universities till 1959. He was very good at chess and a problem composer.

Recalling F. P. Keynes' remark about "imagination . . . controlled," one might read A. Cockburn's *Idle Passion: Chess and the Dance of Death* (New York: Village Voice/Simon & Schuster, 1974) and its psychoanalytical extremes with a grain of salt. The tractate reduces all of chess almost to depravity, and solely by inference. It is void of concrete chess substance, yet it serves as an anti-climax to too much obsession.

A staple in the field of instruction in chess for the young has been Milton Hanauer's *Chess for You and Me* (Philadelphia: McKay, 1948), later republished as *Chess Streamlined* (New York: Sterling, 1961) and then again as *Chess Made Easy* (Hollywood: Wilshire, 1967). Hanauer also produced *Chess Made Simple* (New York: Doubleday, 1957), and as a New York City school principal helped in establishing courses of chess instruction. He was a member of the U.S. Olympic team in 1928. Dr. Helen Weissenstein's *John and the Chess Men* (New York: McKay, 1952), illustrated by Kurt

Werth, attempted to bridge fairy tale, fairy chess game, and chess proper. The author had been equal 1st to 3rd with Bain and Karff in the U.S. Women's Open Championship 1939.

Attractive anthologies were compiled by I. A. Horowitz, I. Chernev, J. Saltzman, F. Reinfeld, N. Lessing, and A. Saidy (who became an International Master in 1969). The ultimate, and very amusing, trend was to tie science-fiction into chess; e.g., in Roger Lee Vernon's *The Chess Civilization* (New York: New American Library, 1955). Another such novelette, a genuine science-fiction forecast, remarkable in its foresight because computer chess was then in its infancy, is Fritz Leiber's, *The 64-Square Madhouse* (New York: Doubleday, 1966). The booklet deals with a live tournament in which a computer or, rather, its programmer, is one of the participants. The programmer is, however, permitted to change, adjust, and improve upon his program from round to round and in between play (time-limit permitting), depending on whom the computer is facing. This is actually a facsimile of what happens to the live opponents' tactics in a tournament. The author's prediction came true when in the Minnesota Open, February 1977, the Control Data Corporation's computer Cyber 176, programmed by Larry Atkin and David Slate as "CHESS 4.5," shared 1st and 2nd prize with a score 5:1, winning the championship on account of the statistical tie-break! (A lot of new problems as to title-holding by computer, by program, by programmers, by research institutions, or by live contestants; and entry into the higher class of competition by virtue of an existing program of changes therein, were bound to arise.)

## CHESS ICONOGRAPHY

The iconologists and bibliophiles of chess belong to an exalted stratum, different from the one that practices the game with the sweat of the brow. They don't play the chessmen—they collect or create their images; a few of them produce essays and illustrations; and some don't care to master the game, but simply admire its symbolism as their halucinogen. More people may have flocked to see their treasures or their organized pageants than active contests. On occasions, fancy meets pragmatism and both the player's and the collector's attitudes may overlap.

Valuable collections of chess sets—antique, classic, contemporary, or modernistic—are in the custody of the Metropolitan Museum of Art in New York (the prominent part of it came from Gustavus A. Pfeiffer, 1872–1953), but are also found in several other American museums. New York's Museum of Modern Art displays impressive modern sets, made of different woods, minerals, plastics, ceramics, alloys, and other substances. Other collections are privately owned; e.g. by the family of Macy Donald Liddell (1879–1958), illustrated in *Chessmen* (New York: Harcourt, Brace, 1937); by John F. Harbeson (shown in the Philadelphia Museum); by David Hafler, also of Philadelphia; and by William N. Copley of New York. Copley also owns sets designed by the famous sculptor Max Ernst during his visit with his close friend Marcel Duchamp in New York.

Sets of staggered origin are in the Cleveland Public Library, and some are also kept by various art galleries and other receptacles. Many of the modern Space Age sets are very descriptive in design, but often do not have the squat sturdiness and all-around visual functionalism of the official Staunton pattern. Artistic pieces serve to please the senses and are for deft and loving fingers, but are too delicate or expensive for practical use. They express an artist's desires and impressions and are a vehicle for his imagination, or are construed to reflect an era's mores.

Monographs on chess sets by American writers include E. Lanier Graham's *Chess Sets* (New York: Walker, 1968) and C. K. Wilkinson and Jessie McNab Dennis, *Chess: East and West, Past and Present* (New York: The Metropolitan Museum of Art, 1968).

Another chapter belongs to chess paintings and watercolors, etchings and lithographs, or whatever the medium may be for these portrayals. Many of them were itemized in Manfred Roesler, *Chess in Art* (ed. "The Chess Arts," Iowa, 1973). There are also chess tapestries, chess stamps, chess coins, chess patterns in advertising, ill-produced chess sets, mass-produced memorabilia, and so on . . .

Referring back to Marcel Duchamp, the native Frenchman but enthusiastic New Yorker, it is due to his friends, the poet Walter Arensberg and his wife Louise, that most of Duchamp's paintings on the theme of chess were loaned or donated to the Philadelphia Museum of Art. Part of his artistic figurations on chess remained with the Museum of Modern Art, with Mme. Varése, and with the Fried Gallery, all of New York, and with other private owners. Duchamp wrote an important treatise on pawn endings (together with Halberstadt), published in French, German, and English. His widow, Alexandra, is an adviser to the American Chess Foundation.

# 13.

# The Younger Elite and
# Their Impact

Buoyed by Fischer's model, coupled with its own stimulus and for a while propelled by continuing expectations of "he shall return," chess went through an upswing in the 1970s. The social European coffeehouse was in native fashion replaced by a multitude of "chess houses," catering to all comers, weak or strong, cultured or "sub"-cultured. New events were inaugurated on state or national level; the GHI International Open, the National Open, the World Open (with a $40,000 prize fund), the American Open; the U.S. Team and the Class Tournaments; and other arrangements, augmenting the U.S. championships and the U.S. Open, with one difference: that the championship, and other regular round-robin (inter-) national tourneys conveyed a clearer and steadier picture of individual playing strengths than was possible by the more haphazard and congested methods of the increasingly prevalent Swiss System of knock-out and elimination.

What fell by the board with the velocity of chess development and the intensity of the younger strata, was the "ageless" aspect of chess which, as a not-so-physical hobby, had allowed its being pursued into an old age when only physical but not the mental faculties might decline. The overpowering factor of superimposed speed, often lasting long hours, deprived the mentally still fit but slower senior—and also the occasional indulger—of proving his full worth. The athletic facet drowned out the intellectual one and the concomitant enjoyment of his cherished leisure.

While a few more chess columns were syndicated just before Fischer's no-show, a creeping slowdown of the economy and the emergence of a number of vital national priorities caused a moratorium in the further spasmodic expansion of chess. Yet, there were other hopes, of a different character.

Chess courses and seminars developed in some institutions that focused on liberal arts, a welcome attempt to catch up with the entrenched and popular courses on bridge and other pastimes. However, too much emphasis was on basic instruction which was up to high school level, and too little on catering to an enlightened though non-chess-playing audience of publishers, journalists, authors, copy-editors, commentators, media-reporters, public relations and promotional agencies, and even compositors and printers.

A large new generation of enthusiasts sprang up—less inhibited by the opponents' fame, nonchalant, yet quick to absorb the game. Many were longhaired, in tired blue jeans, backpacked and knap-sacked, with beard, headband, bedroll, and bare feet—inquisitive and irreverent youngsters who played strong chess with a determination that made them feared during sporadic appearances abroad.

Many of them attended college, taking out time equally for good grades and masterful chess. A few reached grandmaster level, and deserve to be so recorded, having contributed the new ideas always needed to beat an opponent. A few excelled in play only for a while, but stayed on to contribute to instruction and literature. A few left their occupations, turning to the hedonistic pursuit of professional chess with more or less lasting effect. Some others "found themselves" in chess for an interim period before continuing with other professions. One factor remained certain: Most of them entered the show at a vastly earlier age than players of the past and achieved high levels of achievement while still in adolescence.

The final verdict of lasting excellence would come with time; only a few highlights can be given in this chapter. The members of this generation, through increased means of communication, developed a far greater reservoir of technical knowledge than their predecessors. This wealth is rightly reflected by the greater extent of theoretical explanations given in the games that follow.


## WALTER BROWNE

Walter Shawn Browne (b. 1946) served as an example of the melting pot, Australo-American brand. A colorful globe-trotter of chess, he came to the United States from his native Sydney, Australia, at the age of seven. The family settled in Brooklyn and at fourteen he became the youngest national master in the country and quit school at sixteen to devote all his time to chess. At nineteen, he returned to Australia to win that country's championship. Using his national origin as an easier hemispheric starting point in the fierce regional scramble for nominations and invitations to well-stocked foreign tournaments, Browne won his international master title at San Juan, Puerto Rico 1969, and in 1970 clinched the grand-master title after placing 3rd–4th in the Malaga Grandmaster Tournament. At Zagreb 1970, he placed low, but drew with Fischer after ninety-eight gruelling moves. ("Gruelling" is right in many respects: While Walter Browne is well-controlled as a person away from the board, he becomes very tense while playing.) In 1971, he placed first at Venice, Italy, ahead of Gligoric, Hort and Kavalek, and scored the greatest number of wins at the Skopje Olympics 1972, covering for Australia. He then formally acquired U.S. citizenship, topped the U.S. Championship 1971–72, and both the U.S. National and the World Open Championship in 1973. In Spring 1974 he was the leader at Wijk aan Zee, Holland, with 11 points out of 16 (with nine grandmasters and six international masters competing), 1½ points ahead of the runner-up. By that time he had synchronized his titles, his residency (in California), and his citizenship, and was rated an American grandmaster.

He continued his steady success by winning the 23rd U.S. Championship in Chicago in 1974, again 1½ points ahead of the nearest rival in a field of 14, including five grandmasters and four international masters; taking 1st prize at the Pan-American in Winnipeg, Canada, winning 12 and drawing 3 out of 15 games, without a loss. To round out the global picture, Browne pocketed the International German Championship 1974, and at Cleveland, Ohio, again placed first in the massively attended U.S. Championship 1975. He came first at Reykjavik in 1978 (with Lombardy sharing 3rd–6th place) and has remained in the front rank ever since, winning also the U.S. Championship in 1976 and 1977—three times in a row.

Browne's bravura prevented him from being just a fidgety hunch-back glued to a chair. He had many interests, was sociable and easygoing, and enjoyed a happy marriage—and was lowbrow enough to try profiting at poker when short of funds.

The following game is instructive, and worth meticulous study.

### U.S. CHAMPIONSHIP

#### Chicago 1974
*Petrov's Defense*

W. BROWNE      A. BISGUIER

| 1 P–K4 | P–K4 |
|--------|------|
| 2 N–KB3 | N–KB3 |
| 3 NxP | P–Q3 |
| 4 N–KB3 | NxP |
| 5 P–Q4 | P–Q4 |
| 6 B–Q3 | B–K2 |

One of the pillars of the defense, thoroughly analyzed by the early Russians A. Petrov and C. Jaenisch, with its main lines known almost by rote.

| 7 O–O | N–QB3 |
| 8 P–B4 | |

The sharpest line tactically, and exemplary of Browne's preference, but we can almost feel Black's shrug "So what?"—as this variation is best known since the game Yates–Kashdan, Hastings 1932, which Kashdan won. More persevering but exhausted by usage is 8 R–K1.

| 8 . . . | N–N5 |

Reciprocating with the motto that Black must pursue Petrov with vigor; but the old-fashioned 8 . . . B–KN5 is more natural. Bisguier follows the brain grooves retained from early years of studying the games of American masters, and established theory, and Browne will cash in!

| 9 PxP | NxB |
| 10 QxN | QxP |
| 11 R–K1 | B–KB4 |
| 12 N–B3 | NxN |
| 13 QxN | P–QB3 |

So far a tedious repetition of theory studied upside down and inside out since Jaenisch wrote his treatise in 1843. The game Yates–Kashdan continued 14 B–Q2 P–KR3. Although Kashdan finally won, Fine recommends 14 . . . B–K3 15 R–K5 Q–B5 16 Q–K3 Q–B7! and therefore prefers 14 R–K5 Q–Q2 15 P–Q5. But both 15 . . . PxP 16 RxBch QxR 17 QxP K–Q2 18 N–K5ch K–K3, or 15 . . . O–O 16 PxP PxP still level.

Black's last move is normal, as also remembered by Bisguier, who suspects no Jack hidden in White's box.

### 14 B–R6!!

A diabolical inspiration. The flank attack and sacrifice looks quite out of place, with all the play staged in the center. Yet with hindsight the bishop actually clears the line for the queen's rook, and also preempts the diagonal; i.e., 14 . . . PxB 15 R–K5 Q–Q2 16 QR–K1 B–K3 17 P–Q5! PxP 18 RxB!! PxR 19 QxRch B–B1 20 Q–B6 B–K2 21 RxP wins. If 14 . . . B–K5 15 BxP R–KN1 16 B–B6! BxB 17 RxBch QxR 18 R–K1±.

After forty-five minutes of deliberation, Bisguier tries his only chance and hopes that everything is taken care of.

| 14 . . . | R–KN1 |
| 15 R–K5 | Q–Q2 |
| 16 QR–K1 | B–K3 |
| 17 N–N5!! | |

Black might have been safe after the expected 17 B–N5 B–Q3 18 R/5–K3 P–KR3 19 B–R4 P–KN4 20 B–N3 BxB 21 RPxB O–O–O. As noted by Browne in *CL&R*, October 1974, he "felt as though walking a tightrope." All plausible defenses required razor-fine precision; e.g., 17 N–N5, with (a) 17 . . . B–B3 18 NxB BxR 19 N–B5+; (b) 17 . . . PxB 18 NxB PxN 19 RxP R–N2 20 P–Q5!! K–B1 21 QxRch KxQ 22

RxBch QxR 23 RxQch±; (c)
17 . . . BxN 18 BxB P–KR3 19
B–R4 P–KN4 20 B–N3 K–B1
21 RxB P–R5 and again 22 P–
Q5 wins.

Bisguier's answer removes the
king to safety but also away
from his own defenses. If 17
. . . BxN 18 BxB P–KR3 19 B–
R4 P–KN4 20 B–N3 K–B1 21
Q–B3.

| 17 . . . | O–O–O |
|----------|-------|
| 18 NxBP! | BxN |
| 19 RxB | QxP |
| 20 RxB! | QxQ |
| 21 PxQ | PxB |
| 22 R–N1! | R–N4 |

White's 22nd move threatens to
win a queen-side pawn and the
doubled rooks' pawns will be no
match for White's KBP. So
Black finesses in the faint hope
that after 23 R/7xNP R–N4 24

R/7xR PxR 25 P–B4 RxP he
can hold White's king-side
pawns at bay by moving his king
over to the king-side or the center and by utilizing the passed
QRP. However, the text allows
White to open a loophole for
his king, and Black's plan comes
to naught.

| 23 P–KR4 | R–N4 |
|----------|------|
| 24 RxR | PxR |
| 25 RxRP | R–Q8ch |
| 26 K–R2 | R–Q7 |
| 27 RxRP | RxRP |

Black has created a passed pawn
after all, but White has three,
and the rook's pawn is well advanced. The windup is easy: 28
P–R5 RxP 29 R–R8ch K–B2
30 P–R6 K–N3 31 K–R3 P–R4
32 P–N4 P–N5 33 PxP PxP 34
R–K8 R–B8 35 K–N2, and
Black resigned five moves later.

The lesson of this game lies in 13 B–R6! It teaches how ephemeral theory is with its reams of detailed analysis based on infallible
conclusions. This statement contains no disrespect, except for those
who accept the credo and don't keep searching, unlike the grandmaster to whom constant surprises are nothing new. L. Evans in
*The Chess Opening for You* (New York: RHM Press, 1975) states,
"Bobby Fischer showed the move to friends around 1964, keeping it
secret till he could use it." If so—who were these friends (Browne?);
who not (Bisguier?); and why then did Fischer *not* keep his secret?

It takes lucid minds to see through and upset established lines
in explosive fashion; and it will take some ingenious programming
to educate a computer to do likewise with the game as we know it
now. Another powerful thought enters in the next game, where a
similar scoop by Black squashes a grandmaster within thirty moves.

## U.S. CHAMPIONSHIP

Oberlin 1975
*Sicilian Defense*

R. BYRNE       W. BROWNE

1 P–K4       P–QB4
2 N–KB3    P–Q3
3 P–Q4      PxP
4 NxP       N–KB3
5 N–QB3    P–QR3

Black's last move is almost invariably played in related Sicilian systems and it is preferable to play it here before P–K3, even though the difference might ultimately be minute. Upon 5 . . . P–K3 first, White can also choose the adventurous Keres Attack 6 P–KN4?!—as Byrne did against Spassky in their 1st match game in 1974. The move was introduced in Keres–Bogolyubov, Salzburg 1943. Some subtleties must be noted that can make or break its adoption against the planned Scheveningen System, the key moves of which are . . . P–Q3; . . . P–K3; . . . N–QB3; and . . . B–K2 in varying order. At this point, after 5 . . . P–QR3, this Sicilian Bayonet Attack of Keres is not yet possible.

The Byrne–Spassky 1st match game 1974 went (5 . . . P–K3) 6 P–KN4 P–QR3! 7 P–N5 (or 7 B–N2 KN–Q2 8 O–O N–QB3 9 K–R1 B–K2 10 P–B4 O–O 11 P–N5 NxN 12 QxN P–N4= as in the 5th match game) KN–Q2 8 P–QR4?! (also 8 B–K3 or 8 B–QB4 or 8 B–N2 have been

played) N–QB3 9 B–K3 N/2–K4 10 B–K2 NxN 11 QxN N–B3 and ended in a draw on the 44th move.

## 6 B–K3

Another one of the many branches of the Sicilian tree. Playing 6 B–K3 first and before B–K2 allows White to answer 6 . . . P–KN3 with 7 B–QB4, saving a tempo for this bishop, with different ramifications if so preferred by White.

First 6 B–K2, answered by . . . QN–Q2, permits 7 P–B4?! P–K4!? 8 N–B5 N–B4 9 N–N3 Q–N3 as in the draw Karpov–Browne, Amsterdam 1976. An equilibrium, though a precarious one, is maintained after 6 . . . P–K3 7 P–B4 Q–B2 8 O–O N–B3 9 B–K3 B–K2 10 Q–K1 O–O 11 Q–N3 B–Q2 12 QR–Q1 P–QN4=. Tisdall–Jacobs, Binghampton 1976, went 12 QR–K1 QR–B1 13 K–R1, when . . . P–QN4 would have been best. Also 12 K–R1 is thematic and permits White the option which rook move to choose.

Black also has 6 . . . P–K4, a move belonging to a specific defensive system which we may have occasion to summarize in another context. (Spassky–Lombardy, Leningrad 1960 went 6 B–KN5 QN–Q2 7 B–QB4 Q–R4 8 Q–Q2 P–K3=). (For other variations see the game Timman–Kavalek, p. 250.)

| 6 . . . | P–K3 |
| 7 B–K2 | QN–Q2 |

7 . . . N–B3 is more customary than the text, which could have been followed by 8 P–B4 P–QN4 9 Q–Q2 B–N2 10 B–B3 Q–B2 with often recurring formations of familiar patterns. While Black hardly has an alternative to . . . O–O, White can choose either O–O–O or O–O, with the latter being more frequent.

**8 P–KN4!?**

White reaches back to his pet move, but he is in for an awakening. An alternative is 8 P–QR4.

| 8 . . . | P–R3 |
| 9 P–B4 | P–QN4 |
| 10 P–N5 | PxP |
| 11 PxP | R–R6!!? |

A bolt out of the "black," made possible by White's omission either to castle or to play 8 Q–Q2 B–K2 (or . . . Q–B2, or . . . B–N2) before pushing 9 P–N5.

Assuming that the conven-

tional 8 O–O Q–B2 had been interpolated, White would now have (12 . . . R–R6?) 13 R–B3 RxR 14 BxR P–N5 15 QN–K2 N–R2 16 P–N6!

In the diagram, White's attack has been aborted and Black's pieces acquire frightening vitality. Obviously out is 12 PxN RxB 13 PxP Q–R5ch 14 K–Q2 BxP! with annihilation. Positionally won is 12 Q–Q2 P–N5 13 PxN PxN 14 QxP NxP. If 12 B–B2 RxN! 13 NxKP Q–R4!∓. Interesting, but still fragile is 12 B–B3 N–N5 13 B–B4 (13 B–Q2 N/5–K4 14 B–N2 R–R5 15 Q–K2 B–K2!) N–K4 14 B–N2 R–R5 (14 . . . R–R2 15 Q–Q2), with all the makings of a powerful Black buildup.

However, the real refutation, so far overlooked, presented to Browne by Zeshkovsky at Manila in 1976, i.e., 12 B–B2! RxN 13 PxN! (not 13 PxR NxKP) 13 . . . R–KR6 14 NxKP! Q–R4ch 15 P–B3 PxN 16 PxP BxP 17 QxP R–R3 18 R–N8±.

**12 B–KB4      P–N5**
**13 N–Q5**

Upon 13 PxN QxP! (stronger than 13 . . . PxN 14 NxKP!) 14 O–O PxN 15 B–N4 Q–N3 16 B–N3 RxBch! 17 PxR PxP 18 R–N1 N–B3 Black stands better.

| 13 . . . | PxN |
| 14 PxN | NxP |
| 15 N–B6 | |

Not 15 PxP N–R4! 16 BxN
Q–R5ch 17 B–N3 RxB winning.

| 15 . . . | Q–N3 |
| 16 PxP | N–K5!! |

The bitter fruit of White's neglecting to castle. Apart from Black's mating threat, all his men command open lines and files, and are poised for assault. Also only . . . P–N3 is needed to post the king's bishop on its diagonal.

White is slowly crushed after 17 KR–B1 P–N4 18 B–B1 RxP.

| 17 Q–Q4 | QxQ |
| 18 NxQ | P–N4!! |
| 19 B–QB1 | B–KN2 |

| 20 N–B6 | N–N6 |
| 21 R–KN1 | NxB |
| 22 RxP | |

A last-ditch effort to hold the line, as 22 KxN RxPch 23 K–Q1 B–B4 or 23 K–Q3 P–R4 24 BxP wins. White could have resigned here.

| 22 . . . | N–Q5 |
| 23 RxB | NxPch |
| 24 K–Q1 | NxR |
| 25 R–N8ch | K–Q2 |
| 26 R–B8 | R–Q6ch |
| 27 B–Q2 | RxP |
| 28 NxP | R–KB4 |
| 29 B–B3 | P–R4 |
| 30 N–Q3 | P–R5 |

Resigns

## LARRY CHRISTIANSEN

Larry Christiansen (b. 1956) is so far the youngest and most recent international grandmaster on the United States atlas. He first availed himself of the training offered by three regular U.S. Jr. Championships, before entering the international student championship arena. He usurped the 1st spot in the U.S. Jr. Championships in 1973 and 1975, tying for 1st in 1974 with Peter Winston; he scored 7 points out of 15 at the very strong USCF International Tournament in Cleveland 1975; was 2nd at the World Jr. Championship, Tjentiste, in August 1975 (½ point behind V. Chekhov of the USSR); and attached 2nd prize at Torremolinos 1976 (after R. Byrne's 1st). This standing gave him a first norm toward the international master title, and he jumped both the 2nd norm and those required to become grandmaster, by winning the Costa del Sol Tournament at Torremolinos (Spain), February 1977; in March, at Lone Pine, he narrowly missed sharing 1st prize and landed in the 2nd echelon, together with Lombardy. Larry's most gentle and sympathetique posture hides a chess volcano.

## WORLD JR.
## CHAMPIONSHIP

Tjentiste 1975
*Sicilian Defense*

| V. INKYOV | L. CHRISTIANSEN |
|-----------|------------------|
| 1 P–K4 | P–QB4 |
| 2 N–KB3 | P–Q3 |
| 3 P–Q4 | PxP |
| 4 NxP | N–KB3 |
| 5 N–QB3 | N–B3 |

As in the further text, Black's key variation is based on the counter . . . P–K4. We demonstrate here a sideline with the same motif: after 5 . . . P–QR3 6 P–KN3 P–K4! 7 N/4–K2 B–K2 8 B–N2 P–QN3 (8 . . . O–O 9 O–O P–QN4! 10 P–KR3 QN–Q2 11 B–K3 Q–B2 is more precise) 9 P–QR4 B–N2 and now (a) 10 P–KR3 QN–Q2 11 P–KN4 N–N4 12 N–N3 N–K3 13 B–K3 P–N3 14 N–Q5 NxN 15 PxN N–B4=; or (b) 10 O–O QN–Q2 11 N–Q5! NxN 12 PxN R–QB1 13 B–K3 O–O 14 Q–Q2 Q–B2 (Furman). In Rohde–Browne, Lone Pine 1975, Black deviated with 12 . . . P–QN4? 13 B–K3 O–O 14 PxP PxP 15 Q–Q3! B–R3 16 R–R3!! Q–B2 17 KR–K1 Q–N2 18 P–QN4, and young Rohde won surely and impressively, and with unerring technique.

After 5 . . . P–QR3, the "orthodox" . . . P–K4 lines are (a) 6 B–K2 P–K4 7 N–N3 B–K2 8 O–O B–K3 9 P–B4 Q–B2 10 P–QR4 QN–Q2 11 K–R1 O–O 12 B–K3, a typical position of the Czech master's Opočensky Variation; with Black putting in . . . P–QN4 and . . . N–B4, eventually sacrificing Black's QP if need be in return for an attack. R. Byrne held his own with these strategies against Karpov at Leningrad 1974, and versus Spassky at San Juan 1974. (b) 6 P–B4 P–K4! 7 N–B3 QN–Q2 (the omission of . . . N–QB3 reinforces Black's push). Black may also push at once 5 . . . P–K4 (Pelikán's Variation, *MCO*, 11th ed., p. 170).

## 6 B–K3

6 B–QB4 P–K4 7 KN–K2 B–K3 has its own merits and so does 6 B–K2 P–K4.

## 6 . . .    P–K4

There are two criteria that make for the strength of Black's center stroke, the omission of 6 B–N5, and, in the above variation, the absence of . . . N–QB3, as Black then retains the option of . . . QN–Q2. However, in the text Black still gains a good position even with . . . N–QB3 and proves its practical worth.

## 7 N/4–N5

Á *la* Pelikán, and possibly because Black has not yet played . . . P–QR3, although he will now. With 7 N–N3 or 7 N–B3 White would land in conventional channels, but he joins the guerrillas instead.

7 ...                    P–QR3!?

7 ... B–K2 is safer, and a developing move, and sustains the threat of ... NxKP.

| 8 N–R3 | P–QN4 |
| 9 N–Q5!! | NxN |
| 10 PxN | N–K2 |
| 11 P–QB4 | P–N5 |

The position becomes livid. After 12 Q–R4ch B–Q2 13 QxNP N–B4 14 B–Q3 or 14 B–K2, White might experience uncomfortable moments, but a pawn is a pawn is a pawn. Now and later White plays into Black's luck.

| 12 N–B2 | N–B4! |
| 13 B–Q2 | P–QR4 |
| 14 B–Q3 | B–K2 |

The backward QP is apparently safe and no early breakthrough P–QB4 to B5 is imminent once Black plays ... R–QB1. Therefore 14 ... P–N3 and 15 ... B–N2, with ... O–O, would have been solid and active. The QP, which becomes backward in all of the ... P–K4 systems, actually turns out to be a pivotal support for Black's counterattacks on either wing and altogether serves as one of the means of revising the positional thinking of the post–World War I chess generation.

| 15 O–O | O–O |
| 16 P–B4 | PxP? |
| 17 RxP | N–R5 |

Either 16 ... P–N3 or 17 ... P–N3 were yet better; but Black will not be called to account.

| 18 N–Q4! | N–N3 |
| 19 N–B6! | Q–N3ch |
| 20 K–R1 | B–Q1 |
| 21 BxN | |

The turning point. Instead of pressing on with 21 Q–R5 and activating his rook, White gives up material and his mobile bishop pair. The game is now even and what comes is mutual probing, thus: 21 ... RPxB 22 Q–B3 B–Q2 23 R–KB1 P–B4 24 B–K3 Q–B2 25 P–B5? BxN 26 PxB R–R3! 27 Q–Q5ch? Q–B2 28 QxQP B–B2 29 Q–Q3 BxR 30 QxR BxB 31 P–B7 Q–Q2! 32 Q–Q6 Q–B1 33 P–KR4 K–R2 34 R–Q1 R–B2 35 Q–K5 P–B5 36 R–Q8 Q–R3 37 Q–Q5? (Robert Wade pointed out that 37 K–R2! Q–B8 38 QxB! PxQ 39 P–B8(Q) Q–B5ch 40 K–R3 Q–B4ch 41 QxQ forces a drawn rook ending. Q–B8ch 38 K–R2 P–B6!! White promotes a second queen but remains trapped in a closing mating net. 39 R–R8ch KxR 40 P–B8(Q)ch K–R2 41 Q–R3 (if 41 Q–N4 Q–N8ch 42 K–R3 Q–R8ch 43 K–N3 QxP mate) Q–N8ch.

## LUBOMIR KAVALEK

Lubomir ("Lubosh") Kavalek, born in Czechoslovakia in 1943 of Polish parents, became grandmaster in 1965, three years before he left his native land. First joining his father in Munich, whereto he had emigrated in 1948, Kavalek proceeded to the United States to complete his studies, and quickly became homegrown.

In 1973, he and Grefe were U.S. co-Champions, resulting in Kavalek's attachment to the U.S. 1974 Olympic team, with Kavalek scoring 8½:6½ on first board. He then shared 1st prize with Polugayevsky at Solingen 1974, ahead of Spassky. At Montilla 1974 (and in 1977), he placed 2nd. In 1975, he got a little rusty, placing "only" 4th at Wijk aan Zee (Browne placed 8th–10th!); 6th–7th at Amsterdam; and 8th–9th at Teeside. I put "only" in quotes, because these three tournaments were attended by as many as twenty contestants of the highest caliber worldwide, and "Lubosh" produced some splendid games, convincingly flooring many celebrities with his original innovations. He won the U.S. Championships 1978.

Just to be consistent with at least one openings monograph, here is another Sicilian; this time it is Black who disproves his opponent's configuration.

### IBM TOURNEY

#### Amsterdam 1975
*Sicilian Defense*

| J. TIMMAN | L. KAVALEK |
|-----------|------------|
| 1 P–K4 | P–QB4 |
| 2 N–KB3 | P–Q3 |
| 3 P–Q4 | PxP |
| 4 NxP | N–KB3 |
| 5 N–QB3 | P–QR3 |
| 6 B–KN5 | P–K3 |

The Najdorf System, as characterized before. Specifically, 6 . . . N–B3 is the Richter-Rauzer Attack, as already mentioned; also 6 . . . QN–Q2, which is best answered by 7 B–QB4. White's next three moves form

one of the more popular strategies of the day—with provisos!

### 7 P–B4

Now 7 B–QB4 P–N4 accelerates Black's dynamics.

### 7 . . .          B–K2

The "to be or not to be" here or later is 7 . . . P–KR3 (in this game, later in the text), allowing an escape square for the king after . . . O–O, or a stepping-stone for a king-side attack if White castles king and Black refrains. These are only a few of many considerations, mostly of tactical nature.

A different strategy is postponing . . . B–K2 and developing the queen-side first by 7 . . . QN–Q2, . . . Q–B2, and . . . P–QN4, accompanied by either . . . N–B4 and . . . B–Q2; or by . . . B–N2. Thereafter, Black has the options of . . . QR–B1 first, or of . . . O–O–O and . . . K–N1, and then . . . R–QB1 to occupy the QB file. 7 . . . QN–Q2 8 B–B4! Q–N3! 9 B–N3 B–K2 10 Q–Q2 N–B4 is at least equal for Black. 7 . . . Q–N3 might result in the "poisoned pawn" variation.

To return to 7 . . . P–KR3, Grefe–Brown, U.S. Championship 1973, continued 8 B–R4 B–K2 9 Q–B3 QN–Q2 (now 9 . . . Q–N3 10 O–O–O! is not so effective for Black; but he can switch into the Scheveningen with 9 . . . N–B3 10 NxN PxN 11 P–K5 N–Q4 12 BxB QxP or back into this game by first 9 . . . Q–B2, still maintaining the option of . . . B–Q2 and . . . N–B3!) 10 O–O–O Q–B2 11 B–K2 QR–N1 12 Q–N3 R–N1 (or 12 . . . P–KN4 13 PxP PxP 14 BxN R–N1) 13 KR–B8 P–KN4 14 PxP. The further course of the game was a sparkler that won Grefe a brilliancy prize. With the same line, but continuing 13 . . . P–QN4 14 NxKP, Lombardy harvested a brilliancy prize against Quinteros at Manila 1973.

## 8 Q–B3    Q–B2

Another one of the staples of the Najdorf (see *MCO*, 11th ed., p. 151, and Byrne–Evans 1965, p. 185 in this book). Again, 8 . . . P–R3 can be inserted, with different strategies. But the same move is due here later.

## 9 O–O–O    QN–Q2!
## 10 B–Q3    P–R3

Here it is, and better than 10 . . . P–N4 11 KR–K1 B–N2 12 N–Q5 or 12 Q–N3.

## 11 Q–R3

While this move has been extensively analyzed and employed, I have doubts about White's placing the queen onto the diagonal of Black's hidden "battery." 11 P–KR4 may be explored, or 11 B–R4 P–KN4 12 PxP N–K4 13 Q–K2 N/3–N5! 14 N–B3 PxP! 15 B–N3 B–Q2 16 QR–B1! N–N3.

## 11 . . .    N–N3!

11 . . . N–B1 or 11 . . . R–KN1 are pale substitutes.

## 12 B–R4

Alternatives are (a) 12 P–B5 (blocking the "battery" P–K4 13 N–N3 B–Q2 14 B–K3 N–QR4=; (b) 12 KR–K1 P–K4 13 N–B5 BxN 14 PxB O–O–O 15 BxN BxB 16 PxP PxP 17 N–K4 N–Q5=, or 15 B–R4 PxP 16 B–B2 KR–K1 17 BxN QxN 18 B–B4 P–Q4!= (as in Planinć–Browne, Madrid 1973); (c) 12 KR–B1 B–Q2 13 P–B5 P–K4 14 N–N3 O–O–O 15 B–K3 N–QR4! 16 B–Q2 NxN=.

With the text, White blithely faces the music.

12 . . . P–K4
13 N–B5 P–N3

The battery in action! The knight is pinned, having to shield the queen. White probably anticipated all that, but believed that his positional pressure was going to make up for a queen sacrifice—but somehow it is all so unnatural!

14 NxB!? BxQ
15 BxN B–K3
16 P–B5

16 BxR KxN 17 B–N2 (or 17 P–B5) P–R3 18 P–B5 still merited a try.

16 . . . R–KB1
17 B–N5ch

*Chess Informant* believes that first 17 PxP PxP 18 B–N5ch N–Q2 19 KR–B1 RxB 20 N/7–Q5 saves the day, but the claim is dubious.

17 . . . B–Q2!

17 . . . PxB? 18 N/3xP Q–N1 (the only safe [?] square) 19 NxPch K–Q2 20 N–N5ch K–K1 21 N–B8! is vitriolic.

18 N/7–Q5 NxN
19 NxN Q–R4

How far into the opening the details of analysis have reached becomes clear from the fact that this line had been known and looked at by a circle of masters

before this game took place and that according to Kavalek, Timman had published his analysis with the conclusion that White now wins after 19 . . . Q–B4 20 P–QN4! It all goes to show that one better not disclose a train of thought which only offers future opponents an opportunity to find the holes, as suspected by Milan Vukcevich, who back home in Oberlin had suggested the text move. Indeed, after 20 . . . Q–B1 21 N–N6 wins; whereas after the text, 20 P–QN4 is useless because of 20 . . . Q–R6ch and 21 . . . BxB. Still, Black has an obstacle course to run before he can disprove White's queen sacrifice.

20 BxBch KxB
21 P–QR4 Q–B4

Countering a primitive attempt to trap the queen with P–QN4.

22 P–QN4 Q–B3
23 P–R5 PxP!
24 PxP

White must keep control over K6, but now Black lets loose on the open file.

24 . . . R–KN1
25 N–N6ch K–K1
26 P–N3 R–N5
27 KR–K1 R–QN1

After 27 NxR R–QB5 28 KR–K1 RxPch 29 K–N1 Q–B5! 30 RxPch K–B1! Black wins (CL&R). At this point, White is already outplayed. The game continued *28 BxP PxB 29 RxPch K–B1 30 N–Q7ch K–N2 31 P–B6ch K–R2 32 NxR Q–QB6! 33 R/1–Q5 R–Q5!* and White resigned, as *33 RxR Q–R8ch* wins both rooks!

## EDMAR MEDNIS

Edmar Mednis became a personable aspirant to chess recognition in his late thirties, turning away from a nonhedonistic occupation—at least for a while. (He held a Master's degree in Chemical Engineering.) Mednis wrote *How to Beat Bobby Fischer* (New York: Bantam Books, 1974), with a bit of humor in the title, and followed it up with *How Karpov Wins* (New York: McKay, 1975).

Mednis came 3rd at Houston, Texas 1974, right after the two foreign grandmasters R. Huebner and A. Matanović, leading the American contingent. At Cleveland, Ohio 1975, three grandmasters from overseas again booked the first few places, and Andy Soltis shared 4th–6th place with another two guests; but Mednis was next with 8 points out of 15 possible, in front of N. Weinstein, Zuckerman, Tarjan, Kaplan, Grefe, and Shamkovich, gaining one notch toward grandmastership, and none too early.

Mednis' love is the endgame, and he proved his empathy with this phase in his game with Huebner at Houston, when he construed a surprising stalemate trap out of an apparent loss. The game given here was won in the middlegame just before adjournment time.

### INTERNATIONAL TOURNAMENT

**Houston 1974**
*Sicilian Defense*

M. DAMJANOVIC          E. MEDNIS

| 1 P–K4 | P–QB4 |
|---|---|
| 2 N–KB3 | N–QB3 |
| 3 P–Q4 | PxP |
| 4 NxP | N–B3 |
| 5 N–QB3 | P–Q3 |
| 6 B–KN5 | |

The Richter–Rauzer Attack, which is one of White's choices if Black has already played . . . N–QB3.

One of the more recent and sharper alternatives is *6 B–QB4*, once a favorite of Fischer's, and later refined into the Velimirovich Attack. A game Fischer–Larsen, Palma de Mallorca 1970, progressed *6 . . . P–K3 7 B–K3 B–K2 8 Q–K2 P–QR3 9 O–O–O Q–B2 10 B–N3 O–O 11 KR–N1 (11 P–N4* may be played now) *N–Q2 12 P–N4 N–B4=.* In this game, both parties castle queen.

**6 . . .          P–K3**

Older sidelines are the immediate 6 . . . B–Q2 or 6 . . . P–QR3 or 6 . . . Q–N3 or 6 . . . Q–R4, with the option 7 BxN NPxB and a bishop pair.

**7 Q–Q2          P–QR3**

Both defending and preparing . . . P–QN4 and a queen-side attack if White castles queen; yet 7 . . . B–K2 is also still playable; e.g., 8 O–O–O O–O 9 P–B4 NxN 10 QxN Q–R4 11 B–B4 B–Q2 (*MCO*; 11th ed.). In a game Evans–Santos, Portimao 1975, White quickly transposed into a somewhat better endgame with 11 P–K5 PxP 12 QxP QxQ 13 PxQ N–Q4 14 BxB NxB 15 B–N5 and quickly won, but a stronger defender ought to have held the game against such minimal odds.

**8 O–O–O          B–Q2**

At this point, 8 . . . B–K2 was played in N. Weinstein–O. Rodriguez, Portimao 1975; i.e., 9 P–B4 B–Q2 10 N–B3! (10 B–K2 O–O 11 B–B3 P–R3 or 10 P–B5 R–QB1 11 PxP PxP 12 B–QB4 NxN are also customary) P–N4 (so as to post the queen behind, with . . . Q–N3; but 10 . . . R–QB1 and then either . . . Q–R4 or . . . N–QR4 is better) 11 BxN (in the same tourney, Evans against N. Weinstein, played 11 P–QR3 P–N5 12 PxP NxP 13 B–B4

and . . . B–B3 14 KR–K1 O–O would have leveled) PxB!=.

**9 P–B4          P–N4**
**10 BxN          PxB**
**11 P–B5**

Sharper and stronger than 11 P–KN3 Q–N3 12 NxN BxN 13 B–N2 O–O–O 14 N–K2 K–N1 15 N–Q4 B–N2 16 Q–K2 P–KR4 with a draw (in Matanović–Mednis in an earlier round). In this game, both players try to improve.

**11 . . .          Q–N3**

Mednis comments that 11 . . . N–K4 was stronger (e.g., 12 P–KN3 P–KR4! or 12 B–K2 P–KR4 13 K–N1 P–N5!). This leaves White with the windup 12 BxP PxB 13 N/4xNP Q–N3 14 NxPch BxN 15 QxB Q–N2 16 KR–B1 KR–B1 17 R–Q4 R–R3 and an unpredictable ending.

**12 PxP**

Mednis calls his 11th (and 12th) move powerful, and it might be so; nevertheless, in the 10th round, Jansa–Commons, White came up with 12 NxN QxN 13 B–Q3 O–O–O 14 KR–B1 B–K2 15 Q–K2 K–N1 16 PxP PxP 17 N–Q5, with quite a good game. Whatever the case and the fortunes, the game now enters an active stage of probing, with Black getting the better of it.

**12 . . .          PxP**
**13 NxN          QxN**

If *13* . . . BxP *14* Q–B4 B–K2
*15* B–Q3, or also *15* P–KN3
P–N5 *16* N–Q2 P–QR4 *17* B–
R3 with complications.

## 14 B–Q3      O–O–O
## 15 K–N1

Better is *15* KR–B1 B–K2 and
Black's threat . . . B–R3 is disposed of with tempo. White
might have seen ghosts of *15*
. . . B–N2 with some hidden
diagonal threats, and rather
moved his king. But after the
text, Mednis wears him out very
consequentially. The game continued: *15* . . . K–N1 *16* KR–B1
B–K2 *17* N–K2 QR–N1 *18* N–

B4 R–N4 *19* P–KN3 R–QB1
*20* Q–N4 K–R2 *21* P–B3 R–
QN1 *22* B–B2 Q–B5 *23* P–
QR3! QxQ *24* RPxQ R–QN2!
*25* R–B2 B–QB1 *26* B–N3 R–
K4! *27* R–Q4 P–B4! *28* PxP
RxP! (gives Black a passed
pawn, and his KP is indirectly
protected because White's rook
is pinned) *29* R/4–Q2 P–K4
*30* N–Q5 B–N4! *31* R/Q–K2
R/2–KB2 *32* RxR BxRch *33*
B–B2 B–N5 *34* R–K1 B–Q7 *35*
R–N1 B–B6 *36* B–N3 B–K5ch
*37* K–R1 R–B7 *38* P–R4 B–N7
*39* N–B6 P–K5 *40* RxB P–K6!!!
White is lost.

## ANDREW SOLTIS

Andrew Soltis (b. 1947) was also nearing the end of the "Now
Generation." Apart from steady good performances, he has also been
a professional writer, with various chess titles to his credit. A roving
reporter for the *New York Post*, he also directed its chess column,
succeeding H. R. Bigelow. He made his first international mark as a
member of the 14th Student Olympics 1967, and placed 4th–6th in
Cleveland 1975, a notch ahead of Mednis; he had the satisfaction
of drawing with the winners (Czom and Ostojić) and of scoring a
clear victory over Argentina's grandmaster Quinteros. At the 7th
USCF International Tournament, New York 1977, he won his first
grandmaster norm. He always scored well in International Tournament, sporadic intranational events. The game against Quinteros
is instructive.

## 5TH USCF INTERNATIONAL TOURNAMENT

Cleveland 1975
*Sicilian Defense*

A. SOLTIS        M. QUINTEROS

| 1 P–K4 | P–QB4 |
|---|---|
| 2 N–KB3 | P–Q3 |
| 3 P–Q4 | PxP |
| 4 NxP | N–KB3 |

If 4 . . . P–QR3 5 B–Q3! N–KB3 6 O–O P–Q3 7 P–QB4 B–K2 8 N–B3 or 8 Q–K2, with the intention of an early breakthrough P–K5.

| 5 N–QB3 | P–QR3 |
|---|---|

Generally, without further subclassification, this sequence is called the Najdorf System, especially if followed up by 6 B–KN5 or 6 B–QB4, or by the text move in this game. After 6 B–K2 P–K3 and . . . B–K2, it becomes a Scheveningen Variation; after 6 . . . O–O it still remains a modern Paulsen Defense; and after 6 . . . P–KN3 we have the "Dragon." Soltis embarks on a favorite of Belyavsky's:

| 6 P–QR4 | |
|---|---|

This is a preventive against a wing attack by . . . P–QN4 and lets the opponent decide upon either of the above-mentioned systems. White might find that Black chose a system which renders P–QR4 useless; e.g., the Dragon Variation 6 . . . P–KN3

(as in Belyavsky–Browne, Las Palmas 1974), continued 7 B–K2 B–N2 8 P–B4 N–B3 9 B–K3 O–O 10 O–O B–Q2 11 N–N3 B–K3 12 P–N4 R–B1 13 P–B5 BxN 14 PxB N–Q2 15 P–N5 N–B4 16 R–B4 B–K4 17 R–R4 N–N5 18 B–B4 P–K3 19 P–B6 P–N4 20 PxP PxP 21 BxP.

Not bad is 6 . . . P–K4 7 N–N3! B–K3 8 B–K2 B–K2 9 O–O QN–Q2 10 P–B4 Q–B2 with a standard line, reinforcable with . . . R–B1 and . . . N–R4. Less certain—and thus falling for White's bait 6 P–QR4—is 6 . . . N–B3 at once, as it abdicates the . . . QN–Q2 configuration; e.g., 7 B–K2 P–K4 (what else?) 8 N–N3 B–K2 9 O–O O–O 10 P–B4 N–QN5 11 R–K1 B–K3 12 B–K3±.

| 6 . . . | P–K3 |
|---|---|

Black chooses the Scheveningen, which means putting the finger in the lion's mouth if we just fall back on the earliest exploration that gave the line its name—Maróczy–Euwe, Scheveningen 1923; namely, 1 P–K4 P–QB4 2 N–KB3 N–QB3 3 P–Q4 PxP 4 NxP N–B3 5 N–B3 P–Q3 6 B–K2 P–K3 7 O–O B–K2 8 K–R1 O–O 9 P–B4 Q–B2 10 N–N3 P–QR3 11 P–QR4!! P–QN3 12 B–B3 B–N2 13 B–K3 N–QN5 14 Q–K2 P–Q4 15 P–K5 N–K5 16 BxN, with considerable positional superiority, which ended in White's victory. Since then, there have of course been improvements for Black.

| 7 B–K2 | B–K2 |
| 8 P–B4 | Q–B2 |
| 9 O–O | N–B3 |
| 10 B–K3 | |

Departure one: *10 N–N3 O–O 11 P–R5? P–QN4! 12 PxP e.p. QxPch 13 K–R1 B–N2* (Durao–Rogoff, Orense 1976). From *10 B–K3* onwards, the salient transpositions depend on (a) if and when to exchange N/4xN or rather play N–N3; (b) if and when to play B–KB3 or Q to K1 to N3; (c) for Black: when to defend accurately by . . . N–QN5, or when to choose . . . N–QR4; (d) if and when to develop . . . B–Q2, or . . . P–QN3 followed by . . . B–N2.

| 10 . . . | B–Q2 |

Departure two: *10 . . . O–O 11 N–N3 P–QN3* and now (a) *12 K–R1 R–Q1 13 Q–K1 R–N1 14 Q–B2 N–QR4=;* (b) *12 B–B3 R–N1 13 Q–K1* (or *13 Q–K2 N–QR4 14 N–Q2 R–Q1 15 K–R1 B–N2 16 Q–B2 N–Q2 17 QR–K1 N–B5=*) . . . *N–QR4 14 NxN PxN 15 P–QN3 B–N2=* (ECO suggested *15 . . . R–N5=*).

In an earlier departure, instead of *11 N–N3* White may play *11 K–R1*, answered by *11 . . . B–Q2* (or *11 . . . NxN?!*) *12 N–N3! P–QN3 13 P–B4 Q–B2 14 B–B3 KR–Q1 15 P–N4 B–K1 16 P–N5 N–Q2 17 B–N2!* (to allow for R to B3 to R3, Black should have taken precaution by . . . N–B1) *N–B4 18 R–B3 R–N1 19 R–KR3 P–N3?*

(*19 . . . P–B3!!*) *20 Q–N4 P–N4 21 PxP PxP 22 Q–R4 P–KR4* (apparently the saving clause. White has no KNP left to break open the position, but instead, he has a bishop to serve as the chisel) *23 B–B3 B–B1 24 P–B5!! NxN 25 P–B6!!* Black resigned (Grefe–Benko, U.S. Championship 1975).

| 11 Q–K1 | O–O |
| 12 Q–N3 | |

White already has an even more advantageous choice in *12 N–N3 N–QN5 13 Q–Q2 P–Q4 14 P–K5 N–K5 15 NxN±,* as given in ECO, quoting Belyavsky–Dieks, Teeside 1973 (however, this game departed from text by *9 . . . P–QN3 10 B–B3 B–N2 11 P–K5!*). Whatever the right references, Maróczy–Euwe shines through in these sequences.

| 12 . . . | QR–N1 |

White has no reason to exchange *13 NxN PxN* and to open Black's QN file, or to allow the alternative *13 . . . BxN 14 B–B3 P–QN4!* Therefore *12 . . . QR–B1*; e.g., *13 NxN BxN 14 B–Q4 P–KN3 15 P–B5 P–K4=* is better.

| 13 K–R1! | K–R1 |
| 14 B–B3 | P–KN3 |
| 15 NxN! | PxN |
| 16 P–K5 | N–K1 |
| 17 N–K4 | P–Q4 |
| 18 N–N5 | RxP |
| 19 Q–R4 | BxN |
| 20 QxB | N–N2? |

Probably the first misjudgment, disregarding the chance of 20 ... RxP to prevent White's next move (or play either 20 ... B–B1 or 20 ... P–QB4). If 20 ... RxP 21 B–Q1 R–B5 22 Q–K7 (22 R–B3 seems ineffective after 22 ... R–N1 23 R–R3 B–N1 24 Q–R6 R–N2!) R–N1 23 QxBP B–B1 and Black seems safe.

| 21 B–B5!! | R–K1 |
| 22 B–K7 | K–N1 |
| 23 B–B6 | R/1–N1?? |

The second suicidal misjudgment. After 23 ... N–B4 24 B–

K2 (24 B–N4 or P–N4 P–R3! loses White's queen) P–R3 25 Q–N4 R/1–N1 26 B–Q3 Q–B1, with ... Q–KB1 or 26 ... K–R2, gives Black all the protection he needs and a devastating counterattack.

White's next move prevents the saving clause ... N–B4, and the game continued 24 B–N4! N–K1 25 B–K7 Q–B1 26 R–R3 R–N8 27 B–Q1 P–QR4 28 Q–R6 N–N2 29 R–R3 N–R4 30 RxN PxR 31 Q–N5ch K–R1 32 B–B6 mate.

## JAMES E. TARJAN

James E. Tarjan of California (b. 1952) started chess early in high school, became a senior U.S. master at nineteen, and then took part in the World Student Chess Championships. He first hit national headlines by sharing the two 1st places with Walter Browne in the U.S. Open 1970. In 1973 he tied Browne and L. Szabó of Hungary at the National Open in Las Vegas and garnered the laurels (with 7½ points) at the American Open in Santa Monica (followed by Kim Commons' 7 points). At the 2nd USCF International Tournament in Chicago in 1973, Tarjan drew even with grandmaster N. Karaklajić for 3rd–4th place (7 points each), just behind N. Weinstein 8 and G. Sigurjonsson of Iceland 7½. (This was one of N. Weinstein's great successes.) Tarjan's youthful promise secured him a spot on the U.S. Olympic team at Nice 1974 and, playing board four, he won a gold medal.

Like chess authors George Kane, Bruce Pandolfini, and others, Tarjan was a brainchild of the University of California at Berkeley. In 1975, Tarjan placed 2nd–4th at Novi Sad in October, and 1st at Subotica in November. Finishing 4th–5th in the sixteen-man tourney at Skopje, he was confirmed a grandmaster, bringing the number of U.S. grandmaster titles up to twelve. At Hastings 1976–77, Tarjan collected 9 out of 14 points, respectably ending in 3rd place. At Quito (Ecuador) 1976, he came 2nd with 14 out of 17 points (Panno was 1st with 13½ points). He took 2nd place in the U.S.

Championship 1978, in front of Mednis, Shamkovich, Lein, R. Byrne, N. Weinstein, Soltis, Christiansen, Benko, Lombardy, Commons, and Rogoff.

The following game was against John Grefe, one of the many participants in round robins and "Swisses," who every so often proves a stumbling block to other masters' aspirations. This encounter, though, is a draw.

## U.S. CHAMPIONSHIP

### El Paso 1973
*Sicilian Defense*

J. GREFE      J. TARJAN

| 1 P–K4 | P–QB4 |
|--------|-------|
| 2 N–KB3 | P–Q3 |
| 3 P–Q4 | PxP |
| 4 NxP | N–KB3 |

As this game deals with yet another Sicilian System, the Fianchetto Defense . . . P–KN3, it is opportune to look at an alternative that arises if the move is played now, namely the once dreaded Maróczy Bind (4 . . . P–KN3) 5 P–QB4! Historically, it was Swiderski who played 5 P–QB4! against Maróczy's fianchetto at Monte Carlo 1904 (with moves transposed), whereupon Black analyzed the ramifications after and in between 5 . . . B–N2 6 B–K3 N–KB3 7 N–QB3 N–QB3 8 B–K2 O–O 9 O–O B–Q2 10 P–KR3. Whitaker–Janowski, New York 1912, utilized the better 10 P–B3! Breyer, in 1920, improved Black's chances in this line, while Tartakover and Réti found attacking chances for White (with N–B2!). A typical game with the Maróczy

Bind was Karpov–Kaplan, San Antonio 1972, which continued 4 . . . P–KN3 5 P–B4 N–KB3 6 N–QB3 N–B3 7 B–K2 B–N2 (an alternative is 7 . . . NxN 8 QxN B–N2 9 B–N5 P–KR3 10 B–K3 O–O 11 Q–Q2 K–R2 12 O–O B–K3=; or 9 . . . O–O 10 Q–Q2 B–K3 11 QR–B1 P–QR3 12 P–QN3 P–QN4 13 PxP PxP 14 BxP Q–R4= [Ree–Browne, Wijk aan Zee 1972]) 8 N–B2! O–O (also 8 . . . N–Q2 9 O–O N–B4 10 P–B3 O–O 11 B–K3 BxN 12 PxB P–N3!=) 9 O–O (Kaplan suggested 9 B–K3 N–Q2 10 Q–Q2 N–B4 11 P–B3 as better; but 11 . . . B–K3 12 O–O Q–R4 is also even) N–Q2 10 Q–Q2 (Kaplan believed that 10 Q–Q2 or 10 B–K3 is better; but 10 . . . BxN! should vindicate Black) N–B4 11 P–QN3 (a departure from the thematic, but equalizing, 11 P–B3 Q–R4 12 P–QN4 NxNP 13 N–Q5 N–B3=; or also 11 . . . P–B4 12 P–QN4 N–K3 13 PxP N–B5=) P–B4!! (Kaplan merely noted: 11 . . . BxN 12 QxB NxKP with an unclear position; but it is interesting to go further into 13 Q–N2!? P–B4!? 14 B–R6 R–B2 15 QR–Q1 B–K3 16 P–QN4

Q–B2 17 R–Q3 P–B5; or 14 P–
B3 P–B5! 15 PxN PxB 16 NxP
RxRch 17 RxR Q–N3) 12 PxP
BxP 13 N–K3 N–Q5 14 NxB
NxN 15 R–N1 P–K3 16 Q–K1
P–QR3, and the game remained
on an even keel till a draw was
agreed upon at the 35th move.

The rise or fall of the
Maróczy had a principal effect
on Black's treatment of the
English and the Réti Openings,
as this same Sicilian Variation
can be reached by various ways
therefrom, and also concerns
the Benoni Defense.

**5 N–QB3　　　P–KN3**

This is the classical Dragon,
which also arises from 2 . . . N–
QB3 first, later followed up with
. . . P–Q3. The omission of 2
. . . N–QB3 denies White an
early KNxN, although it would
not necessarily be preferable to
other conservative variants.

A hyperaccelerated version of
the fianchetto is 1 P–K4 P–QB4
2 N–KB3 P–KN3, but 3 P–B4
B–N2 4 P–Q4 basically leaves
White with a wide choice.

**6 B–K3　　　B–N2**

6 B–K2 deprives White of the
unencumbered choice B–QB4,
6 B–K2 B–N2 7 B–K3 served to
prevent 7 N–N5, but White has
another means to prevent that
simplification:

**7 P–B3**

Prevents . . . N–N5, supports
the KP, and, in particular, prepares for the so-called Yugoslav
Attack on the king-side. It
should be noted that it is not so
effective if Black plays 2 . . .
N–QB3 instead of 2 . . . P–Q3.
In that case, Black may follow
up on 7 P–B3 with . . . O–O 8
Q–Q2 P–Q4!—gaining a tempo
for his QP, and a good game.
Thus, White would use another
strategy; e.g., 7 B–QB4 O–O 8
O–O P–Q3 9 P–KR3 B–Q2 10
B–N3 NxN 11 BxN B–B3 12
Q–Q3 P–QN4!?—as in Chris-
tiansen (of California) versus
Argentina's Szmetan, Torremo-
linos 1976, which continued 13
KR–K1 Q–Q2 14 N–Q5! BxN
15 PxB! Q–N2 16 Q–KB3 KR–
K1 17 QR–Q1 QR–B1 18 P–
QR4 P–QR3 19 PxP, with the
game ultimately won by White.
Also compare with the game
Evans–Zuckerman, 1966–67,
given on p. 183.

**7 . . .　　　N–B3**
**8 Q–Q2　　　O–O**
**9 B–QB4　　　B–Q2**
**10 P–KR4**

Black has no trouble after 10
B–N3 NxN! 11 BxN P–QN4!;
or 10 O–O–O Q–N1 11 B–N3
P–QR4 12 N/4–N5 R–B1; or
10 . . . O–O–O 11 B–N3 KR–
B1 12 P–KR4 N–K4 13 P–R5
NxRP 14 P–N4 N–KB3=.

**10 . . .　　　R–B1**
**11 B–N3　　　N–K4**
**12 P–R5**

In the 2nd match game Karpov–Korchnoi 1974, White re-

verted to *12 O–O–O N–B5 13 BxN RxB 14 P–R5 NxRP 15 P–KN4 N–B3 16 N/4–K2.*

| 12 . . . | NxRP |
|----------|------|
| 13 P–N4 | R–B5 |

*13 . . . N–KB3 14 N–Q5 NxN 15 PxN NxBP 16 NxN QBxP 17 N–Q4 P–KR4 18 P–B3 P–R3 19 B–Q1 BxB 20 RxB Q–R4; or 19 B–B2 BxN 20 BxB P–K4* are also playable.

| 14 PxN | RxN |
|--------|-----|

*14 O–O–O* fails. One can also consider *. . . RxN/5, . . . NxP,* and *. . . BxP,* and Geller's *14 BxR NxB 15 Q–K2 NxB 16 QxN N–B3.* The moves that follow now are hair-raising.

| 15 Q–N2 | Q–N3!? |
|---------|--------|

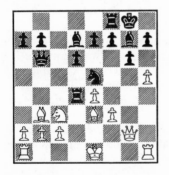

**16 PxP**

Grefe, saturated with the theories of the month, detours pragmatically from *16 N–Q5*

*Q–R4ch!;* or *16 O–O N–B5 17 B–B2 N–Q7;* or *16 Q–B2 R–B1 17 O–O N–B5 18 BxN R/B1xB 19 N–Q5 Q–Q1;* or *16 N–K2 Q–R4ch 17 K–B2 R–B5 18 PxP BPxP 19 N–B4 P–Q4.* Grefe also avoids being shown any consequences of *16 BxR?! QxB 17 Q–K2 K–R1 18 R–Q1 Q–B4 19 P–R6 B–B3 20 N–Q5 B–QN4 21 Q–B2;* or *20 . . . R–B1 21 Q–B2,* when proof is needed that Black can hold the game together.

| 16 . . . | RxP! |
|----------|------|
| 17 PxBPch | |

Not *17 PxR QxBch 18 Q–K2 BxNch 19 PxB QxQch 20 KxQ RPxP!* Nor *17 O–O–O QxBch 18 K–N1 R–Q5 19 RxR QxR,* winning for Black.

| 17 . . . | K–R1 |
|----------|------|

*17 . . . NxP! 18 NxR QxBch 19 Q–K2 Q–B5 20 P–B3 K–R1* is even more dangerous for White.

| 18 O–O–O | QxBch |
|----------|-------|
| 19 K–N1 | R–QB5 |
| 20 QR–N1 | RxP |
| 21 BxR | NxB |
| 22 Q–N6 | N–R6ch!! |
| 23 PxN | Q–N3ch |
| 24 K–B1 | Q–K6ch |
| 25 K–N1 | |

Of course not *25 K–Q1 QxPch.* Thus: draw by perpetual check.

## THE YOUNG HOPEFULS

Thus far I have concentrated on those contemporary players who already made it on the international scene under the American emblem, mostly clinching the grandmaster title. While limitations of space forbid going too far afield even at the risk of innocent omissions, a few more portraits are in order of players whose names were mentioned in the annotations to games. Some players may come and be already gone again while these lines are being read, others may still be going strong and grow bigger still by the time this book is out.

A wave of enthusiasts of a very young age has also become quite visible in all national matches or tournaments of standing. They are a pressing, ambitious, fearless, and provocative "no beat" chess generation. We will look at both groups consecutively, and with our apologies to those whom we left out, in name or game.

JOHN GREFE (born 1947), no longer among the youngest group in age, but still young at heart when one observes him walking serenely through crowds, through his games, and through his fortunes and sometimes misfortunes. Probably his training in Relaxation Response, of which T.M., Transcendental Meditation is a form, is partly responsible for his general disposition, as T. M. can offset stresses caused by the incessant pressures of life.

Grefe, an international master, can apply a good punch when he sees occasion for it, as he did in his game versus Browne at the U.S. Championship 1973, which made Grefe a U.S. cochampion. At Lone Pine 1976, Grefe produced a much-quoted brilliancy, with a chain of smashing sacrificial maneuvers, over veteran grandmaster Najdorf.

NORMAN WEINSTEIN (b. 1951 at Allston, Massachusetts) had his successes fluctuate according to location, mood, and opponents.[1] Norman won his international master trophy by coming in 1st at the 2nd USCF International Tournament, Chicago 1973, and at the U.S. Open Championship 1973. After a lull (7th–8th at the USCF International Tournament 1974, yet in front of Commons, Tarjan, Zuckerman, and the Hungarian grandmaster Lengyel), he placed 2nd (after Evans) and in front of ten other grandmasters and international masters at Portimao 1975.

JULIO KAPLAN (b. 1951 in Argentina) moved as a child to Puerto Rico, then to mainland U.S., and in 1977 to Berkeley, California, to

---

[1] Not to be confused with the ten-years-older Raymond Weinstein of Florida, who was awarded the international master title in 1961.

complete postgraduate studies in computer technology. He has been a sort of player in the wings, with a dormant strength, fitting in chess when his scholastic pursuits allowed it. Kaplan earned his international master title at the age of sixteen, for Puerto Rico, when he finished 1st at 9th World Jr. Championship in Jerusalem 1967—leaving Keene, Timman, Huebner, Ghizdavu, Sigurjonsson, and Matera behind. In the same event at Stockholm 1969, Kaplan placed 4th out of thirty-eight contestants, but drew with Karpov (1st) and Adorjan (2nd). In the International Tournament in Los Angeles 1974, he shared 2nd–3rd prize with Gheorgiu, ½ point behind Gligoric (7½). Kaplan did well at Hastings 1975–76 (7½ points out of 15), and at Lone Pine 1977. There, an unfortunate Swiss rating system cost him the chance of gaining a grandmaster norm. (Seirawan had a similar misfortune in not being matched with a foreign titleholder in the last round and thus losing the chance of a go at the International Master title.)

KIM COMMONS of California (b. 1951) was state champion in 1972, won the California Open at Ventura 1972, ahead of Tarjan and Grefe, whom he also overtook at the Western Qualifying Tournament in Los Angeles in 1973. From 1974 onwards, both the competition and Kim's relative success increased considerably, and at Lone Pine 1975 and Albena, Bulgaria, 1975, he earned his international master spurs; and the international tourneys at Plovdiv, Primersco, and Varna, all in 1976, saw him in 1st place. At the Haifa Olympics 1976 he made the best score, 83.8 percent, with 6 wins and 3 draws; he played 2nd reserve board.

KEN ROGOFF (b. 1953) won the U.S. Student Championship three times and was 3rd at the World Jr. Championship 1971. A Yale graduate, he then "leaned back" for a while. He made a comeback at the U.S. Championship 1975 in Oberlin, where Browne scored 8½ and Rogoff was 2nd with 8 points out of 13 possible. At Orense, Spain, 1976, he tied for 1st. At Lone Pine 1978 he secured his first grandmaster norm.

GREGG DE FOTIS of Chicago (b. 1954) also stayed in the top ranks of three U.S. Jr. Championships and took part in the World Student Team Championship 1971.

SAL MATERA (b. 1951) of New York defeated Soltis in 1975 in a match held at the Marshall Chess Club; tied for 2nd–4th place at Birmingham, England, 1975 (Matulovich was 1st); tied Bernard Zuckerman for 1st in the Atlantic Open 1975; and won his international master title at Reykjavik 1976.

JOHN PETERS (b. 1951), among the up and coming, just between the younger and the youngest freshmen, placed 7th–14th "only," out of forty-eight grandmasters and international masters and the like, at Lone Pine 1977; but he drew with the winners Balashov and Panno, and with Benko, and won against Lein and Lombardy, losing only to Sahović and Mrs. Nona Gaprindashvili. He tied for 1st in the American Open in 1977 and achieved his Grandmaster norm in the Lloyds Bank Master Tournament, London 1978.

Real future hopes dawned with a series of fast-developing youngsters: Joel Benjamin, Yassir Seirawan, Mark Diesen, Michel Rohde, John Tisdall, Jay Whitehead, Kenneth Regan, and many more to come, who will hopefully prove the stability of Western chess even without Bobby Fischer. Also among the women, young stars have come up; e.g., Diane Savereide, a California college graduate intent on taking out a period after graduation to perfect her performance. It is worth noting that, with few exceptions, all the aforementioned top players were dividing their efforts between preparation for a profession and pursuit of perfection at chess.[2]

YASSIR SEIRAWAN (b. 1960) of Seattle, Washington, emerged 1st out of 487 contestants at the 12th Annual American Open at Santa Monica 1976, drawing with two grandmasters and, after the tie-break, leaving grandmaster Brown and John Pike behind to share 2nd and 3rd prize. The Amateur Section of the same event was headed by nineteen-year-old Dennis Uchimura of Los Angeles. At Lone Pine 1977, Seirawan won a brilliancy prize for his game against grandmaster Shamkovich. In 1977, he again won the American Open.

JOHN TISDALL (b. 1959) topped the U.S. Jr. Championship 1973; shared 2nd–3rd place with Diesen in the same event in 1975 (Christiansen was 1st); took 3rd prize at the Junior at Memphis 1976; and then joined the Hastings (England) Challengers' (formerly "Reserve") Tournament 1976–77, a 10-round Swiss Knockout tourney. With 9 points out of 9 possible, he nosed out forty-eight global participants, the cream of the world's chess youth.

KENNETH REGAN (b. 1960) finished 3rd in the U.S. Jr. Championship 1976, joined the U.S. team for the International Student Team Tournament, Caracas 1976, which was won by the USSR with the U.S. coming in 2nd, and with Regan proving himself a feared opponent. The 7th USCF International Tournament, New York 1977, held at the Marshall Chess Club, gave Regan the opportunity to win his international master title. While chalking up "only" 7½ points out of 14, he beat both the 1st- and 2nd-prize winners Soltis

---

[2] For now I will refrain here from recording more games by the new breed. It will suffice to refer to other, continuous, sources; e.g. *Chess Life & Review*, and about one-hundred U.S. chess magazines and columns (small or large, local and regional). Public libraries can assist readers with information about availability.

and Shamkovich. At Lone Pine 1977, he drew with grandmaster Shamkovich, but defeated grandmasters Lein and Szabó, placing 7th–14th out of forty-eight first-rank players.

MARK DIESEN (b. 1958) came from a tight circle of students of chess, with his father Carl a well-known correspondence chess player and endgame composer. Mark became cochampion (with Rohde) after the U.S. Jr. Invitational Championship at Memphis, Tennessee, 1976 (Tisdall came 3rd), and became World Jr. Champion at Groningen 1976–77, with 10 points out of 12 possible. The 7th USCF International Tournament saw him finish an excellent 4th–5th.

MICHAEL ROHDE (b. 1958) was coChampion with Diesen at Memphis 1976; showed his mettle at the Manhattan Chess Club International Tournament 1976 by securing his first international master norm with 9 points out of 14; and secured the international master title by pulling together 7½ out of 14 points at the 7th USCF International of 1977.

## WOMEN AND OTHER PEER GROUPS

A glimpse into chess history reveals that even before the advent of our century, women chess players had some significant, though sometimes secret, successes at the board. An early news item from the New York *Evening Post* of May 31, 1859, recounts how an elegantly attired lady had driven up, incognito, to Morphy's hotel and, as White, had drawn a game on even terms. There also was a Mrs. J. W. Gilbert (1837–1900) of Hartford, Connecticut, who excelled in correspondence chess, brilliantly beating players like the British master G. H. D. Gossip.

Before the tides and ebbs of women's liberation, the stronger of America's "weaker" sex also plunged into the chess stream. Compared to her European counterpart, however, the American woman chess player still remained noncompetitive. The lack of competitive results internationally may have been due to greater involvement with managing a household, to lesser domestic opportunity to play, and to inundation of international competitions overseas by more numerous competitors—rather than because of lack of talent.

EVA ARONSSON, MARY BAIN, SONJA GRAF-STEVENSON, GISELLA KAHN-GRESSER, MONA KARFF, and MARILYN SIMMONS upheld the ladies' chess banner between 1938 and 1953. With the march of time, a few more promising candidates began to appear; e.g., DIANA SAVEREIDE of California, who won the Women's Championship at Milwaukee, Wisconsin 1975, and repeated her success at the 1976–

77 Championship; and RUTH ORTON of Arkansas, Miss Savereide's runner-up at Milwaukee. Both were awarded the FIDE woman's international master title and led the U.S. Women's Olympic team at Haifa in 1976.

LISA LANE, U.S. Woman Champion 1959–62, and cochampion with Gisella Kahn-Gresser in 1966, became an adherent at the age of nineteen. She studied Russian particularly for the purpose of following their chess literature. As one of the U.S. representatives in the International Women's World Championship candidates' tournament at Vrñacká Banja 1961, she got stuck at 12th place, with fifteen players present, and was beaten by her compatriot, Gresser; but she held the Soviet Amazon, Nona Gaprindashvili, to a draw. Later, Lisa became Mrs. Hickey, and faded out of active chess.

JACQUELINE PIATIGORSKY was another grand dame d'échec, who devoted both mind and capital to the game. She was the wife of the late concert cellist, and a descendent of the Paris branch of the Rothschild family. Jacqueline Piatigorsky was, literally by title, an expert at the game. The (Gregor and Jacqueline) Piatigorsky Foundation financed what was planned to be a triennial invitational (grand-) master tourney on the West Coast. Only two such occasions materialized, in 1963 and 1966; but they also financed the Fischer–Reshevsky match in 1961, with a prize fund of $8000 plus expenses paid (the conflicts between players, and the organizational mishaps which led to a premature interruption of the match at the score of 5½:5½ are part of often-told chess history). The foundation supported many U.S. Junior Championships and many events in the vicinity of Los Angeles. Quite a few of Hollywood's chess-enthusiastic artists and entertainers moved through the Piatigorsky home; e.g., H. Bogart, M. Brando, B. Darrin, M. Elman, P. Falk, and J. Ferrer.

CLARE BENEDICT (1871–1961) was a special case of an American benefactor of chess, on an uninterrupted basis, but only devoted to chess overseas. Benedict was an author and a great-granddaughter and James Fenimore Cooper. She resided in Switzerland since 1945, and in memory of her husband wholly subsidized an annual European six-country team tournament of four players each—with priority to Swiss locations. The first "Little Olympiad" took place at Mount Pelerin sur Vevey in 1953 and the idea has continued, under the direction of Adolf Nagler, to the present day. She also financed the International Grandmaster Tournament in Zurich in 1954.

While Clare Benedict reaped her laurels overseas, we might (as a footnote, figuratively speaking) add a word about another woman with foreign residence who left her imprint on U.S. chess. The 6th American Chess Congress, New York 1889, a double-round event, was attended by twenty players, many of them carrying illustrious names in American and European chess circles. One of the participants was Mrs. W. J. Baird (1859–1923), an ingenious and original chess problem composer of world renown living in England. She finished last but one; but she chalked up 7 points, with one win each against Bird, Hanham, Martinez, McLeod, and Mason, and draws against Bird, Burille, Gossip, and Hanham.

(The one outstanding woman international master, famous between 1929 and 1939, Vera Menchik-Stevenson, unfortunately never visited the United States.)

Clare Benedict's demise went unnoticed in the U.S. chess press, but her munificence was acknowledged everywhere overseas as carrying the American imprimatur.

The customary separation of chess championships by sexes seems to have no sound rationale, when the game is based largely on brain power, bestowed upon both men and women. It appears like giving a "minority" the chance of garnering prizes and awards within their own segregated circle. A change seemed, however, in the offing, when the Soviet Union's female contingent started sending its spearheads into the middle of men's competitions, including some in the United States.

In 1977, the World's Woman Chess Champion, Nona Gaprindashvili, a resident of Tbilisi, arrived at Lone Pine, to tie for 1st–4th (with Balashov, Panno, and Sahović, at 6½ points each), overtaking Lombardy, Christiansen (6 each), and forty-two additional male masters and grandmasters in this gigantic 9-round Swiss tournament. She secured a fully equal first grandmaster norm, playing tenaciously, logically, and forcefully. Actually, women's chess power had been tasted already in Lone Pine 1975, when Alla Kushnir of Israel (formerly of the USSR), and a runner-up to Mrs. Gaprindashvili, outpaced grandmasters and six international masters, also beating Larry Evans in the process.

During my long interview with Nona Gaprindashvili at Lone Pine, she took a straightforward, positive view regarding women's chess performance vis-à-vis men. She agreed that women players' "backwardness" was due to their other absorbing activities in life. She was convinced that the lack of equal opportunity and training and the waiting time required in generating peer recognition, accounted for the slow start. She believed that full development had already been reached in her country, especially in the Georgian

S.S.R., and mentioned several young women aspirants as having full, prodigy-like talents, greater than her own. (Nona is college-educated, a physician's wife, and mother of a six-year-old girl.)

The term "peer recognition," which I introduced into our dialogue, presupposes the presence of a sufficient number of practitioners, learners, and achievers with a given racial, economic, or simply, an age group, to create the necessary impetus for one or more of the members to reach the top and command his or her peers' respect—instead of remaining "freaks." As different from the traditions of a home passed on to the offspring, it represents a recent aspect of social propulsion and advances mutual understanding.

If such views are taken as a valid "minority" opinion, they were shared by one from our own chess group. The articulate American master Frank Street, another visitor to Lone Pine, a black man and former U.S. Amateur Champion (in 1965), thought that circumstances, and in such cases as his, color, had retarded the emergence of such peer recognition in chess, but that here the trend was changing. (If so, then chess might help in opening up other chances than mere supremacy in athletics.)

Harry Golombek mentions that "a great number of the best Soviet players were Jewish and pertained to Jewish, rather than Russian, culture. This brings me naturally to Professor Elo's [of Milwaukee, Wisconsin] theory of the vertical movements of population. This lays down that wherever people break through the rigid layers of a class-bound society they produce a stock, by the intermingling of classes, which is prone to give the world geniuses in many ranges of the arts, sciences and games of an intellectual nature."[3]

Whether the road toward integrated and dynamic chess is indeed winding around *specific* peer pressures first, or in combination with other factors, is a question which we might broach again.

At this moment we merely point out the astonishing success of the exclusively black Robert Vaux JHS from Philadelphia which won the National Junior High School Championship 1977. Self-propelled and self-financed, the group, accompanied by some elders, toured the United States, again beating the rivals of all races, wherever they went.

[3] *A History of Chess* (London: Routledge & Kegan Paul, 1976), p. 209.

# 14.

# New Frontiers

Even within the scrupulously chronicled annals of America's chess heritage, the contours of gradual changes made themselves felt. They are, horizontally, the widening out into regions outside the East Coast; vertically, an intensification of events; organizationally, a realignment aimed at catering both to the amateur's recreational need and the avowed craftsmen's professional drive; technologically, the influence of developing new—mostly electronic—tools and mediums, and, sociologically, the tendencies of broadening the interest in chess as a recreational activity. Not necessarily in the same order, but one by one, we will look into these undercurrents.

## WESTWARD EXPANSION

It took the Daniel Boones of chess almost two hundred years to reach the West. They did not really visit the East frequently. Due to the density of East Coast population, and the easier European-American interaction which still overshadows the Latin-American and Pacific one, the gravitational centers still are very much in the East. However, a steady population movement has progressed from the East to the West and Southwest, as borne out by U.S. censuses of 1960 and 1970. This shift was followed by increasing chess activity in these regions, vindicating the labor of many local veteran chess columnists and players who had kept the flag flying especially around the populous West Coast states. Browne and many of the younger elite reside there. With the influx of new blood (even from other countries), the influence of these "outside areas" was likely to grow.

Great influence was exerted by George Koltanowski (b. 1903) who arrived in the United States after the outbreak of World War

II and proceeded to San Francisco. In 1975 he was elected President of the United States Chess Federation for a three-year term.

"Kolty," who could boast of an immensely retentive, photographic memory, held a clean record in simultaneous blindfold chess and described the background of such exertions in his *Adventures of a Chess Master* (New York: McKay, 1955). In 1972 he published *With the Chess Masters* (San Francisco: Falcon) and (with Milton Finkelstein) *Checkmate* (New York: Doubleday, 1978). Kolty inspired the Paul Masson Mountain Vineyard of Saratoga, California, to hold a regular annual Class Championship. The 4th, in 1976, served as an experimental testing ground for the Wang Company's computer setup, producing an instant printout of 730 participants' first and subsequent pairings, results, and round-by-round changes in pairings. Koltanowski introduced the Swiss system to the United States in 1943, pioneered chess showings on educational (public) television, and brought out a monograph *TV Chess* (KQED, 1968). He conducted a daily chess column in the *San Francisco Chronicle*.

As an aftermath of H. Steiner's earlier trail-blazing, the Los Angeles area developed a beehive in "The Chess Set," run by Lina Grumette who once played in the Skopje Olympics in 1972, representing the U.S. possession, the Virgin Islands. Other busy centers were located around San Francisco, in San Diego, in Seattle, Washington, and in Houston, Texas. Publicity was given by a number of periodicals, among them Guthrie McClain's *The California Chess Reporter*, which held a record of twenty-five years (1951–76) of a complete magazine under one editorship. Among chess columns, Fred Chevalier's (syndicated) column, emanating from the *Christian Science Monitor* since 1929, probably holds another record in endurance.

Chicago had prided itself for a long time in being the Midwest's geographical and true chess center, and the northwestern frontier was often hosting masters from neighboring British Columbia.

## THE STRATIFICATION OF CHESS ORGANIZATION

In 1939, three different associations were merged into the United States Chess Federation (USCF). In 1945, *Chess Life* was founded and, until the end of the 1950s, was edited by Montgomery Major; during some of the intervals, B. Hochberg, F. Reinhard, F. Wren and others kept it afloat. In October 1969, the journal absorbed Horowitz' *Chess Review* to become *Chess Life & Review* (CL&R), with Hochberg becoming editor.

In 1966, the USCF's governing board appointed (Lt. Col.) Edmond B. Edmondson (b. 1920) Executive Director. In 1977, Edmondson was succeeded by Martin M. Morrison. During Edmondson's, and continued under Morrison's tenure, the USCF's procedures were streamlined to comply with the technical requirements of the age, and to cope with the rise—but also the fluctuations—in membership. Membership had expanded from about 6,000 to more than 60,000 during the Fischer boom, declined to 43,000 in 1977, but then leveled out. In regular intervals, the USCF also published a roster of all other North American periodicals and columns. Somewhat different from many other federations, it also continued a trade department (in books and equipment) that had been inherited as one of *Chess Review*'s commercial enterprises.

The USCF Policy Board is elected every three years by the vote of regional delegates and does not seem to be based on an individual members' voting system. A stable operational arm of the USCF was the Continental Chess Association (CCA), managed by W. Goichberg. Working up from grassroots, and from the nucleus of recreation, the CCA arranged regional events which allowed players to move from lower to higher class or vice versa. The chess clubs mostly retained the solid round robin, and ladder tournament, system. The CCA, in order to accommodate large attendances during limited periods of play, favored the speedier Swiss System, where only players with similar scores are paired during one event. It also allowed "unrated" newcomers a chance of entry.

In addition to the organizationally faster Swiss events, Speed Chess also gained ground, and a Speed Chess Association was created, capable of providing instant rating figures and pairings for this type of tournament.

The USCF and/or *CL&R* also ran a "Postal Chess" section which, according to a *CL&R* report of November 1975, then comprised 18,000 mail chess members, a sizeable proportion in comparison to total membership. There also existed a number of independent mail chess groups, such as the Correspondence Chess League of America (CCLA), originally incorporated in 1893 and affiliated with the International Correspondence Chess Association (ICCA), just as are Walter Muir's United States Postal Union and others.

Equally private—and independent within the meaning of its bylaws—an Association of U.S. Chess Journalists (AUSCJ) was formed in 1970. There seemed to be need for a balanced codification of (chess) journalistic ethics, and for securing equity of full reporting about all facets of the chess scene; for the development of promotional chess guide-lines; for an equitable liaison with publishers, institutions, and media; for guidance of, and information about "small press"; etc. Apart from that, one of the former sponsors of the AUSCJ, L. Evans, launched a Professional Chess Association with the purpose of advancing the professional players' stature and status, and issuing a quarterly bulletin.

Cooperating with the USCF, but acting independently, the American Chess Foundation (ACF) rendered support on a national level. Its tax-exempt status allowed for more effective financing of worthwhile projects. As the ACF operated discreetly, by direct solicitation, the exact extent of its otherwise considerable impact was difficult to evaluate. One of its past sponsors, Thomas Emery, initiated the annual U.S. Armed Forces (global) chess competition. The ACF induced the American Legion posts to lend their facilities and prestige, and also subsidized educational T.V. programs, etc. The ACF also advocated official U.S. governmental underwriting of chess instruction, but (as might be important to keep in mind from the communitarian point of view), the U.S. Department of Health, Education and Welfare did not share the same outlook. Many experts in the National Institute of Education believed that educational concentration on real mastery of chess *competed* too strongly *with the acquisition of other intellectual skills*; and that the possession of one or another talent, for instance chess, was neither transferable, nor proof of support in sharpening one's intellect toward mastery of other disciplines.

The ACF, in cooperation with the Lincoln Chess Foundation, organized a symposium *Chess and the Humanities*, held in May 1978 at the University of Nebraska. It was attended by many prominent scholars, from different disciplines, who submitted about the function of chess. The ACF also underwrote the composition of a book by Arpad E. Elo, *The Rating of Chessplayers, Past and Present*, a technical work and an historical study, published by Batsford of England.

These—well-founded—reasonings enter into inquiry and conclusions at a later point, but we will here continue our review of concrete actions to propagate chess from within, and look at some of the social and technical changes in recent years as they made themselves felt in chess.

## THE PROPAGATION OF THE GAME

Youthful neophytes picked up chess during school, in youth clubs, and at home—but only when a conducive environment was present. Where this premise was missing, chess remained unknown even though athletics were cultivated. Therefore, capable enthusiasts fostered chess in civic institutions on the basis of a voluntary recreation (once it becomes a compulsory subject, as practiced in some European countries, it may lose its joy, or create an exclusive obsession).

In a systematic way, starting with "The Milwaukee Plan of Chess Promotion"[1] in schools and community centers, the municipal recreational framework began to expand in the 1970s; with the aim of instructing the youth, providing leisure for the elderly, and a chance for chess activists to spread the avocation. Exhibits, fairs, conventions, shopping malls, etc. also provided a forum for the professionals.

Under the impression of chess' redeeming social value, chess was carried into correctional institutions and state hospitals, which had no funds for procuring curricula or instructors, and the USCF maintained a roster and liaison, a laudable activity within reasonable bounds. However, according to enlightened officials of correctional institutions:[2] "Games and hobbies are encouraged by the authorities to keep prison population from exploding. The therapeutic qualities for mentally ill and retarded, and the physically ill and impaired, are well recognized, but the pertinent programs should be instigated and managed by the medical and psychological personnel involved. Recreation is a primary, not an adjectival program. Use of leisure is an end in itself and not justified by its effect upon other programs." Chess might support self-reliance in persons primarily talented for the game, or might serve as a narrow bridge toward reacceptance. Many convicts might claim to be political not criminal ones; but again, the prison might simply release a repeater who also plays chess as a shrewd excuse to find sympathy. Benefit of doubt is justified in both cases.

## NEWER MASS EVENTS

Prompted by the American Bicentennial and after, additional competitions of intra- or international recognition came to the fore.

---

[1] The plan was operated under the guidance of Professor Arpad E. Elo, a former president of the American Chess Federation. Modifying Kenneth Harkness' USCF Rating System, he became an international chess authority when FIDE adopted the Elo International Rating System; in Europe his ratings are called "Elo figures."

[2] J. C. Charlesworth (editor), *Leisure in America: Blessing or Curse?* (Philadelphia: American Academy of Political and Social Science, Monograph 4, April 1964) pp. 42–43.

In 1976, the time-honored Anglo-American cable match experienced a revival, with a 12-board Telex match New York–London held in September. It was hosted by the Manhattan Chess Club and ended 9:4 in favor of the United States. The 1977 match ended 8:4 for the United States.

The National Chess League telephone matches were launched as a novel series of continental telephone competitions, initially between nine cities, each providing a six-man team; in 1977 this network already had expanded to sixteen teams. Due to the reasonable number of six participants per team, the arrangement appealed to resident masters and strong amateurs alike, as it allowed for rotation without tying down everyone to a lengthy schedule. Possible projection on the screen, availability of promptly annotated games, potential transmission on television (cable), the visible presence of an audience, rooting for their team—all these morsels made for a potential to generate interest, if regularly pursued through consistent promotion by the organizers (often a missing element).

In the "Futurity" tournaments, conducted by the CCA with support from the ACF, and offering promising players a proving ground against stronger opponents, a number of FIDE rated players were pitted against an equal number of unrated opponents, giving the latter a chance to gain a higher standing if they beat their total of rated opponents in a proportion higher than 50%.

The U.S. Scholastics, comprising National High, National Junior High, and National Elementary schools, also gained more attention and meaning.

Starting modestly in 1971, an impressive show has been staged annually at Lone Pine, California, on the Nevada border in the midst of the Sierra Nevada at more than 3000 ft. altitude. The event has had significance as an individual, not otherwise subsidized and by now regular undertaking of the affluent Louis D. Staham and his wife Doris, who resided there. They could almost be considered the patrons of the small town of Lone Pine, which also served as a location (the Alabama Hills) for Western movies; and as a starting point for scalers of adjacent Mt. Whitney and for visitors to nearby Death Valley.

The Annual Louis D. Staham Masters-Plus Tournament, held in a Staham-built annex to the town hall, provided an enormous, ultracompetitive, free-enterprise stimulus. This may have been so, partly at least, because of the substantial prize money put up as the carrot, and (with certain contractual exceptions made for the super-athletes of chess), "with no expenses paid" as the stick. An obstacle race, namely how to get to the isolated spot, was an added incentive! I. Kashdan of Los Angeles functioned as the tournament director. Basically, though, the tournament had been earmarked as pitting high-rated, but preferably young, U.S. masters against highly rated foreign international and grandmasters. Whether a few rounds annually of a chancy Swiss System tourney indeed met the goal remained to be proven.

In 1976, eleven grandmasters and ten international masters arrived, along with thirty-six very highly classed players, to divide the total of $23,000 in awards among themselves. The tourney's then seven-round Swiss System produced ex-World Champion Petrosian's 1st prize (with 5½ points) and *nine* dissimilar players (including Smyslov) in 2nd place with an equal score of 5:2—an inconclusive picture of their relative strength.

The March 1977 Masters-Plus increased the rounds to nine and the prize money to $30,000, with $10,000 for the 1st-prize winner(s). Play proceeded at a gruelling pace of forty-two moves in five hours; adjourned games were to be continued after a two-hour dinner break and finally broken off after another four hours of play; any games unfinished by then were treated as draws regardless of a party's chances. This provision was needed in order to have time to prepare the next day's Swiss pairings, although they could not be mathematically exact. Lone Pine in March was insulated from distractions, with ample accommodations available that did not limit the duration of a tournament. The location contrasted with the often noisy, or drab (but sometimes diversified) environment elsewhere. The magnitude of the competition was illustrative of contemporary American chess promotion, but Lone Pine raised some pertinent questions about its utility. The investment was not restricted to a selective round robin, to well-planned publications, or to seminars, as the by-product of high-class attendance producing qualitatively top-level chess; it was subject to the hectic outcome of a mass-marathon. Brilliancy prizes were indeed budgeted for exactly two prize-winners per round, regardless of their absolute quality. The excellence of a massive undertaking was subordinated to the mechanistic demands of "the next day's ratings," the division of who was to have the white, and who the black pieces was too unbalanced for a high-class event, and the game of skill was in danger of becoming a rodeo.

As a positive side, free global access to U.S. Chess and its dollar treasure displayed a promotional shingle of a free society. The high contingent of foreign title holders also allowed a few American players a chance of scoring against them well enough to gain them an international title. It was a costly undertaking and it did not entice enough reciprocal invitations for Americans anxious to test their mettle overseas. There remained, of course, the hope that more consolidated and substantial "Lone Pines" would achieve such results; and would also revive the type of generosity as displayed in earlier years by John G. White, Alain C. White, and many others, for the indigent good of American chess, amateurs or professionals, young and old alike.

The 1978 spectacle, also of 9 rounds, again increased its prize fund, this time to $36,000, with $12,000 for first prize; and the USSR's Petrosian, Polugayevsky and Zaltsman participating, and booking simultaneous exhibitions on the side on their freely accessible tour of the United States. The lead scores from among 68 competitors in this tour de force were: Larsen (Denmark) 7½; Polugayevsky (USSR) 7½; Peters, Lein, and Portisch (Hungary) 6½; Petrosian, Zaltsman (USSR) and Rogoff 7.

# THE AUTOMATION AND POLITICS OF CHESS

### PSYCHOMECHANICS OF CHESS

As an illuminator of mental processes, chess has been subjected to much observation since the days of A. Binet[3] The interest has centered on the player's mind, his reactions and emotions; his *modus operandi* in the game and his capabilities otherwise; and comparisons between his goals in life and chess.

Experiments were conducted in Russia in 1925, when researchers tried to create a "psychogram" of a player's personality by psychometric measurements, and by both psychological and physiological tests. They did not arrive at conclusive proof that any specific characteristics in the makeup of leading chess players were transferable to other activities. Hence, while chess might be used as an auxiliary and absorbing educational tool (with the absorbing aspect carried further by the USSR in due course), its educational value as such remained undefinable.

Psychographic analyses in the United States mostly tried to determine whether factors of perception, social behavior, mental faculties, and chessboard performance were interrelated in a psychology of chess thought.

Since 1966, Dr. Ernest Rubin has published comparisons on chess performance, time elements and age factors, which appeared in *The American Statistician*.

Within a different scientific field, chess—alongside poker—formed

---

[3] *Psychologie des Grands Calculateur et Joueurs d'Echecs* (Paris: Hachette, 1904). Binet was exclusively and excessively preoccupied with (some) chess players' gift of playing blindfold.

a fascinating nucleus within the upcoming theories of games and probabilities, and many of the findings were in parallel fashion incorporated in subsequent computer (or "machine intelligence") researches. Here Anatol Rapaport already inserts an element of cynical doubt about the social physicists' tabulations of tens of thousands of chess games, with masses of statistics showing the frequency, distribution, correlations, and percentages of any conceivable factor.[4] With Rapaport inclined to mutter: "Yes, but is what you have studied chess?" In contrast, the intuitively creative approach has also come under observation, with the effect of reaching a desirable modicum between the two extremes. In dealing with game strategies, Rapaport also analyzed the transformation of probabilities by virtue of friends' and foes' coalitions—a remarkable reminder of the mechanism and impact of intensive collective teamwork by modern, organized chess groups, competing with the American, self-reliant chess professional.

None of the American research has sought any ideological consequence. In Russia, however, the desire for behavior control and the political integration of any and all private and public activity, tended to mesh involvement in chess with Russia's social psychopolitics.

COMPUTERIZATION OF CHESS

In the United States, scientific interest in chess arose subsequent to progress in technology which tended to automate many outlooks; and the chess game was adopted as a suitable matrix for problem-solving. A. Newell and H. A. Simon devote 124 pages to chess in their 920-page *Human Problem Solving* (Englewood Cliffs: Prentice-Hall, 1972). C. Shannon first recognized the significance of chess both for studying intelligence and behavior, and as a medium to solve elements of long-range planning, forecasting, and decision-making. The concept was then further formalized by Chase, Greenblatt, Samuel, Turing, Ulam, and others. During the Fischer boom, this research was joined by academicians ambidexterous in both chess and science: L. Atkin, H. Berliner, N. Charness, R. Church, E. Hearst, C. Kalme, M. Newborn, D. Slate, and others. Already before them, computerization of chess had begun in the USSR, probably with the computer specialist, chess champion Dr. Botvinnik, lending a hand. In Fall 1966, contests were started to test the quality of programmers' texts and computer speed, and the conclusions were summarized in books by M. Newman, D. N. L. Levy,

---

[4] Anatol Rapaport, *Fight, Games and Debates* (Ann Arbor: Center for Research in Conflict Resolution, University of Michigan, 1950; rev. 5th ed., 1974).

and in the multidisciplinary compilation *Chess Skill in Man and Machine* (New York: Springer, 1977), edited by Professor Peter W. Frey of Northwestern University (Illinois). American master Craig Chellstorp annotated the games therein.

Although the sophistication of the programs improved, they still disclosed gaps in comparison to live play. While Botvinnik foresaw a Computer Chess Death for the game, the opposite view was held by Professor Euwe, also a computer expert. A comparable uncertainty—and wistful comment—as to the fate and role of chess and chess players was expressed in the chapter written by Eliot Hearst for Peter Frey's book in the section on "Genius and Chess" (p. 182): "Chessmasters as well as chess computers deserve less reverence than the public accords them." The divergence of views by Botvinnik, Euwe, Frey and Hearst, and other researchers, is basically one of ideological attitude within a given value system. Apprehensions had arisen that the computer sorcerer's apprentices were unable to control the multiplying offspring of the computer cultist. Chess had originally been one of the programming tools chosen by the scientists, but the blinking monster decided to confer autonomy upon its favorite. The players' psychological reciprocities became divorced from the idea of relatively correct judgment in chess and this in turn was recognized as "truth" only when it could be so proven linearly; that is, by the computer's heuristically, but not artistically, designed program. The computer's internal speed, its built-in element of the clock and the time-frame, became an autonomous instrument, with dominance over the human being instead of vice versa. The computer's tendency was to make decisions, but not to leave the player a choice—for better or worse. This outcome might satisfy the compulsive, but not the social, amateur, and it might actually cause a danger to the chess professional's personal development and function—unless he agrees to see himself primarily as a computer programmer of rather limited application.

With these encroachments upon the recreational fabric, dissent arose also from within the academic fraternity. M.I.T. professor Joseph Weitzenbaum, in *Computer Power and Human Reason* (San Francisco: Freeman, 1976) committed the ultimate heresy of questioning what computers were indeed for; that man's (in our case, chessplaying man's) aims were thus geared to comply and catch up with what the machine was capable of, not the other way round. He questioned if computers could, and should, reason "organically."

Yet, with the genie out of the bottle, progress, if constructive and controlled, would not be denied and technical development, properly applied, was bound to have a beneficial effect upon chess practice, upon chess communication, and upon greater utilization of the electronic tools.

## ELECTRONICS IN CHESS

Chess as one of the sounding boards for computer science might prove to have been only a by-product when compared to other, more immediate, possibilities offered by the electronic age. The digital integrated circuits, activated by transistors at an undreamt-of speed, with the resultant savings in cost and manipulation, paved the way for information storage and retrieval of lesser essentials, e.g., chess data. The only remaining requirement for manpower is transcription of copy not yet geared to machine pick-up. The electronic upheaval also accounted for the construction of single-purpose microcomputers, for ambitious amateurs eager to tinker with, and invent their own, chess programs. With these devices they could possibly play against each other, each aided by a home computer, or set up their own computer opponents—a new and different category of formal exercise or fun but no combat person-to-person.

The first challenging microprocessors, feedable with chess programs of varied levels, started appearing on the market in the late 1970s. Like the "Automation" two centuries before, which was directed by an anonymous, well-hidden player, these modern contraptions operated on programs supplied by chess technicians. However, disclosure of their identity and thus of their credentials in computer science or chess was often withheld by the manufacturers. As against identifiable writers of chess books, the verification of the accuracy of a program and its monolinear moves stayed with the manufacturer/publisher, but not with the public which was expected to purchase blindly and to rely on hit and miss. Computer chess newsletters appeared occasionally, filling the role of critical reviews, but they were not yet integrated in the whole body of chess.[5] Last but not least, modern TV sets could tape, and at will replay any public programs on, let us assume, chess.

In the area of viewing and projection, microfilm viewers, stocked with match and tournament records and pertinent texts, reveal possibilities of reproducing factual or instructional matter on a screen open to a participating audience and to seminars. Standard cassettes can record game scores or enable instructors to annotate clients' games. Mass participation in analysis, by a large public, from remote places, can be foreseen. The typographic instrument

[5] In summer 1978, the New England magazine *Personal Computing* started a spacious section exclusively devoted to chess.

of a published book still provides a longer-lasting store of reference than audio-visual "recall"; but the latter forms a promising accessory in the fields of compilation and promotion.

In spite of these advances in electronics, basic chess mechanics still remained just that. The United States has been working on, but still is behind its capacity of, providing easier mechanics for simultaneous electronic (or magnetic) time controls, score-keeping, demonstration, transcription, transmission, and multiple reproduction of chess-playing motions, all synchronized.

Waiting at the door were also Home Base, or CB (Civilian Band) Radio as a medium of promotion and contact. By 1978, its use had reached a total of thirty million sets in operation. These instruments permit intercommunication within a limited, though considerably wide, radius between two or more private persons; "kibitzers" can tune in on the same wavelength. The operators are able to contact each other for any purpose, functional or recreational, including the playing of a game.[6] Direct casting tended to open new ways for spontaneous recreational indulgence, linked up with radio, or similar, magazine publicity and cutting across geographic boundaries, wider than a conventional chess club's perimeter. As the pastime spreads, it allows the formation of new and additional social groupings, and ignores the depersonalization and professionalism of an established status quo. With an eye half-cocked to the future, one can imagine chess boards on the dashboards of moving or stationary vehicles, or on one's desk, or table in the den, independent of a fixed time and place of meeting; with synchronized digital clocks and signal lights indicating whose move it was within a given interval of time.

Let us now change from technicalities to prospects.

[6] At this point we notice that the German term *Fernschach* is more all-inclusive, generically than our *Mail Chess*, and as against O–T–B (over-the-board) chess; a term such as "long-distance chess," "tele-chess," "chess *par distance*," or another suitable differentiation might be more applicable in days of the vanishing mail.

# 15.

# Prospects and Perspectives

## THE DOMESTIC SCENE

There is reason neither for exalted euphoria or nostalgia about good old times of golden chess, nor for despair that the enjoyment of chess, on domestic grounds and under home rule, makes the game take a backseat; or that chess must scramble to keep up with the encroaching competition.

To draw a balance, we will, however, in loose order and in staccato style, touch on some of the factors that have surfaced as the occasional retardants, or prospective propellants of chess in America:

There was a fervent increase in USCF-organized membership drives toward mass events, but it affected much of the same circle of participants—with the proliferation often choking the game on its own momentum.

Intensification of foreign competitions, with their continued outpouring of new (International and Grand) Master titles, triggered more competitions in the United States—but, as yet, without a corresponding ground swell of domestic popularity. It merely prompted higher local expectations of professional recognition and rewards, directed toward increased specialization, perhaps to the detriment of other vocational priorities. The relentless chase after "ratings" and, then, to achieve two master norms within a prescribed period of time, may have helped stem the avalanche of title holders, but it smothered other aspects of leisurely chess pursuit, many of which have been described in the preceding sections of this book; and its adherents have, practically, been kept outside the mainstream of chess.

## THE CHESS AMATEUR SETUP

In the 1970s, only *one* national event a year, called the U.S. *Amateur* Championship, carried that specific label. It was not a round robin, but again a breathtaking Swiss tournament, open to all except rated masters, coupled with the requirement to join the USCF as an *organized* member.

The American Open also set aside a special Amateur Section. But "amateur," with its connotation of dilettantism, seemed a misnomer as it obscured the fact that participants of "mere" expert class may live by instruction only, paying their taxes—and not be hobbyists-amateurs—whereas many rated masters play chess for fun and not for professional recognition. These were excluded from the amateur brethren—for the amateur's protection—and ranked among the competing professionals, with the disadvantage of being pitted against "full-timers" who monopolized prizes and competed for the Interzonal standings to which the amateur was equally entitled (as there is so far no such distinction as there is, for instance, in tennis).

Chess columnist L. Evans once remarked that "according to a Harris Poll, about thirteen million Americans were interested in the game." The poll alluded to is the (Louis) Harris Survey of September, 1972, which had been contracted by the *Chicago Tribune*. It does not really give any ultimate figure, but I secured the original report and integrated it with the subsequent 1973 U.S. census figures. Harris stated that "a significantly high 64% of the public 18 years of age or older followed the [Fischer–Spassky] matches, although only a fraction . . . 18% . . . actually play chess." Harris, who culls opinions and not statistics, excluded the age group of 10–17. Taking a playing average of these of 15%, a consolidation of all figures and percentages arrives at about 27,000,000 individuals potentially interested in chess. This figure needs some pruning by exclusion of peer groups who are not yet fully integrated into the privileges of community development; but a conservative reduction by 50% would still leave an impressive—post-Fischer—11,000,000 prospects.[1]

Among the intangibles was the 10–24 year old group which

[1] As reported by the then Executive Secretary Sidney Wallach of the ACF: "At least ten million Americans play chess regularly, according to a 1977 survey by *U.S. News & World Report*. Millions of others have played but do not play regularly. Among all these millions, there must be [potential] chess players in every American community." Mr. Wallach apparently means past players can be brought back as active players or, at least, as readers and donors.

maintains interest during school or college years, but does not rotate around a rigid "chess association," and which is a disaffected audience. Another intangible was the private societies, youth clubs, hobby and puzzle magazines or general periodicals—but they were, as yet, diffused in their orientation and accessibility. Many chess columns that were read by such a public were often out of tune with the local scene. CB radio had not been given a chance to be affected.

## A PIONEERING TASK AHEAD

With the statistics about a latent potential in mind, the vital question arose: Where can chess go from its present station? What identity and what leadership may make it accessible to the greatest possible number of participants? The human being is entitled to a full life which means taking time out for recreation and recuperation as one chooses. It also means giving the community its due, yet being safeguarded in one's choice of recreation, which is a community's task to create constructively. Thus it is the community that must create a space for chess, not as an exclusive pastime for specialists only, but as one exciting aspect of many diverse phases of recreational activity, open to all individuals alike.

Such an approach offers the chess professional his assigned niche; but also, as in a decathlon, it presents for everyone the prospect of diversification and enrichment within a realm of pooled leisure activities. Thus, the "consumer" might switch from chess to bridge to Gomuku; to fine arts and crafts; to creative writing; and back again; so can the professional instructor. The movement can then be traced from the ivory tower of chess, with the lone player pitted against other loners or against powerful members of state-subsidized teams elsewhere, with the specialist dictating to the generalist/leisurist—to a communitarian trend of intranational symbiosis of leisure activities and—only after that—to international reciprocation and interaction.

The current trends call for more emphasis on "recreational stock exchanges," such as the labor or industrial recreation hall, the instructional extension course, or even the correctional "community center" as the functionally ideal and more economical focal points. While such structures might be more egalitarian (there are only good or bad backgammon, bridge, or chessplayers), the activities, while interchangeable, would still be functionally different and apportioned according to demand. While a Paul Masson Vineyard would go on flourishing as a place to attend a Chess Class Tournament, or Church's Fried Chicken have all its franchises provide a wonderful free podium for master-instructors and a joyful public,[2] the general interest will gain by this and additional integration.

The views as hitherto expressed are not utopian—else they would not belong in a "chronicle"—but they do defy inertia. They arise because of certain realignments in our total national approach to recreation and national needs, and the role of our corporate bodies, of the educational system and of the media.[3] Apart from the pressures which are already affecting the programming by public-education television and broadcasting, there are institutions, corporations, unions, foundations, and other chartered bodies—all of which might find themselves called upon (or might volunteer) to coordinate and sensibly apportion financial, manpower, and media support. The emphasis might change from commercial consumerism of the market place to other social tasks, among them a coordination of all leisure activities such as chess, but not "nothing but chess."

With the demand for a greater role to be played by corporations, and private and government agencies in support of chess, a further variety of goals presented itself: to instigate publications of less mechanistic but more illuminating, noncompetitive nature, as done by university presses for scholastic advancement; to raise funds on a broader basis, including a stronger, and matching, response by the clamoring chess community itself; and, most of all, to foster promotion among organizationally smaller but numerically attractive groups and enroll them to the chess creed by absorbing also their interest. Altogether, the time had come for a better social script.

[2] On February 1, 1978, Church's Fried Chicken, Inc. set aside $60,000 a year for the promotion of chess, for salaries, travel and publicity, with chessmasters Christiansen and Peters as the intructors, to an open public. The venture was inaugurated by George Koltanowski.

[3] In 1976, the U.S. Federal Government made funds available, under Title VII of Public Law 92-318, earmarking budgetary contributions to public school districts with high "minority group segregation; to overcome that segregation and its ill effects," and to encourage and assist promoters (including chess) to introduce recreational (that is, also chess) programs into the public schools under the Emergency School Act. The USCF publicized this enactment.

Also in 1978, D. J. Terrible of Grove City, Ohio, composed a doctoral thesis *Chess and Social Change*, to serve as a working paper and government grant proposal to augment the aforementioned Title VII.

As indicated in the foregoing, and repeated in the concluding sections of this book, this governmental provision belongs in a framework of fostering recreation in general and on a synchronized basis.

# Index

# Index of Games